Study Guide

Principles of Accounting
2002e

Principles of Financial Accounting
2002e

Study Guide

Principles of Accounting
2002ⓔ

Principles of Financial Accounting
2002ⓔ

Belverd E. Needles, Jr.
DePaul University

Marian Powers
Northwestern University

Susan V. Crosson
Santa Fe Community College, Florida

CONTRIBUTING EDITORS
Edward H. Julius
California Lutheran University

Debbie Luna
El Paso Community College

Houghton Mifflin Company   **Boston**   **New York**

Sponsoring Editor: Bonnie Binkert
Senior Development Editor: Margaret Kearney
Associate Editor: Damaris Curran
Senior Manufacturing Coordinator: Priscilla J. Bailey
Marketing Manager: Steven Mikels

Printed in the U.S.A.

ISBN: 0-618-12425-X

123456789-CRS-05 04 03 02 01

Contents

Appendix

To the Student

This self-study guide is designed to help you improve your performance in your first accounting course. You should use it in your study of either *Principles of Accounting* 2002© or *Principles of Financial Accounting* 2002© by Needles, Powers, and Crosson.

Reviewing the Chapter

This section of each chapter summarizes in a concise but thorough manner the essential points related to the chapter's learning objectives. Each integrated learning objective is restated and all key terms are covered in this section. Where applicable, a summary of journal entries introduced in the chapter also is presented.

Self-Test

The Self-Test within each chapter reviews the basic concepts taught in the chapter and helps you to prepare for the examination your teacher will give based on the learning objectives assigned and taught in class.

Testing Your Knowledge

Each chapter contains a matching quiz of key terms, a short-answer section, true-false statements, and multiple-choice questions to test your understanding of the learning objectives and vocabulary in the chapter. This Study Guide also contains fourteen crossword puzzles to test your knowledge of key terms.

Applying Your Knowledge

An important goal in learning accounting is the ability to work exercises and problems. In this section of each chapter, you can test your ability to apply two or three of the new principles introduced in the chapter to "real-life" accounting situations.

Answers

The Study Guide concludes with answers to all questions, exercises, problems, and crossword puzzles. All answers are cross-referenced to the learning objectives in the chapter.

CHAPTER 1   USES OF ACCOUNTING INFORMATION AND THE FINANCIAL STATEMENTS

REVIEWING THE CHAPTER

Objective 1: Define *accounting,* **identify business goals and activities, and describe the role of accounting in making informed decisions.**

1. **Accounting** is an information system that measures, processes, and communicates financial information about an identifiable economic entity. It provides information that is essential for decision making. **Bookkeeping,** a small but important aspect of accounting, is the mechanical and repetitive recordkeeping process.

2. A **business** is an economic unit that sells goods and services at prices that will provide an adequate return to its owners. For a business to survive, management must make satisfactory earnings to hold investment capital (called **profitability**) and must keep sufficient cash on hand to pay debts as they fall due (called **liquidity**). The company also has other goals, such as improving its products and expanding operations. It is management that directs the company toward these goals by making decisions.

3. Businesses pursue their goals by engaging in financing, investing, and operating activities.
   a. **Financing activities** are needed to obtain funding for the business and include such activities as issuing stocks and bonds and repaying creditors.
   b. **Investing activities** consist of spending the funds raised and include activities such as buying and selling land, buildings, and equipment.

   c. **Operating activities** involve the everyday sale of goods and services as well as the related everyday activities.

4. **Performance measures** indicate the extent to which management is achieving its business goals and is managing business activities. Accordingly, performance measures often serve as the basis for the evaluation of managers. Examples of performance measures are cash flow (for liquidity), net income or loss (for profitability), and the ratio of expenses to revenue (for operating activities).

5. A distinction is usually made between **management accounting,** which focuses on information for internal users, and **financial accounting,** which involves the preparation, reporting, analysis, and interpretation of accounting information in reports for external users. These reports are called **financial statements.**

6. The **computer** is an electronic tool that rapidly collects, organizes, and communicates vast amounts of information. The computer does not take the place of the accountant. However, the accountant must understand how the computer operates because it is an integral part of the accounting information system.

7. A **management information system (MIS)** is an information network that takes in all major functions (called *subsystems*) of a business. The accounting information system is the financial hub of the management information system.

Objective 2: Identify the many users of accounting information in society.

8. There are basically three groups that use accounting information: management, outsiders with a direct financial interest, and outsiders with an indirect financial interest.

   a. As already stated, **management** steers a business toward its goals by making the business's important decisions. Specifically, it must ensure that the business is adequately financed, productive assets are obtained, goods and services are produced and marketed, employees are managed, and pertinent information is provided to decision makers.

   b. Present or potential investors and present or potential creditors are considered outside users with a direct financial interest in a business. Most businesses publish financial statements that report their profitability and financial position. Investors use these financial statements to assess the strength or weakness of the company, whereas creditors examine the financial statement to determine the company's ability to repay debts on time.

   c. Society as a whole, through government officials and public groups, can be viewed as an accounting information user with an indirect financial interest in a business. Specifically, such users include tax authorities, regulatory agencies, and other groups (such as labor unions, economic planners, and financial analysts).

9. The **Securities and Exchange Commission (SEC)** is an agency of the federal government set up by Congress to protect the investing public by regulating the issuing, buying, and selling of stocks in the United States.

10. Managers within government and within not-for-profit organizations such as hospitals, universities, professional organizations, and charities also make extensive use of financial information.

Objective 3: Explain the importance of business transactions, money measure, and separate entity to accounting measurement.

11. To make an accounting measurement, the accountant must answer the following basic questions:
   a. What is measured?
   b. When should the measurement be made?
   c. What value should be placed on what is measured?
   d. How should what is measured be classified?

12. Accounting is concerned with measuring transactions of specific business entities in terms of money.

   a. **Business transactions** are economic events that affect the financial position of a business. Business transactions can involve an exchange of value (e.g., sales, borrowings, and purchases) or a nonexchange (e.g., the physical wear and tear on machinery, and losses due to fire or theft).

   b. The **money measure** concept states that business transactions should be measured in terms of money. Financial statements are normally prepared in terms of the monetary unit of the business's country (dollars, pesos, etc.). When transactions occur between countries with differing monetary units, the amounts must be translated from one currency to another, using the appropriate **exchange rate**.

   c. For accounting purposes, a business is treated as a **separate entity,** distinct from its owners, creditors, and customers. That is, the business owner's personal bank account, resources, debts, and financial records should be kept separate from those of the business.

Objective 4: Identify the three basic forms of business organization.

13. The three basic forms of business organization are sole proprietorships, partnerships, and corporations. Accountants recognize each form as an economic unit separate from its owners.

   a. A **sole proprietorship** is an unincorporated business that is owned by one person. The owner receives all profits, absorbs all losses, and is personally liable for all debts of the business.

   b. A **partnership** is an unincorporated business owned and managed by two or more persons. The owners divide profits and losses according to a predetermined formula, and each is personally liable for all debts of the business.

   c. A **corporation** is a business that has been granted a state charter and which is legally separate from its owners (the stockholders). Corporations are managed by officers, who are appointed by a board of directors, who are elected by the stockholders. Each stockholder is liable only to the extent of his or her investment, and ownership can be transferred without affecting operations.

Objective 5: Define *financial position,* **state the accounting equation, and show how they are affected by simple transactions.**

14. Every transaction affects a firm's financial position. **Financial position** (a company's economic resources and the claims against those resources) is shown on the firm's balance sheet, so called because the two sides or parts of the balance sheet always must equal each other. Specifically, the total dollar amount of assets must equal the total dollar amount of liabilities and owner's equity. This is known as the **accounting equation.** It is formally stated as

    Assets = Liabilities + Owner's Equity

15. **Assets** are the economic resources owned by a business and expected to benefit future operations. Examples of assets are cash, accounts receivable, inventory, buildings, equipment, patents, and copyrights.

16. **Liabilities** are present obligations (debts) of a business to pay cash, transfer assets, or provide services to other entities in the future. Examples of liabilities are money borrowed from banks, amounts owed to creditors for goods bought on credit, and taxes owed to the government.

17. **Owner's equity** represents the claims by the owner to the assets of the business. It equals the residual interest in assets after deducting the liabilities. Because it is equal to assets minus liabilities, owner's equity is said to equal the **net assets** of the business.

18. Owner's equity is affected by four types of transactions. **Owner's investments** increase owner's equity. **Revenues,** which result when goods or services have been provided, also increase owner's equity. **Expenses,** which represent the costs of doing business, decrease owner's equity, as do **owner's withdrawals.** When revenues exceed expenses, a **net income** results. When expenses exceed revenues, a **net loss** has been suffered.

19. **Accounts** are used by accountants to accumulate amounts that result from like transactions. Examples are Cash, Accounts Payable, and John Doe, Capital.

20. Although every transaction affects the accounting equation in some way, the equation must always remain in balance. In other words, dollar amounts may change, but assets must always equal liabilities plus owner's equity.

a. The investment of cash by the owner will increase both assets and owner's equity.
b. The purchase of assets with cash will both increase and decrease assets by the same amount (i.e., total assets will not change).
c. The purchase of assets on credit will increase both assets and liabilities.
d. The payment of a liability will decrease both assets and liabilities.
e. Earning revenue, whether for cash or for credit, will increase both assets and owner's equity.
f. The collection on an account receivable will both increase and decrease assets by the same amount (i.e., total assets will not change).
g. Incurring and immediately paying for expenses will decrease both assets and owner's equity.
h. Incurring expenses to be paid later will increase liabilities and decrease owner's equity.
i. The withdrawal of cash by the owner will decrease both assets and owner's equity.

Objective 6: Identify the four financial statements.

21. Accountants communicate their information through financial statements. The four principal statements are the income statement, statement of owner's equity, balance sheet, and statement of cash flows.

22. Every financial statement has a three-line heading. The first line gives the name of the company. The second line gives the name of the statement. The third line gives the relevant dates (the date of the balance sheet or the period of time covered by the other three statements).

23. The **income statement,** whose components are revenues and expenses, is perhaps the most important financial statement. Its purpose is to measure the business's success or failure in earning an income over a given period.

24. The **statement of owner's equity** relates the income statement to the balance sheet by showing how the owner's capital changed during the period. The owner's capital at the beginning of the period is the first item on the statement. Because net income belongs to the owner, it is added to beginning capital, as are any additional investments made by the owner during the period. Finally, any withdrawals by the owner during the period are subtracted, as is a net loss, to arrive at the owner's capital at the end of the period. This ending figure then is stated as the owner's capital in the balance sheet.

25. The **balance sheet** shows the financial position of a business as of a certain date. The resources used in the business are called *assets,* debts of the business are called *liabilities,* and the owner's financial interest in the business is called *owner's equity.* The balance sheet is also known as the *statement of financial position.*

26. The **statement of cash flows** focuses on the business's liquidity goal and shows much information that is not found in the other three financial statements. **Cash flows** refer to the business's cash inflows and cash outflows. *Net* cash flows represent the difference between these inflows and outflows.

27. The statement of cash flows discloses all the business's operating, investing, and financing activities during the accounting period. As discussed in paragraph 3, operating activities consist mainly of receipts from customers and payments to suppliers and others in the ordinary course of business. Investing activities might include selling a building or investing in stock. Financing activities might include issuing stock or paying dividends. The statement will indicate the net increase or decrease in cash produced during the period.

Objective 7: State the relationship of generally accepted accounting principles (GAAP) to financial statements and the independent CPA's report, and identify the organizations that influence GAAP.

28. Accounting theory provides the reasoning behind and framework for accounting practice. **Generally accepted accounting principles (GAAP)** are the set of guidelines and procedures that constitute acceptable accounting practice at a given time. The set of GAAP changes continually as business conditions change and practices improve.

29. The financial statements of publicly held corporations are audited by licensed professionals, called **certified public accountants (CPAs),** to ensure the quality of those statements. Before an **audit** can take place, however, the CPA must be independent of the client (without financial or other ties). On completion of the audit, the CPA reports on whether or not the audited statements "present fairly, in all material respects" and are "in conformity with generally accepted accounting principles."

30. The **Financial Accounting Standards Board (FASB)** is the authoritative body for development of GAAP. This group is separate from the AICPA and issues *Statements of Financial Accounting Standards.*

31. The **American Institute of Certified Public Accountants (AICPA)** is the professional association of CPAs. Its senior technical committees help influence accounting practice.

32. The Securities and Exchange Commission (SEC) is an agency of the federal government. It has the legal power to set and enforce accounting practices for companies whose securities are traded by the general public.

33. The **Governmental Accounting Standards Board (GASB)** was established in 1984 and is responsible for issuing accounting standards for state and local governments.

34. The **International Accounting Standards Committee (IASC)** is responsible for developing worldwide accounting standards. To date, it has approved more than 30 such standards, which have been translated into six languages.

35. The **Internal Revenue Service (IRS)** enforces and interprets the set of rules that govern the assessment and collection of federal income taxes.

Objective 8: Define *ethics* and describe the ethical responsibilities of accountants.

36. **Ethics** is a code of conduct that applies to everyday life. **Professional ethics** is the application of a code of conduct to the practice of a profession. The accounting profession has developed such a code, intended to guide the accountant in carrying out his or her responsibilities to the public. In short, the accountant must act with integrity, objectivity, independence, and due care.
   a. **Integrity** means that the accountant is honest, regardless of consequences.
   b. **Objectivity** means that the accountant is impartial in performing his or her job.
   c. **Independence** is the avoidance of all relationships that could impair the objectivity of the accountant, such as owning stock in a company he or she is auditing.
   d. **Due care** means carrying out one's professional responsibilities with competence and diligence.

37. The **Institute of Management Accountants (IMA)** has adopted a Code of Professional Conduct of competence, confidentiality, integrity, and objectivity for management accountants.

SELF-TEST

Test your knowledge of the chapter by choosing the best answer for each of the following items.

1. Which of the following is an important reason for studying accounting?
   a. Accounting information is useful in making economic decisions.
   b. Accounting plays an important role in society.
   c. The study of accounting can lead to a challenging career.
   d. All of the above are important reasons for studying accounting.

2. Which of the following groups uses accounting information for planning a company's profitability and liquidity?
   a. Management
   b. Investors
   c. Creditors
   d. Economic planners

3. Economic events that affect the financial position of a business are called
   a. separate entities.
   b. business transactions.
   c. money measures.
   d. financial actions.

4. For legal purposes, which of the following forms of business organization is treated as a separate economic unit from its owner(s)?
   a. Sole proprietorship
   b. Corporation
   c. Partnership
   d. All of the above

5. If a company has liabilities of $19,000 and owners' equity of $57,000, its assets are
   a. $38,000.
   b. $76,000.
   c. $57,000.
   d. $19,000.

6. The payment of a liability
   a. increases both assets and liabilities.
   b. increases assets and decreases liabilities.
   c. decreases assets and increases liabilities.
   d. decreases both assets and liabilities.

7. Investments by an owner will
   a. increase both total assets and total owner's equity.
   b. increase both total assets and total liabilities.
   c. increase total assets and decrease total owner's equity.
   d. have no effect on total assets, liabilities, or owner's equity.

8. Expenses and withdrawals appear, respectively, on the
   a. balance sheet and income statement.
   b. income statement and balance sheet.
   c. statement of owner's equity and balance sheet.
   d. income statement and statement of owner's equity.

9. Generally accepted accounting principles
   a. define accounting practice at a point in time.
   b. are similar in nature to the principles of chemistry or physics.
   c. rarely change.
   d. are not affected by changes in the ways businesses operate.

10. Independence is an important characteristic of which of the following when performing audits of financial statements?
    a. Government accountants
    b. Certified management accountants
    c. Certified public accountants
    d. Accounting educators

TESTING YOUR KNOWLEDGE

*Matching**

Match each term with its definition by writing the appropriate letter in the blank.

_____ 1. Accounting

_____ 2. Bookkeeping

_____ 3. Computer

_____ 4. Management information system (MIS)

_____ 5. Management accounting

_____ 6. Financial accounting

_____ 7. Accounting equation

_____ 8. Withdrawals

_____ 9. Certified public accountant (CPA)

_____ 10. Sole proprietorship

_____ 11. Partnership

_____ 12. Corporation

_____ 13. Generally accepted accounting principles (GAAP)

_____ 14. Balance sheet

_____ 15. Income statement

_____ 16. Statement of owner's equity

_____ 17. Statement of cash flows

_____ 18. Separate entity

_____ 19. Money measure

_____ 20. Asset

_____ 21. Liability

_____ 22. Owners' equity

a. A debt of a business

b. A business owned by stockholders but managed by a board of directors and officers

c. Assets taken from the business by the owner for personal use

d. The standard that all business transactions should be measured in terms of money

e. The statement that shows the financial position of a company as of a certain date

f. The repetitive recordkeeping process

g. An economic resource of a business

h. An information system that measures, processes, and communicates economic information

i. An unincorporated business owned and managed by two or more persons

j. An expert accountant licensed by the state

k. The branch of accounting concerned with providing managers with financial information needed to make decisions

l. The statement that shows a company's profit or loss over a certain period of time

m. The statement that discloses the operating, investing, and financing activities during the period

n. The branch of accounting concerned with providing external users with financial information needed to make decisions

o. An electronic tool that processes information rapidly

p. The residual interest in the assets of a business

q. The statement that shows the changes in the owner's capital account during the period

r. The information network that links a company's functions together

s. Assets = Liabilities + Owner's Equity

t. The accounting concept that treats a business as distinct from its owners, creditors, and customers

u. The guidelines that define acceptable accounting practice at a given point in time

v. An unincorporated business that is owned by one person

Note to student: The matching quiz might be completed more efficiently by starting with the definition and searching for the corresponding term.

Short Answer

Use the lines provided to answer each item.

1. On the lines that follow, insert the correct heading for the annual income statement of Zeno Company on June 30, 20xx.

   _____

   _____

   _____

2. Briefly distinguish between bookkeeping and accounting.

   _____

   _____

   _____

3. Briefly define the terms below, all of which relate to the accountants' Code of Professional Conduct.

   a. Integrity _____

   _____

   b. Objectivity _____

   _____

   c. Independence _____

   _____

   d. Due care _____

   _____

4. What three broad groups use accounting information?

   _____

   _____

   _____

5. What two objectives must be met for a company to survive?

   _____

   _____

6. List the four principal financial statements and state briefly the purpose of each.

   Statement

   a. _____

   _____

   b. _____

   _____

   c. _____

   _____

   d. _____

   _____

   Purpose

   a. _____

   _____

   b. _____

   _____

   c. _____

   _____

   d. _____

   _____

True-False

Circle T if the statement is true, F if it is false. Please provide explanations for false answers, using the blank lines at the end of the section.

T F 1. Financial position can best be determined by referring to the income statement.

T F 2. The IRS is responsible for interpreting and enforcing GAAP.

T F 3. One form of the accounting equation is Assets – Liabilities = Owner's Equity.

T F 4. Revenues have the effect of increasing owner's equity.

T F 5. The existence of Accounts Receivable on the balance sheet indicates that the company has one or more creditors.

T F 6. When expenses exceed revenues, a company has suffered a net loss.

T F 7. The measurement stage of accounting involves preparation of the financial statements.

T F 8. Withdrawals appear as a deduction in the income statement.

T F 9. The current authoritative body dictating accounting practice is the FASB.

T F 10. A sole proprietor is personally liable for all debts of the business.

T F 11. The statement of cash flows would disclose whether or not land was purchased during the period.

T F 12. The statement of owner's equity links a company's income statement to its balance sheet.

T F 13. The IASC is responsible for setting guidelines for state and local governments.

T F 14. A corporation is managed directly by its stockholders.

T F 15. Generally accepted accounting principles are not like laws of math and science; they are guidelines that define correct accounting practice at the time.

T F 16. Net assets equal assets plus liabilities.

T F 17. The major sections of a balance sheet are assets, liabilities, owner's equity, revenues, and expenses.

T F 18. A business transaction must always involve an exchange of value between two or more parties.

T F 19. A management information system deals not only with accounting, but with other activities of a business as well.

T F 20. The income statement is generally considered to be the most important financial statement.

T F 21. For accounting purposes, a business should be understood as an entity that is separate and distinct from its owners, customers, and creditors.

T F 22. Economic planners are accounting information users with a direct financial interest.

T F 23. The essence of an asset is that it is expected to benefit future operations.

T F 24. Cash flow is a measure of profitability.

_____

_____

_____

_____

_____

_____

_____

_____

_____

_____

_____

Multiple Choice

Circle the letter of the best answer.

1. Which of the following accounts would *not* appear on the balance sheet?
   a. Wages Expense
   b. M. Garcia, Capital
   c. Notes Receivable
   d. Wages Payable

2. Companies whose stock is publicly traded must file financial statements with the
   a. FASB.
   b. GASB.
   c. SEC.
   d. AICPA.

3. One characteristic of a corporation is
   a. unlimited liability of its owners.
   b. the ease with which ownership is transferred.
   c. ownership by the board of directors.
   d. dissolution upon the death of an owner.

4. Which of the following statements does *not* involve a distinct period of time?
   a. Income statement
   b. Balance sheet
   c. Statement of cash flows
   d. Statement of owner's equity

5. The principal purpose of an audit by a CPA is to
   a. express an opinion on the fairness of a company's financial statements.
   b. detect fraud by a company's employees.
   c. prepare the company's financial statements.
   d. assure investors that the company will be profitable in the future.

6. Collection on an account receivable will
   a. increase total assets and increase total owner's equity.
   b. have no effect on total assets, but will increase total owner's equity.
   c. decrease both total assets and total liabilities.
   d. have no effect on total assets, liabilities, or owner's equity.

7. In a partnership,
   a. profits are always divided equally among partners.
   b. management consists of the board of directors.
   c. no partner is liable for more than a proportion of the company's debts.
   d. dissolution results when any partner leaves the partnership.

8. Which of the following is *not* a major heading on a balance sheet or income statement?
   a. Accounts Receivable
   b. Owner's Equity
   c. Liabilities
   d. Revenues

9. Withdrawals by an owner will
   a. decrease total liabilities and decrease total owner's equity.
   b. decrease total assets and decrease total owner's equity.
   c. decrease total assets and decrease total liabilities.
   d. have no effect on total assets, liabilities, or owner's equity.

10. The purchase of an asset for cash will
    a. increase total assets and increase total owner's equity.
    b. increase total assets and increase total liabilities.
    c. increase total assets and decrease total liabilities.
    d. have no effect on total assets, liabilities, or owner's equity.

11. Which of the following is *not* an activity listed in the statement of cash flows?
    a. Investing Activities
    b. Funding Activities
    c. Operating Activities
    d. Financing Activities

12. The payment of a liability will
    a. decrease both total liabilities and total owner's equity.
    b. decrease total assets and increase total owner's equity.
    c. decrease both total assets and total liabilities.
    d. have no effect on total assets, liabilities, and owner's equity.

APPLYING YOUR KNOWLEDGE

Exercises

1. Global Siding Company always publishes annual financial statements. This year, however, it has suffered a huge loss and is trying to keep this fact a secret by refusing anyone access to its financial statements. Why might each of the following nevertheless insist on seeing Global's statements?

   a. Potential investors in Global

   b. The Securities and Exchange Commission

   c. The bank, which is considering a loan request by Global

   d. Present stockholders of Global

   e. Global's management

2. Black Wolf Company had assets of $100,000 and liabilities of $70,000 at the beginning of the year. During the year, assets decreased by $15,000 and owner's equity increased by $20,000. What is the amount of liabilities at year end?

   $_____

3. Below are the accounts of Mendez TV Repair Company as of December 31, 20xx.

Accounts Payable	$ 1,300
Accounts Receivable	1,500
Building	10,000
Cash	?
Land	1,000
Hector Mendez, Capital	17,500
Equipment	850
Truck	4,500

   Using this information, prepare a balance sheet *in good form*. (You must derive the dollar amount for Cash.)

   Mendez TV Repair Company
   Balance Sheet
   December 31, 20xx

   Assets

   Liabilities

   Owner's Equity

   ---

4. Following are the transactions for Hoffman Painting Company for the first month of operations.

   a. Bruce Hoffman invested $20,000 cash in the newly formed business.
   b. Purchased paint supplies and equipment for $650 cash.
   c. Purchased a company truck on credit for $5,200.
   d. Received $525 for painting a house.
   e. Paid half of the amount due on the truck previously purchased.
   f. Billed a customer $150 for painting his garage.
   g. Paid $250 for one month's rental of the office.
   h. Received full payment from the customer whose garage was painted (transaction **f**).
   i. Sold a company ladder for $20. The buyer said he would pay next month.
   j. Withdrew $1,000 from the business for personal use.

   In the form below, show the effect of each transaction on the balance sheet accounts by putting the dollar amount, along with a plus or minus sign, under the proper account. Determine the balance in each account at month's end. As an example, transaction **a** already has been recorded.

| Transaction | Assets | | | | Liabilities | Owner's Equity |
	Cash	Accounts Receivable	Supplies and Equipment	Trucks	Accounts Payable	Bruce Hoffman Capital
a	+$20,000					+$20,000
b						
c						
d						
e						
f						
g						
h						
i						
j						
Balance at end of month						

Crossword Puzzle
for Chapter 1

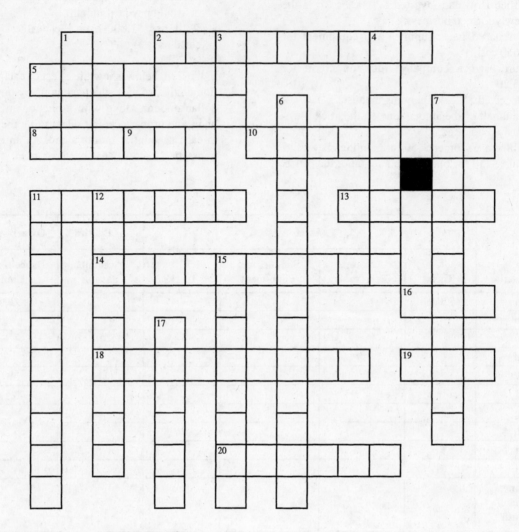

ACROSS

2. Accounting mainly for external use
5. _____ proprietorship
8. Resources of a company
10. One to whom another is indebted
11. _____ sheet
13. Professional organization of accountants
14. The language of business
16. IRS's concern
18. Measure of debt-paying ability
19. Data-generating network
20. Separate _____ concept

DOWN

1. See 3-Down
3. With 1-Down, income statement measure
4. Independent CPA activity
6. Measure of business performance
7. Form of business organization
9. Regulatory agency of publicly held corporations
11. Recorder of business transactions
12. Debt of a company
15. Impartial
17. Ownership in a company

CHAPTER 2   MEASURING BUSINESS TRANSACTIONS

REVIEWING THE CHAPTER

Objective 1: Explain, in simple terms, the generally accepted ways of solving the measurement issues of recognition, valuation, and classification.

1. Before recording a business transaction, the accountant must determine three things:
    a. When the transaction should be recorded (the **recognition** issue)
    b. What value to place on the transaction (the **valuation** issue)
    c. How the transaction should be categorized, or assigned, to accounts (the **classification** issue)

2. A sale is recognized (entered in the accounting records) when the title to merchandise passes from the supplier to the purchaser, regardless of when payment is made or received. This point of sale is referred to as the **recognition point**.

3. The **cost principle** states that the dollar value (**cost**) of any item involved in a business transaction is its original cost (also called *historical cost*). Generally, any change in value after the transaction is not reflected in the accounting records.

Objective 2: Describe the chart of accounts and recognize commonly used accounts.

4. Every business transaction is classified in a filing system consisting of accounts. An account is the basic storage unit for accounting data. Each asset, liability, component of owner's equity, revenue, and expense has a separate account.

5. All of a company's accounts are contained in a book or file called the **general ledger** (or simply the *ledger*). In a manual accounting system, each account appears on a separate page. The accounts generally are in the following order: assets, liabilities, owner's equity, revenues, and expenses. A list of the accounts with their respective account numbers, called a **chart of accounts,** is presented at the beginning of the ledger for easy reference.

6. Although the accounts used by companies will vary, there are some that are common to most businesses. Some typical assets are Cash, Notes Receivable, Accounts Receivable, Prepaid Expenses, Land, Buildings, and Equipment. Some typical liabilities are Notes Payable, Accounts Payable, and Mortgage Payable.

7. The Owner's Capital account (an owner's equity account) represents the owner's investment in the company at any point in time. If William Marshall is an owner, the name of the account would be William Marshall, Capital. If there is more than one owner, a separate Capital account must be kept for each owner.

8. The Owner's Withdrawals account (also an owner's equity account) records amounts withdrawn from the business for personal use, in anticipation of earning a profit. If Paula Post is an owner, her withdrawals account would be called Paula Post, Withdrawals, or Paula Post, Drawing. As with the Capital account, there must be a separate Withdrawals account for each owner.

9. A separate account also is kept for each type of revenue and expense. The exact revenue and

expense accounts used vary depending on the kind of business and its operations. Revenues produce an increase in owner's equity, whereas expenses produce a decrease in owner's equity.

Objective 3: Define *double-entry system* and state the rules for double entry.

10. The **double-entry system** of accounting requires that for each transaction there must be one or more accounts debited and one or more accounts credited, and that the total dollar amount of debits must equal the total dollar amount of credits.

11. An account in its simplest form, a **T account,** has three parts:
    a. A title that expresses the name of the asset, liability, owner's equity, revenue, or expense
    b. A left side, which is called the **debit** side
    c. A right side, which is called the **credit** side

12. At the end of an accounting period, **balances** (also known as *account balances*) are calculated in order to prepare the financial statements. Using T accounts, there are three steps to follow in determining the account balances:
    a. Foot (add up) the debit entries. The **footing** (working total) should be made in small numbers beneath the last entry.
    b. Foot the credit entries.
    c. Subtract the smaller total from the larger. A debit balance exists when the debit footing exceeds the credit footing; a credit balance exists when the opposite is the case.

13. To determine which accounts are debited and which are credited in a given transaction, accountants use the following rules:
    a. Increases in assets are debited.
    b. Decreases in assets are credited.
    c. Increases in liabilities and owner's equity are credited.
    d. Decreases in liabilities and owner's equity are debited.
    e. Revenues and (investments of) capital increase owner's equity and, therefore, are credited.
    f. Expenses and withdrawals decrease owner's equity and, therefore, are debited.

14. Transactions may be analyzed and processed by the following five steps:
    a. Determine the effect (increase or decrease) of the transaction on assets, liabilities, and owner's equity accounts. Each transaction should be supported by a **source document,** such as an invoice or canceled check.
    b. Apply the rules of double entry.

c. In **journal form,** enter the transaction (record the entry) into the journal.
d. Post the journal entry to the general ledger.
e. Prepare the trial balance.

Objective 4: Apply the steps for transaction analysis and processing to simple transactions.

15. To record a transaction, one must (a) obtain a description of the transaction, (b) determine which accounts are involved and what type each is (for example, asset or revenue), (c) determine which accounts are increased and which are decreased, and (d) apply the rules stated in paragraph 13 a–f.

16. For example, if the transaction were "purchased office supplies on credit," the transaction analysis would proceed as follows. Based on the wording, one can determine that the accounts involved are Office Supplies and Accounts Payable. In addition, Office Supplies, an asset, has been increased. Similarly, Accounts Payable, a liability, has also been increased. Accordingly, the appropriate rules of double entry indicate that an increase in an asset (Office Supplies, in this case) is debited, and an increase in a liability (Accounts Payable, in this case) is credited.

Objective 5: Prepare a trial balance and describe its value and limitations.

17. Periodically, the accountant must check the equality of the total of debit and credit balances in the ledger. This is done formally by means of a **trial balance,** which is a listing of all the ledger accounts with their debit and credit balances listed and totaled. A normal balance is determined by whether an account is increased by entries to the debit side or by entries to the credit side. The side on which increases are recorded dictates what is considered the **normal balance.** For example, asset accounts have a normal debit balance because they are increased with debits.

18. If the trial balance does not balance, one or more errors have been made in the journal, ledger, or trial balance. The accountant must locate the errors to put the trial balance in balance. It is important to know, however, that it is possible to make errors that would not cause the trial balance to be out of balance (i.e., errors that cannot be detected through the trial balance).

19. Ruled lines appear in financial reports before each subtotal, and a double line customarily is placed below the final amount. Although dollar signs are required in financial statements, they are omitted

in journals and ledgers. On paper with ruled columns, commas and decimal points are omitted, and a dash frequently is used to designate zero cents. On unruled paper, however, commas and decimal points are used.

Objective 6: Record transactions in the general journal.

20. As transactions occur, they are recorded initially and chronologically in a book called the **journal.** The **general journal** is the simplest and most flexible type of journal. Each transaction **journalized** (recorded) in the general journal contains (a) the date, (b) the account names, (c) the dollar amounts debited and credited, (d) an explanation, and (e) the account numbers, if the transaction has been posted. A line should be skipped after each **journal entry,** and more than one debit or credit can be entered for a single transaction (called a **compound entry**).

Objective 7: Post transactions from the general journal to the ledger.

21. The general journal records details of each transaction; the results of these details are summarized in the general ledger which updates each account. Each day's journal entries must be posted to the appropriate account in **ledger account form.**

22. **Posting** is a transferring process that results in an updated balance for each account. The dates and amounts are transferred from the journal to the ledger, and new account balances are calculated. The Post. Ref. columns are used for cross-referencing between the journal and the ledger.

A. (LO 4) Cash   XX (amount invested)
          Joan Miller, Capital   XX (amount invested)
              Investment of cash into business by owner

B. (LO 4) Prepaid Rent   XX (amount paid)
          Cash   XX (amount paid)
              Advance payment for rent

C. (LO 4) Art Equipment   XX (purchase price)
          Cash   XX (amount paid)
              Purchase of art equipment for cash

D. (LO 4) Office Equipment   XX (purchase price)
          Cash   XX (amount paid)
          Accounts Payable   XX (amount to be paid)
              Purchase of office equipment, partial payment made

E. (LO 4) Art Supplies   XX (purchase price)
          Office Supplies   XX (purchase price)
          Accounts Payable   XX (amount to be paid)
              Purchase of art and office supplies on credit

F. (LO 4) Prepaid Insurance   XX (amount paid)
          Cash   XX (amount paid)
              Advance payment for insurance coverage

G. (LO 4) Accounts Payable   XX (amount paid)
          Cash   XX (amount paid)
              Payment on a liability

H. (LO 4) Cash   XX (amount received)
          Advertising Fees Earned   XX (amount earned)
              Received payment for services rendered

I. (LO 4) Wages Expense   XX (amount incurred)
          Cash   XX (amount paid)
              Recorded and paid wages for the period

J. (LO 4) Cash   XX (amount received)
          Unearned Art Fees   XX (amount received)
              Received payment for services to be performed

K. (LO 4) Accounts Receivable   XX (amount to be received)
          Advertising Fees Earned   XX (amount earned)
              Rendered service, payment to be received at later time

L. (LO 4) Utilities Expense   XX (amount incurred)
          Cash   XX (amount paid)
              Recorded and paid utility bill

M. (LO 4) Telephone Expense   XX (amount incurred)
              Accounts Payable   XX (amount to be paid)
                   Recorded telephone bill, payment to be made at later time

N. (LO 4) Joan Miller, Withdrawals   XX (amount withdrawn)
              Cash   XX (amount withdrawn)
                   Owner withdrew cash from business

SELF-TEST

Test your knowledge of the chapter by choosing the best answer for each of the following items.

1. Deciding whether to record a sale when the order for services is received or when the services are performed is an example of a
   a. recognition issue.
   b. valuation issue.
   c. classification issue.
   d. communication issue.

2. Which of the following statements is true?
   a. The chart of accounts usually is presented in alphabetical order.
   b. The general ledger contains all the accounts found in the chart of accounts.
   c. The general journal contains a list of the chart of accounts.
   d. Most companies use the same chart of accounts.

3. Which of the following is a liability account?
   a. Accounts Receivable
   b. Diane Mathews, Withdrawals
   c. Rent Expense
   d. Accounts Payable

4. An entry on the left side of an account is referred to as
   a. the balance.
   b. a debit.
   c. a credit.
   d. a footing.

5. Although debits increase assets, they also
   a. decrease assets.
   b. increase owner's equity.
   c. increase expenses.
   d. increase liabilities.

6. Payment for a two-year insurance policy is a debit to
   a. Prepaid Insurance.
   b. Insurance Expense.
   c. Cash.
   d. Accounts Payable.

7. An agreement to spend $100 a month on advertising beginning next month requires
   a. a debit to Advertising Expense.
   b. a debit to Prepaid Advertising.
   c. no entry.
   d. a credit to Cash.

8. Transactions initially are recorded in the
   a. trial balance.
   b. T account.
   c. journal.
   d. ledger.

9. In posting from the general journal to the general ledger, the page number on which the transaction is recorded appears in the
   a. Post. Ref. column of the general ledger.
   b. Item column of the general ledger.
   c. Post. Ref. column of the general journal.
   d. Description column of the general journal.

10. To test that the total debits and the total credits are equal, the accountant periodically prepares a
    a. trial balance.
    b. T account.
    c. general journal.
    d. ledger.

TESTING YOUR KNOWLEDGE

Matching*

Match each term with its definition by writing the appropriate letter in the blank.

_____ 1. Original (historical) cost

_____ 2. Account

_____ 3. Debit

_____ 4. Credit

_____ 5. Account balance

_____ 6. General ledger

_____ 7. Posting

_____ 8. Prepaid expenses

_____ 9. Accounts Payable

_____ 10. Nancy Zahn, Capital

_____ 11. Nancy Zahn, Withdrawals

_____ 12. Double-entry system

_____ 13. Trial balance

_____ 14. Journal

_____ 15. Post. Ref.

_____ 16. Footing

_____ 17. Compound entry

_____ 18. Unearned revenue

a. Transferring data from the journal to the ledger
b. The amount in an account at a given time
c. An entry with more than one debit or credit
d. An account that represents an owner's equity in a company
e. A procedure for checking the equality of debits and credits in the ledger accounts
f. The basic storage unit for accounting data
g. The book or file that contains all of a company's accounts
h. Adding a column of numbers
i. A liability that arises when payment is received before a service is performed
j. An account that represents amounts taken out of a business for personal expenses
k. The proper valuation to place on a business transaction
l. Amounts owed to others
m. Amounts paid in advance for goods or services
n. The book of original entry
o. The right side of a ledger account
p. The column in the journal and ledger that provides for cross-referencing between the two
q. The left side of a ledger account
r. The method that requires at least one debit and one credit for each transaction

Short Answer

Use the lines provided to answer each item.

1. List the five steps that must be executed to analyze and process transactions.

   _____

   _____

   _____

   _____

   _____

2. Given the following journal entry, indicate which part of the entry applies to each measurement issue listed.

   July 14   Cash   150
                  Accounts Receivable   150
                  Collection on account

   a. Recognition issue _____

   b. Valuation issue _____

   c. Classification issue _____

**Note to student:* The matching quiz might be completed more efficiently by starting with the definition and searching for the corresponding term.

3. Describe a transaction that would require a debit to one asset and a credit to another asset.

_____

_____

_____

4. Describe a transaction that would require a debit to a liability and a credit to an asset.

_____

_____

_____

5. List the four account types that affect the owner's Capital account.

_____

_____

_____

6. List the three account types that are credited when increased.

_____

_____

_____

True-False

Circle T if the statement is true, F if it is false. Please provide explanations for the false answers, using the blank lines at the end of the section.

T F **1.** A sale should be recorded on the date of payment.

T F **2.** _Historical cost_ is another term for _original cost._

T F **3.** There must be a separate account for each asset, liability, component of owner's equity, revenue, and expense.

T F **4.** The credit side of an account implies something favorable.

T F **5.** In a given account, total debits must always equal total credits.

T F **6.** Management can determine the cash balance quickly by referring to the journal.

T F **7.** The number and titles of accounts vary among businesses.

T F **8.** Promissory Note is an example of an account title.

T F **9.** Prepaid expenses are classified as assets.

T F **10.** Increases in liabilities are indicated with a credit.

T F **11.** In all journal entries, at least one account must be increased and another decreased.

T F **12.** Journal entries are made after transactions have been entered into the ledger accounts.

T F **13.** In the journal, all liabilities and owner's equity accounts must be indented.

T F **14.** A debit is never indented in the journal.

T F **15.** Posting is the process of transferring data from the journal to the ledger.

T F **16.** The Post. Ref. column of a journal or ledger should be empty until posting is done.

T F **17.** In practice, the ledger account form is used, but the T account form is not.

T F **18.** The chart of accounts is a table of contents to the general journal.

T F **19.** Unearned Revenue has a normal debit balance.

T F **20.** Corporations do not use a Withdrawals account.

T F **21.** Errors caused by transposing digits are divisible by 2.

T F **22.** Dollar signs are omitted from journals and ledgers.

_____   _____
_____   _____
_____   _____
_____   _____
_____   _____
_____   _____
_____   _____
_____   _____
_____   _____
_____   _____
_____   _____
_____   _____
_____   _____

Multiple Choice

Circle the letter of the best answer.

1. Which of the following is *not* considered in initially recording a business transaction?
   a. Classification
   b. Recognition
   c. Summarization
   d. Valuation

2. When a liability is paid, which of the following is true?
   a. Total assets and total liabilities remain the same.
   b. Total assets and total owner's equity decrease.
   c. Total assets decrease by the same amount that total liabilities increase.
   d. Total assets and total liabilities decrease.

3. Which of the following is *not* true about a proper journal entry?
   a. All credits are indented.
   b. All debits are listed before the first credit.
   c. An explanation is needed for each debit and each credit.
   d. A debit is never indented, even if a liability or owner's equity account is involved.

4. When an entry is posted, what is the last step to be taken?
   a. The explanation must be transferred.
   b. The account number is placed in the reference column of the ledger.
   c. The journal page number is placed in the reference column of the journal.
   d. The account number is placed in the reference column of the journal.

5. Which of the following errors will probably be disclosed by the preparation of a trial balance (i.e., would cause it to be out of balance)?
   a. Failure to post an entire journal entry (i.e., nothing is posted).
   b. Failure to record an entry in the journal (i.e., nothing is entered).
   c. Failure to post part of a journal entry.
   d. Posting the debit of a journal entry as a credit, and the credit as a debit.

6. When cash is received in payment of an account receivable, which of the following is true?
   a. Total assets increase.
   b. Total assets remain the same.
   c. Total assets decrease.
   d. Total assets and total owner's equity increase.

7. Which of the following is increased by debits?
   a. Julia Schell, Withdrawals
   b. Unearned Revenue
   c. Bonds Payable
   d. Julia Schell, Capital

8. Which of the following accounts is an asset?
   a. Unearned Revenue
   b. Prepaid Rent
   c. Jim Lutton, Capital
   d. Fees Earned

9. Which of the following accounts is a liability?
   a. Interest Payable
   b. Interest Expense
   c. Interest Receivable
   d. Interest Income

10. A company that rents an office (i.e., a lessee or tenant) would never have an entry to which account for that particular lease?
    a. Prepaid Rent
    b. Unearned Rent
    c. Rent Payable
    d. Rent Expense

11. Which of the following accounts has a normal credit balance?
    a. Prepaid Insurance
    b. Dot Lucci, Withdrawals
    c. Sales
    d. Advertising Expense

12. Payment of a $50 debt was accidentally debited and posted to Accounts Receivable instead of to Accounts Payable. As a result of the error, the trial balance will
    a. be out of balance by $25.
    b. be out of balance by $50.
    c. be out of balance by $100.
    d. not be out of balance.

APPLYING YOUR KNOWLEDGE

Exercises

1. Following are all the transactions of Precision Printing Company for the month of May. For each transaction, provide the journal entries required *in good form*. Use the journal provided on the next page.

May 2 Al Mayer formed Precision Printing Company by investing $28,000 cash.

3 Rented part of a building for $300 per month. Paid three months' rent in advance.

5 Purchased a small printing press for $10,000 and photographic equipment for $3,000 from Vermont Press, Inc. Paid $2,000 and agreed to pay the remainder as soon as possible.

8 Hired a pressman, agreeing to pay him $200 per week.

9 Received $1,200 from Ski Chalet Department Store as an advance for brochures to be printed.

11 Purchased paper for $800 from ABC Pulp Supply Company. Issued ABC Pulp a promissory note for the entire amount.

14 Completed a $500 printing job for Harrington Shoes. Harrington paid for half, agreeing to pay the remainder next week.

14 Paid the pressman his weekly salary.

15 Paid Vermont Press, Inc., $1,000 of the amount owed for the May 5 transaction.

18 Received the remainder due from Harrington Shoes for the May 14 transaction.

20 Withdrew $700 from the business for personal living expenses.

24 Received an electric bill of $45. Payment will be made in a few days.

30 Paid the electric bill.

2. Below are three balance sheet accounts, selected at random from Sivula Company's ledger. For each, determine the account balance.

Accounts Receivable	
2,000	1,000
750	

Accounts Payable	
1,200	4,200
2,000	

Cash	
15,000	1,000
4,000	1,200
	2,200

a. Accounts Receivable has a (debit or credit) balance of

$_____.

b. Accounts Payable has a (debit or credit) balance of

$_____.

c. Cash has a (debit or credit) balance of

$_____.

General Journal				
Date		**Description**	**Debit**	**Credit**
May	2	Cash	28,000	
		Al Mayer, Capital		28,000
		To record the owner's original investment		

	General Journal			
Date	Description		Debit	Credit

3. Two journal entries are presented below. Post both entries to the ledger accounts provided. Only those accounts needed have been provided, and previous postings have been omitted to simplify the exercise.

		General Journal			Page 7
Date		**Description**	**Post. Ref.**	**Debit**	**Credit**
Apr.	3	Cash		1,000	
		Revenue from Services			1,000
		Received payment from Lincoln Company for services			
	5	Accounts Payable		300	
		Cash			300
		Paid Middlebury Supply Company for supplies purchased on March 31 on credit			

Cash   **Account No. 11**

						Balance	
Date		**Item**	**Post. Ref.**	**Debit**	**Credit**	**Debit**	**Credit**

Accounts Payable   **Account No. 21**

						Balance	
Date		**Item**	**Post. Ref.**	**Debit**	**Credit**	**Debit**	**Credit**

Revenue from Services   **Account No. 41**

						Balance	
Date		**Item**	**Post. Ref.**	**Debit**	**Credit**	**Debit**	**Credit**

CHAPTER 3 MEASURING BUSINESS INCOME

REVIEWING THE CHAPTER

Objective 1: Define *net income* and its two major components, *revenues* and *expenses*.

1. Profitability, or earning a **profit,** is an important goal of most businesses. A major function of accounting is to measure and report a company's success or failure in achieving this goal. This is done by means of an income statement.

2. **Net income** is the net increase in owner's equity resulting from the operations of the company. Net income results when revenues exceed expenses, and a **net loss** results when expenses exceed revenues.

3. **Revenues** are the price of goods sold and services rendered during a specific period of time. Examples of revenues are Sales (the account used when merchandise is sold), Commissions Earned, and Advertising Fees Earned. Revenues produce an increase in owner's equity, as well as (typically) an inflow of cash or receivables.

4. Also described as the *cost of doing business* or as *expired costs,* **expenses** are the costs of goods and services used in the process of earning revenues. Examples of expenses are Telephone Expense, Wages Expense, and Advertising Expense. Expenses produce a decrease in owner's equity, as well as (typically) an outflow of cash or the incurring of a liability.

5. Not all increases in owner's equity arise from revenues, nor are all decreases in owner's equity produced by expenses. Similarly, not all increases in cash arise from revenues, nor are all decreases in cash produced by expenses.

Objective 2: Explain the difficulties of income measurement caused by the accounting period issue, the continuity issue, and the matching issue.

6. The **periodicity** assumption (the solution to the **accounting period issue,** or the difficulty of assigning revenues and expenses to a short period of time) states that although measurements of net income for short periods of time are approximate, they are nevertheless useful. Income statement comparison is made possible through accounting periods of equal length. A **fiscal year** covers any twelve-month accounting period used by a company. Many companies use a fiscal year that corresponds to a calendar year, which is a twelve-month period that ends on December 31.

7. Under the **going concern** assumption (the solution to the **continuity issue,** or the difficulty of not knowing how long a business will survive), the accountant assumes that the business will continue to operate indefinitely, unless there is evidence to the contrary (such as an imminent bankruptcy).

8. When the **cash basis of accounting** is used, revenues are recorded when cash is received, and expenses are recorded when cash is paid. This method, however, can lead to distortion of net income for the period.

9. According to the **matching rule,** revenues should be recorded in the period(s) in which they are

actually earned, and expenses should be recorded in the period(s) in which they are used to produce revenue; the timing of cash payments or receipts is irrelevant.

Objective 3: Define *accrual accounting* and explain two broad ways of accomplishing it.

10. **Accrual accounting** consists of all techniques used to apply the matching rule. Specifically, it involves (1) recognizing revenues when earned (**revenue recognition**) and expenses when incurred, and (2) adjusting the accounts at the end of the period.

11. Because adjusting entries never involve the Cash account, they do not affect cash flow. They are, however, necessary for the accurate measurement of performance. Good judgment must be exercised in the preparation of adjusting entries to avoid the abuse and misrepresentation that can occur.

Objective 4: State four principal situations that require adjusting entries.

12. A problem arises when revenues or expenses apply to more than one accounting period. The problem is solved by making **adjusting entries** at the end of the accounting period. Adjusting entries allocate to the current period the revenues and expenses that apply to that period, deferring the remainder to future periods. A **deferral** is the postponement of the recognition of an expense already paid or of a revenue already received [see 13(a) and (c) below]. An **accrual** is the recognition of an expense or revenue that has arisen but has not yet been recorded [see 13(b) and (d) below].

13. Adjusting entries are required to accomplish several purposes:
    a. To divide recorded costs (such as the cost of machinery or prepaid rent) among two or more accounting periods.
    b. To record unrecorded expenses (such as wages earned by employees after the last pay period in an accounting period).
    c. To divide recorded revenues (such as commissions collected in advance) among two or more accounting periods.
    d. To record unrecorded revenues (such as commissions earned but not yet billed to customers).

Objective 5: Prepare typical adjusting entries.

14. When an expenditure is made that will benefit more than just the current period, the initial debit is usually made to an asset account instead of to

an expense account. Then, at the end of the accounting period, the amount that has been used up is transferred from the asset account to an expense account.
   a. **Prepaid expenses,** such as Prepaid Rent and Prepaid Insurance, are debited when they are paid for in advance. At the end of the accounting period, an expense is debited and the prepayment credited for the amount expired.
   b. An account for supplies, such as Office Supplies, is debited when supplies are purchased. At the end of the accounting period, an inventory of supplies is taken. The difference between supplies available for use during the period and ending inventory is the amount used up during the period.
   c. The cost of a long-lived asset such as a building, trucks, or office furniture is debited to an asset account when purchased. At the end of each accounting period, an adjusting entry must be made to transfer a part of the original cost of each long-lived asset to an expense account. The amount transferred or allocated is called **depreciation** or *depreciation expense*.
   d. **Accumulated depreciation accounts** are contra-asset accounts used to total the past depreciation expense on specific long-term assets. They are called **contra accounts** because on the balance sheet they are subtracted from their associated asset account. Thus proper balance sheet presentation will show the original cost, the accumulated depreciation as of the balance sheet date, and the undepreciated balance (called **carrying value** or *book value*).

15. In making the adjusting entry to record depreciation, Depreciation Expense is debited and Accumulated Depreciation is credited.

16. Similarly, expenses have often been incurred but not recorded in the accounts because cash has not yet been paid. An adjusting entry must be made to record these **accrued expenses.** For example, interest on a loan may have accrued that does not have to be paid until the next period. A debit to Interest Expense and a credit to Interest Payable will record the current period's interest for the income statement. A similar adjusting entry would be made for estimated income taxes and accrued wages. These entries will also record the liabilities for the balance sheet.

17. Sometimes payment is received for goods before they are delivered or for services before they are rendered. In such cases, a liability account such

as **Unearned Revenues** or Unearned Fees would appear on the balance sheet. This account is a liability because it represents revenues that still must be earned by providing the product or service that is owed.

18. Often at the end of an accounting period, revenues have been earned but not recorded because no payment has been received. An adjusting entry must be made to record these **accrued** (unrecorded) **revenues**. For example, interest that has been earned might not be received until the next period. A debit must be made to Interest Receivable and a credit to Interest Income to record the current period's interest for the income statement. This entry will also record the asset for the balance sheet.

Objective 6: Prepare financial statements from an adjusted trial balance.

19. After all the adjusting entries have been posted to the ledger accounts and new account balances have been computed, an **adjusted trial balance** should be prepared. If it is in balance, the adjusted trial balance is then used to prepare the financial statements.

Supplemental Objective 7: Analyze cash flows from accrual-based information.

20. Liquidity, or the ability to pay debts when they fall due, relies upon cash flow (not accrual-based) information. Fortunately, cash receipts and payments can be calculated, given accrual-based net income and related information. The general rule for determining cash flow received from any revenue or paid for any expense (except depreciation) is to determine the potential cash payments or cash receipts and then deduct the amount not paid or received. For example, cash payments for rent would equal rent expense plus an increase (or minus a decrease) in prepaid rent occurring during the period. The formulas for cash flow are presented in the box below.

Cash Flow Formulas (SO 7)			
Type of Account	**Potential Payment or Receipt**	**Not Paid or Received**	**Result**
Prepaid Expense	Ending Balance + Expense for the Period	– Beginning Balance	= Cash Payments for Expenses
Unearned Revenue	Ending Balance + Revenue for the Period	– Beginning Balance	= Cash Receipts from Revenues
Accrued Expense	Beginning Balance + Expense for the Period	– Ending Balance	= Cash Payments for Expenses
Accrued Revenue	Beginning Balance + Revenue for the Period	– Ending Balance	= Cash Receipts from Revenues

A. (LO 5)   Rent Expense   XX (amount expired)
              Prepaid Rent   XX (amount expired)
                  Expiration of prepaid rent

B. (LO 5)   Insurance Expense   XX (amount expired)
              Prepaid Insurance   XX (amount expired)
                  Expiration of prepaid insurance

C. (LO 5)   Art Supplies Expense   XX (amount consumed)
              Art Supplies   XX (amount consumed)
                  Consumption of art supplies

D. (LO 5)   Office Supplies Expense   XX (amount consumed)
              Office Supplies   XX (amount consumed)
                  Consumption of office supplies

E. (LO 5)   Depreciation Expense, Art Equipment   XX (amount allocated to period)
              Accumulated Depreciation, Art Equipment   XX (amount allocated to period)
                  Depreciation recorded

F. (LO 5)   Depreciation Expense, Office Equipment   XX (amount allocated to period)
              Accumulated Depreciation, Office Equipment   XX (amount allocated to period)
                  Depreciation recorded

G. (LO 5)   Wages Expense   XX (amount incurred)
              Wages Payable   XX (amount to be paid)
                  Accrual of unrecorded expense

H. (LO 5)   Unearned Art Fees   XX (amount earned)
              Art Fees Earned   XX (amount earned)
                  Performance of services paid for in advance

I. (LO 5)   Fees Receivable   XX (amount to be received)
              Advertising Fees Earned   XX (amount earned)
                  Accrual of unrecorded revenue

SELF-TEST

Test your knowledge of the chapter by choosing the best answer for each of the following items.

1. The net increase in owner's equity that results from business operations is called
   a. net income.
   b. revenue.
   c. an expense.
   d. an asset.

2. Which of the following accounts is an example of a contra account?
   a. Unearned Art Fees
   b. Depreciation Expense, Buildings
   c. Prepaid Insurance
   d. Accumulated Depreciation, Office Equipment

3. A business can choose a fiscal year that corresponds to
   a. the calendar year.
   b. the natural business year.
   c. any 12-month period.
   d. any of the above.

4. Assigning revenues to the accounting period in which goods are delivered or services performed, and expenses to the accounting period in which they are used to produce revenues is called the
   a. accounting period issue.
   b. continuity assumption.
   c. matching rule.
   d. recognition rule.

5. Accrual accounting involves all of the following *except*
   a. recording all revenues when cash is received.
   b. applying the matching rule.
   c. recognizing expenses when incurred.
   d. adjusting the accounts.

6. Which of the following is an example of a deferral?
   a. Accruing year-end wages
   b. Recognizing revenues earned but not yet recorded
   c. Recording prepaid rent
   d. Recognizing expenses incurred but not yet recorded

7. Prepaid Insurance shows an ending balance of $2,300. During the period, insurance in the amount of $1,200 expired. The adjusting entry would include a debit to
   a. Prepaid Insurance for $1,200.
   b. Insurance Expense for $1,200.
   c. Unexpired Insurance for $1,100.
   d. Insurance Expense for $1,100.

8. Adjusting entries are used to
   a. make financial statements from one period to the next more comparable.
   b. make net income reflect cash flow.
   c. correct errors in the recording of earlier transactions.
   d. record initial transactions.

9. On July 31, Wages Payable had a balance of $500 and on August 31, the balance was $300. Wages Expense for August was $2,600. How much cash was expended for wages during August?
   a. $2,100
   b. $2,400
   c. $2,600
   d. $2,800

10. Which of the following accounts would probably be contained in an adjusted trial balance, but probably *not* in a trial balance?
    a. Unearned Revenue
    b. Cash
    c. Depreciation Expense
    d. Utilities Expense

TESTING YOUR KNOWLEDGE

*Matching**

Match each term with its definition by writing the appropriate letter in the blank.

_____ 1. Net income

_____ 2. Revenues

_____ 3. Expenses

_____ 4. Expired cost

_____ 5. Unexpired cost

_____ 6. Deferral

_____ 7. Accrual

_____ 8. Fiscal year

_____ 9. Going concern assumption

_____ 10. Cash basis of accounting

_____ 11. Accrual accounting

_____ 12. Matching rule

_____ 13. Adjusting entry

_____ 14. Depreciation expense

_____ 15. Accumulated Depreciation

_____ 16. Contra account

_____ 17. Unearned revenue

_____ 18. Adjusted trial balance

a. All the techniques used to apply the matching rule

b. A liability that represents an obligation to deliver goods or render services

c. That portion of an asset that has not yet been charged as an expense

d. A general term for the price of goods sold or services rendered

e. The assumption that a business will continue indefinitely (solution to the continuity problem)

f. Recognition of an expense or revenue that has arisen but has not yet been recorded

g. A method of determining whether accounts are still in balance

h. The idea that revenues are recorded (recognized) when earned and that expenses are recorded when incurred

i. The amount by which revenues exceed expenses (opposite of net loss)

j. An account that is subtracted from an associated account

k. Any 12-month accounting period used by a company

l. An example of a contra account to assets

m. An end-of-period allocation of revenues and expenses relevant to that period

n. The cost of doing business

o. Recording revenues and expenses when payment is received or made

p. The expired cost of a plant asset for a particular accounting period

q. Postponement of the recognition of an expense already paid or of a revenue already received

r. A descriptive term for expense

Note to student: The matching quiz might be completed more efficiently by starting with the definition and searching for the corresponding term.

Use the lines provided to answer each item.

1. Briefly summarize the four situations that require adjusting entries.

_____

_____

_____

_____

2. Briefly explain the matching rule.

_____

_____

_____

_____

3. Define *depreciation* as the term is used in accounting.

_____

_____

_____

4. Distinguish between prepaid expenses and unearned revenues.

_____

_____

_____

_____

True-False

Circle T if the statement is true, F if it is false. Please provide explanations for the false answers, using the blank lines at the end of the section.

T F 1. Failure to record accrued wages will result in total liabilities that are understated.

T F 2. Expired costs are listed in the income statement.

T F 3. A calendar year refers to any 12-month period.

T F 4. The cash basis of accounting often violates the matching rule.

T F 5. Under the accrual basis of accounting, the timing of cash payments is vital for recording revenues and expenses.

T F 6. Adjusting entries must be made immediately after the financial statements are prepared.

T F 7. Prepaid insurance represents an unexpired cost.

T F 8. Office Supplies Expense must be debited for the amount in ending inventory of office supplies.

T F 9. Because Accumulated Depreciation appears on the asset side of the balance sheet, it has a debit balance.

T F 10. As a machine is depreciated, its accumulated depreciation increases and its unexpired cost decreases.

T F 11. Unearned Revenues is a contra account to Earned Revenues in the income statement.

T F 12. When an expense has accrued but payment has not yet been made, a debit is needed for the expense and a credit for Prepaid Expenses.

T F 13. The adjusted trial balance is the same as the trial balance, except that it has been modified by adjusting entries.

T F 14. If one has made a sale for which the money has not yet been received, one would debit Unearned Revenues and credit Earned Revenues.

T F 15. The original cost of a long-lived asset should appear on the balance sheet even after depreciation has been recorded.

T F 16. Adjusting entries help make financial statements comparable from one period to the next.

_____   _____

_____   _____

_____   _____

_____   _____

_____   _____

_____   _____

_____   _____

_____   _____

_____   _____

_____   _____

Multiple Choice

Circle the letter of the best answer.

1. Which of the following is an unlikely description for an adjusting entry?
   a. Debit to an expense, credit to an asset
   b. Debit to a liability, credit to a revenue
   c. Debit to an expense, credit to a revenue
   d. Debit to an expense, credit to a liability

2. Depreciation does *not* apply to
   a. trucks.
   b. office supplies.
   c. machinery.
   d. office equipment.

3. An account called Unearned Fees is used when
   a. recorded costs must be divided among periods.
   b. recorded revenues must be divided among periods.
   c. unrecorded (accrued) expenses must be recorded.
   d. unrecorded (accrued) revenues must be recorded.

4. Depreciation best applies to
   a. recorded costs that must be divided among periods.
   b. recorded revenues that must be divided among periods.
   c. unrecorded expenses that must be recorded.
   d. unrecorded revenues that must be recorded.

5. Which of the following would *not* appear in the adjusted trial balance?
   a. Prepaid Insurance
   b. Unearned Management Fees
   c. Net Income
   d. Depreciation Expense

6. An adjusting entry made to record accrued interest on a note receivable due next year would consist of a debit to
   a. Cash and a credit to Interest Income.
   b. Cash and a credit to Interest Receivable.
   c. Interest Expense and a credit to Interest Payable.
   d. Interest Receivable and a credit to Interest Income.

7. The periodicity assumption solves the accounting period problem by recognizing that
   a. net income over a short period of time is a useful estimate.
   b. a business is likely to continue indefinitely.
   c. revenues should be recorded in the period earned.
   d. a twelve-month accounting period must be used.

8. Prepaid Rent is a(n)
   a. expense.
   b. contra account.
   c. liability.
   d. asset.

9. Which of the following accounts would probably contain a lower dollar amount in the adjusted trial balance than in the trial balance?
   a. Accounts Receivable
   b. Withdrawals
   c. Office Supplies
   d. Rent Expense

10. An adjusting entry would *never* include
   a. Unearned Revenue.
   b. Cash.
   c. Prepaid Advertising.
   d. Wages Expense.

APPLYING YOUR KNOWLEDGE

Exercises

1. On January 1, 20x7, Bristol Transit Company began its business by buying a new bus for $24,000. One-eighth of the cost of the bus is depreciated each year. Complete *in good form* the balance sheet as of December 31, 20x9.

Bristol Transit Company
Partial Balance Sheet
December 31, 20x9

Assets

Cash	$5,000
Accounts Receivable	3,000
Company Vehicles	
	————
Total Assets	$ ————

---

2. For each set of facts, provide the dollar amount that would be recorded.

   a. The cost of supplies at the beginning of the period was $510. During the period, supplies that cost $800 were purchased. At the end of the period, supplies that cost $340 remained. Supplies Expense should be recorded for

   $_____.

   b. The company signed a lease and paid $14,000 on July 1, 20x7, to cover the four-year period beginning July 1, 20x7. How much Rent Expense should it record on December 31, 20x7?

   $_____

   c. The company was paid $600 in advance for services to be performed. By the end of the period, only one-fourth of it had been earned. How much of the $600 will appear as Unearned Revenues on the balance sheet?

   $_____

3. In the next column is the trial balance for Nakamura Company. The facts that follow are based on this trial balance. For each item, make the adjusting entry in the journal provided on the next page.

Keep in mind that Nakamura Company operates on a calendar year.

   a. Cost of supplies on hand, based on a physical count, is $375.
   b. Wages of $2,500 for the five-day workweek ($500 per day) are recorded and paid every Friday. December 31 falls on a Thursday.
   c. Services amounting to $600 were rendered during 20x7 for customers who had paid in advance.
   d. Five percent of the cost of buildings is taken as depreciation for 20x7.
   e. One-quarter of the prepaid advertising expired during 20x7.
   f. All of the insurance shown on the trial balance was paid for on July 1, 20x7, and covers the two-year period beginning July 1, 20x7.
   g. Work performed for customers that has not been billed or recorded amounts to $2,200.
   h. Accrued interest on a note payable amounts to $52. This interest will be paid when the note matures.

Nakamura Company
Trial Balance
December 31, 20x7

	Debit	Credit
Cash	$ 77,300	
Notes Receivable	5,000	
Prepaid Advertising	8,000	
Prepaid Insurance	1,000	
Supplies	500	
Office Equipment	9,000	
Buildings	90,000	
Accumulated Depreciation, Buildings		$ 6,000
Notes Payable		1,500
Unearned Revenues		2,800
Pat Nakamura, Capital		100,000
Pat Nakamura, Withdrawals	13,000	
Revenues from Services		212,000
Wages Expense	118,500	
	$322,300	$322,300

General Journal				
Date		Description	Debit	Credit

4. At year-beginning and year-end, Karayan Industries had the following balance sheet balances:

	Jan. 1	Dec. 31
Wages Payable	$1,200	$3,700
Unearned Revenue	500	900
Prepaid Rent	2,400	1,800

In addition, the following figures were taken from the income statement:

Wages Expense	$ 8,700
Revenue from Services	35,000
Rent Expense	3,600

a. Cash paid for wages during the year =

$_____.

b. Cash received for revenue during the year =

$_____.

c. Cash paid for rent during the year =

$_____.

Crossword Puzzle
for Chapters 2 and 3

ACROSS

1. An account that is subtracted from another
3. See 21-Down
6. Postponement of a revenue or expense
7. Journal column title (same as 2-Down)
9. Where accounts are kept
13. Source of revenues
16. Test of debit and credit equality (2 words)
18. Left side of ledger
19. Monthly or yearly compensation
22. _____ bookkeeping (hyphenated)
23. Realize (revenues)

DOWN

1. Historical _____
2. Post. _____ column
4. Become an expense
5. Hourly or piecework-rate compensation
8. Income statement item
10. _____ estate (land)
11. Record transactions
12. Rule applied through accrual accounting
14. Right side of ledger
15. Assignment of a dollar amount to
17. Recognition of unrecorded revenues or expenses
20. Written promise to pay
21. With 3-Across, the term accountants use to refer to profit

CHAPTER 4   COMPLETING THE ACCOUNTING CYCLE

REVIEWING THE CHAPTER

Objective 1: State all the steps in the accounting cycle.

1. The steps in the **accounting cycle** (or the sequence of steps followed in the accounting system) are as follows:
   a. The transactions are analyzed from the source documents.
   b. The transactions are recorded in the journal.
   c. The entries are posted to the ledger and a trial balance is prepared.
   d. The accounts are adjusted at the end of the period to produce the adjusted trial balance.
   e. The revenue, expense, and withdrawals accounts are closed to conclude the current accounting period and prepare for the beginning of the new accounting period. Also, a post-closing trial balance is prepared.
   f. Financial statements are prepared from the adjusted trial balance.

Objective 2: Explain the purposes of closing entries.

2. Balance sheet accounts are sometimes referred to as **permanent** (or *real*) **accounts** because their balances can extend past the end of an accounting period. They are *not* set back to zero.

3. Revenue and expense accounts are sometimes referred to as **temporary** (or *nominal*) **accounts** because they are temporary in nature. Their purpose is to record revenues and expenses during a particular accounting period. At the end of that period, their totals are transferred to owner's equity, leaving zero balances to begin the next accounting period.

4. **Closing entries** serve two purposes. First, they set the stage for the new accounting period by clearing revenue and expense accounts of their balances. (So that the owner's Capital account can be updated, the Withdrawals account also is closed.) Second, they summarize the period's revenues and expenses by transferring the balance of revenue and expense accounts to the **Income Summary** account. The Income Summary account exists only during the closing process and does not appear in the work sheet or in the financial statements.

Objective 3: Prepare the required closing entries.

5. There are four closing entries, as follows:
   a. Income statement accounts with credit balances are closed. This is accomplished with a compound entry that debits each account for the amount required to give it a zero balance and credits Income Summary for the total.
   b. Income statement accounts with debit balances are closed. This is accomplished with a compound entry that credits each account for the amount required to give it a zero balance, and debits Income Summary for the total.
   c. The Income Summary account is closed. After the income statement accounts have been closed, the Income Summary account will have either a debit balance or a credit balance. If a credit balance exists, then Income Summary must be debited for the amount required to give it a zero balance, and the owner's Capital account is credited for the same amount.

The reverse is done when Income Summary has a debit balance.

d. The Withdrawals account is closed. This is accomplished by crediting the owner's Withdrawals account for the amount required to give it a zero balance, and debiting the owner's Capital account for the same amount. Note that the Income Summary account is not involved in this closing entry.

Objective 4: Prepare the post-closing trial balance.

6. After the closing entries are posted to the ledger, a **post-closing trial balance** must be prepared to verify again the equality of the debits and credits in the ledger. Only balance sheet accounts appear because all income statement accounts (as well as the Withdrawals account) have zero balances at this point.

Objective 5: Prepare reversing entries as appropriate.

7. At the end of each accounting period, the accountant makes adjusting entries to bring revenues and expenses into conformity with the matching rule. The accrual type of adjusting entry is followed in the next period by the receipt or payment of cash. Thus it would become necessary in the next period to make a special entry dividing amounts between the two periods. To avoid this inconvenience, the accountant can make **reversing entries** (dated the beginning of the new period). Reversing entries, though not required, allow the bookkeeper to simply make the routine bookkeeping entry when cash finally changes hands. Not all adjusting entries may be reversed. In the system we use, only adjustments for accruals may be reversed. Deferrals may not.

Objective 6: Prepare a work sheet.

8. Accountants use **working papers** to help organize their work and to provide evidence in support of the financial statements. The **work sheet** is one such working paper. It decreases the chance of overlooking an adjustment, acts as a check on the arithmetical accuracy of the accounts, provides evidence of past work so that accountants can retrace their steps, and helps in preparing financial statements. The work sheet is never published but is a useful tool for the accountant.

9. The five steps in the preparation of the work sheet are as follows:
a. Enter and total the account balances in the Trial Balance columns.

b. Enter and total the adjustments in the Adjustments columns. (A letter identifies the debit and credit for each adjustment and can act as a key to a brief explanation at the bottom of the work sheet.)
c. Enter (after **crossfooting,** or adding and subtracting from left to right) and total the adjusted account balances in the Adjusted Trial Balance columns.
d. Extend (transfer) the account balances from the Adjusted Trial Balance columns to the Income Statement columns or the Balance Sheet columns (depending on which type of account is involved).
e. Total the Income Statement columns and the Balance Sheet columns. Enter the net income or net loss in both pairs of columns (one will be entered in a debit column and one will be entered in a credit column) as a balancing figure, and recompute the column totals.

Objective 7: Use a work sheet for three different purposes.

10. Once the work sheet is completed, it can be used to (a) record the adjusting entries in the general journal, (b) record the closing entries in the journal, and (c) prepare the financial statements, thus preparing the records for the new period.
a. Formal adjusting entries must be recorded in the journal and posted to the ledger so that the account balances on the books will agree with those on the financial statements. This is easily accomplished by referring to the Adjustments columns (and footnoted explanations) of the work sheet.
b. Formal closing entries are entered into the journal and posted to the ledger, as explained in Objective 3. This is accomplished by referring to the work sheet's Income Statement columns (for the revenue and expense accounts) and its Balance Sheet debit column (for the Withdrawals account).
c. The income statement may be prepared from the information found in the work sheet's Income Statement columns. Calculations of the change in owner's capital for the period are shown in the statement of owner's equity. Information for this calculation may be found in the Balance Sheet columns of the work sheet (beginning capital, net income, and withdrawals). The balance sheet may be prepared from information found in the work sheet's Balance Sheet columns and in the statement of owner's equity.

A. (LO 3) Advertising Fees Earned   XX (current credit balance)
           Art Fees Earned   XX (current credit balance)
             Income Summary   XX (sum of revenue amounts)
               To close the revenue accounts

B. (LO 3) Income Summary   XX (sum of expense amounts)
             Wages Expense   XX (current debit balance)
             Utilities Expense   XX (current debit balance)
             Telephone Expense   XX (current debit balance)
             Rent Expense   XX (current debit balance)
             Insurance Expense   XX (current debit balance)
             Art Supplies Expense   XX (current debit balance)
             Office Supplies Expense   XX (current debit balance)
             Depreciation Expense, Art Equipment   XX (current debit balance)
             Depreciation Expense, Office Equipment   XX (current debit balance)
               To close the expense accounts

C. (LO 3) Income Summary   XX (current credit balance)
             Joan Miller, Capital   XX (net income amount)
               To close the Income Summary account
               (profit situation)

D. (LO 3) Joan Miller, Capital   XX (withdrawals for period)
             Joan Miller, Withdrawals   XX (withdrawals for period)
               To close the Withdrawals account

E. (LO 5) Wages Expense   XX (amount incurred)
             Wages Payable   XX (amount to be paid)
               Accrued unrecorded wages

F. (LO 5) Wages Payable   XX (amount previously accrued)
           Wages Expense   XX (amount incurred this period)
             Cash   XX (amount paid)
               Paid wages; entry E above was *not* reversed

G. (LO 5) Wages Payable   XX (amount to be paid)
             Wages Expense   XX (amount incurred)
               Reversing entry for E above (assume Wages
               Expense had been closed at end of period)

H. (LO 5) Wages Expense   XX (amount paid)
             Cash   XX (amount paid)
               Paid wages; entry E above *was* reversed

I. (LO 5) Advertising Fees Earned   XX (amount accrued)
             Fees Receivable   XX (amount to be received)
               Reversed adjusting entry for accrued fees receivable

SELF-TEST

Test your knowledge of the chapter by choosing the best answer for each of the following items.

1. Which of the following sequences of actions describes the proper sequence of the accounting cycle?
    a. Post, record, analyze, prepare, close, adjust
    b. Analyze, record, post, adjust, close, prepare
    c. Prepare, record, post, adjust, analyze, close
    d. Enter, record, close, prepare, adjust, analyze

2. One important purpose of closing entries is to
    a. adjust the accounts in the ledger.
    b. set balance sheet accounts to zero to begin the next accounting period.
    c. set income statement accounts to zero to begin the next accounting period.
    d. summarize assets and liabilities.

3. After all the closing entries have been posted, the balance of the Income Summary account should be
    a. a debit if a net income has been earned.
    b. a debit if a net loss has been incurred.
    c. a credit if a net loss has been incurred.
    d. zero.

4. After the closing entries have been posted, all of the following accounts should have a zero balance *except* for
    a. Service Revenue Earned.
    b. Depreciation Expense.
    c. Unearned Service Revenue.
    d. Service Wages Expense.

5. The post-closing trial balance
    a. lists income statement accounts only.
    b. lists balance sheet accounts only.
    c. lists both income statement and balance sheet accounts.
    d. is prepared before closing entries are posted to the ledger.

6. For which of the following adjustments would a reversing entry facilitate bookkeeping procedures?
    a. An adjustment for depreciation expense
    b. An adjustment to allocate prepaid insurance to the current period
    c. An adjustment made as a result of an inventory of supplies
    d. An adjustment for wages earned but not yet paid to employees

7. The work sheet is a type of
    a. ledger.
    b. journal.
    c. working paper.
    d. financial statement.

8. Which of the following is shown directly on the work sheet?
    a. Ending owner's capital
    b. Total assets
    c. Net income
    d. Total liabilities

9. In preparing closing entries, it is helpful to refer first to the
    a. Adjustments columns of the work sheet.
    b. Adjusted Trial Balance columns of the work sheet.
    c. Income Statement columns of the work sheet.
    d. general journal.

10. The work sheet may assist in
    a. preparing financial statements.
    b. recording adjusting entries.
    c. recording closing entries.
    d. all of the above.

TESTING YOUR KNOWLEDGE

Matching*

Match each term with its definition by writing the appropriate letter in the blank.

_____ 1. Post-closing trial balance

_____ 2. Working papers

_____ 3. Work sheet

_____ 4. Foot

_____ 5. Crossfooting

_____ 6. Reversing entry

_____ 7. Closing entries

_____ 8. Income Summary

_____ 9. Temporary (nominal) accounts

_____ 10. Permanent (real) accounts

a. Accounts whose balances extend beyond the end of an accounting period
b. Add, or total, a column of numbers
c. The means of transferring net income or loss to the owner's Capital account
d. A working paper that facilitates the preparation of financial statements
e. A final proof that the accounts are in balance
f. The opposite of an adjusting entry, journalized to facilitate routine bookkeeping
g. Documents that help accountants organize their work
h. Adding and subtracting from left to right
i. Accounts that begin each period with zero balances
j. An account used only during the closing process

Short Answer

Use the lines provided to answer each item.

1. What four accounts or kinds of accounts are closed out each accounting period?

_____

_____

_____

_____

2. List the five columnar headings of a work sheet in their proper order.

_____

_____

_____

_____

_____

3. In general, what accounts appear in the post-closing trial balance? What accounts do *not* appear?

_____

_____

_____

4. Briefly, explain the purpose of reversing entries.

_____

_____

_____

5. The six steps in the accounting cycle are presented here in the wrong order. Place the numbers 1 through 6 in the spaces provided to indicate the correct order.

_____ The entries are posted to the ledger.

_____ The temporary accounts are closed.

_____ The transactions are analyzed from the source documents.

_____ The accounts are adjusted.

_____ The transactions are recorded in the journal.

_____ Financial statements are prepared from the adjusted trial balance.

_____

Note to student: The matching quiz might be completed more efficiently by starting with the definition and searching for the corresponding term.

Circle T if the statement is true, F if it is false. Please provide explanations for the false answers, using the blank lines at the end of the section.

T F **1.** The work sheet is prepared before the formal adjusting entries have been made in the journal.

T F **2.** Preparation of a work sheet helps reduce the possibility of overlooking an adjustment.

T F **3.** Total debits will differ from total credits in the Balance Sheet columns of a work sheet by the amount of the net income or loss.

T F **4.** The statement of owner's equity is prepared after the formal income statement, but before the formal balance sheet.

T F **5.** The Income Summary account can be found in the statement of owner's equity.

T F **6.** Closing entries convert real and nominal accounts to zero balances.

T F **7.** When revenue accounts are closed, the Income Summary account will be credited.

T F **8.** The Withdrawals account is closed to the Income Summary account.

T F **9.** When the Income Summary account is closed, it always requires a debit.

T F **10.** Reversing entries are never required.

T F **11.** The work sheet is published with the balance sheet and income statement, as a supplementary statement.

T F **12.** A key letter is needed in the Adjusted Trial Balance columns of a work sheet to show whether the entry is extended to the Balance Sheet columns or the Income Statement columns.

T F **13.** If total debits exceed total credits (before balancing) in the Income Statement columns of a work sheet, that means that a net loss has occurred.

T F **14.** The post-closing trial balance will contain the Withdrawals account.

T F **15.** Reversing entries update the accounts at the end of the accounting period.

T F **16.** Accounts Payable is an example of a permanent (real) account.

Multiple Choice

Circle the letter of the best answer.

1. Which account will appear in the post-closing trial balance?
   a. Interest Income
   b. Income Summary
   c. Dawn Brooks, Capital
   d. Dawn Brooks, Withdrawals

2. Which of the following statements is true?
   a. Closing entries are prepared before formal adjusting entries.
   b. The work sheet is prepared after the post-closing trial balance.
   c. Formal adjusting entries are prepared before the work sheet.
   d. The financial statements are prepared after the post-closing trial balance.

3. Reversing entries
   a. are dated as of the end of the period.
   b. are the opposite of adjusting entries.
   c. may be made for depreciation previously recorded.
   d. are the opposite of closing entries.

4. If total debits exceed total credits (before balancing) in the Balance Sheet columns of a work sheet,
   a. a net income has occurred.
   b. a net loss has occurred.
   c. a mistake has definitely been made.
   d. no conclusions can be drawn until the closing entries have been made.

5. Which of the following accounts would *not* be involved in closing entries?
   a. Unearned Commissions
   b. Richard Hale, Capital
   c. Telephone Expense
   d. Richard Hale, Withdrawals

6. When a net loss has occurred,
   a. all expense accounts are closed with debits.
   b. the Income Summary account is closed with a credit.
   c. the Withdrawals account is closed with a debit.
   d. all revenue accounts are closed with credits.

7. Which of the following is *not* an objective of closing entries?
   a. To transfer net income or loss to the owner's Capital account
   b. To produce zero balances in all nominal accounts
   c. To update the revenue and expense accounts
   d. To be able to measure net income for the following period

8. A company began the accounting period with $50,000 in owner's capital, ended with $75,000 in owner's capital, and the owner withdrew $30,000 during the period for personal use. What was the company's net income or loss for the period?
   a. $55,000 net income
   b. $30,000 net loss
   c. $5,000 net loss
   d. $5,000 net income

9. Which of the following is an example of a temporary account?
   a. Prepaid Rent
   b. Unearned Revenues
   c. Wages Expense
   d. Accumulated Depreciation, Building

APPLYING YOUR KNOWLEDGE

Exercises

1. Below are the accounts and amounts in a work sheet's Adjusted Trial Balance columns for the month of July. In the journal provided, record the necessary closing entries. All accounts have normal balances.

Accounts Payable	$1,000
Accounts Receivable	2,000
Sidney Simon, Capital	3,000
Sidney Simon, Withdrawals	2,500
Cash	3,500
Rent Expense	500
Revenue from Services	4,700
Telephone Expense	50
Utilities Expense	150

General Journal				
Date		Description	Debit	Credit

2. Using the information from Exercise 1, complete the following statement of retained earnings.

Sid's Fix-It Shop
Statement of Owner's Equity
For the Month Ended July 31, 20xx

---

3. The items below provide the information needed to make adjustments for Frieda's Garden Service as of December 31, 20xx. Complete the entire work sheet on the next page using this information. Remember to use key letters for each adjustment.

a. On December 31, there is $200 of unexpired rent on the storage garage.

b. Depreciation taken on the lawn equipment during the period amounts to $1,500.

c. An inventory of lawn supplies shows $100 remaining on December 31.

d. Accrued wages on December 31 amount to $280.

e. Grass-cutting fees earned but as yet unrecorded amount to $50.

f. Of the $300 landscaping fees collected in advance, $120 had been earned by December 31.

Frieda's Garden Service
Work Sheet
For the Year Ended December 31, 20xx

Account Name	Trial Balance		Adjustments		Adjusted Trial Balance		Income Statement		Balance Sheet	
	Debit	Credit	Debit	Credit	Debit	Credit	Debit	Credit	Debit	Credit
Cash	2,560									
Accounts Receivable	880									
Prepaid Rent	750									
Lawn Supplies	250									
Lawn Equipment	10,000									
Accum. Deprec., Lawn Equip.		2,000								
Accounts Payable		630								
Unearned Landscaping Fees		300								
Frieda Parsons, Capital		6,000								
Frieda Parsons, Withdrawals	6,050									
Grass-Cutting Fees		15,000								
Wages Expense	3,300									
Gasoline Expense	140									
	23,930	23,930								
Rent Expense										
Depreciation Expense										
Lawn Supplies Expense										
Landscaping Fees Earned										
Wages Payable										
Net Income										

4. On December 1, Dickerson Company borrowed $20,000 from a bank on a note for 90 days at 12 percent annual interest. Assuming that interest is not included in the face amount, prepare the following journal entries using the form below:

a. December 1 entry to record the note
b. December 31 entry to record accrued interest (interest is $200 per month)
c. December 31 entry to close interest
d. January 1 reversing entry
e. March 1 entry to record payment of the note plus interest

		General Journal		
Date		**Description**	**Debit**	**Credit**

CHAPTER 5 MERCHANDISING OPERATIONS

REVIEWING THE CHAPTER

Objective 1: Identify the management issues related to merchandising businesses.

1. Accounting for **service businesses,** such as movers and dry cleaners, is relatively easy because this type of business does not have inventory (goods for resale) to manage.

2. A **merchandising business,** on the other hand, is a wholesaler or retailer that buys and sells goods in finished form. This kind of firm uses the same basic accounting methods as a service company. However, the merchandiser must also account for its inventory, requiring a more complicated process and producing a more sophisticated income statement.

3. The merchandiser engages in a series of transactions known as the **operating cycle,** consisting of (a) the purchase of **merchandise inventory,** or goods available for sale, (b) the payment for purchases made on credit, (c) the sale of the inventory for cash or on credit, and (d) the collection of cash from credit sales.

4. Merchandisers must carefully manage cash flow, or liquidity. Such **cash flow management** is essential for the business to pay its bills when they fall due. **Profitability management** is also important for the merchandiser. It involves purchasing goods at favorable prices, selling those goods at a price that will cover costs and help earn a profit, and controlling operating expenses.

5. One effective way to control expenses is to use operating budgets. An **operating budget** consists of a detailed listing of selling and general and administrative expenses, along with their projected amounts. Periodically, management should compare these budgeted amounts with actual amounts expensed, analyze the items that are significantly over or under budget, and adjust operations accordingly.

6. The merchandising company must choose a system to account for its inventory. The two basic systems are the periodic inventory system and the perpetual inventory system.

7. The **perpetual inventory system** is used when management wishes to keep a record of the quantity (and usually the cost) of inventory as it is both purchased and sold. As a result, management can quickly determine product availability, avoid running out of stock, and control the costs of carrying its inventory. Under the perpetual inventory system, the Merchandise Inventory account and Cost of Goods Sold are updated whenever goods are sold.

8. The **periodic inventory system** is used when it is unnecessary or impractical to keep track of the quantity of inventory or the cost of each item. Under this method, the company waits until the end of the accounting period to take a physical inventory. This physical count figure is then multiplied by a derived cost-per-unit figure (explained in Chapter 10) to arrive at the cost of ending inventory.

9. The periodic inventory system is simpler and less costly to maintain than the perpetual inventory system. However, its lack of detailed records may

lead to inefficiencies, lost sales, and higher operating costs.

10. A merchandising business typically handles a great deal of cash and inventory. Unfortunately, these assets are very susceptible to theft and embezzlement. Accordingly, a good system of **internal control** must be established by management to help protect the company's assets and to help produce reliable accounting records. The specific procedures that are commonly adopted are discussed in Chapter 8.

11. Merchandise inventory appears as an asset on the balance sheet and includes all salable goods owned by the company, no matter where the goods are located. Goods in transit to which a company has acquired title are included in ending inventory. However, goods that the company has formally sold are not included, even if the company has not yet delivered them. To simplify the taking of a **physical inventory** (an actual count of the merchandise on hand), which usually takes place on the last day of the fiscal year, many companies end their fiscal year during the slow season, when inventories are relatively low.

Objective 2: Compare the income statements for service and merchandising concerns, and define the components of the merchandising income statement.

12. Service companies calculate net income by simply deducting expenses from revenues. However, the income of a merchandising firm is computed as follows:

    Net Sales

    − Cost of Goods Sold

    = Gross Margin

    − Operating Expenses

    = Net Income

13. **Net sales** (or simply *sales*) consist of gross proceeds from the sale of merchandise (**gross sales**) less **sales returns and allowances** and sales discounts. Both sales returns and allowances and sales discounts appear as contra accounts to gross sales in the income statement.

14. **Cost of goods sold** (also called *cost of sales*) is the amount that the merchandising company originally paid for the goods that it sold during a given period. If, for example, a merchandising firm sells for $100 a radio that cost the company $70, then revenues from sales are $100, cost of goods sold is $70, and **gross margin** (also called *gross profit*) is $30. This $30 gross margin helps pay for **operating expenses** (all expenses other than cost of goods sold). What is left after subtracting operating expenses represents **net income.** Preparing an income statement in this way provides useful information to management, which is continually trying to improve net income.

15. Operating expenses consist of selling expenses and general and administrative expenses. Selling expenses are advertising expenses, salespeople's salaries, sales office expenses, **freight out expense** on merchandise sold (also called *delivery expense),* and all other expenses directly related to the sales effort. General and administrative expenses are all expenses not directly related to the sales effort. Examples are general office expenses and executive salaries.

Objective 3: Define and distinguish the terms of sale for merchandising transactions.

16. As a matter of convenience, manufacturers and wholesalers frequently quote prices of merchandise based on a discount from the list or catalogue price (called a **trade discount**). Neither the list price nor the trade discount is entered into the accounting records.

17. When goods are sold on credit, terms will vary as to when payment must be made. For instance, n/30 means that full payment is due within 30 days after the invoice date, and n/10 eom means that full payment is due 10 days after the end of the month.

18. Often a customer is given a discount for early payment, and the merchandiser records a **sales discount.** Terms of 2/10, n/30, for example, mean that a 2 percent discount will be given if payment is made within 10 days of the invoice date. Otherwise, the full amount is due within 30 days.

19. Freight charges are borne by the buyer or seller of the goods, depending upon the terms specified. A merchandiser in Chicago, for instance, must pay the freight in from Boston if the terms specify FOB Boston or **FOB shipping point.** However, the supplier in Boston pays if the terms are FOB Chicago or **FOB destination.** FOB terms are also related to when the title of the merchandise passes from the seller to the buyer. FOB stands for "free on board."

Objective 4: Prepare an income statement and record merchandising transactions under the perpetual inventory system.

20. As illustrated in paragraph 12, the net income of a merchandising firm is computed as follows:

    Net Sales
    – Cost of Goods Sold
    = Gross Margin
    – Operating Expenses
    = Net Income

21. Under the perpetual inventory system, cost of goods sold and merchandise inventory are updated whenever a purchase, sale, or other inventory transaction takes place. In addition, **freight in** (also called *transportation in*) is usually included in cost of goods sold.

22. Transactions are recorded under the perpetual inventory system as explained below:

    a. For the purchase of merchandise on credit, Merchandise Inventory is debited and Accounts Payable is credited.

    b. Transportation costs for goods received are recorded with a debit to Freight In (also called *transportation in*) and a credit to Accounts Payable or Cash.

    c. The return of goods to the supplier (for credit) is recorded with a debit to Accounts Payable and a credit to Merchandise Inventory.

    d. Payment on account is recorded with a simple debit to Accounts Payable and credit to Cash.

    e. When goods are sold on credit, Accounts Receivable is debited and Sales is credited. However, an additional entry must be made, debiting Cost of Goods Sold and crediting Merchandise Inventory.

    f. Delivery costs for goods sold are recorded with a debit to Freight Out Expense and a credit to Accounts Payable or Cash.

    g. When a credit customer returns goods for a refund, Sales Returns and Allowances is debited and Accounts Receivable is credited. The Sales Returns and Allowances account is debited instead of the Sales account to provide management with data on customer dissatisfaction. Under the perpetual inventory system, a second entry is needed to reinstate Merchandise Inventory (a debit) and to reduce Cost of Goods Sold (a credit).

    h. The receipt of payment on account is recorded with a simple debit to Cash and credit to Accounts Receivable.

23. Companies that allow customers to use national credit cards (such as MasterCard) must follow special accounting procedures. The credit card company reimburses the merchant for the sale, less a service charge. The credit card company levies this service charge because it is responsible for establishing credit and collecting money from the customer. Assuming that the merchant deposits its credit card sales invoices into a special bank account for immediate credit, it would debit Cash and Credit Card Discount Expense and credit Sales.

24. Inventory losses result from theft and spoilage, and are included in cost of goods sold. These losses are easier to track under the perpetual inventory system than under the periodic system, for the following reason. Under the perpetual system, the Merchandise Inventory account is constantly updated for sales, purchases, and returns. Accordingly, the loss can be identified as the difference between the dollar amount in the inventory records and the dollar amount indicated by the physical count at the end of the period. Normally, Cost of Goods Sold is debited and Merchandise Inventory credited to record the loss.

Supplemental Objective 5: Prepare an income statement and record merchandising transactions under the periodic inventory system.

25. Under the periodic inventory system, cost of goods sold and merchandise inventory are *not* updated for purchases, sales, and other inventory transactions. In addition, its income statement contains a specific calculation of cost of goods sold, as illustrated below:

    Beginning Inventory
    + Net Cost of Purchases (see paragraph 26)
    = **Goods Available for Sale**
    – **Ending Inventory**
    = Cost of Goods Sold

26. **Net cost of purchases** is calculated as follows:

    (Gross) Purchases
    – Purchases Returns and Allowances
    – Purchases Discounts
    = **Net Purchases**
    + Freight In
    = Net Cost of Purchases

27. The ending inventory of one period automatically becomes the beginning inventory of the next period.

28. Transactions are recorded under the periodic inventory system as explained below:

   a. All purchases of merchandise are debited to the **Purchases** account and credited to Accounts Payable. The purpose of the Purchases account is to accumulate the cost of merchandise purchased for resale during the period.

   b. Transportation costs for goods purchased are recorded with a debit to Freight In and a credit to Accounts Payable or Cash.

   c. The return of goods to the supplier (for credit) is recorded with a debt to Accounts Payable and a credit to **Purchases Returns and Allowances.** The latter appears as a contra account to Purchases on the income statement.

   d. Payment on account is recorded with a simple debit to Accounts Payable and credit to Cash.

   e. When a cash sale is made, Cash is debited and Sales is credited for the amount of the sale. When a credit sale is made, Accounts Receivable is debited and Sales is credited. Generally, a sale is recorded when the goods are delivered and title passes to the customer, regardless of when payment is made.

   f. Delivery costs for goods sold are recorded with a debit to Freight Out Expense and a credit to Accounts Payable or Cash.

   g. When a credit customer returns goods for a refund, Sales Returns and Allowances is debited and Accounts Receivable is credited.

   h. The receipt of payment on account is recorded with a simple debit to Cash and credit to Accounts Receivable.

Supplemental Objective 6: Prepare a work sheet and closing entries for a merchandising concern using the perpetual inventory system.

29. The work sheet for a merchandising company is prepared a bit differently from that of a service company, which was explained and illustrated in Chapter 4. The main difference is the inclusion of accounts such as Merchandise Inventory, Sales, and Freight In. In addition, work sheet preparation will differ depending upon whether the periodic or the perpetual inventory system is being used.

30. Under the perpetual inventory system, the Merchandise Inventory account is up to date at the end of the accounting period. This occurs because the account is updated whenever there is a purchase, sale, or return. Therefore, Merchandise Inventory is not involved in the closing process. On the work sheet, the Trial Balance and Balance Sheet columns both reflect the ending balance. Under either inventory system, an Adjusted Trial Balance column may be eliminated if only a few adjustments are necessary.

31. As inventory is sold (under the perpetual inventory system), the cost is transferred from the Merchandise Inventory account to Cost of Goods Sold. Therefore, Cost of Goods Sold will appear in the work sheet and in the closing entries along with all the other expenses.

32. Data for closing entries may be obtained from the completed work sheet. A summary of the closing entries is presented at the end of this chapter review.

Supplemental Objective 7: Prepare a work sheet and closing entries for a merchandising concern using the periodic inventory system.

33. Under the periodic inventory system, the objectives of dealing with inventory at the end of the period are to (a) remove the beginning balance from the Merchandise Inventory account, (b) enter the ending balance into the Merchandise Inventory account, and (c) enter the beginning inventory as a debit and the ending inventory as a credit to the Income Summary account to become part of the calculation of net income.

34. Under the periodic inventory system, beginning inventory appears as a debit in the Income Statement column of the work sheet. Ending inventory appears as a credit in the Income Statement column and as a debit in the Balance Sheet column. A Cost of Goods Sold account will *not* appear in the work sheet, though it will under the perpetual inventory system.

35. Data for closing entries may be obtained from the completed work sheet. A summary of the closing entries is presented at the end of this chapter review.

Supplemental Objective 8: Apply sales and purchases discounts to merchandising transactions.

36. Often a merchandising company offers (and is offered) a discount if payment is received (or made) within a given number of days.

   a. Sales discounts are recorded when payment is received within the discount period. Cash and Sales Discounts are debited; Accounts Receivable is credited. Sales Discounts is a contra account to Gross Sales in the income statement.

   b. A purchase is initially recorded at the gross purchase price. If the company makes payment within the discount period, it debits Accounts Payable, credits Purchases Discounts and Cash. **Purchases Discounts** is a contra account to Purchases in the Income Statement.

Perpetual Inventory System

A. (LO 4) Merchandise Inventory   XX (purchase price)
         Accounts Payable   XX (amount due)
               Purchased merchandise on credit

B. (LO 4) Freight In   XX (price charged)
         Accounts Payable   XX (amount due)
               Received transportation charges

C. (LO 4) Accounts Payable   XX (amount returned)
         Merchandise Inventory   XX (amount returned)
               Returned merchandise to supplier for full credit

D. (LO 4) Accounts Payable   XX (amount paid)
         Cash   XX (amount paid)
               Made payment on account

E. (LO 4) Accounts Receivable   XX (amount to be received)
         Sales   XX (sales price)
               Sold merchandise on credit

         Cost of Goods Sold   XX (inventory cost)
         Merchandise Inventory   XX (inventory cost)
               Transferred cost of merchandise inventory sold
               to Cost of Goods Sold account

F. (LO 4) Freight Out Expense   XX (amount incurred)
         Cash   XX (amount paid)
               Paid delivery costs

G. (LO 4) Sales Returns and Allowances   XX (price of goods returned)
         Accounts Receivable   XX (amount credited to account)
               Accepted returned merchandise for credit

         Merchandise Inventory   XX (inventory cost)
          Cost of Goods Sold   XX (inventory cost)
               Transferred cost of merchandise returned to
               the Merchandise Inventory account

H. (LO 4) Cash   XX (amount received)
         Accounts Receivable   XX (amount settled)
               Received payment on account

I. (LO 4) Cash   XX (amount net of fee)
         Credit Card Discount Expense   XX (fee charged)
          Sales   XX (gross amount sold)
               Made sales on credit card

Periodic Inventory System

J. (SO 5) Purchases   XX (purchase price)

                Accounts Payable   XX (amount due)

                    Purchased merchandise on credit

K. (SO 5) Freight In   XX (price charged)

                Accounts Payable   XX (amount due)

                    Received transportation charges

L. (SO 5) Accounts Payable   XX (amount returned)

                Purchases Returns and Allowances   XX (amount returned)

                    Returned merchandise to supplier for full credit

M. (SO 5) Accounts Payable   XX (amount paid)

                Cash   XX (amount paid)

                    Made payment on account

N. (SO 5) Accounts Receivable   XX (amount to be received)

                Sales   XX (sales price)

                    Sold merchandise on credit

O. (SO 5) Freight Out Expense   XX (amount incurred)

                Cash   XX (amount paid)

                    Paid delivery costs

P. (SO 5) Sales Returns and Allowances   XX (price of goods returned)

                Accounts Receivable   XX (amount credited to account)

                    Accepted returned merchandise, credited account

Q. (SO 5) Cash   XX (amount received)

                Accounts Receivable   XX (amount settled)

                    Received payment on account

Perpetual Inventory System

R. (SO 6) Income Summary   XX (sum of credits)

                Sales Returns and Allowances   XX (current debit balance)

                Cost of Goods Sold   XX (current debit balance)

                Freight In   XX (current debit balance)

                All other expenses   XX (current debit balances)

                    Closing entry 1: To close the temporary expense
                    and revenue accounts having debit balances

S. (SO 6) Sales   XX (current credit balance)

                Income Summary   XX (sales amount)

                    Closing entry 2: To close the temporary revenue
                    account having a credit balance

T. (SO 6) Income Summary   XX (current credit balance)

                Gloria Fenwick, Capital   XX (net income amount)

                    Closing entry 3: To close the Income Summary
                    account

U. (SO 6) Gloria Fenwick, Capital   XX (amount withdrawn)

          Gloria Fenwick, Withdrawals   XX (amount withdrawn)

                    Closing entry 4: To close the Withdrawals account

---

Periodic Inventory System

V. (SO 7) Income Summary   XX (sum of credits)

          Merchandise Inventory   XX (beginning amount)

          Sales Returns and Allowances   XX (current debit balance)

          Purchases   XX (current debit balance)

          Freight In   XX (current debit balance)

          All other expenses   XX (current debit balances)

                    Closing entry 1: To close the temporary expense and revenue accounts having debit balances and to remove the beginning inventory

W. (SO 7) Merchandise Inventory   XX (ending amount)

          Sales   XX (current credit balance)

          Purchases Returns and Allowances   XX (current credit balance)

               Income Summary   XX (sum of debits)

                    Closing entry 2: To close the temporary expense and revenue accounts having credit balances and to establish the ending inventory

X. (SO 7) Income Summary   XX (current credit balance)

          Gloria Fenwick, Capital   XX (net income amount)

                    Closing entry 3: To close the Income Summary account

Y. (SO 7) Gloria Fenwick, Capital   XX (amount withdrawn)

          Gloria Fenwick, Withdrawals   XX (amount withdrawn)

                    Closing entry 4: To close the Withdrawals account

---

Z. (SO 8) Cash   XX (net amount received)

          Sales Discounts   XX (discount given)

                  Accounts Receivable   XX (gross amount settled)

                  Received payment for sale, discount taken

AA. (SO 8) Accounts Payable   XX (gross amount settled)

          Purchases Discounts   XX (discount taken)

          Cash   XX (net amount paid)

                  Paid supplier, discount taken

SELF-TEST

Test your knowledge of the chapter by choosing the best answer for each of the following items.

1. Management determines that, on average, customers are taking five more days to pay for sales made on credit. To which of the following management concerns does this payment pattern directly relate?
   a. Cash flow management
   b. Profitability management
   c. Choice of inventory system
   d. Control of merchandise operations

2. A net income always results when
   a. the cost of goods sold exceeds operating expenses.
   b. revenues exceed the cost of goods sold.
   c. revenues exceed operating expenses.
   d. the gross margin exceeds operating expenses.

3. Which of the following appears as an operating expense on the income statement of a merchandising concern?
   a. Freight In
   b. Freight Out Expense
   c. Sales Returns and Allowances
   d. Purchases Returns and Allowances

4. If beginning and ending merchandise inventories are $400 and $700, respectively, and the cost of goods sold is $3,400, net cost of purchases
   a. is $3,700.
   b. is $3,400.
   c. is $3,100.
   d. cannot be determined.

5. A firm that maintains perpetual inventory records sells on account for $2,000 goods that had cost $1,400. The entries to record this transaction should include a
   a. debit to Merchandise Inventory for $1,400.
   b. debit to Sales for $2,000.
   c. credit to Accounts Receivable for $2,000.
   d. debit to Cost of Goods Sold for $1,400.

6. A purchase of merchandise for $750 including freight of $50 under terms of n/30, FOB shipping point would include a
   a. debit to Freight In of $50.
   b. debit to Purchases of $750.
   c. credit to Accounts Payable of $700.
   d. credit to Freight Payable of $50.

7. Dawson Company shows a beginning merchandise inventory of $12,000 and an ending merchandise inventory of $14,000. Under the periodic inventory system, what is the balance of the Merchandise Inventory account at the end of the accounting period before and after the closing entries?
   a. $12,000 and $14,000
   b. $14,000 and $12,000
   c. $14,000 and $14,000
   d. $12,000 and $12,000

8. Which of the following balance sheet accounts would appear in the Income Statement columns of a work sheet for a company using the periodic inventory method?
   a. Cash
   b. Merchandise Inventory
   c. Accumulated Depreciation
   d. Accounts Payable

9. The closing entries for a merchandising concern using the perpetual inventory system would contain a credit to
   a. Sales.
   b. Purchases.
   c. Cost of Goods Sold.
   d. Purchases Returns and Allowances.

10. A sale is made on June 1 for $200, terms 2/10, n/30, on which a sales return of $50 is granted on June 7. The dollar amount received for payment in full on June 9 is
    a. $200.
    b. $150.
    c. $147.
    d. $196.

TESTING YOUR KNOWLEDGE

*Matching**

Match each term with its definition by writing the appropriate letter in the blank.

_____ 1. Merchandiser

_____ 2. Cost of goods sold

_____ 3. Gross margin (gross profit)

_____ 4. Operating expenses

_____ 5. Sales Returns and Allowances

_____ 6. Sales Discounts

_____ 7. Operating cycle

_____ 8. Purchases

_____ 9. Goods available for sale

_____ 10. Perpetual inventory system

_____ 11. Periodic inventory system

_____ 12. Physical inventory

_____ 13. Freight in (transportation in)

_____ 14. FOB (free on board)

_____ 15. Purchases Returns and Allowances

_____ 16. Purchases Discounts

a. Transportation cost for goods purchased

b. From the purchase of merchandise to collection from sales

c. A buyer and seller of goods that are in finished form

d. A system whereby continuous quantity and cost records are maintained for merchandise

e. All expenses except the cost of goods sold

f. The point after which the buyer must bear the transportation cost

g. The account used to accumulate the cost of goods bought during the period

h. What a merchandising company paid for the goods that it sold during the period

i. Beginning inventory plus net cost of purchases

j. Net sales minus the cost of goods sold

k. The account used by the seller when the buyer pays for goods early under the terms of the sales agreement

l. The account used by the seller when the buyer returns goods

m. A system whereby continuous quantity and cost records are *not* maintained for merchandise

n. The account used by the buyer when he/she pays for goods early under the terms of the sales agreement

o. A count of merchandise on hand

p. The account used by the buyer when he/she returns goods

Note to student: The matching quiz might be completed more efficiently by starting with the definition and searching for the corresponding term.

Short Answer

Use the lines provided to answer each item.

1. List the five parts of a merchandiser's condensed income statement in their proper order. Use mathematical signs to indicate their relationship.

   _____

   _____

   _____

   _____

   _____

2. Assuming a periodic inventory system, list the items in the condensed cost of goods sold section of an income statement. Use mathematical signs to indicate their relationship.

   _____

   _____

   _____

   _____

   _____

3. Using mathematical signs, list the sequence of items involved in computing net cost of purchases in a periodic inventory system.

   _____

   _____

   _____

   _____

   _____

4. Using mathematical signs, list the sequence of items involved in computing net sales.

   _____

   _____

   _____

   _____

5. Explain briefly how merchandise inventory is handled in the accounts at the end of the period under the periodic inventory system.

   _____

   _____

   _____

   _____

   _____

   _____

True-False

Circle T if the statement is true, F if it is false. Please provide explanations for the false answers, using the blank lines at the end of the section.

T F **1.** The failure to include an item of a warehouse's merchandise in ending inventory results in an overstated net income.

T F **2.** Terms of n/10 eom mean that payment must be made 10 days before the end of the month.

T F **3.** An overstated beginning inventory results in an overstated cost of goods sold.

T F **4.** A low-volume car dealer is more likely to use the periodic inventory system than the perpetual inventory system.

T F **5.** FOB destination means that the seller must bear the transportation cost.

T F **6.** Under the periodic inventory system, Cost of Goods Sold would appear in the work sheet.

T F **7.** Sales Discounts is a contra account to Gross Sales.

T F **8.** Using the periodic inventory system, ending inventory is needed for both the balance sheet and the income statement.

T F **9.** Goods available for sale minus the cost of goods sold equals ending inventory.

T F **10.** The perpetual inventory system requires more detailed recordkeeping than does the periodic system.

T F **11.** The beginning inventory of a period is the same as the ending inventory of the previous period.

T F **12.** Purchases Returns and Allowances is closed with a credit.

T F **13.** Sales Returns and Allowances normally has a credit balance.

T F **14.** Under the periodic inventory system, a cash purchase of office supplies that are meant to be used in the day-to-day operation of a business requires a debit to Purchases and a credit to Cash.

T F **15.** The cost of goods sold does not appear in the income statement of a company that provides services only.

T F **16.** If the gross margin is not enough to cover operating expenses, then a net loss has been suffered.

T F **17.** Under a periodic inventory system, as soon as a sale is made, the cost of the goods sold must be recorded and the inventory account must be decreased.

T F **18.** One example of a trade discount is 2/10, n/30.

T F **19.** When goods are shipped FOB shipping point, title passes when the goods are received by the buyer.

T F **20.** Inventory losses are normally included in the cost of goods sold.

T F **21.** Credit Card Discount Expense is treated by the merchant as a contra account to Sales.

T F **22.** Ending merchandise inventory is needed to calculate goods available for sale.

_____

_____

_____

_____

_____

_____

_____

_____

_____

_____

_____

_____

_____   _____
_____   _____
_____   _____
_____   _____
_____   _____
_____   _____
_____   _____

Multiple Choice

Circle the letter of the best answer.

1. Van buys $600 of merchandise from Allen, with terms of 2/10, n/30. Van immediately returns $100 of goods and pays for the remainder eight days after the purchase. Van's entry on the date of payment would include a
   a. debit to Accounts Payable for $600.
   b. debit to Sales Discounts for $12.
   c. credit to Purchases Returns and Allowances for $100.
   d. credit to Purchases Discounts for $10.

2. Which of the following normally has a credit balance?
   a. Sales Discounts
   b. Merchandise Inventory
   c. Purchases Returns and Allowances
   d. Freight In

3. If an item in ending inventory is accidentally counted twice,
   a. net income will be understated.
   b. beginning inventory for the next period will be understated.
   c. goods available for sale will be overstated.
   d. the cost of goods sold will be understated.

4. On the work sheet, assuming the periodic inventory system, beginning inventory appears on the
   a. debit side of the Income Statement columns.
   b. credit side of the Income Statement columns.
   c. debit side of the Balance Sheet columns.
   d. credit side of the Balance Sheet columns.

5. Which of the following is irrelevant in computing the cost of goods sold?
   a. Freight In
   b. Freight Out Expense
   c. Beginning Merchandise Inventory
   d. Ending Merchandise Inventory

6. Using the periodic inventory system, which of the following is always credited in the closing process?
   a. Purchases Returns and Allowances
   b. Sales
   c. Beginning Inventory
   d. Income Summary

7. Which of the following accounts would appear as an operating expense in a merchandiser's income statement?
   a. Advertising Expense
   b. Sales Discounts
   c. Freight In
   d. Purchases

8. Which of the following accounts is _not_ used in conjunction with a perpetual inventory system?
   a. Cost of Goods Sold
   b. Freight In
   c. Purchases
   d. Merchandise Inventory

9. The operating cycle does _not_ include which of the following transactions?
   a. Sale of inventory
   b. Cash payment for inventory purchases
   c. Purchase of inventory
   d. Cash collection from inventory sales

10. A company has credit card sales for the day of $1,000. If the credit card company charges 5 percent, the company's journal entry to record sales and the receipt of cash upon depositing the credit card invoices at the bank would include a
    a. credit to Sales for $950.
    b. credit to Credit Card Discount Expense for $50.
    c. debit to Sales for $1,000.
    d. debit to Cash for $950.

APPLYING YOUR KNOWLEDGE

Exercises

1. Following are the May transactions of Monumental Merchandising Company. For each transaction, prepare the journal entry in the journal provided on the next page. Assume that the periodic inventory system is used.

May 1 Purchased merchandise for $500 on credit, terms 2/10, n/60.
     3 Sold merchandise for $500 on credit, terms 2/10, 1/20, n/30.
     4 Paid $42 for freight charges relating to a merchandise purchase of April.
     5 Purchased office supplies for $100, on credit.
     6 Returned $20 of the May 5 office supplies, for credit.
     7 Returned $50 of merchandise purchased on May 1, for credit.
     9 Sold merchandise for $225, on credit, terms 2/10, 1/15, n/30.
    10 Paid for the merchandise purchased on May 1, less the return and any discount.
    14 The customer of May 9 returned $25 of merchandise, for credit.
    22 The customer of May 9 paid for the merchandise, less the return and any discount.
    26 The customer of May 3 paid for the merchandise.

General Journal				
Date		Description	Debit	Credit

2. Below are the accounts and data needed to prepare the 20xx closing entries for Reed Merchandising Company. In the journal provided, prepare Reed's closing entries. Assume the use of a periodic inventory system.

Advertising Expense	$ 5,000
Pam Reed, Capital	15,000
Pam Reed, Withdrawals	12,000
Freight In	2,000
Freight Out Expense	4,000

Merchandise Inventory, Jan. 1	$ 10,000
Merchandise Inventory, Dec. 31	8,000
Purchases	50,000
Purchases Discounts	500
Purchases Returns and Allowances	500
Rent Expense	3,000
Sales	100,000
Sales Discounts	300
Sales Returns and Allowances	200
Wages Expense	7,000

General Journal				
Date		Description	Debit	Credit

Merchandising Operations

3. Using the information from Exercise 2, prepare a partial income statement showing just the computation of gross margin.

Reed Merchandising Company Partial Income Statement For the Year 20xx			

4. The work sheet for Kay's Mart has been started, as shown on the next page. Use the following information to complete the work sheet (remember to key the adjustments). Assume the use of a periodic inventory system. Notice that the Adjusted Trial Balance columns have been provided, even though they are not absolutely necessary.
   a. Expired rent, $250
   b. Accrued salaries, $500
   c. Depreciation on equipment, $375
   d. Ending merchandise inventory, $620

Kay's Mart
Work Sheet
For the Month Ended March 31, 20xx

Account Name	Trial Balance		Adjustments		Adjusted Trial Balance		Income Statement		Balance Sheet	
	Debit	Credit	Debit	Credit	Debit	Credit	Debit	Credit	Debit	Credit
Cash	1,000									
Accounts Receivable	700									
Merchandise Inventory	400									
Prepaid Rent	750									
Equipment	4,200									
Accounts Payable		900								
Kay Walters, Capital		4,200								
Sales		9,800								
Sales Discounts	300									
Purchases	3,700									
Purchases Returns and Allowances		150								
Freight In	400									
Salaries Expense	3,000									
Advertising Expense	600									
	15,050	15,050								

5. Following are the accounts and data needed to prepare the 20xx closing entries for Byram Manufacturing Company. Assume a normal account balance for each, as well as use of the *perpetual* inventory system. (Omit explanations.)

Cost of Goods Sold	$ 59,200
Freight In	3,200
General and Administrative Expenses	24,800
Sales	244,100
Sales Returns and Allowances	5,300
Selling Expenses	39,400

In addition, the owner, Mary Byram, withdrew $50,000 during the year.

General Journal				
Date		Description	Debit	Credit

Crossword Puzzle
for Chapters 4 and 5

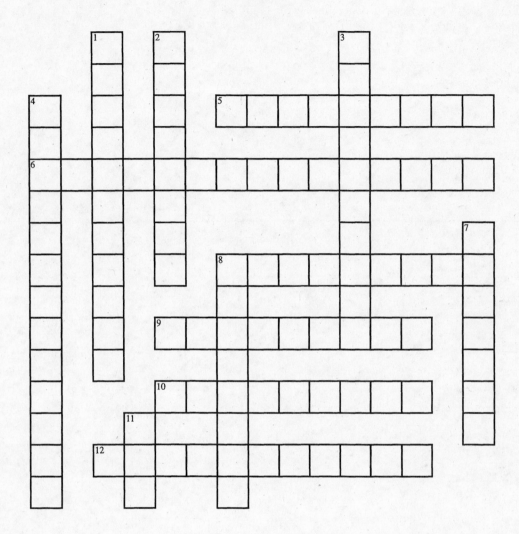

ACROSS

5. Entry opposite of adjusting
6. Inventory-related expense (4 words)
8. System of accounting for inventory
9. Inventory-acquisition account
10. Add and subtract horizontally
12. FOB _____

DOWN

1. Income statement subtotal (2 words)
2. Reward for paying early
3. Aids to financial statement preparation (2 words)
4. Account used when clearing the accounts (2 words)
7. Clearing the accounts
8. System of accounting for inventory
11. _____ Sales

CHAPTER 6 FINANCIAL REPORTING AND ANALYSIS

REVIEWING THE CHAPTER

Objective 1: State the objectives of financial reporting.

1. Financial reporting should fulfill three objectives. It should (a) provide information that is useful in making investment and credit decisions; (b) provide information that is useful in assessing cash flow prospects; and (c) provide information about business resources, claims to those resources, and changes in them. General-purpose external financial statements are the main way of presenting financial information to interested parties. They consist of the balance sheet, income statement, statement of owner's equity, and statement of cash flows.

Objective 2: State the qualitative characteristics of accounting information and describe their interrelationships.

2. Accounting attempts to provide decision makers with information that displays certain **qualitative characteristics,** or standards:
   a. **Understandability,** carrying the intended meaning, is a key qualitative characteristic.
   b. Another very important standard is **usefulness.** For it to be useful, information must be relevant and reliable. **Relevance** means that the information is capable of influencing the decision. Relevant information provides feedback, helps in making predictions, and is timely. **Reliability** means that accounting information accurately reflects what it is meant to reflect, that it is credible, verifiable, and neutral.

Objective 3: Define and describe the use of the conventions of *comparability* and *consistency, materiality, conservatism, full disclosure,* and *cost-benefit*.

3. To help users interpret financial information, accountants depend on five **conventions,** or rules of thumb: comparability and consistency, materiality, conservatism, full disclosure, and cost-benefit.
   a. **Comparability** means that the information allows the decision maker to compare the same company over two or more accounting periods, or different companies over the same accounting period. **Consistency** means that a particular accounting procedure, once adopted, should not be changed unless the company can justify the change and discloses the dollar effect on the statements.
   b. The **materiality** convention states that strict accounting practice need not be applied to items of insignificant dollar value. Whether a dollar amount is material or not is a matter of professional judgment, which should be exercised in a fair and accurate manner.
   c. The **conservatism** convention states that an accountant who has a choice of acceptable accounting procedures should choose the one that is least likely to overstate assets and income. Applying the lower-of-cost-or-market rule to inventory valuation is an example of conservatism.
   d. The **full disclosure** convention states that financial statements and their notes should contain all information relevant to the user's understanding of the statements.

e. The **cost-benefit** convention states that the cost of providing additional accounting information should not exceed the benefits to be gained from the information.

Objective 4: Explain management's responsibility for ethical financial reporting and define _fraudulent financial reporting_.

4. Users depend on management and its accountants to act ethically and with good judgment in the preparation of financial statements. This responsibility is often expressed in the report of management that accompanies financial statements.

5. The intentional preparation of misleading financial statements is called **fraudulent financial reporting.** It can result from the distortion of records, falsified transactions, or the misapplication of accounting principles. Individuals who perpetrate fraudulent financial reporting are subject to criminal and financial penalties.

Objective 5: Identify and describe the basic components of a classified balance sheet.

6. **Classified financial statements** divide assets, liabilities, owner's equity, revenues, and expenses into subcategories to offer the reader more useful information.

7. On a classified balance sheet, assets are usually divided into four categories: (a) current assets; (b) investments; (c) property, plant, and equipment; and (d) intangible assets. (Sometimes another category called "other assets" is added for miscellaneous items.)

8. These categories are usually listed in order of liquidity (the ease with which an asset can be turned into cash).

9. **Current assets** are cash and other assets that are expected to be turned into cash or used up within the normal operating cycle of the company or one year, whichever is longer. (From here on we will call this time period the current period.)
   a. A company's normal operating cycle is the average time between the purchase of inventory and the collection of cash from the sale of that inventory.
   b. Cash, short-term investments, accounts receivable, notes receivable, prepaid expenses, supplies, and inventory are examples of current assets.

10. Examples of **investments** are stock and bonds held for long-term investment, land held for future use, plant or equipment not used in the business,

special funds for debt retirement, and a controlling interest in another company.

11. **Property, plant, and equipment** (also called _operating assets, fixed assets, tangible assets, long-lived assets,_ or _plant assets_) include things like land, buildings, delivery equipment, machinery, office equipment, and natural resources. Most of the assets in this category are subject to depreciation.

12. **Intangible assets** have no physical substance. More importantly, they represent certain long-lived rights or privileges. Examples are patents, copyrights, goodwill, franchises, and trademarks.

13. **Other assets** is used as a category by some companies to group all assets other than current assets and property, plant, and equipment. In this case, other assets can include investments and intangible assets.

14. The liabilities of a classified balance sheet are usually divided into current and long-term liabilities.
   a. **Current liabilities** are obligations for which payment (or performance) is due in the current period. They are paid from current assets or by incurring new short-term liabilities. Examples are notes payable, accounts payable, taxes payable, and unearned revenues.
   b. **Long-term liabilities** are debts that are due after the current period or that will be paid from non-current assets. Examples are mortgages payable, long-term notes payable, bonds payable, employee pension obligations, and long-term leases.

15. The owner's equity section of a classified balance sheet is usually called owner's equity, partners' equity, or stockholders' equity. The exact name depends on whether the business is a sole proprietorship, a partnership, or a corporation. Other descriptive terms for owner's equity are _proprietorship, capital,_ and the somewhat misleading term _net worth._

16. In a sole proprietorship or partnership, the owner's equity or partners' equity section shows the name of the owner or owners. Each is followed by the word _Capital_ and the dollar amount of investment as of the balance sheet date.

17. In a corporation, the stockholders' equity section consists of contributed capital and retained earnings.
   a. **Contributed capital** (sometimes called _paid-in capital_) is the amount invested by the stockholders. It is divided further into the par value

of the issued stock and the paid-in or contributed capital in excess of par value.
  b. **Retained earnings** (sometimes called *earned capital*) reflect the earnings record of the company since its beginning. *Dividends* (assets distributed to stockholders) reduce the Retained Earnings account balance, as do net losses.

18. One difficult aspect of reading a balance sheet is understanding the numerical relationships and patterns among the various accounts listed. That is, the dollar amount assigned to an account has little meaning by itself, but becomes significantly more pertinent when put into proper perspective. Fortunately, software has been developed to present balance sheet figures in graphical form. This visual presentation enables the reader to easily grasp the relative magnitude of the numbers, and to plainly see their relationship to the whole.

Objective 6: Prepare multistep and single-step classified income statements.

19. A **condensed financial statement,** which contains the statement's major categories with little or no detail, may be presented in either multistep or single-step form.
  a. The **multistep form** is the more detailed of the two, containing several subtractions and subtotals. It has separate sections for cost of goods sold, operating expenses, and **other** (nonoperating) **revenues and expenses.** One important subtotal is **income from operations,** which equals gross margin minus operating expenses. A condensed version of the multistep form is illustrated below:

Net Sales	X
− Cost of Goods Sold	X
= Gross Margin	X
− Operating Expenses	X
= Income from Operations	X
± Other Revenues and Expenses	X
= Net Income	X

  b. In the **single-step form,** the revenues section lists all revenues, including other revenues, and the costs and expenses section lists all expenses, including other expenses. The difference is labeled net income or net loss. A condensed version of the single-step form is illustrated below:

Revenues	X
− Costs and Expenses	X
= Net Income	X

Objective 7: Evaluate liquidity and profitability using classified financial statements.

20. Classified financial statements help the reader evaluate liquidity and profitability.

21. **Liquidity** refers to a company's ability to pay its bills when they are due and to meet unexpected needs for cash. Two measures of liquidity are working capital and the current ratio.
  a. **Working capital** equals current assets minus current liabilities. It is the amount of current assets that would remain if all the current debts were paid.
  b. The **current ratio** equals current assets divided by current liabilities. A current ratio of 1.1, for example, shows that current assets are barely enough to pay current liabilities. A 2.1 current ratio is considered more satisfactory.

22. **Profitability** means more than just a company's net income. And to draw conclusions, one must compare profitability measures with industry averages and past performance. Five common measures of profitability are profit margin, asset turnover, return on assets, debt to equity ratio, and return on equity.
  a. The **profit margin** equals net income divided by net sales. A 12.5 percent profit margin, for example, means that 12½¢ has been earned on each dollar of sales.
  b. **Asset turnover** equals net sales divided by average total assets. This measures how efficiently assets are used to produce sales.
  c. **Return on assets** equals net income divided by average total assets. This measure shows how efficiently the company is using its assets to produce income.
  d. The **debt to equity** ratio measures the proportion of a business financed by creditors relative to the proportion financed by owners. It equals total liabilities divided by owner's equity. A debt to equity ratio of 1.0, for instance, indicates equal financing by creditors and owners.
  e. **Return on equity** shows what rate of return was earned on the owner's investment. It equals net income divided by average owner's equity.

SELF-TEST

Test your knowledge of the chapter by choosing the best answer for each of the following items.

1. Goodwill is categorized as
   a. a current asset.
   b. revenue.
   c. an intangible asset.
   d. property, plant, and equipment.

2. Accounting information is said to be useful if it is
   a. timely and biased.
   b. relevant and reliable.
   c. relevant and certain.
   d. accurate and faithful.

3. To ignore an amount because it is small in relation to the financial statements taken as a whole is an application of
   a. materiality.
   b. conservatism.
   c. full disclosure.
   d. comparability.

4. Accounting is concerned with providing information to decision makers. The overall framework of rules within which accountants work to provide this information is best described as
   a. business transactions.
   b. data processing.
   c. generally accepted accounting principles.
   d. income tax laws.

5. A note receivable due in two years normally would be classified as
   a. a current asset.
   b. an investment.
   c. property, plant, and equipment.
   d. an intangible asset.

6. The current portion of long-term debt is normally classified as
   a. current assets.
   b. current liabilities.
   c. long-term liabilities.
   d. owner's equity.

7. A disadvantage of the single-step income statement is that
   a. gross margin is not disclosed separately.
   b. other revenues and expenses are separated from operating items.
   c. interest expense is not disclosed.
   d. the cost of goods sold cannot be determined.

8. Net income is a component in determining each of the following ratios *except*
   a. profit margin.
   b. return on assets.
   c. debt to equity.
   d. return on equity.

9. Asset turnover is expressed
   a. in dollars.
   b. as a percentage.
   c. in times.
   d. in days.

10. Which of the following terms does *not* mean the same as the others listed?
    a. Net worth
    b. Owner's equity
    c. Proprietorship
    d. Working capital

TESTING YOUR KNOWLEDGE

Matching*

Match each term with its definition by writing the appropriate letter in the blank.

_____ 1. Qualitative characteristics

_____ 2. Relevance

_____ 3. Reliability

_____ 4. Fraudulent financial reporting

_____ 5. Classified financial statements

_____ 6. Liquidity

_____ 7. Current assets

_____ 8. Property, plant, and equipment

_____ 9. Intangible assets

_____ 10. Current liabilities

_____ 11. Long-term liabilities

_____ 12. Other revenues and expenses

_____ 13. Profitability

_____ 14. Income from operations

_____ 15. Condensed financial statements

a. The ability of a business to earn a satisfactory income

b. Long-lived tangible assets

c. The intentional preparation of misleading financial statements

d. Financial reports that contain only major categories of information

e. Guidelines for evaluating the quality of accounting reports

f. Short-term obligations

g. Gross margin less operating expenses

h. Financial reports broken down into subcategories

i. The income statement section that contains non-operating items

j. The subcategory of assets that are expected to be turned into cash or used up within one year or the normal operating cycle, whichever is longer

k. The standard that accounting information should be related to the user's needs

l. Long-term assets that lack physical substance and that grant rights or privileges to their owner

m. Obligations due after the current period

n. The standard that accounting information should accurately reflect what it is meant to represent

o. The ability to pay bills when due and to meet unexpected needs for cash

---

*Note to student: The matching quiz might be completed more efficiently by starting with the definition and searching for the corresponding term.

Short Answer

Use the lines provided to answer each item.

1. List the three forms of business organization, with each one's name for the equity section of the balance sheet.

Business Organization

a. _____

b. _____

c. _____

Name for Equity Section

a. _____

b. _____

c. _____

2. What does each of the following ratios show about a company's profitability?

Profit margin

_____

_____

_____

Asset turnover

_____

_____

_____

Return on assets

_____

_____

_____

Return on equity

_____

_____

_____

Debt to equity ratio

_____

_____

_____

3. Define each of the following liquidity ratios.

Working capital

_____

_____

Current ratio

_____

_____

4. Explain the basic point of each of the following conventions:

Consistency and comparability

_____

_____

Materiality

_____

_____

Cost-benefit

_____

_____

Conservatism

_____

_____

Full disclosure

_____

_____

True-False

Circle T if the statement is true, F if it is false. Please provide explanations for the false answers, using the blank lines at the end of the section.

T F **1.** Receivables are never current assets if collection requires more than one year.

T F **2.** When a dividend is distributed, the Common Stock account is reduced.

T F **3.** Profit margin is expressed as a dollar figure.

T F **4.** Coal mines are categorized as property, plant, and equipment.

T F **5.** Accounting information is relevant if it could make a difference to the outcome of a decision.

T F **6.** The net income figure is needed to compute the profit margin, the return on assets, and the return on equity.

T F **7.** The investments section of a balance sheet would include both short- and long-term investments in stock.

T F **8.** One meaning of the term *profitability* is the ease with which an asset can be converted into cash.

T F **9.** A company's normal operating cycle cannot be less than one year.

T F **10.** Net worth refers to the current value of a company's assets.

T F **11.** Other revenues and expenses is a separate classification in a multistep income statement.

T F **12.** The net income figures for a multistep and a single-step income statement will differ, given the same accounting period for the same company.

T F **13.** Retained earnings exist for a corporation, but not for a sole proprietorship or a partnership.

T F **14.** Working capital equals current assets divided by current liabilities.

T F **15.** The proportion of a company financed by the owners is shown by the debt to equity ratio.

T F **16.** The qualitative characteristic of relevance means that accounting information can be confirmed or duplicated by independent parties.

Multiple Choice

Circle the letter of the best answer.

1. The basis for classifying assets as current or noncurrent is the period of time normally required by the business to turn cash invested in
   a. noncurrent assets back into current assets.
   b. receivables back into cash, or 12 months, whichever is shorter.
   c. inventories back into cash, or 12 months, whichever is longer.
   d. inventories back into cash, or 12 months, whichever is shorter.

2. Which of the following will *not* be found anywhere in a single-step income statement?
   a. Cost of goods sold
   b. Other expenses
   c. Gross margin
   d. Operating expenses

3. The current ratio would probably be of *most* interest to
   a. stockholders.
   b. creditors.
   c. management.
   d. customers.

4. Which item below will *not* appear in the stockholders' equity section of a corporation's balance sheet?
   a. Retained earnings
   b. Common stock
   c. Paid-in capital in excess of par value
   d. Anna Fletcher, Capital

5. Net income divided by net sales equals
   a. profit margin.
   b. return on assets.
   c. working capital.
   d. income from operations.

6. Applying the lower-of-cost-or-market rule to inventory valuation and short-term investments follows the convention of
   a. consistency.
   b. materiality.
   c. conservatism.
   d. full disclosure.

7. Which of the following is *not* an objective of financial reporting, according to FASB Statement of Financial Accounting Concepts No. 1?
   a. To provide information about the timing of cash flows
   b. To provide information to investors and creditors
   c. To provide information about business resources
   d. To provide information to management

8. If a company has a profit margin of 4.0 percent and an asset turnover of 3.0 times, its return on assets is approximately
   a. 1.3 percent.
   b. 3.0 percent.
   c. 4.0 percent.
   d. 12.0 percent.

9. Operating expenses consist of
   a. other expenses and cost of goods sold.
   b. selling expenses and cost of goods sold.
   c. selling expenses and general and administrative expenses.
   d. selling expenses, general and administrative expenses, and other expenses.

APPLYING YOUR KNOWLEDGE

Exercises

1. Assume that Spangler Company uses the following group headings on its classified balance sheet:

    a. Current Assets
    b. Investments
    c. Property, Plant, and Equipment
    d. Intangible Assets
    e. Current Liabilities
    f. Long-Term Liabilities
    g. Owner's Equity

    Indicate by letter where each of the following should be placed. Write an X next to items that do not belong on the balance sheet.

    _____ 1. Franchises
    _____ 2. Short-term advances from customers
    _____ 3. Accumulated depreciation
    _____ 4. Jo Spangler, Capital
    _____ 5. Prepaid rent
    _____ 6. Delivery truck
    _____ 7. Office supplies
    _____ 8. Fund for the purchase of land
    _____ 9. Notes payable due in ten years
    _____ 10. Bonds payable currently due (payable out of current assets)
    _____ 11. Goodwill
    _____ 12. Short-term investments
    _____ 13. Depreciation expense
    _____ 14. Inventory
    _____ 15. Accounts payable

2. The following information relates to Quality Appliance Company for 20xx:

Current Assets	$ 60,000
Average total assets	200,000
Current liabilities	20,000
Long-term liabilities	30,000
Average owner's equity	150,000
Net sales	250,000
Net income	25,000

    In the spaces provided, indicate each measure of liquidity and profitability.

    a. Working capital = $ _____
    b. Current ratio = _____
    c. Profit margin = _____ %
    d. Return on assets = _____ %
    e. Return on equity = _____ %
    f. Asset turnover = _____ times

3. The following data relate to Rinaldi Company for 20xx:

Cost of goods sold	$150,000
Interest income	2,000
Interest expense	5,000
Net Sales	200,000
Operating Expenses	30,000

    a. In the space provided below, complete the condensed multistep income statement in good form.

Rinaldi Company Income Statement (Multistep) For the Year Ended December 31, 20xx		

b. In the space provided, complete the condensed single-step income statement in good form.

Rinaldi Company Income Statement (Single-step) For the Year Ended December 31, 20xx		

HOW TO READ AN ANNUAL REPORT

REVIEWING THE SUPPLEMENT

1. Most of the four million corporations in the United States are *private,* or *closely held, corporations,* so named because ownership is not available to the general public. *Public companies,* though fewer in number, often are owned by thousands of stockholders, creating a far greater economic impact than their closely held counterparts.

2. Public companies are required to register their common stock with the Securities and Exchange Commission (SEC), primarily for the protection of the investing public. In addition, public companies must submit to their stockholders an *annual report,* which contains the requisite financial statements and other vital information about the financial position and performance of the company. Called the 10-K when filed with the SEC, the annual report is available to the general public through a number of sources (including the Internet and electronic media sources such as *Compact Disclosure*).

3. In addition to the financial statements, the annual report ordinarily contains a letter to the stockholders, a multiyear summary of financial highlights, a description of the business, management's discussion of operating results and financial condition, a report of management's responsibility, notes to the financial statements, the auditors' report, and a list of directors and officers of the corporation.

4. *Consolidated financial statements* are the combined statements of a company and its controlled subsidiaries. A company's financial statements may show data from consecutive periods side by side for comparison. Such statements are called *comparative financial statements.*

5. The consolidated statement of earnings should contain information regarding net income and earnings per share. A measure of a company's profitability, earnings per share equals net income divided by the weighted average number of shares of common stock outstanding.

6. The consolidated balance sheet usually contains classifications such as current assets, current liabilities, and long-term debt, which are useful in assessing a company's liquidity. In addition, stockholders' equity normally contains information on stock issued and bought back by the corporation, on earnings retained by the business, and on certain unusual items, such as foreign currency translation adjustments.

7. Whereas the consolidated statement of earnings reflects a company's profitability, the consolidated statement of cash flows reflects its liquidity. The statement provides information about a company's cash receipts and cash payments, and is divided into operating, investing, and financing activities experienced during an accounting period.

8. A *consolidated statement of stockholders' equity* is usually presented in a corporate annual report in place of the statement of retained earnings. It explains the changes in each of the components of stockholders' equity.

9. A section called *notes to the financial statements* accompanies, and is considered an integral part of, the financial statements. Its purpose is to help the reader interpret some of the more complex financial statement items.

10. A *summary of significant accounting policies* discloses the generally accepted accounting principles used in preparing the statements. It usually follows the last financial statement, perhaps as the first note to the financial statements.

11. Corporations are often required to issue *interim financial statements*. These statements give financial information covering less than a year (for example, quarterly data). Ordinarily they are reviewed, but not audited, by the independent CPA.

12. An annual report usually also includes a report of management's responsibilities for the financial statements and the internal control structure of the company as well as management's discussion and analysis of operating performance.

13. The *independent auditors' report* conveys to third parties that the financial statements were examined in accordance with generally accepted auditing standards (*scope section*), and expresses the auditors' opinion on how fairly the financial statements reflect the company's financial condition (*opinion section*). In addition, the auditors' report clarifies the nature and purpose of an audit, and emphasizes management's ultimate responsibility for the financial statements.

CHAPTER 7   ACCOUNTING INFORMATION SYSTEMS

REVIEWING THE CHAPTER

Objective 1: Identify the principles of accounting systems design.

1. **Accounting systems** summarize a business's financial data, organize the data into useful form, and (through accountants) communicate the results to management. Management then uses the output to make a variety of business decisions. An accounting system is able to accomplish the above objectives through an activity called **data processing.**

2. Most businesses now process their data by means of computerized accounting systems. For such a system to work, however, the individuals involved must possess a solid understanding of the accounting process. The opposite is also true: an accountant must have a basic knowledge of computer systems.

3. In designing an accounting system, the systems designer must adhere to four general principles of systems design:
   a. The **cost-benefit principle** states that the benefits derived from the accounting system must match or exceed its cost.
   b. The **control principle** states that the accounting system must contain the safeguards necessary to protect assets and make sure the data are reliable.
   c. The **compatibility principle** states that the accounting system must be in harmony with the organization and its people.

   d. The **flexibility principle** states that the accounting system should be able to accommodate changes in the volume of transactions and in organizational changes within the business.

Objective 2: Describe how general ledger software and spreadsheet software are used in accounting.

4. Accountants use a variety of software (computer programs), but rely especially upon general ledger software and spreadsheet software.
   a. **General ledger software** consists of programs that perform, in an integrative way, major accounting functions, such as sales, accounts receivable, purchases, accounts payable, and payroll. Most general ledger software uses the Windows® operating system. Windows®, through its **graphical user interface (GUI),** employs symbols, called **icons,** to represent common computer operations. A *mouse* or *trackball* may be used with Windows®, or the keyboard may be operated in the usual manner. When programs use Windows® as their graphical user interface, the program is termed "Windows®-compatible."
   b. Unlike general ledger software, which is useful for double-entry transactions, **spreadsheets** assist in data analysis. With such commercial names as Windows® Excel and Lotus, a spreadsheet is a computerized grid of rows and columns, into which are placed data or formulas for accounting tasks such as financial planning and cost estimation.

Objective 3: Describe the use of microcomputer systems in small businesses.

5. Although most businesses use computerized accounting systems, these systems vary widely in both structure and purpose. More and more, multinational companies are making use of **enterprise resource management (ERM)** systems. These ERM systems consist of extremely powerful computers (aided by very complex software), linked together to provide global communication and data transfer.

6. In companies both large and small, however, microcomputer systems have become critical in the processing of information. Their importance will become even more evident as companies expand their use of the Internet to communicate and transact business.

7. Most small businesses purchase general ledger software that performs, through *integrated programs,* various accounting functions. Every transaction entered into the accounting records should be supported by **source documents** (invoices, etc.). Posting can be accomplished on a batch posting (end of the day, week, or month) or a real-time posting (immediate) basis. General ledger software makes accounting procedures less time-consuming and more accurate and dependable.

Objective 4: Explain how accountants use the Internet.

8. The **Internet** is the world's largest computer network, enabling individuals and organizations around the world to communicate with one another. One needs a modem and, usually, an Internet service provider (ISP) to access the Internet.

9. Individuals and organizations can send and receive **electronic mail (e-mail)** through the Internet and can subscribe to any number of *electronic mailing lists.*

10. The **World Wide Web** (or "the Web") consists of information that can be accessed through the Internet. *Browsers,* such as Netscape Navigator and Microsoft Internet Explorer, consist of software needed to access the Web.

11. Files can be downloaded (obtained) from the Internet through a process called **information retrieval.** Information can be shared over the Internet by individuals with common interests through **bulletin boards.**

12. **E-business** is Internet use for a wide variety of business purposes. One such purpose, **electronic**

commerce, involves the transaction of business with vendors, suppliers, and customers. Electronic commerce provides new challenges for accountants to maintain accurate recordkeeping.

13. **Search engines,** such as Yahoo and Lycos, assist the Internet user in obtaining information from the World Wide Web on almost any topic of interest.

Objective 5: Explain the objectives and uses of special-purpose journals.

14. Companies that use **manual data processing** (those companies that keep handwritten accounting records) record an entry in one or more journals. A company can record all of its transactions in the general journal. However, companies with a large number of transactions also use **special-purpose journals** for efficiency, economy, and control.

15. Most business transactions fall into one of four types and are recorded in one of four special-purpose journals:
   a. Sales of merchandise on credit are recorded in the sales journal.
   b. Purchases on credit are recorded in the purchases journal.
   c. Receipts of cash are recorded in the cash receipts journal.
   d. Disbursements of cash are recorded in the cash payments journal.

Objective 6: Explain the purposes and relationships of controlling accounts and subsidiary ledgers.

16. The general ledger contains an Accounts Receivable **controlling account,** or *control account.* The controlling account is updated at the end of each month and keeps a running total of all accounts receivable. Its balance should equal the sum of all the accounts in the accounts receivable subsidiary ledger, described in paragraph 17. In actuality, *any* account can act as a controlling account, supported by a subsidiary ledger.

17. Most companies that sell to customers on credit keep an accounts receivable record for each customer. In this way, a company can determine how much a given customer owes at any time. All customer accounts are filed either alphabetically or numerically in the accounts receivable **subsidiary ledger.**

18. Most companies also use an Accounts Payable controlling account and subsidiary ledger, which function much like the Accounts Receivable controlling account and subsidiary ledger.

Objective 7: Construct and use a sales journal, purchases journal, cash receipts journal, cash payments journal, and other special-purpose journals.

19. The **sales journal,** which is used to record credit sales, saves time because (a) each entry requires only one line; (b) account names need not be written out (each entry automatically is debited to Accounts Receivable and credited to Sales); (c) explanations are not needed; and (d) only total sales for the month, not each individual sale, are posted to the Sales account in the general ledger. Postings are made daily, however, to customer accounts in the accounts receivable subsidiary ledger. Similar time-saving principles apply to the other special-purpose journals.

20. The **purchases journal** is used to record purchases on credit. A single-column purchases journal records the purchases of merchandise only. A multicolumn purchases journal can accommodate the purchase of merchandise and supplies and freight, for example. Only total purchases for the month are posted to the Purchases account; however, postings are made daily to creditor accounts in the accounts payable subsidiary ledger.

21. All receipts of cash are recorded in the **cash receipts journal.** Typically, a cash receipts journal includes debit columns for Cash, Sales Discounts, and Other Accounts, and credit columns for Accounts Receivable, Sales, and Other Accounts. Postings to customer accounts and Other Accounts are made on a daily basis. All column totals, except for Other Accounts, are posted to the general ledger at the end of the month.

22. All payments of cash are recorded in the **cash payments journal.** Typically, a cash payments journal includes debit columns for Accounts Payable and Other Accounts, and credit columns for Cash, Purchases Discounts, and Other Accounts. Postings to creditor accounts and Other Accounts are made daily. All column totals, except for Other Accounts, are posted to the general ledger at the end of the month.

23. Transactions that cannot be recorded in a special-purpose journal, such as the return of goods by a customer for credit, are recorded in the general journal. Adjusting entries and closing entries also are made in the general journal. Postings are made at the end of each day. And, in the case of Accounts Receivable and Accounts Payable, postings are made to both the controlling account and the subsidiary account.

24. The special-purpose journals used by a business can differ slightly from those described in the textbook because the types of transactions can vary. However, an understanding of the general concepts and mechanics of special-purpose journals makes adapting them to a different system relatively easy.

Summary of Journal Entries Introduced in Chapter 7

Note: Most entries in this chapter are *not* in general journal form (i.e., they are recorded in special journals) and therefore will not be duplicated here. However, two sample *general* journal entries were provided, as follows:

A. (LO 7) Accounts Payable, Thomas Auto   212/✓   XX (amount returned)
           Purchases Returns and Allowances   513   XX (amount returned)
               Returned used car for credit (Accounts Payable is
               posted both to general ledger controlling account
               and to Thomas Auto in Accounts Payable ledger.)

B. (LO 7) Sales Returns and Allowances   413   XX (amount returned)
           Accounts Receivable, Maxwell Gertz   114/✓   XX (amount returned)
               Customer returned goods for credit (Accounts
               Receivable is posted both to general ledger
               controlling account and to Maxwell Gertz in
               Accounts Receivable ledger.)

SELF-TEST

Test your knowledge of the chapter by choosing the best answer for each of the following items.

1. Designing a system that allows a retailer to expand to multiple locations and products is probably the result of applying the
   a. cost-benefit principle.
   b. control principle.
   c. compatibility principle.
   d. flexibility principle.

2. A decision to go ahead with a costly computer system because of potential sales loss and customer discontent under the current system is probably a result of applying the
   a. cost-benefit principle.
   b. control principle.
   c. compatibility principle.
   d. flexibility principle.

3. Which of the following assists the Internet user in obtaining information on a specific topic?
   a. Spreadsheet
   b. Browser
   c. General ledger software
   d. Search engine

4. Special-purpose journals are used primarily because most businesses have many transactions that
   a. are difficult to classify.
   b. are essentially identical.
   c. use only a very few ledger accounts.
   d. are easy to classify.

5. The failure to post the receipt of a customer's payment in the customer's account in the subsidiary ledger would most likely be discovered when
   a. the cash receipts journal is footed and cross-footed.
   b. the trial balance is prepared.
   c. the total of the subsidiary ledger is compared to the balance of the accounts receivable controlling account.
   d. assets are compared with the liabilities and owner's equity on the balance sheet.

6. The total of a single-column sales journal is posted as a
   a. debit to Sales and a credit to Accounts Receivable.
   b. debit to Accounts Receivable and a credit to Sales.
   c. debit to Cash and a credit to Sales.
   d. debit to Sales and a credit to Cash.

7. The daily total of cash sales is recorded in the
   a. sales journal.
   b. purchases journal.
   c. cash payments journal.
   d. cash receipts journal.

8. One advantage of a multicolumn purchases journal is that it
   a. minimizes the use of the general journal.
   b. eliminates the need for the accounts payable subsidiary ledger.
   c. includes purchases on credit and for cash.
   d. records only credit sales.

9. A company that has four special journals and a general journal would probably record which of the following in the general journal?
   a. A sale on credit
   b. A purchase on credit
   c. A sales return
   d. A purchases discount

10. Each entry in the purchases journal requires that an entry be made in the
    a. general journal.
    b. accounts payable subsidiary ledger.
    c. general ledger.
    d. Purchases account.

TESTING YOUR KNOWLEDGE

*Matching**

Match each term with its definition by writing the appropriate letter in the blank.

_____ 1. Source document

_____ 2. Search engine

_____ 3. World Wide Web

_____ 4. Icon

_____ 5. General ledger software

_____ 6. Internet

_____ 7. Electronic mail (E-mail)

_____ 8. Electronic commerce

_____ 9. Enterprise resource management (ERM)

_____ 10. Information retrieval

_____ 11. Spreadsheet

_____ 12. Data processing

_____ 13. Special-purpose journal

_____ 14. Subsidiary ledger

_____ 15. Controlling (control) account

_____ 16. Schedule of accounts receivable

_____ 17. Subsidiary account

a. A formal list of customers who owe the company

b. Gathering, organizing, and communicating information

c. A symbol representing a common computer operation

d. The record of a customer or creditor in a subsidiary ledger

e. The vast collection of information accessible through the Internet

f. Where customer or creditor accounts are kept

g. Any general ledger account that has a related subsidiary ledger

h. Any journal except for the general journal

i. The written evidence that supports a transaction

j. A computerized grid of columns and rows, used in accounting tasks

k. The transaction of business over the Internet

l. Correspondence by means of the Internet

m. A group of integrated accounting programs

n. The downloading of files from the Internet

o. A system of very powerful computers linked together

p. Internet site that assists in information gathering on a specific topic

q. The world's largest computer network

Short Answer

Use the lines provided to answer each item.

1. List the four major special-purpose journals, with the type of transaction that should be recorded in each.

Special-Purpose Journal

_____

_____

_____

_____

Type of Transaction

_____

_____

_____

_____

Note to student: The matching quiz might be completed more efficiently by starting with the definition and searching for the corresponding term.

2. Briefly explain why totals in the Other Accounts columns of special-purpose journals should not be posted at the end of the month.

_____

_____

_____

_____

3. Differentiate between controlling and subsidiary accounts.

_____

_____

_____

_____

4. Differentiate between the Internet and the World Wide Web.

_____

_____

_____

_____

5. From which journal would some accounts be "double-posted," and what does the double-posting signify?

_____

_____

_____

_____

6. List the four general principles of systems design, and briefly describe the significance of each.

a. _____

_____

b. _____

_____

c. _____

_____

d. _____

_____

True-False

Circle T if the statement is true, F if it is false. Please provide explanations for the false answers using the blank lines at the end of the section.

T F   **1.** All transactions can be recorded in the general journal, but the use of special-purpose journals probably saves time.

T F   **2.** The purchase of new office equipment on credit would be recorded in a single-column purchases journal.

T F   **3.** Posting to subsidiary accounts should be done at the end of the month.

T F   **4.** At the end of each month, column totals in the general journal should be posted to the general ledger.

T F   **5.** Adjustments for depreciation should be recorded in the general journal.

T F   **6.** A check is placed in the Post. Ref. column of the sales journal to show that the entry has been posted to the accounts payable subsidiary ledger.

T F   **7.** A company with 25 sales recorded in the sales journal in a single month should have 25 postings to the Sales account.

T F   **8.** Cash sales should be recorded in the sales journal.

T F   **9.** The Accounts Receivable and Accounts Payable controlling accounts are not updated daily.

T F **10.** In the cash payments journal, Accounts Payable is a debit column.

T F **11.** Accounts receivable in the general journal are posted to both the controlling and the subsidiary accounts.

T F **12.** After a schedule of accounts receivable is prepared, its total is compared with the balance in the controlling account.

T F **13.** The software used to navigate the World Wide Web is called a *spreadsheet*.

T F **14.** A graphical user interface (GUI) uses icons to make software easier to use.

T F **15.** Microcomputer systems are rarely used in large multinational companies.

_____

_____

_____

_____

_____

_____

_____

_____

_____

_____

_____

_____

_____

_____

_____

_____

_____

_____

_____

_____

_____

_____

_____

_____

Multiple Choice

Circle the letter of the best answer.

1. Posting the total of the sales journal at the end of the month involves a debit to
   a. Cash and a credit to Sales.
   b. Accounts Receivable and a credit to Sales.
   c. Sales only.
   d. Accounts Payable and a credit to Sales.

2. Which of the following statements about the accounts receivable subsidiary accounts is *not* true?
   a. Each is a record of a credit customer.
   b. They receive daily postings from the special journals.
   c. A check is placed in the Post. Ref. column of each subsidiary account after each posting.
   d. Their balances are used to prepare a schedule of accounts receivable.

3. A customer returns goods and receives a cash refund. In which journal should the transaction be entered?
   a. Sales journal
   b. Cash receipts journal
   c. Cash payments journal
   d. General journal

4. A customer returns goods for credit. The transaction should be recorded in the
   a. sales journal.
   b. cash receipts journal.
   c. cash payments journal.
   d. general journal.

5. Accounts Receivable is usually *not* involved at any time with the
   a. sales journal.
   b. cash receipts journal.
   c. cash payments journal.
   d. general journal.

6. Which of the following statements about the Accounts Payable controlling account is *not* true?
   a. It receives daily postings from the special-purpose journals.
   b. It is found in the general ledger.
   c. Its balance at the end of the month should equal the total in the schedule of accounts payable.
   d. It has an account number.

7. Purchases Discounts would most likely occupy a column in the
   a. sales journal.
   b. purchases journal.
   c. cash receipts journal.
   d. cash payments journal.

8. The Purchases account has *no* involvement at any time with
   a. the purchases journal.
   b. the cash receipts journal.
   c. the cash payments journal.
   d. any of the above.

9. Being able to accommodate changes in a business is a description of the
   a. control principle.
   b. compatibility principle.
   c. flexibility principle.
   d. cost-benefit principle.

10. Information is shared over the Internet by individuals with common interests through
    a. bulletin boards.
    b. Internet service providers.
    c. e-business.
    d. general ledger software.

APPLYING YOUR KNOWLEDGE

Exercises

1. In the spaces provided, indicate the symbol of the journal that should be used by Targum Appliance Store.

   S = Sales journal
   P = Purchases journal (single-column)
   CR = Cash receipts journal
   CP = Cash payments journal
   J = General journal

   _____ a. Goods that had been purchased by Targum on credit are returned.
   _____ b. Goods that had been purchased by Targum for cash are returned for a cash refund.
   _____ c. Toasters are purchased on credit by Targum.
   _____ d. The same toasters are paid for.
   _____ e. A blender is sold on credit.
   _____ f. The electric bill is paid.
   _____ g. Adjusting entries are made.
   _____ h. Office furniture is purchased by Targum on credit.
   _____ i. Closing entries are made.
   _____ j. Targum pays for half of the office furniture.
   _____ k. A customer pays a bill and receives a discount.

2. Enter the following transactions of Cournoyer Liquidators, Inc., into the cash receipts journal provided below. Complete the Post. Ref. column as though the entries had been posted daily. Also, make the proper posting notations in the journals as though the end-of-month postings had been made. Accounts Receivable is account no. 114, Sales is account no. 411, Sales Discounts is account no. 412, and Cash is account no. 111.

   Feb. 3 Received payment of $500 less a 2 percent discount from Don Morris for merchandise previously purchased on credit.
         9 Sold land (account no. 135) for $8,000 cash.
         14 Issued $10,000 more in common stock (account no. 311).
         23 Sue O'Neill paid Cournoyer $150 for merchandise she had purchased on credit.
         28 Cash sales for the month totaled $25,000.

Cash Receipts Journal									Page 1
				Debits			Credits		
Date		Account Debited/Credited	Post. Ref.	Cash	Sales Disc.	Other Accts.	Accts. Receiv.	Sales	Other Accts.

3. A page from a special-purpose journal is shown below.

Date	Ck. No.	Payee	Account Credited/ Debited	Post. Ref.	Credits			Debits	
					Cash	Purchases Discounts	Other Accounts	Accounts Payable	Other Accounts
May 1	114	DePasquale Supply Co.		✓	784	16		800	
7	115	Monahan Bus Equip.	Office Equipment	167	2,000				2,000
13	116	Celestial News	Advertising Expense	512	350				350
19	117	Denecker Motors		✓	420			420	
					3,554	16		1,220	2,350
					(111)	(413)		(211)	(315)

The following questions relate to this journal.

a. What type of journal is this? _____

_____

b. What error was made in the preparation of this journal?_____

_____

_____

c. Provide an explanation for the four transactions.

May 1 _____

_____

May 7 _____

_____

May 13 _____

_____

May 19 _____

_____

d. Explain the following:

1. The check marks in the Post. Ref. column

_____

_____

2. The numbers 167 and 512 in the Post. Ref. column_____

_____

3. The numbers below the column totals ____

_____

_____

_____

_____

_____

_____

Crossword Puzzle
for Chapters 6 and 7*

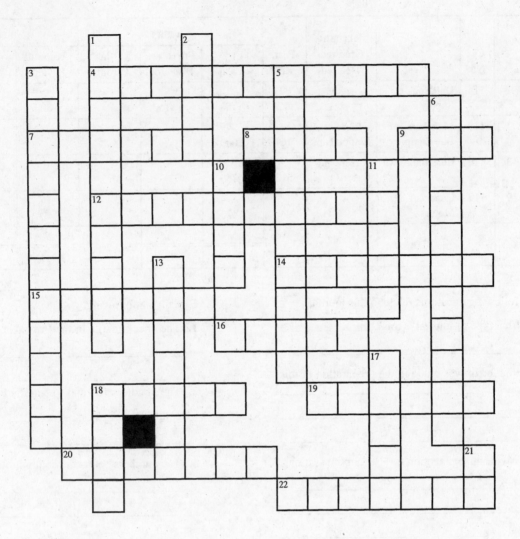

ACROSS

4. Extent of accurate representation
7. _____ document (e.g., invoice)
8. See 17-Down
9. Paid-in Capital in Excess of _____ Value
12. Vital qualitative characteristic
14. Quarterly financial statements, e.g.
15. Data processing by hand
16. Special-purpose journal
18. Spreadsheet product
19. Debt to _____ ratio
20. Financial performance evaluator
22. Independent CPA

DOWN

1. Dishonest financial reporting
2. World _____ Web
3. Special-purpose journal (2 words)
5. Trademark, e.g.
6. Relative importance
10. _____ disclosure
11. _____ turnover
13. Working _____
17. With 8-Across, income statement form
18. An operating asset
21. Special journal abbreviation

*Includes Supplement to Chapter 6: How to Read an Annual Report

CHAPTER 8   INTERNAL CONTROL

REVIEWING THE CHAPTER

Objective 1: Define *internal control*, identify the five components of internal control, and explain seven examples of control activities.

1. **Internal control** encompasses all the policies and procedures management uses to assure (a) the reliability of financial reporting, (b) compliance with laws and regulations, and (c) the effectiveness and efficiency of operations. To achieve these objectives, management must establish the following five components of internal control: the control environment, risk assessment, information and communication, control activities, and monitoring.
    a. The **control environment** reflects management's philosophy and operating style, the company's organizational structure, methods of assigning authority and responsibility, and personnel policies and practices.
    b. **Risk assessment** entails identification of areas where risks of asset loss or inaccuracy of records is especially high.
    c. **Information and communication** involves the establishment of the accounting systems by management, as well as the communication of each individual's responsibility within those systems.
    d. **Control activities** are the specific procedures and policies established by management to ensure that its objectives of internal control are met. These activities are discussed in more detail in the following paragraph.
    e. **Monitoring** consists of management's regular assessment of the quality of internal control.

2. Examples of control activities are (a) requiring authorization for all transactions, (b) recording all transactions, (c) the design and use of adequate documents, (d) physical controls, as over the accounting records and assets, (e) periodic independent verification of records and assets, (f) separation of duties, and (g) sound personnel procedures. **Bonding** an employee (a good example of sound personnel procedures) means reducing or eliminating the risk of loss due to theft by that individual against the company.

Objective 2: Describe the inherent limitations of internal control.

3. A system of internal control relies on the people who carry out the control procedures. Human error, mistakes in judgment, collusion, and changing conditions all can limit the effectiveness of a system of internal control.

Objective 3: Apply internal control activities to common merchandising transactions.

4. Proper controls over merchandising transactions help prevent losses from theft or fraud and help ensure accurate accounting records. In addition, controls over merchandising transactions should help keep inventory levels balanced, keep enough cash on hand to make timely payments for purchases discounts, and avoid credit losses.

5. Some common control procedures over cash are (a) separating the authorization, recordkeeping, and custodianship of cash; (b) limiting access to

cash; (c) specifying those responsible for handling cash; (d) maximizing the use of banking facilities, while minimizing cash on hand; (e) bonding employees who have access to cash; (f) physically protecting cash on hand by using cash registers, etc.; (g) performing unannounced audits of the cash on hand; (h) recording cash receipts promptly; (i) depositing cash receipts promptly; (j) paying by check; and (k) having someone who does not deal with cash reconcile the Cash account.

6. Cash received by mail should be handled by two or more employees. Cash received from sales over the counter should be controlled through the use of cash registers and prenumbered sales tickets. At the end of each day, total cash receipts should be reconciled and recorded in the cash receipts journal following the principle of separation of duties.

7. All cash payments for purchases should be made by check and only with authorization. The system of authorization and the documents used differ among companies, but these are the most common documents:
   a. A **purchase requisition** is completed by a department requesting that the company purchase something for the department.
   b. A **purchase order** is completed by the department responsible for the company's purchasing activities; it is sent to the vendor.
   c. An **invoice** is the bill sent from the vendor to the buyer's accounting department.
   d. A **receiving report** is completed by the receiving department and forwarded to the accounting department; it contains information about the quantity and condition of the goods received.
   e. A **check authorization**, issued by the accounting department, is a document attached to the purchase order, invoice, and receiving report, indicating that the information on those three documents is in agreement, and that payment is approved.
   f. When payment is approved, a **check** is issued by the treasurer to the vendor for the amount of the invoice, less the appropriate discount. A remittance advice, which shows what the check is paying, should be attached to the check.

Objective 4: Demonstrate the control of cash by preparing a bank reconciliation.

8. The end-of-month balance in a bank statement rarely agrees with the balance in the company's books for that date. Thus, the accountant must prepare a **bank reconciliation** to account for the difference and to locate any errors made by the bank or the company. The bank reconciliation begins with the balance per books and balance per bank figures as of the bank statement date. Each figure is adjusted by additions and deductions, resulting in two adjusted cash balance figures, which must agree. The balance per books figure is adjusted by information that the bank knew on the bank statement date but the company did not. The balance per bank figure is adjusted by information that the company knew on the bank statement date but the bank did not. For example:
   a. Outstanding checks are a deduction from the balance per bank.
   b. Deposits in transit are an addition to the balance per bank.
   c. Service charges by the bank appear on the bank statement and are a deduction from the balance per books.
   d. A customer's nonsufficient funds (NSF) check is deducted from the balance per books.
   e. Interest earned on a checking account is added to the balance per books.
   f. Miscellaneous charges are deducted from the balance per books. Miscellaneous credits are added to the balance per books.
   g. Errors must be identified and corrected.

9. After the bank reconciliation has been prepared, adjusting entries must be made so that the accounting records reflect the new information supplied by the bank statement. Each adjustment includes either a debit or a credit to Cash. Adjustments are recorded only for the items that affected the balance per books.

Supplemental Objective 5: Demonstrate the use of a simple imprest system.

10. Although it is good practice for a company to pay by check, it often is not practical for items of small value. For items like postage, a few inexpensive supplies, and taxi fares, many firms use a **petty cash fund**. One of the best ways to operate a petty cash fund is by the **imprest system**. Under this system, when the fund is established (through a check drawn to the petty cash custodian), Petty Cash is debited, and Cash is credited. When payment is made from the fund, the fund's custodian prepares a **petty cash voucher** showing the date, amount, and purpose of the expenditure. The petty cash fund is replenished periodically and at the

end of the accounting period. In each case, all the expenditures since the fund was last replenished are debited, and Cash is credited. Discrepancies are recorded as Cash Short or Over.

Supplemental Objective 6: Define *voucher system* and describe the components of a voucher system.

11. A **voucher system** is any system that gives documentary proof of and written authorization for business transactions. The goal of a voucher system is to maintain maximum control over cash expenditures. Accordingly, each transaction requires the written approval of key individuals, thus providing an **audit trail**. A voucher system consists of (a) written authorizations for expenditures, called **vouchers;** (b) the form of payment, called a **voucher check;** (c) a special journal to record the vouchers, called the **voucher register;** and (d) a special journal to record the voucher checks, called the **check register.**

Supplemental Objective 7: Describe and carry out the five steps in operating a voucher system.

12. There are five steps in the operation of a voucher system:
    a. Preparing the voucher for each liability incurred.
    b. Recording the voucher in the voucher register.
    c. Paying the voucher as it comes up in the unpaid voucher file by drawing either a check or a voucher check and recording it in the check register.
    d. Posting the voucher and check registers. This process is very similar to posting the purchases and cash payments journals, except that Vouchers Payable takes the place of Accounts Payable.
    e. Summarizing unpaid vouchers—that is, preparing a schedule of unpaid vouchers from the unpaid voucher file.

A. (LO 4)   After a bank reconciliation is prepared, journal entries must
be made to record the items on the bank statement that the
company has not yet recorded (service charges, NSF checks,
etc.). The sample entries presented in the textbook are not
duplicated here, but please notice that all entries contain either
a debit or a credit to Cash.

B. (SO 5)   Petty Cash   XX (initial fund amount)
    Cash   XX (initial fund amount)
      To establish the petty cash fund

C. (SO 5)   Postage Expense   XX (amount incurred)
    Supplies   XX (amount purchased)
    Freight In   XX (amount incurred)
    Cash Short or Over   XX (amount short)
      Cash   XX (amount replenished)
      To replenish the petty cash fund

D. (SO 7)   In the textbook, numerous transactions were entered into
a voucher register and a check register. Because they are
not in the form of general journal entries, they are not shown
here. Please notice, however, that all entries in the voucher
register and the check register contain either a credit or a debit,
respectively, to Vouchers Payable.

SELF-TEST

Test your knowledge of the chapter by choosing the best answer for each of the following items.

1. Which of the following is *not* a component of internal control?
   a. Assessing the risk of loss
   b. Creating a control environment
   c. Maximizing the amount of cash on hand
   d. Monitoring the quality of internal control

2. The separation of duties in terms of cash transactions means that separate individuals should be responsible for authorization, custody, and
   a. approval.
   b. recordkeeping.
   c. control.
   d. protection.

3. Which of the following is least likely to lead to a breakdown in internal control?
   a. Human errors and mistakes
   b. Employees carrying out their duties as prescribed
   c. Management taking full control of an operation
   d. Two employees working together to steal assets

4. Which of the following documents should be presented and agreed on before a check authorization is prepared?
   a. Purchase requisition and purchase order
   b. Purchase order and receiving report
   c. Purchase requisition, purchase order, and invoice
   d. Purchase order, invoice, and receiving report

5. On a bank reconciliation, which of the following would be added to the balance per bank?
   a. Outstanding checks
   b. Deposits in transit
   c. A service charge
   d. Interest on the average balance

6. Which of the following items in a bank reconciliation would require a journal entry?
   a. Outstanding checks
   b. Deposits in transit
   c. Interest on the average balance
   d. The adjusted Cash balance

7. The entry to replenish a $50 petty cash fund that has $20 cash and a receipt for $30 of postage would include a credit to
   a. Cash.
   b. Petty Cash.
   c. Postage Expense.
   d. Prepaid Postage.

8. The voucher system strengthens internal control by requiring that a voucher be prepared to authorize payment of a liability at the time the liability is
   a. paid.
   b. incurred.
   c. planned.
   d. audited.

9. To help the company pay within the discount period, unpaid vouchers are filed by
   a. voucher number.
   b. date of authorization.
   c. due date.
   d. check number.

10. Under the voucher system, at the end of the accounting period, the amount of accounts payable on the balance sheet should equal
    a. the total of the schedule of unpaid vouchers.
    b. the amount paid to creditors during the accounting period.
    c. the total of the subsidiary accounts payable file.
    d. none of the above.

TESTING YOUR KNOWLEDGE

Matching*

Match each term with its definition by writing the appropriate letter in the blank.

_____ 1. Internal control

_____ 2. Bonding

_____ 3. Invoice

_____ 4. Purchase requisition

_____ 5. Purchase order

_____ 6. Receiving report

_____ 7. Check authorization

_____ 8. Bank reconciliation

_____ 9. Outstanding check

_____ 10. NSF check

_____ 11. Petty cash fund

_____ 12. Petty cash voucher

_____ 13. Voucher register

_____ 14. Check register

_____ 15. Schedule of unpaid vouchers

a. A bad check
b. A description of goods received by a company
c. A record of vouchers that have been paid
d. Insuring a business against theft by its employees
e. The journal that contains a record of each approved voucher
f. A system designed to safeguard assets, promote operational efficiency, encourage adherence to managerial policies, and help achieve accounting accuracy
g. Cash set aside to pay for items of small value
h. An order for goods that is sent to the vendor
i. A list of debts
j. A document that asks the purchasing department to order certain items
k. An accounting for the difference between book balance and bank balance at a particular date
l. A document that authorizes payment
m. A record of an expenditure from petty cash
n. A vendor's bill
o. A check that has been issued but has not yet been presented to the bank for payment

Short Answer

Use the lines provided to answer each item.

1. List the five components of internal control.

_____

_____

_____

_____

2. What three documents should be in agreement before a bill is paid?

_____

_____

_____

3. List seven control activities that help make a system of internal control effective.

_____

_____

_____

_____

_____

_____

_____

Note to student: The matching quiz might be completed more efficiently by starting with the definition and searching for the corresponding term.

4. List three items that would be deducted from the balance per books in a bank reconciliation.

_____

_____

_____

5. List, in order, the five steps followed in the operation of a voucher system.

_____

_____

_____

_____

_____

6. List any six procedures that can be employed to control and safeguard cash.

_____

_____

_____

_____

_____

_____

True-False

Circle T if the statement is true, F if it is false. Please provide explanations for the false answers, using the blank lines at the end of the section.

T F **1.** A good system of internal control guarantees that the accounting records are accurate.

T F **2.** When a petty cash fund is established, Cash is debited and Petty Cash is credited.

T F **3.** Collusion is a secret agreement between two or more persons to defraud a company.

T F **4.** Cash Short or Over is debited to reflect a cash shortage.

T F **5.** The use of prenumbered sales tickets can strengthen a store's system of internal control.

T F **6.** Mail should be opened in the accounting department so that transactions can be recorded immediately.

T F **7.** A company orders goods by sending the supplier a purchase requisition.

T F **8.** A check that is outstanding for two consecutive months should be included in both months' bank reconciliations.

T F **9.** A credit memorandum on a bank statement indicates an addition to the bank balance.

T F **10.** After a bank reconciliation has been completed, the company must make journal entries to adjust for all outstanding checks.

T F **11.** Only the purchase of merchandise can be recorded in the voucher register.

T F **12.** The check register has a Vouchers Payable debit column.

T F **13.** After a voucher has been recorded, it is placed in an unpaid voucher file in alphabetical order.

T F **14.** A bank reconciliation for the month of September should begin with the balance per books and the balance per bank on September 1.

T F **15.** Rotating employees in job assignments is poor internal control because employees continually would be forced to learn new job skills.

T F **16.** _Imprest system_ refers to the mechanics of a petty cash fund.

_____

_____

_____

_____

_____

_____

_____   _____
_____   _____
_____   _____
_____   _____
_____   _____
_____   _____
_____   _____
_____   _____

Multiple Choice

Circle the letter of the best answer.

1. In a system that uses special-purpose journals, the voucher register takes the place of the
   a. cash register.
   b. cash payments journal.
   c. accounts receivable subsidiary ledger.
   d. purchases journal.

2. After the bank reconciliation has been completed, a company must make journal entries to adjust for all of the following *except*
   a. bank service charges.
   b. deposits in transit.
   c. a note collected by the bank.
   d. an error made by the bank.

3. The balance in the schedule of unpaid vouchers should equal the Vouchers Payable
   a. debit total from the voucher register minus the Vouchers Payable credit total from the check register.
   b. credit total from the check register minus the Vouchers Payable debit total from the voucher register.
   c. credit total from the voucher register minus the Vouchers Payable debit total from the check register.
   d. debit total from the check register minus the Vouchers Payable credit total from the voucher register.

4. When a petty cash fund is replenished,
   a. Petty Cash is credited.
   b. Petty Cash is debited.
   c. Cash is credited.
   d. Cash is debited.

5. Interest earned on a checking account should be included in a bank reconciliation as a(n)
   a. addition to the balance per bank.
   b. deduction from the balance per bank.
   c. addition to the balance per books.
   d. deduction from the balance per books.

6. Which of the following documents is prepared (in a company buying goods) before all the others?
   a. Purchase order
   b. Receiving report
   c. Check authorization (or voucher)
   d. Purchase requisition

7. Which of the following actions is an example of poor internal control?
   a. Having the receiving department compare goods received with the related purchase order
   b. Forcing employees to take earned vacations
   c. Requiring someone other than the petty cash custodian to enter petty cash transactions into the accounting records
   d. Bonding employees

8. A company's bank statement erroneously shows a $1,000 deposit as $100, and the bank is notified. The $900 error appears in the bank reconciliation as a(n)
   a. addition to the balance per bank.
   b. deduction from the balance per bank.
   c. addition to the balance per books.
   d. deduction from the balance per books.

APPLYING YOUR KNOWLEDGE

Exercises

1. A petty cash fund of $100 was set up. Petty cash vouchers for the month totaled $86, and cash in the petty cash box totaled $12.50. The fund should be reimbursed in the amount of $_____.

2. The facts that follow are needed to prepare a bank reconciliation for Bosley Company as of March 31, 20xx. For each fact, write the correct letter (a, b, c, or d) to indicate where it should appear.

   a = Addition to the balance per bank

   b = Deduction from the balance per bank

   c = Addition to the balance per books

   d = Deduction from the balance per books

   _____ 1. The service charge by the bank was $8.

   _____ 2. A $1,700 note receivable was collected for the company by the bank. No collection fee was charged.

   _____ 3. There were two outstanding checks, totaling $3,200.

   _____ 4. A $355 NSF check drawn by a customer was deducted from the company's bank account and returned to the company.

   _____ 5. A deposit of $725 was made after banking hours on March 31.

   _____ 6. Check no. 185 was drawn for $342 but was recorded erroneously in the company's books as $324.

3. Herrera & Company uses a voucher system. Record each transaction in the journal provided on the next page, and indicate after each entry the journal of original entry in which the transaction would be recorded.

   a. Voucher no. 200 is prepared to establish a petty cash fund of $75.

   b. Voucher no. 201 is prepared to purchase merchandise from Wilton Company, $350.

   c. Voucher check no. 601 is issued in payment of voucher no. 200.

   d. Voucher check no. 602 is issued in payment of voucher no. 201.

   e. Voucher no. 202 is prepared to replenish the petty cash fund, which contains $20 in cash and the following receipts: cab fare, $12; postage, $34; and miscellaneous expense, $7.

   f. Voucher check no. 603 is issued in payment of voucher no. 202.

General Journal				
Date		Description	Debit	Credit

CHAPTER 9 SHORT-TERM LIQUID ASSETS

REVIEWING THE CHAPTER

Objective 1: Identify and explain the management issues related to short-term liquid assets.

1. It is management's responsibility to use company assets to maximize income while maintaining liquidity. **Short-term liquid assets** are financial assets that arise from cash transactions, the investment of cash, and the extension of credit. Examples are cash and cash equivalents, short-term investments, accounts receivable, and notes receivable.

2. A common measure of the adequacy of short-term liquid assets is the **quick ratio,** which equals short-term liquid assets divided by current liabilities. A quick ratio of 1.0 is generally considered a benchmark, but industry characteristics and company trends should also be carefully examined.

3. To maintain adequate liquidity, management must (a) manage cash needs during seasonal cycles, (b) set credit policies, and (c) consider the financing of receivables.
   a. During the course of a year, most businesses experience periods of both strong and weak sales, as well as variations in cash flow. For a business to remain liquid, management must carefully plan for cash inflows, cash outflows, borrowing, and investing.
   b. Companies sell on credit to be competitive and to increase sales. However, a business must carefully review the financial backgrounds of its potential credit customers before selling to them on credit. The effect of a company's credit policies is commonly measured by the **receivable turnover** (net sales divided by average net accounts receivable) and the **average days' sales uncollected** (365 divided by the receivable turnover).
   c. Occasionally, companies cannot afford to wait until their receivables are collected. They can use the receivables to obtain cash by borrowing funds and pledging the accounts receivable as collateral. Also, a business can sell its receivables to a **factor** (e.g., a bank or finance company) through a process called **factoring.** Receivables can be factored without recourse (as with major credit cards) or with recourse. The factoring fee is much greater when receivables are factored without recourse because of the greater risk involved. When receivables are sold with recourse, the seller of the receivable has a **contingent liability** (potential obligation) to 'make good' on the debt in the event of nonpayment by the debtor. Finally, a business can obtain financing through the **discounting** (selling) of its notes receivable.

Objective 2: Explain *cash, cash equivalents,* and the importance of electronic funds transfer.

4. **Cash** consists of coin and currency on hand, checks and money orders from customers, and deposits in checking accounts. A company's Cash account also can include a **compensating balance,** the minimum amount a bank requires a company to keep in its bank account.

5. **Cash equivalents** consist of investments, such as certificates of deposit and U.S. Treasury notes,

that have a term of less than 90 days. Cash and cash equivalents often are combined on the balance sheet.

6. Most companies need to keep some currency and coins on hand, for cash registers and for paying expenses that are impractical to pay by check. One way to control a cash fund or cash advances is through the use of an **imprest system.** A common form of imprest system is the petty cash fund, which is established at a fixed amount. Each payment from the fund is documented by a receipt. The petty cash fund is replenished periodically to restore it to its original amount.

7. Making payment by check reduces the need for currency and provides a permanent record of the payment itself. However, the use of checks can be partially avoided through an **electronic funds transfer (EFT),** or the transfer of funds between banks through electronic communication.

8. Banks provide a variety of services to their customers, as well as convenient means for conducting their banking transactions. In recent years, the use of automated teller machines (ATMs), banking by phone, and *debit cards* have become commonplace. When a purchase is made with a debit card, the purchase amount is deducted directly from the customer's bank account.

Objective 3: Account for short-term investments.

9. Companies frequently have excess cash on hand for short periods of time. To put this idle cash to good use, most companies purchase **short-term investments,** or **marketable securities.** Short-term investments are categorized as held-to-maturity securities, trading securities, or available-for-sale securities.

10. **Held-to-maturity securities** are debt securities, such as U.S. Treasury bills, that are expected to be held until the maturity date and whose cash value is not needed until then. Upon purchase of these securities, Short-Term Investments is debited and Cash credited. At year end, accrued interest is recognized with a debit to Short-Term Investments and a credit to Interest Income; the investment would be valued on the balance sheet at its amortized cost. At maturity, Cash is debited for the maturity amount, and Short-Term Investments and Interest Income are credited.

11. **Trading securities** consist of both debt and equity securities that will be held for just a short period of time. These securities, which serve to generate profits on short-term price increases, are valued on the balance sheet at their fair value (normally, market value). Also, dollar increases or decreases in the total trading portfolio during the period are reflected on that period's income statement.
   a. Upon the purchase of trading securities, Short-Term Investments is debited and Cash is credited.
   b. At the end of the accounting period, the cost and market (fair) value of the securities are compared, and an adjustment is made. When a decline in value has been suffered, Unrealized Loss on Investments (an income statement account) is debited and Allowance to Adjust Short-Term Investments to Market (a contra-asset account) is credited. When, on the other hand, an increase in value is experienced, Allowance to Adjust Short-Term Investments to Market is debited and Unrealized Gain on Investments is credited. In either case, the investments are reported on the balance sheet at market value.
   c. When an investment is sold, Cash is debited for the proceeds, Short-Term Investments is credited for the original cost, and Realized Gain (or Realized Loss) on Investments is credited (or debited) for the difference.

12. **Available-for-sale securities** are equity and debt securities that do not qualify as either held-to-maturity or trading securities. These securities are recorded in the same way as trading securities, except that unrealized gains and losses are reported in the stockholders' equity section of the balance sheet (as Accumulated Other Comprehensive Income) rather than on the income statement.

13. Dividend and interest income for all three categories of investments is recorded in the Other Income and Expenses section of the income statement.

Objective 4: Define *accounts receivable* and apply the allowance method of accounting for uncollectible accounts, using both the percentage of net sales method and the accounts receivable aging method.

14. **Accounts receivable** are short-term liquid assets that represent payment due from credit customers. This type of credit is called **trade credit.**

15. **Installment accounts receivable** are receivables that will be collected in a series of payments; they usually are classified on the balance sheet as current assets.

16. When loans and sales are made to the company's employees, officers, or owners, they should be

shown separately on the balance sheet with a title such as Receivables from Employees.

17. When a customer overpays, his or her account shows a credit balance. When a balance sheet is prepared, Accounts Receivable should be the sum of all accounts with debit balances. The sum of all accounts with credit balances should be shown as current liabilities.

18. Regardless of how thorough and efficient its control system is, a company will always have some customers who cannot or will not pay. **Uncollectible accounts** (also called *bad debts*), the accounting term for credit accounts that are not paid, are an expense of selling on credit. The company can afford such an expense because extending credit allows it to sell more, thereby increasing company earnings.

19. Some companies recognize the loss from an uncollectible account at the time it is determined to be uncollectible. This **direct charge-off method** is used by small companies and by all companies for tax purposes, but companies that follow GAAP do not use it on their financial statements because it does not match revenues and expenses.

20. The matching rule requires that uncollectible accounts expense is recognized in the same accounting period as the corresponding sale, even if the customer defaults in a future period. Of course, at the time of a credit sale, the company does not know which customers are not going to pay. Therefore, an estimate of uncollectible accounts must be made at the end of the accounting period. Then an adjusting entry is made, debiting Uncollectible Accounts Expense and crediting Allowance for Uncollectible Accounts for the estimated amount. This method of accounting for uncollectible accounts is called the **allowance method.** Uncollectible Accounts Expense appears on the income statement and is closed out as are other expenses. **Allowance for Uncollectible Accounts** (also called *Allowance for Bad Debts*) is a contra account to Accounts Receivable, reducing Accounts Receivable to the amount estimated to be collectible.

21. The two most common methods for estimating uncollectible accounts are the percentage of net sales method and the accounts receivable aging method.

22. Under the **percentage of net sales method,** the estimated percentage for uncollectible accounts is multiplied by net sales for the period. The answer determines the amount of the adjusting entry for uncollectible accounts. Any previous balance in

Allowance for Uncollectible Accounts represents estimates from previous years that have not yet been written off. Under this method, that balance has no bearing on the adjusting entry for this period.

23. Under the **accounts receivable aging method,** customers' accounts are placed in a "not yet due" category or in one of several "past due" categories (called the **aging of accounts receivable**). The amounts in each category are totaled. Each total then is multiplied by a different percentage for estimated bad debts. The sum of these answers represents estimated bad debts in ending Accounts Receivable. Again, the debit is to Uncollectible Accounts Expense, and the credit is to Allowance for Uncollectible Accounts. However, the entry is for the amount that will bring Allowance for Uncollectible Accounts to the figure arrived at in the aging calculation.

24. The percentage of net sales method can be described as an income statement approach to estimating uncollectible accounts because net sales (an income statement component) is the basis for the calculation. The accounts receivable aging method, on the other hand, is more of a balance sheet approach, because it uses a balance sheet component (accounts receivable) as *its* computational basis.

25. When it becomes clear that a specific account will not be collected, it should be written off by a debit to Allowance for Uncollectible Accounts (not to Uncollectible Accounts Expense, which was already charged when the Allowance was set up). After a specific account is written off, Accounts Receivable and Allowance for Uncollectible Accounts decrease by the same amount, but the net figure for expected receivables stays the same.

26. When a customer whose account has been written off pays in part or in full, two entries must be made. First, the customer's receivable is reinstated by a debit to Accounts Receivable and a credit to Allowance for Uncollectible Accounts for the amount now thought to be collectible. Second, Cash is debited and Accounts Receivable is credited for each collection.

Objective 5: Define and describe a *promissory note,* and make calculations and journal entries involving promissory notes.

27. A **promissory note** is an unconditional written promise to pay a definite sum of money on demand or at a future date. The person who signs the

note and thereby promises to pay is called the *maker* of the note. The person to whom money is owed is called the *payee*. The payee records short- or long-term **notes receivable,** and the maker records short- or long-term **notes payable.**

28. The **maturity date** (or date on which the note must be paid) and the **duration of note** (or length of time between issuance and maturity) must be stated on the promissory note, or it must be possible to figure them out from the information on the note.

29. To the borrower, **interest** is the cost of borrowing money. To the lender, it is the reward for lending money. Principal is the amount of money borrowed or loaned. The interest rate is the annual charge for borrowing money and is expressed as a percentage. A note can be either interest-bearing or non-interest-bearing.

30. Interest (not the interest rate) is a dollar figure, which is computed as follows:

    Interest = Principal
    × Rate of Interest
    × Time (length of loan)

    For example, interest on $800 at 5 percent for 90 days is $10: $800 × 5/100 × 90/360. A 360-day year is used to simplify the computation. If the length of the note was expressed in months, then the third fraction would be the number of months divided by 12.

31. The **maturity value** of an interest-bearing note is the face value of the note (principal) plus interest. For a non-interest-bearing note, maturity value is equal to the face amount (which, however, includes implied interest).

32. There are four situations that result in journal entries for notes receivable: (a) receipt of a note, (b) collection on a note, (c) recording a dishonored note, and (d) recording adjusting entries.

33. When a promissory note is received—for example, in settlement of an existing account receivable—Notes Receivable is debited and Accounts Receivable is credited. Other situations could require the credit to be made to a revenue account instead.

34. When collection is made on a note, Cash is debited for the maturity value, Notes Receivable is credited for the face value, and Interest Income is credited for the difference.

35. A **dishonored note** is one that is not paid at the maturity date. The payee debits Accounts Receivable for the maturity value, and credits Notes Receivable and Interest Income.

36. End-of-period adjustments must be made for notes that apply to both the current and future periods. In this way, interest can be divided correctly among the periods.

A. (LO 3)   Short-Term Investments   XX (purchase price)
                     Cash   XX (amount paid)
                         Purchase of U.S. Treasury bills

B. (LO 3)   Short-Term Investments   XX (accrued interest)
                     Interest Income   XX (accrued amount)
                         Accrual of interest on U.S. Treasury bills

C. (LO 3)   Cash   XX (maturity amount)
                     Short-Term Investments   XX (debit balance)
                     Interest Income   XX (interest this period)
                         Receipt of cash at maturity of U.S. Treasury bills
                         and recognition of related income

D. (LO 3)   Short-Term Investments   XX (purchase price)
                     Cash   XX (amount paid)
                         Investment in stocks for trading

E. (LO 3)   Unrealized Loss on Investments   XX (market decline)
                     Allowance to Adjust Short-Term Investments to Market   XX (market decline)
                         Recognition of unrealized loss on trading portfolio

F. (LO 3)   Cash   XX (proceeds on sale)
                     Short-Term Investments   XX (purchase price)
                     Realized Gain on Investments   XX (the difference)
                         Sale of stock at a gain

G. (LO 3)   Allowance to Adjust Short-Term Investments to Market   XX (market increase)
                     Unrealized Gain on Investments   XX (market increase)
                         Recognition of unrealized gain on trading portfolio

H. (LO 4)   Uncollectible Accounts Expense   XX (amount estimated)
                     Allowance for Uncollectible Accounts   XX (amount estimated)
                         To record the estimated uncollectible accounts
                         expense for the year

I. (LO 4)   Allowance for Uncollectible Accounts   XX (defaulted amount)
                     Accounts Receivable   XX (defaulted amount)
                         To write off receivable of specific customer as
                         uncollectible

J. (LO 4)   Accounts Receivable   XX (amount reinstated)
                     Allowance for Uncollectible Accounts   XX (amount reinstated)
                         To reinstate the portion of a specific customer's
                         account now considered collectible

K. (LO 4)   Cash   XX (amount received)
                     Accounts Receivable   XX (amount received)
                         Collection from customer in J

Short-Term Liquid Assets   111

L. (LO 5) Notes Receivable   XX (establishing amount)
                   Accounts Receivable   XX (eliminating amount)
                      Received note in payment of account

M. (LO 5) Cash   XX (maturity amount)
                   Notes Receivable   XX (face amount)
                   Interest Income   XX (amount earned)
                      Collected note

N. (LO 5) Accounts Receivable   XX (maturity amount)
                   Notes Receivable   XX (face amount)
                   Interest Income   XX (amount earned)
                      To record dishonored note

O. (LO 5) Interest Receivable   XX (amount accrued)
                   Interest Income   XX (amount earned)
                      To accrue interest earned on a note receivable

P. (LO 5) Cash   XX (maturity amount)
                   Notes Receivable   XX (face amount)
                   Interest Receivable   XX (interest previously accrued)
                   Interest Income   XX (interest this period)
                      Receipt of note receivable plus interest (see O above)

SELF-TEST

Test your knowledge of the chapter by choosing the best answer for each of the following items.

1. Because Tamara Company's sales are concentrated in the summer, management must carefully plan its borrowing needs and short-term investments. This is an example of management's responsibility to
   a. finance receivables.
   b. manage cash needs during seasonal cycles.
   c. set reasonable credit policies.
   d. finance purchases of long-term assets.

2. At year end, RJN Company has coin and currency on hand of $3,400, deposits in checking accounts of $32,000, U.S. Treasury bills due in 60 days of $58,000, and U.S. Treasury bonds due in 180 days of $88,000. On its balance sheet, cash and cash equivalents will be shown as
   a. $3,400.
   b. $35,400.
   c. $93,400.
   d. $181,400.

3. A $100,000 U.S. Treasury bill due in 180 days is purchased for $97,000. When cash in the amount of $100,000 is received, the journal entry would contain a
   a. credit to Interest Income for $3,000.
   b. debit to Gain on Investment for $3,000.
   c. credit to Investment Loss for $3,000.
   d. credit to Gain on Investment for $3,000.

4. The matching rule
   a. necessitates the recording of an estimated amount for bad debts.
   b. is violated when the allowance method is employed.
   c. results in the recording of an exact amount for bad debt losses.
   d. requires that bad debt losses be recorded when an individual customer defaults.

5. Which of the following methods of recording uncollectible accounts expense would best be described as an income statement method?
   a. Accounts receivable aging method
   b. Direct charge-off method
   c. Percentage of net sales method
   d. Both a and b

6. Using the percentage of net sales method, uncollectible accounts expense for the year is estimated to be $54,000. If the balance of Allowance for Uncollectible Accounts is a $16,000 credit before adjustment, what is the balance after adjustment?
   a. $16,000
   b. $38,000
   c. $54,000
   d. $70,000

7. Using the accounts receivable aging method, estimated uncollectible accounts are $74,000. If the balance of Allowance for Uncollectible Accounts is an $18,000 credit before adjustment, what is the balance after adjustment?
   a. $18,000
   b. $56,000
   c. $74,000
   d. $92,000

8. Each of the following is a characteristic of a promissory note, with the exception of a(n)
   a. payee who has an unconditional right to receive a definite amount on a definite date.
   b. amount to be paid that can be determined on the date the note is signed.
   c. due date that can be determined on the date the note is signed.
   d. maker who agrees to pay a definite sum subject to conditions to be determined at a later date.

9. The maturity value of a $6,000, 90-day note at 10 percent is
   a. $600.
   b. $5,850.
   c. $6,600.
   d. $6,150.

10. Unrealized Loss on Investments (for trading securities) appears on the
    a. balance sheet within the stockholders' equity section.
    b. income statement.
    c. balance sheet within the liabilities section.
    d. balance sheet within the assets section.

TESTING YOUR KNOWLEDGE

Matching*

Match each term with its definition by writing the appropriate letter in the blank.

_____ 1. Trade credit

_____ 2. Factoring

_____ 3. Uncollectible accounts expense

_____ 4. Allowance for uncollectible accounts

_____ 5. Installment accounts receivable

_____ 6. Promissory note

_____ 7. Maker

_____ 8. Payee

_____ 9. Maturity date

_____ 10. Maturity value

_____ 11. Interest rate

_____ 12. Interest

_____ 13. Principal

_____ 14. Contingent liability

_____ 15. Dishonored note

_____ 16. Discounting

_____ 17. Compensating balance

_____ 18. Cash equivalents

_____ 19. Cash

a. Short-term investments of less than 90 days

b. Coins, currency, checks, money orders, and bank deposits

c. The charge for borrowing money, expressed as a percentage

d. A note that is not paid at the maturity date

e. A written promise to pay

f. Estimated bad debts as shown on the income statement

g. Selling or transferring accounts receivable

h. A potential obligation

i. The time when payment is due on a note

j. Allowing customers to pay for merchandise over a period of time

k. A note's principal plus interest

l. The creditor named in a promissory note

m. Estimated bad debts as represented on the balance sheet

n. Selling a note prior to maturity

o. The charge for borrowing money, expressed in dollars

p. Receivables that will be collected in a series of payments

q. A minimum amount that a bank requires a company to keep in its account

r. The debtor named in a promissory note

s. The amount of money borrowed or loaned

Note to student: The matching quiz might be completed more efficiently by starting with the definition and searching for the corresponding term.

Short Answer

Use the lines provided to answer each item.

1. List three methods used in computing uncollectible accounts expense.

   _____

   _____

   _____

2. Explain the concept of contingent liability as it relates to discounted notes receivable.

   _____

   _____

   _____

   _____

3. Under what circumstance would there be a debit balance in Allowance for Uncollectible Accounts?

   _____

   _____

   _____

4. List the three categories of short-term investments.

   _____

   _____

   _____

5. List four examples of short-term liquid assets.

   _____

   _____

   _____

   _____

True-False

Circle T if the statement is true, F if it is false. Please provide explanations for the false answers, using the blank lines at the end of the section.

T F   1. Under the direct charge-off method, Allowance for Uncollectible Accounts does not exist.

T F   2. The percentage of net sales method violates the matching rule.

T F   3. Under the accounts receivable aging method, the balance in Allowance for Uncollectible Accounts is ignored in making the adjusting entry.

T F   4. Allowance for Uncollectible Accounts is a contra account to Accounts Receivable.

T F   5. Loans to officers of the company should not be included in Accounts Receivable on the balance sheet.

T F   6. When a customer overpays, his or her account on the company's books has a credit balance.

T F   7. Interest of 5 percent on $700 for 90 days would be computed as follows:

   $700 \times .05 \times 90.$

T F   8. *Trade credit* refers to credit sales made to customers by wholesalers or retailers.

T F   9. When a note is discounted at the bank, the maker must make good on the note if the payee defaults.

T F   10. A note dated December 14 and due February 14 has a duration of 60 days.

T F **11.** The figure for receivable turnover is a component of the average days' sales uncollected calculation.

T F **12.** Under the allowance method, the entry to write off a specific account as uncollectible decreases total assets.

T F **13.** The maturity value of an interest-bearing note equals principal plus interest.

T F **14.** Under the allowance method, a specific account is written off with a debit to Uncollectible Accounts Expense and a credit to Accounts Receivable.

T F **15.** When a note is dishonored, the payee nevertheless should record interest earned.

T F **16.** Uncollectible accounts are an expense of selling on credit.

T F **17.** Accounts receivable are an example of a cash equivalent.

T F **18.** The use of a major credit card (e.g., MasterCard) is an example of factoring with recourse.

T F **19.** The quick ratio equals current assets divided by current liabilities.

T F **20.** *Imprest system* refers to the mechanics of a petty cash fund.

T F **21.** Held-to-maturity securities consist of debt securities, but not equity securities.

T F **22.** Trading securities appear on the balance sheet at original cost.

Multiple Choice

Circle the letter of the best answer.

1. Unrealized gains and losses on available-for-sale securities are reported on
   a. the income statement.
   b. the balance sheet as a contra-asset account.
   c. the balance sheet within shareholders' equity.
   d. no financial statement.

2. Which of the following does *not* equal the others?
   a. $600 for 60 days at 6 percent
   b. $1,200 for 120 days at 3 percent
   c. $300 for 120 days at 6 percent
   d. $600 for 30 days at 12 percent

3. A company estimates at the balance sheet date that $1,500 of net sales for the year will not be collected. A debit balance of $600 exists in Allowance for Uncollectible Accounts. Under the percentage of net sales method, Uncollectible Accounts Expense and Allowance for Uncollectible Accounts would be debited and credited for
   a. $600.
   b. $1,100.
   c. $1,500.
   d. $2,100.

4. A contingent liability exists when
   a. a note is discounted.
   b. a note is dishonored.
   c. interest accrues on a note.
   d. a note reaches maturity.

5. Based on the accounts receivable aging method, a company estimates that $850 of end-of-period accounts receivable will not be collected. A credit balance of $300 exists in Allowance for Uncollectible Accounts. Uncollectible Accounts Expense should be recorded for
   a. $300.
   b. $550.
   c. $850.
   d. $1,150.

6. Under the accounts receivable aging method, a specific customer's account is written off by debiting
   a. Uncollectible Accounts Expense and crediting Allowance for Uncollectible Accounts.
   b. Accounts Receivable and crediting Allowance for Uncollectible Accounts.
   c. Allowance for Uncollectible Accounts and crediting Accounts Receivable.
   d. Uncollectible Accounts Expense and crediting Accounts Receivable.

7. Which of the following *cannot* be determined from the information on a note?
   a. Discount rate
   b. Interest rate
   c. Interest
   d. Maturity date

8. Which method for handling bad debts often violates the matching rule?
   a. Percentage of net sales method
   b. Direct charge-off method
   c. Accounts receivable aging method
   d. Both a and c

9. Which of the following is *not* considered a short-term liquid asset?
   a. Notes receivable
   b. Short-term investments
   c. Inventory
   d. Cash

10. The adjusting entry to accrue interest earned on held-to-maturity securities of 120 days would include a debit to
    a. Gain on Short-Term Investments.
    b. Cash.
    c. Interest Income.
    d. Short-Term Investments.

APPLYING YOUR KNOWLEDGE

Exercises

1. For the following set of facts, make the necessary entries for Dugan's Department Store in the journal provided on the next page.

   Dec. 31 Interest of $75 has accrued on notes receivable.

   31 Net sales for the year were $600,000. It is estimated that 4 percent will not be collected. Make the entry for uncollectible accounts.

   Jan. 3 Anna Kohn purchased $10,000 worth of goods on credit in November. She now issues Dugan's her $10,000, 30-day, 6 percent note, thus extending her credit period.

   8 Tom O'Brien goes bankrupt and notifies Dugan's that he cannot pay for the $1,000 worth of goods he had purchased last year on account.

   25 Tom O'Brien notifies Dugan's that he will be able to pay $600 of the $1,000 that he owes.

   28 A check for $200 is received from Tom O'Brien.

2. Calculate interest on the following amounts:

   a. $7,200 at 4% for 20 days = _____

   b. $52,000 at 7% for 3 months = _____

   c. $4,317 at 6% for 60 days = _____

   d. $18,000 at 8% for 1 day = _____

3. On November 17, 20x1, Rosser Corporation purchased 2,000 shares of Lopez Corporation stock for $30 per share. The purchase was made for trading purposes. At December 31, 20x1, the stock had a market value of $28 per share. On January 12, 20x2, Rosser sold all 2,000 shares for $66,000. In the journal provided below, prepare the entries for November 17, December 31, and January 12.

General Journal				
Date		Description	Debit	Credit

General Journal				
Date		Description	Debit	Credit

Short-Term Liquid Assets

119

Crossword Puzzle
for Chapters 8 and 9

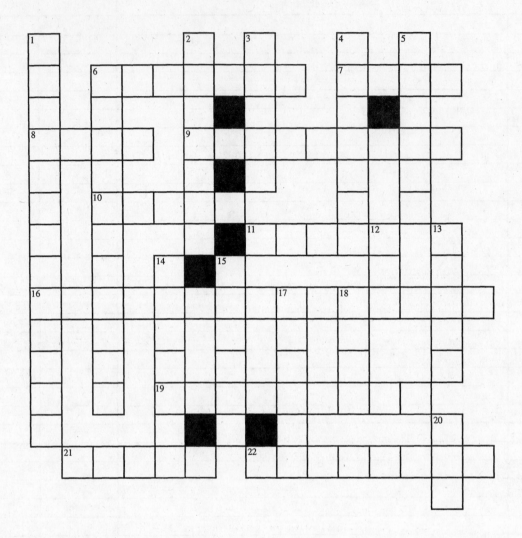

ACROSS

6. Bank statement item
7. Cash Short or _____
8. See 21-Across
9. Conspiracy for fraudulent purposes
10. Purchase _____
11. Column in 1-Down
16. A company's system of regulatory procedures (2 words)
19. Temporary, as investments (hyphenated)
21. With 8-Across, type of fund (2 words)
22. Uncollectible accounts (2 words)

DOWN

1. Voucher system journal (2 words)
2. Written authorization for an expenditure
3. Invoices
4. Available-_____ securities
5. Receiving _____
6. Method of selling notes receivable
12. Electronic bank transfer, for short
13. Balance per _____
14. Deposit in _____
15. Buyer of accounts receivable
17. Account such as Allowance for Uncollectible Accounts
18. Promissory _____
20. Banking convenience, for short

CHAPTER 10 INVENTORIES

REVIEWING THE CHAPTER

Objective 1: Identify and explain the management issues associated with accounting for inventories.

1. The **merchandise inventory** of a merchandising business consists of all goods owned and held for sale in the regular course of business. The inventory of a manufacturer, on the other hand, consists of raw materials, work in process, and finished goods. The costs of work in process and finished goods inventories include the costs of raw material, labor, and overhead (indirect manufacturing costs) incurred in producing the finished product. Inventory appears in the current asset section of the balance sheet.

2. To measure income properly and observe the matching rule, the following two questions must be answered for each nonfinancial asset:
   a. How much of the asset has been used up (expired) during the current period and should be transferred to expense?
   b. How much of the asset is unused (unexpired) and should remain on the balance sheet as an asset?

3. It is important for a merchandiser to maintain a sufficient level of inventory to satisfy customer demand. However, the higher the level maintained, the more costly it is for the business. Management can evaluate the level of inventory by calculating and analyzing the inventory turnover and average days' inventory on hand.
   a. **Inventory turnover** indicates the number of times a company's average inventory is sold during the period. It equals cost of goods sold divided by average inventory.
   b. **Average days' inventory on hand** indicates the average number of days required to sell the average inventory. It equals 365 divided by the inventory turnover.

4. Many companies, in an attempt to reduce their inventory, are changing to a **just-in-time operating environment.** They work closely with suppliers to coordinate and schedule shipments so that the goods arrive just in time to be used or sold.

Objective 2: Define *inventory cost* and relate it to goods flow and cost flow.

5. **Inventory cost** is the purchase price of the inventory less purchase discounts, plus freight or transportation in, including insurance in transit, and applicable taxes and tariffs.

6. Goods in transit should be included in inventory only if the company has title to the goods. When goods are sent FOB (free on board) shipping point, title passes to the buyer when the goods reach the common carrier. When goods are sent FOB destination, title passes when the goods reach the buyer. Goods that have been sold but are still on hand should not be included in the seller's inventory count.

7. When goods are held on **consignment,** the consignee (who earns a commission on making the sale) has possession of the goods, but the consignor

retains title and, thus, includes the goods on its balance sheet.

8. When identical items of merchandise are purchased at different prices during the year, it is usually impractical to monitor the actual **goods flow** and record the corresponding costs. Instead, the accountant makes an assumption of the **cost flow** and uses one of the following methods: (a) specific identification, (b) average-cost, (c) first-in, first-out (FIFO), or (d) last-in, first-out (LIFO).

Objective 3: Calculate the pricing of inventory, using the cost basis under the periodic inventory system, according to the specific identification method; average-cost method; first-in, first-out (FIFO) method; and last-in, first-out (LIFO) method.

9. If the units of ending inventory can be identified as having come from specific purchases, the **specific identification method** can be used. The flow of costs reflects the actual flow of goods in this case. However, the specific identification method is not practical in most cases.

10. Under the **average-cost method,** the average cost per unit is figured for the goods available for sale during the period. That is, the cost of goods available for sale is divided by the units available for sale. Then the average cost per unit is multiplied by the number of units in ending inventory to get the cost of ending inventory.

11. Under the **first-in, first-out (FIFO) method,** the cost of the first items purchased is assigned to the first items sold. Therefore, ending inventory cost is determined from the prices of the most recent purchases. During periods of rising prices, FIFO yields the highest income before income taxes of the four methods.

12. Under the **last-in, first-out (LIFO) method,** the cost of last items purchased are assigned to the first items sold. Therefore, the ending inventory cost is determined from the prices of the earliest purchases. During periods of rising prices, LIFO yields the lowest income before income taxes of the four methods. However, it best matches current merchandise costs with current sales prices.

Objective 4: Apply the perpetual inventory system to the pricing of inventories at cost.

13. When the periodic inventory system is used, a physical inventory is taken at the end of the period, and the cost of goods sold is calculated by subtracting ending inventory from the cost of goods available for sale.

14. The perpetual inventory system is used by companies that want more control over their inventories. A continuous record is kept of the balance of each inventory item. As goods are sold, costs are transferred from the Inventory account to Cost of Goods Sold.

15. The perpetual inventory system lends itself to specific identification, average-cost, FIFO, and LIFO calculations. Under specific identification and FIFO, figures for inventory and cost of goods sold should match those under the periodic inventory system. The perpetual LIFO method, though time-consuming to apply manually, is facilitated by the use of computers.

Objective 5: State the effects of inventory methods and misstatements of inventory on income determination, income taxes, and cash flows.

16. During periods of rising prices, FIFO produces a higher net income than LIFO. During periods of falling prices, the reverse is true. The average-cost method produces income before income taxes figures that are somewhere between those of FIFO and LIFO. Because the specific identification method depends on the particular items sold, no generalization can be made about the effect of changing prices. Even though LIFO best follows the matching rule, FIFO provides a more up-to-date ending inventory figure for balance sheet purposes.

17. There are several rules for the valuation of inventory for federal income tax purposes. For example, even though a business has a wide choice of methods, once a method has been chosen, it must be applied consistently. In addition, several regulations apply to LIFO, such as the requirement that LIFO also be used for the accounting records when it is being used for tax purposes.

18. A **LIFO liquidation** occurs when sales have reduced inventories below the levels established in earlier years. When prices have been rising steadily, a LIFO liquidation produces unusually high profits.

19. Beginning inventory plus purchases equals the cost of goods available for sale. The cost of goods sold is determined indirectly by deducting ending inventory from the cost of goods available for sale.

20. Because the cost of ending inventory is needed to compute the cost of goods sold, it affects income

before income taxes dollar for dollar. It is important to match the cost of goods sold with sales so that income before income taxes is reasonably accurate.

21. This year's ending inventory automatically becomes next year's beginning inventory. Because beginning inventory also affects income before income taxes dollar for dollar, an error in this year's ending inventory results in misstated income before income taxes for both this year and next year.
   a. When ending inventory is understated, income before income taxes for the period is understated.
   b. When ending inventory is overstated, income before income taxes for the period is overstated.
   c. When beginning inventory is understated, income before income taxes for the period is overstated.
   d. When beginning inventory is overstated, income before income taxes for the period is understated.

22. A company's choice of inventory method will affect not only its profitability, but also its liquidity and cash flows. The use of LIFO, for example, will usually produce a lower income before income taxes than will FIFO. However, the reduced tax liability under LIFO will have a positive effect on cash flow. Liquidity-related measures such as the current ratio, inventory turnover, and average days' inventory on hand will be affected by the inventory method chosen.

Objective 6: Apply the lower-of-cost-or-market (LCM) rule to inventory valuation.

23. The **market** value of inventory (current replacement cost) can fall below its cost as a result of physical deterioration, obsolescence, or decline in price level. Accordingly, it should be valued based on the **lower-of-cost-or-market (LCM) rule.** The two basic methods of valuing inventory at the lower of cost or market are the **item-by-item method** and the **major category method.** Both methods are acceptable by GAAP and for federal income tax purposes.

Supplemental Objective 7: Estimate the cost of ending inventory using the retail inventory method and gross profit method.

24. The **retail method** of inventory estimation can be used when the difference between the cost and sale prices of goods is a constant percentage over a period of time. It can be used whether or not the business makes a physical count of goods. To apply the retail method, goods available for sale are figured both at cost and at retail. Next, a cost-to-retail ratio is computed. Sales for the period then are subtracted from goods available for sale at retail, to produce ending inventory at retail. Finally, ending inventory at retail is multiplied by the cost-to-retail ratio to produce an estimate of ending inventory at cost.

25. The **gross profit method** of inventory estimation assumes that the gross margin for a business remains relatively stable from year to year. This method is used when inventory records are lost or destroyed, and when records of beginning inventory and purchases are not kept at retail. To apply the gross profit method, the cost of goods available for sale is determined by adding purchases to beginning inventory. Then, the cost of goods sold is estimated as follows:

$$\text{Sales} \times (1 - \text{Gross Margin \%})$$

Finally, the estimated cost of goods sold is subtracted from the cost of goods available for sale to arrive at the estimated ending inventory.

SELF-TEST

Test your knowledge of the chapter by choosing the best answer for each of the following items.

1. An overstatement of ending inventory in one period results in
   a. an overstatement of the ending inventory of the next period.
   b. an understatement of income before income taxes of the next period.
   c. an overstatement of income before income taxes of the next period.
   d. no effect on income before income taxes of the next period.

2. Which of the following costs would *not* be included in the cost of inventory?
   a. Goods held on consignment
   b. Purchased goods in transit, FOB shipping point
   c. Freight In
   d. Invoice price

3. Sept.   1   Inventory 10 @ $4.00
         8   Purchased 40 @ $4.40
       17   Purchased 20 @ $4.20
       25   Purchased 30 @ $4.80   Sold 70

   Using this information, cost of goods sold under the average-cost method is
   a. $133.20.
   b. $444.00.
   c. $310.80.
   d. $304.50.

4. Assuming the same facts as in **3,** cost of goods sold under the first-in, first-out (FIFO) method is
   a. $144.00.
   b. $300.00.
   c. $388.50.
   d. $444.00.

5. Assuming the same facts as in **3,** ending inventory under the last-in, first-out (LIFO) method is
   a. $316.
   b. $444.
   c. $300.
   d. $128.

6. Inventory turnover equals average inventory divided into
   a. number of days in a year.
   b. cost of goods available for sale.
   c. number of months in a year.
   d. cost of goods sold.

7. In a period of rising prices, which of the following inventory methods generally results in the lowest income before income taxes figure?
   a. Average-cost method
   b. FIFO method
   c. LIFO method
   d. Cannot tell without more information

8. When applying the lower-of-cost-or-market rule to inventory, *market* generally means
   a. original cost, less physical deterioration.
   b. resale value.
   c. original cost.
   d. replacement cost.

9. Which of the following companies would be most likely to use the retail inventory method?
   a. A farm supply company
   b. A TV repair company
   c. A dealer in heavy machinery
   d. A men's clothing shop

10. A retail company has goods available for sale of $1,000,000 at retail and $600,000 at cost and ending inventory of $100,000 at retail. What is the estimated cost of goods sold?
    a. $60,000
    b. $100,000
    c. $900,000
    d. $540,000

TESTING YOUR KNOWLEDGE

Matching*

Match each term with its definition by writing the appropriate letter in the blank.

_____ 1. LIFO liquidation

_____ 2. Merchandise inventory

_____ 3. Specific identification method

_____ 4. FIFO method

_____ 5. LIFO method

_____ 6. Average-cost method

_____ 7. Lower of cost or market

_____ 8. Retail method

_____ 9. Gross profit method

_____ 10. Periodic inventory system

_____ 11. Perpetual inventory system

_____ 12. Market

_____ 13. Consignment

_____ 14. Cost flow

_____ 15. Goods flow

a. The association of costs with their assumed flow

b. The current replacement cost of inventory

c. The inventory estimation method used when inventory is lost or destroyed

d. The inventory method in which the assumed flow of costs matches the actual flow of goods

e. The inventory system that maintains continuous records

f. The actual physical movement of inventory

g. The inventory method that yields the highest ending inventory during periods of rising prices

h. Goods held for sale in the regular course of business

i. The inventory estimation method that uses a cost-to-retail ratio

j. The inventory method that best follows the matching principle

k. An arrangement whereby one company sells goods for another company, for a commission

l. The inventory system that does not maintain continuous records

m. An occurrence that produces unusually high profits under steadily rising prices

n. The inventory method that utilizes an average-cost-per-unit figure

o. The rule that governs how inventory should be valued on the financial statements

Short Answer

Use the lines provided to answer each item.

1. List the four basic cost-flow assumptions used to determine the cost of merchandise inventory.

_____

_____

_____

_____

2. List the two basic methods of valuing inventory at the lower of cost or market.

_____

_____

---

*Note to student: The matching quiz might be completed more efficiently by starting with the definition and searching for the corresponding term.

3. List two methods of estimating ending inventory.

_____

_____

4. Briefly distinguish between the periodic and perpetual inventory systems in terms of recordkeeping and inventory taking.

_____

_____

_____

_____

5. List the three types of inventory involved in the manufacture of goods.

_____

_____

_____

True-False

Circle T if the statement is true, F if it is false. Please provide explanations for the false answers, using the blank lines at the end of the section.

T F   1. The figure for inventory turnover is needed to calculate average days' inventory on hand.

T F   2. When beginning inventory is understated, the cost of goods sold for the period also is understated.

T F   3. When ending inventory is overstated, income before income taxes for the period also is overstated.

T F   4. An error in 20x1's ending inventory will cause income before income taxes to be misstated in both 20x1 and 20x2.

T F   5. Goods in transit belong in the buyer's ending inventory only if the buyer has paid for them.

T F   6. If prices were never to change, all four methods of inventory valuation would result in identical income before income taxes figures.

T F   7. Under FIFO, goods are sold in exactly the same order as they are purchased.

T F   8. Of the four inventory methods, LIFO results in the lowest income during periods of falling prices.

T F   9. Under the retail method, each item sold must be recorded at both cost and retail.

T F 10. Under the gross profit method, the cost of goods sold is estimated by multiplying the gross margin percentage by sales.

T F 11. Under rising prices, the average-cost method results in a lower income before income taxes than LIFO does.

T F 12. If FIFO is being used for tax purposes, it must be used for reporting purposes as well.

T F 13. When goods are held on consignment, the consignee has both possession and title until the goods are sold.

T F 14. The inventory method that produces the highest profitability won't necessarily generate the highest cash flow.

_____

_____

_____

_____

_____

_____

_____

_____

_____

_____

_____

_____

_____

_____

_____

Multiple Choice

Circle the letter of the best answer.

1. Which of the following is least likely to be included in the cost of inventory?
   a. Freight in
   b. Cost to store goods
   c. Purchase cost of goods
   d. Excise tax on goods purchased

2. Under rising prices, which of the following inventory methods probably results in the highest income before income taxes?
   a. FIFO
   b. LIFO
   c. Specific identification
   d. Average-cost

3. Forgetting to include in inventory an item of merchandise in a warehouse results in
   a. overstated income before income taxes.
   b. overstated total assets.
   c. understated stockholders' equity.
   d. understated cost of goods sold.

4. Which inventory method is best suited for low-volume, high-priced goods?
   a. FIFO
   b. LIFO
   c. Specific identification
   d. Average-cost

5. Which of the following is *not* used or computed in applying the retail inventory method?
   a. Ending inventory at retail
   b. Freight at retail
   c. Beginning inventory at cost
   d. Sales during the period

6. The cost of inventory becomes an expense in the period in which the
   a. inventory is sold.
   b. merchandiser obtains title to the inventory.
   c. merchandiser pays for the inventory.
   d. merchandiser is paid for inventory that it has sold.

7. Goods in transit should be included in the inventory of
   a. neither the buyer nor the seller.
   b. the buyer when the goods have been shipped FOB destination.
   c. the seller when the goods have been shipped FOB shipping point.
   d. the company that has title to the goods.

8. Insurance companies often verify the extent of inventory lost or destroyed by applying the
   a. specific identification method.
   b. retail method.
   c. item-by-item method.
   d. gross profit method.

9. For a manufacturer, the cost of work in process and finished goods inventories would include all of the following costs *except*
   a. indirect materials.
   b. office wages.
   c. indirect labor.
   d. factory rent.

APPLYING YOUR KNOWLEDGE

Exercises

1. McIntyre Company had a beginning inventory of 100 units at $20. The firm made successive purchases as follows:

   Feb. 20   Purchased 200 units at $22
   May   8   Purchased 150 units at $20
   Oct. 17   Purchased 250 units at $24

   Calculate the cost that would be assigned to the ending inventory of 310 units and the cost of goods sold under the following methods (assume a periodic inventory system):

	Cost of Ending Inventory	Cost of Goods Sold
a. LIFO	$_____	$_____
b. FIFO	$_____	$_____
c. Average-cost	$_____	$_____

2. The records of Rojas Company show the following data for the month of May:

Sales	$156,000
Beginning inventory, at cost	70,000
Beginning inventory, at retail	125,000
Net purchases, at cost	48,000
Net purchases, at retail	75,000
Freight in	2,000

   Compute the estimated cost of ending inventory using the retail inventory method.

3. At the beginning of the accounting period, the cost of merchandise inventory was $150,000. Net sales during the period were $300,000; net purchases totaled $120,000; and the historical gross margin has been 20 percent. Compute the estimated cost of ending inventory using the gross profit method.

4. Koslowski Enterprises uses the perpetual LIFO method for valuing its inventory. On May 1, its inventory consisted of 100 units that cost $10 each. Successive purchases and sales for May were as follows:

   May 4   Purchased 60 units at $12 each
         8   Sold 50 units
        17   Purchased 70 units at $11 each
        31   Sold 100 units

   In the space provided, calculate ending inventory and cost of goods sold.

5. Assume the same facts as in Exercise **4**, except that Koslowski uses the perpetual *average-cost* method. In the space provided, calculate ending inventory and cost of goods sold (round dollar amounts to the nearest cent).

CHAPTER 11 LONG-TERM ASSETS

REVIEWING THE CHAPTER

Objective 1: Identify the types of long-term assets and explain the management issues related to accounting for them.

1. **Long-term assets** (also called *fixed assets*) are assets that (a) have a useful life of more than one year, (b) are acquired for use in the operation of the business, and (c) are not intended for resale to customers. Assets such as land and buildings that are not being used in the normal course of business should be classified as long-term investments. Property, plant, and equipment is the balance sheet classification for **tangible assets,** which have physical substance, such as land, buildings, equipment, and **natural resources. Intangible assets** is the balance sheet classification for assets that do not have physical substance, such as patents, trademarks, goodwill, copyrights, leaseholds, and franchises.

2. The allocation of costs to different accounting periods is called **depreciation** in the case of plant and equipment (plant assets), **depletion** in the case of natural resources, and **amortization** in the case of intangible assets. Because land has an unlimited useful life, its cost never is converted into an expense. The unexpired portion of a plant asset's cost is called **carrying value,** or *book value.* It is calculated by deducting accumulated depreciation from original cost.

3. Long-term assets are generally reported at carrying value. However, if **asset impairment** (loss of revenue-generating potential) occurs, the long-term asset's carrying value is reduced to reflect its current fair value (measured by the present value of future cash flows). A loss for the amount of the writedown would also be recorded.

4. Capital budgeting is the process of evaluating long-term assets under consideration for purchase. One common capital budgeting technique compares the amount and timing of cash inflows and outflows over the life of the proposed asset. If the net present value of those cash flows is positive, then the asset should probably be purchased. Information concerning long-term asset acquisitions may be found in the investing activities section of the statement of cash flows.

5. Long-term assets not purchased for cash must be financed. Common financing techniques include issuing stock, bonds, and long-term notes.

6. In dealing with long-term assets, the major accounting problem is to figure out how much of the asset has benefited the current period, and how much should be carried forward as an asset to benefit future periods. To resolve these issues, one must determine (a) the cost of the asset; (b) the method of matching the cost with revenues; (c) the treatment of subsequent expenditures such as repairs, maintenance, and additions; and (d) the treatment of the asset at time of disposal.

Objective 2: Distinguish between capital and revenue expenditures, and account for the cost of property, plant, and equipment.

7. Before recording an expenditure in connection with a long-term asset, one must determine

whether it was a capital expenditure or a revenue expenditure. A **capital expenditure** is an **expenditure** (a payment or an incurrence of liability) for the purchase or expansion of long-term assets. A capital expenditure is recorded as an asset because it will benefit several accounting periods. A **revenue expenditure** is an expenditure for repairs, maintenance, and anything else necessary to maintain and operate the plant and equipment for its originally estimated useful life. A revenue expenditure is charged as an expense in the period in which it is incurred, under the theory that it benefits only the current accounting period.

8. Treating a capital expenditure as a revenue expenditure, or vice versa, can result in a mismatching of revenues and expenses. Accordingly, great care must be taken to draw the appropriate distinction.

9. The cost of a long-term asset includes the purchase cost, freight charges, insurance while in transit, installation, and other costs involved in acquiring the asset and getting it ready for use. Interest incurred during the construction of a plant asset is included in the cost of the asset. However, interest incurred for the purchase of a plant asset is expensed when incurred.

10. When land is purchased, the Land account should be debited for the price paid for the land, real estate commissions, lawyers' fees, and such expenses as back taxes assumed; draining, clearing, and grading costs; assessments for local improvements; the cost (less salvage value) of tearing down buildings on the property; and (usually) the cost of landscaping.

11. Land improvements, such as driveways, parking lots, and fences, are subject to depreciation and require a separate Land Improvements account.

12. When long-term assets are purchased for a lump sum, the cost should be divided among the assets acquired in proportion to their appraisal values.

Objective 3: Define *depreciation*, state the factors that affect its computation, and show how to record it.

13. *Depreciation*, as used in accounting, refers to the allocation of the cost (less the residual value) of a tangible asset to the periods benefited by the asset. It does not refer to the physical deterioration or the decrease in market value of the asset. That is, it is a process of allocation, not valuation.

14. A tangible asset should be depreciated over its estimated useful life in a systematic and rational

manner. Tangible assets have limited useful lives because of **physical deterioration** (limitations resulting from use and exposure to the elements) and **obsolescence** (the process of becoming out of date).

15. Depreciation is computed after the asset's cost, residual value, depreciable cost, and estimated useful life are determined. **Residual value** is the estimated value at the disposal date and often is referred to as *salvage value* or *disposal value*. **Depreciable cost** equals the asset's cost less its residual value. **Estimated useful life** can be measured in time or in units, and requires careful consideration by the accountant.

Objective 4: Compute periodic depreciation under the straight-line method, production method, and declining-balance method.

16. The most common depreciation methods are (a) straight-line, (b) production, and (c) declining-balance. The last is described as an accelerated method.

17. Under the **straight-line method,** the depreciable cost is spread evenly over the life of the asset. Depreciation for each year is computed as:

$$\frac{\text{Cost} - \text{Residual Value}}{\text{Estimated Useful Life (Years)}}$$

18. Under the **production method,** depreciation is based not on time but on use of the asset in units. Under this method, depreciation for each year is computed as:

$$\frac{\text{Cost} - \text{Residual Value}}{\substack{\text{Estimated Units of} \\ \text{Useful Life}}} \times \substack{\text{Actual Units} \\ \text{of Output}}$$

19. The declining-balance method is called an **accelerated method** because depreciation is greatest in the first year and decreases each year thereafter. This method is justified by the matching rule (high depreciation charges in the most productive years) and by the smoothing effect that results when annual depreciation and repair expense are combined (i.e., over the years, depreciation charges decrease and repair costs increase).

20. Under the **declining-balance method,** depreciation is computed by multiplying the remaining carrying value (the unexpired part of the cost) of the asset by a fixed percentage. The **double-declining-balance method** is a form of the

declining-balance method that uses a fixed percentage that is twice the straight-line percentage. Under the double-declining-balance method, depreciation for each year is computed as:

$$2 \times \frac{100\%}{\text{Useful Life in Years}} \times \begin{array}{c}\text{Remaining} \\ \text{Carrying} \\ \text{Value}\end{array}$$

Under the declining-balance or double-declining-balance method, as with other methods, an asset should not be depreciated below its residual value.

Objective 5: Account for the disposal of depreciable assets not involving exchanges.

21. When an asset is still in use after it has been fully depreciated, no more depreciation should be recorded. The asset should not be written off until its disposal. Disposal occurs when the asset is discarded, sold, or traded in.

22. When a business disposes of an asset, depreciation should be recorded for the current period preceding disposal. This brings the asset's Accumulated Depreciation account up to the date of disposal.

23. When a machine, for example, is discarded (thrown out), Accumulated Depreciation, Machinery is debited and Machinery is credited for the present balance in the Accumulated Depreciation account. If the machine has not been fully depreciated, then Loss on Disposal of Machinery must be debited for the carrying value to balance the entry.

24. When a machine is sold for cash, Cash is debited, Accumulated Depreciation, Machinery is debited, and Machinery is credited. If the cash received is less than the carrying value of the machine, then Loss on Sale of Machinery also would be debited. On the other hand, if the cash received is greater than the carrying value, Gain on Sale of Machinery would be credited to balance the entry.

Objective 6: Account for the disposal of depreciable assets involving exchanges.

25. When an asset is traded in (exchanged) for a similar one, the gain or loss is computed first, as follows:

$$\begin{array}{rl} & \text{Trade-In Allowance} \\ - & \underline{\text{Carrying Value of Asset Traded In}} \\ = & \text{Gain (Loss) on Trade-In} \end{array}$$

a. For financial reporting purposes, both gains and losses should be recognized (recorded) on the exchange of dissimilar assets, and losses should be recognized on the exchange of similar assets. However, gains are not recognized on the exchange of similar assets.

b. For income tax purposes, neither gains nor losses should be recognized on the exchange of similar assets, but both should be recognized on the exchange of dissimilar assets.

c. When a gain or loss is recognized, the asset acquired should be debited for its list price—cash paid plus trade-in allowance—using a realistic trade-in value. The old asset is removed from the books, as explained in paragraph 24.

d. When a gain or loss is not recognized, the asset acquired should be debited for the carrying value of the asset traded in plus cash paid (this results in the nonrecognition of the gain or loss).

Objective 7: Identify the issues related to accounting for natural resources and compute depletion.

26. Natural resources are tangible assets in the form of valuable substances that can be cut, pumped, or mined. They include standing timber, oil and gas fields, and mineral deposits.

27. *Depletion* refers both to the exhaustion of the resource and to the allocation of a natural resource's cost to accounting periods based on the amount extracted in each period. Depletion for each year is computed as follows:

$$\frac{\text{Cost} - \text{Residual Value}}{\begin{array}{c}\text{Estimated Units} \\ \text{Available}\end{array}} \times \begin{array}{c}\text{Units Extracted} \\ \text{and Sold} \\ \text{During Period}\end{array}$$

Units extracted but not sold in one year are recorded as inventory, to be charged as an expense in the year they are sold.

28. Assets that are acquired in conjunction with the natural resource, and that have no useful purpose after the natural resource is depleted, should be depreciated on the same basis as depletion is computed.

29. In accounting for the exploration and development of oil and gas resources, two methods have been used. Under the **successful efforts method,** the cost of a dry well is written off immediately as a loss. The **full-costing method,** on the other hand, capitalizes and depletes the costs of both successful and dry wells. Both methods are in accordance with GAAP.

Objective 8: Apply the matching rule to intangible assets, including research and development costs and goodwill.

30. Intangible assets are long-term assets that have no physical substance. They represent certain rights and advantages to their owner. Examples of intangible assets are patents, copyrights, trademarks, goodwill, leaseholds, leasehold improvements, franchises, licenses, brand names, formulas, and processes. An intangible asset should be written off over its useful life (not to exceed 40 years) through amortization. This is to be accomplished by a direct reduction of the asset account and an increase in amortization expense.

    a. A **patent** is an exclusive right granted by the federal government for a period of 20 years (or 14 years for a design) to make a particular product or use a specific process.

    b. A **copyright** is an exclusive right granted by the federal government to the possessor to publish and sell literary, musical, and other artistic materials (including computer programs) for a period of the author's life plus 70 years.

    c. A **leasehold** is a right to occupy land or buildings under a long-term rental contract.

    d. **Leasehold improvements** are improvements to leased property that become the property of the lessor at the end of the lease.

    e. A **trademark** is a registered symbol or brand name that gives the holder the exclusive right to use it to identify a product or service.

    f. A **brand name** is a registered name that gives the holder the right to use it to identify a product or service.

    g. A **franchise** is the right or license to an exclusive territory or market.

    h. A **license** is the right to use a formula, technique, process, or design.

    i. **Goodwill** is the excess of the cost of a group of assets (usually a business) over the fair market value of the assets individually. (See also paragraph 33.)

31. Research and development involve developing new products, testing existing ones, and doing pure research. According to GAAP, the costs associated with these activities should be charged as expenses in the period incurred.

32. The cost to develop computer software that will be sold or leased to others should be treated as research and development up to the point that a product is deemed technologically feasible (i.e., when a detailed working program has been de-

signed). At that point, software production costs should be capitalized and amortized over the estimated useful life of the software, using the straight-line method. However, the cost of software developed for *internal* use may be capitalized in its entirety and amortized over its estimated economic life.

33. *Goodwill,* as the term is used in accounting, refers to a company's ability to earn more than is normal for its particular industry. Goodwill should be recorded only when a company is purchased. It equals the excess of the purchase cost over the fair market value of the net assets if purchased separately. Once it is recorded, goodwill should be amortized over its estimated useful life, not to exceed 40 years (however, the FASB is considering making the amortization of goodwill and other acquired intangible assets with indefinite useful lives optional, with a mandatory write-down only when impaired).

Supplemental Objective 9: Apply depreciation methods to problems of partial years, revised rates, groups of similar items, special types of capital expenditures, and cost recovery.

34. When an asset is purchased after the beginning of the year or discarded before the end of the year, depreciation should be recorded for only part of the year. The accountant figures the year's depreciation and multiplies this figure by the fraction of the year that the asset was in use.

35. Often, the estimated useful life or residual value is found to be over- or understated after some depreciation has been taken. The accountant then must produce a revised figure for the remaining useful life or remaining depreciable cost. Future depreciation then is calculated by spreading the remaining depreciable cost over the remaining useful life, leaving previous depreciation unchanged.

36. When a company has several plant assets that are similar, it probably uses a method known as **group depreciation** rather than individual depreciation. Under group depreciation, the original costs of all similar assets are lumped together in one summary account. Then depreciation is figured for the group of assets as a whole.

37. Businesses make capital expenditures for plant assets, natural resources, and intangible assets. Capital expenditures also include **additions** (such as a building wing) and **betterments** (such as the installation of an air-conditioning system).

38. Ordinary repairs are expenditures necessary to maintain an asset in good operating condition in order to attain its originally intended useful life. They are charged as expenses in the period in which they are incurred. **Extraordinary repairs** are expenditures that either increase an asset's residual value or lengthen its useful life. They are recorded by debiting Accumulated Depreciation (thereby increasing the asset's carrying value) and crediting Cash or Accounts Payable.

39. Under the **Modified Accelerated Cost Recovery System (MACRS)** each depreciable asset is placed in a category for tax purposes only and depreciated according to percentages and over a period of years established by Congress; estimated useful life and residual value are ignored. MACRS depreciation allows the rapid write-off of tangible assets to reduce current taxes but normally is not acceptable for financial reporting purposes. For example, most property other than real estate is depreciated by a 200 percent declining-balance method. Recovery of the cost of property placed in service after December 31, 1986, is calculated according to MACRS for tax purposes. An exception to asset cost allocation prescribed in the Tax Reform Act of 1986 is that the first $17,500 of equipment costs ($25,000 by tax year 2003) may be expensed immediately.

A. (LO 3) Depreciation Expense, Asset Name   XX (amount allocated)
              Accumulated Depreciation, Asset Name   XX (amount allocated)
                 To record depreciation for the period (review of
                 entry introduced in Chapter 3)

B. (LO 5) Depreciation Expense, Machinery   XX (amount allocated)
              Accumulated Depreciation, Machinery   XX (amount allocated)
                 To record depreciation up to date of disposal

C. (LO 5) Accumulated Depreciation, Machinery   XX (existing balance)
              Loss on Disposal of Machinery   XX (carrying value)
                Machinery   XX (purchase price)
                 Discarded machine no longer used in the business

D. (LO 5) Cash   XX (proceeds on sale)
              Accumulated Depreciation, Machinery   XX (existing balance)
                Machinery   XX (purchase price)
                 Sale of machine for carrying value; no gain or loss

E. (LO 5) Cash   XX (proceeds on sale)
              Accumulated Depreciation, Machinery   XX (existing balance)
               Loss on Sale of Machinery   XX (CV minus cash)
                Machinery   XX (purchase price)
                 Sale of machine at less than carrying value (CV);
                 loss recorded

F. (LO 5) Cash   XX (proceeds on sale)
              Accumulated Depreciation, Machinery   XX (existing balance)
                Gain on Sale of Machinery   XX (cash minus CV)
                Machinery   XX (purchase price)
                 Sale of machine at more than carrying value (CV);
                 gain recorded

G. (LO 6) Regarding the topic of exchanges of plant assets, the journal
              entries are all very similar (see entry H). The amounts, however,
              depend on a variety of factors, among them the similarity or
              dissimilarity of assets exchanged and the purpose of the entry
              (financial accounting or income tax). In addition, gains and
              losses sometimes are recognized, sometimes not. Please see
              your textbook for a thorough explanation.

H. (LO 6) Machinery (new)   XX (see textbook)
              Accumulated Depreciation, Machinery   XX (existing balance)
                Machinery (old)   XX (purchase price)
                Cash   XX (payment required)
                 Exchange of machines—cost of old machine and its
                 accumulated depreciation removed from the records,
                 and new machine recorded at list price. (Note: If gain
                 or loss must be recognized, it would be credited or
                 debited, respectively.)

I.   (LO 7)   Depletion Expense, Coal Deposits   XX (amount allocated)
                  Accumulated Depletion, Coal Deposits   XX (amount allocated)
                     To record depletion of coal mine

J.   (SO 9)   Capital expenditures typically are debited to an asset account
                  (such as Buildings or Equipment), and revenue expenditures
                  typically are debited to an expense account (such as Repair
                  Expense). An exception to these rules is for extraordinary repairs,
                  as shown in K.

K.   (SO 9)   Accumulated Depreciation, Machinery   XX (amount of repair)
                  Cash   XX (amount of repair)
                     Extraordinary repair to machinery

SELF-TEST

Test your knowledge of the chapter by choosing the best answer for each of the following items.

1. Which of the following is *not* a characteristic of all long-term assets?
   a. Used in operation of business
   b. Possess physical substance
   c. Useful life of more than a year
   d. Not for resale

2. Which of the following would *not* be included in the cost of land?
   a. Cost of paving the land for parking
   b. Assessment from local government for sewer
   c. Cost of clearing an unneeded building from the land
   d. Commission to real estate agent

3. Which of the following most appropriately describes depreciation?
   a. Allocation of cost of plant asset
   b. Decline in value of plant asset
   c. Gradual obsolescence of plant asset
   d. Physical deterioration of plant asset

4. Assuming a useful life of six years, which of the following methods would result in the most depreciation in the first year?
   a. Cannot tell from data given
   b. Double-declining-balance
   c. Production
   d. Straight-line

5. The sale of equipment costing $16,000, with accumulated depreciation of $13,400 and sale price of $4,000, would result in a
   a. gain of $4,000.
   b. gain of $1,400.
   c. loss of $1,400.
   d. loss of $12,000.

6. A truck that cost $16,800 and on which $12,600 of accumulated depreciation has been recorded was disposed of on January 2, the first business day of the year. Assume the truck was traded for a similar truck having a price of $19,600, that a $2,000 trade-in was allowed, and that the balance was paid in cash. Following APB rules, the amount of the gain or loss recognized on this transaction would be
   a. $2,200 gain.
   b. $2,200 loss.
   c. $2,000 gain.
   d. no gain or loss recognized.

7. Which of the following items is *not* classified as a natural resource?
   a. Timber land
   b. Gas reserve
   c. Goodwill
   d. Oil well

8. According to generally accepted accounting principles, the proper accounting treatment for the cost of a trademark that management feels will retain its value indefinitely is to
   a. amortize the cost over a period not to exceed 40 years.
   b. amortize the cost over five years.
   c. carry the cost of the asset indefinitely.
   d. write the cost off immediately.

9. According to generally accepted accounting principles, the proper accounting treatment of the cost of most research and development expenditures is to
   a. amortize the cost over a period not to exceed 40 years.
   b. amortize the cost over five years.
   c. carry the cost as an asset indefinitely.
   d. write the cost off immediately as an expense.

10. Reliable Insurance Company has many items of office equipment in its home office. Rather than compute depreciation on each item individually, the company may combine like items in one account and use
    a. statistical depreciation.
    b. combined depreciation.
    c. group depreciation.
    d. direct charge off.

TESTING YOUR KNOWLEDGE

*Matching**

Match each term with its definition by writing the appropriate letter in the blank.

_____ 1. Long-term assets (fixed assets)

_____ 2. Depreciation

_____ 3. Obsolescence

_____ 4. Franchise

_____ 5. Residual value (salvage or disposal value)

_____ 6. Accelerated method

_____ 7. Straight-line method

_____ 8. Production method

_____ 9. Full-costing method

_____ 10. Double-declining-balance method

_____ 11. Group depreciation

_____ 12. Natural resources

_____ 13. Depletion

_____ 14. Amortization

_____ 15. Modified Accelerated Cost Recovery System (MACRS)

_____ 16. Capital expenditure

_____ 17. Revenue expenditure

_____ 18. Patent

_____ 19. Copyright

_____ 20. Leasehold

_____ 21. Trademark

_____ 22. Successful efforts method

a. The exclusive right to make a particular product or use a specific process for 20 years

b. Using one depreciation rate for several similar items

c. The allocation of an intangible asset's cost to the periods benefited by the asset

d. Payment for the right to use property

e. Assets to be used in the business for more than one year

f. The allocation of the cost of a tangible asset to the periods benefited by the asset

g. An expenditure for services needed to maintain and operate plant assets (an expense)

h. The depreciation method under which cost allocation is based on units, not time

i. The exclusive right to publish literary, musical, or artistic materials or computer programs for the author's life plus 70 years

j. The accelerated depreciation method based on twice the straight-line rate

k. A depreciation method used for tax purposes only

l. The estimated value of an asset on the disposal date

m. An expenditure for the purchase or expansion of long-term assets (an asset)

n. One reason for an asset's limited useful life

o. Assets in the form of valuable substances that can be extracted and sold

p. An identifying symbol or name for a product or service that can be used only by its owner

q. The method of accounting for oil and gas that immediately writes off the cost of dry wells

r. The depreciation method that charges equal depreciation each year

s. The exclusive right to sell a product within a certain territory

t. The practice of charging the highest depreciation in the first year and decreasing depreciation each year thereafter

u. The allocation of a natural resource's cost to the periods over which the resource is consumed

v. The method of accounting for oil and gas that capitalizes the cost of dry wells

---

Note to student: The matching quiz might be completed more efficiently by starting with the definition and searching for the corresponding term.

Short Answer

Use the lines provided to answer each item.

1. Distinguish between an addition and a betterment.

_____

_____

_____

_____

2. When a plant asset is sold for cash, under what unique circumstance would no gain or loss be recorded?

_____

_____

3. List four pieces of information necessary to compute the depletion expense of an oil well for a given year.

_____

_____

_____

4. Distinguish between ordinary and extraordinary repairs.

_____

_____

_____

_____

5. For each asset category, provide the accounting term for the allocation of its cost to the periods benefited.

Category	Term for Cost Allocation
Intangible assets	_____
Plant and equipment	_____
Natural resources	_____

6. Plant assets have limited useful lives for two reasons. What are they?

_____

_____

True-False

Circle T if the statement is true, F if it is false. Please provide explanations for the false answers, using the blank lines at the end of the section.

T F   1. Land is not subject to depreciation.

T F   2. The loss recorded on a discarded asset is equal to the carrying value of the asset at the time it is discarded.

T F   3. Land held for speculative reasons is not classified as property, plant, and equipment.

T F   4. Depreciation is a process of valuation, not allocation.

T F   5. Depreciation for a machine can be calculated by having an appraiser determine to what extent the machine has worn out.

T F   6. When land is purchased for use as a plant site, its cost should include the cost of clearing and draining the land.

T F   7. Each type of depreciable asset should have its own accumulated depreciation account.

T F   8. Estimated useful life in years is irrelevant when applying the production method of depreciation.

T F   9. Under the straight-line method, if depreciation expense is $1,000 in the first year, it will be $2,000 in the second year.

T F   10. When the estimated useful life of an asset is revised after some depreciation has been taken, the accountant should not go back to previous years to make corrections.

T F   11. For financial accounting purposes, both gains and losses on the exchange of dissimilar assets are recognized in the accounting records.

T F **12.** In an asset's last year of depreciation, accelerated depreciation generally results in less net income than does straight-line depreciation.

T F **13.** Depreciable cost equals cost minus accumulated depreciation.

T F **14.** Estimated useful life and residual value are ignored when applying MACRS depreciation.

T F **15.** A copyright is a name or symbol that can be used only by its owner.

T F **16.** If, by mistake, ordinary maintenance is capitalized instead of being charged as an expense, net income for the period would be overstated.

T F **17.** A betterment is an example of a revenue expenditure.

T F **18.** Recording an extraordinary repair leaves the carrying value of the asset unchanged.

T F **19.** When a machine is sold for less than its carrying value, one of the debits is to Loss on Sale of Machinery and one of the credits is to Accumulated Depreciation, Machinery.

T F **20.** *Capital expenditure* is another term for expense.

T F **21.** For income tax purposes, neither gains nor losses are recognized on the exchange of similar plant assets.

T F **22.** When a plant asset is sold during a year, depreciation expense need not be brought up to date and recorded.

T F **23.** In determining the number of years over which to amortize intangible assets, useful life is far more important than legal life.

T F **24.** As accumulated depreciation increases, carrying value decreases.

T F **25.** Goodwill should not be recorded unless it has been purchased.

T F **26.** Research and development costs should be capitalized when they can be associated with a specific new product.

T F **27.** The full-costing method capitalizes the cost of both successful and dry wells.

T F **28.** A long-term asset's carrying value should be reduced when its value is deemed impaired.

_____

_____

_____

_____

_____

_____

_____

_____

_____

_____

_____

_____

_____

_____

_____

_____

_____

_____

_____

_____

_____

_____

_____

_____

Multiple Choice

Circle the letter of the best answer.

1. A building and land are purchased for a lump-sum payment of $66,000. How much should be allocated to land if the land is appraised at $20,000 and the building at $60,000?
   a. $22,000
   b. $20,000
   c. $16,500
   d. $13,750

2. The expired cost of a plant asset is called its
   a. accumulated depreciation.
   b. carrying value.
   c. depreciable cost.
   d. residual value.

3. Which depreciation method, when applied to an asset in its first year of use, results in the greatest depreciation charge?
   a. Declining-balance
   b. Production
   c. Straight-line
   d. Impossible to determine without more information

4. When a certain machine was purchased, its estimated useful life was 20 years. However, after it had been depreciated for 5 years, the company decided that it originally had overestimated the machine's useful life by 3 years. What should be done?
   a. Go back and adjust depreciation for the first 5 years.
   b. Depreciate the remainder of the depreciable cost over the next 15 years.
   c. Depreciate the remainder of the depreciable cost over the next 12 years.
   d. Both **a** and **b**

5. According to GAAP, intangible assets should never be amortized over more than
   a. 5 years.
   b. 17 years.
   c. 40 years.
   d. 50 years.

6. Land improvements
   a. should be included in the cost of land.
   b. are subject to depreciation.
   c. should be deducted from the cost of land.
   d. should be charged as an expense in the year purchased.

7. A machine that cost $9,000 with a carrying value of $2,000 is sold for $1,700, and an entry is made. Which of the following is true about the entry?
   a. Accumulated Depreciation is debited for $2,000.
   b. Machinery is credited for $2,000.
   c. Loss on Sale of Machinery is credited for $300.
   d. Accumulated Depreciation is debited for $7,000.

8. Which of the following is *not* a revenue expenditure?
   a. Ordinary maintenance of a machine
   b. Replacing an old roof with a new one
   c. The installation of new light bulbs
   d. A tire repair on a company truck

9. Charging a depreciable item as an expense, instead of capitalizing it, results in
   a. overstated total assets.
   b. understated net income for the succeeding period.
   c. overstated depreciation expense for the succeeding period.
   d. understated net income for the period.

10. Overestimating the number of barrels that can be pumped from an oil well over its lifetime results in
    a. understating net income each year.
    b. understating depletion cost per unit each year.
    c. overstating depletion expense each year.
    d. understating total assets each year.

11. The cost of developing computer software that will be sold or leased to others should be
    a. expensed up to the point that the product is technologically feasible.
    b. capitalized in its entirety and amortized over 40 years.
    c. expensed once the product is deemed to be technologically feasible.
    d. expensed in its entirety when incurred.

12. Which of the following normally is charged as an expense in the period of expenditure?
    a. Goodwill
    b. Leaseholds
    c. Leasehold improvements
    d. Research and development costs

APPLYING YOUR KNOWLEDGE

Exercises

1. A machine that cost $26,000 had an estimated useful life of five years and a residual value of $2,000 when purchased on January 2, 20x1. Fill in the amount of depreciation expense for 20x2, as well as the accumulated depreciation and carrying value of the machine as of December 31, 20x2, under both of the listed methods.

	Depreciation Expense for 20x2	Accumulated Depreciation as of 12/31/x2	Carrying Value as of 12/31/x2
a. Straight-line	$ _____	$ _____	$ _____
b. Double-declining-balance	$ _____	$ _____	$ _____

2. A machine that was to produce a certain type of toy was purchased for $35,000 on April 30, 20xx. The machine was expected to produce 100,000 toys during the ten years that the company expected to keep the machine. The company estimated that it then could sell the machine for $5,000. Using the production method, calculate the depreciation expense in 20xx, when the machine produced 7,500 toys.

4. Darnell Manufacturing is investigating the purchase of a piece of equipment that would cost $22,000. It is estimated that the equipment would be used for six years, would have a residual value of $3,000, and would generate positive net cash flows of $4,000 for each of its six years of use. Using Tables 3 and 4 in the appendix to your text, calculate the equipment's net present value, and state whether or not Darnell should make the purchase. Assume an interest rate of 8 percent.

3. Classify each of the following expenditures as a capital or revenue expenditure by placing a **C** or an **R** next to each item.

_____ **a.** Replacement of the roof on a building

_____ **b.** Replacement of the battery in a company vehicle

_____ **c.** The cost of painting the executive offices

_____ **d.** Installation of aluminum siding on a building

_____ **e.** Replacement of the motor in a machine

_____ **f.** The cost to repair an air-conditioning unit

_____ **g.** The cost to install a piece of machinery

_____ **h.** The addition of a building wing

_____ **i.** The tune-up of a company vehicle

5. On January 2, 20xx, McKnight Enterprises traded in, along with $15,500 in cash, a machine that cost $25,000 and had a carrying value of $8,000, for a new machine with a retail price of $23,000. The machines are similar in nature. Prepare the journal entry that McKnight would make to conform to GAAP, as well as the entry that would conform to income tax rulings. Use the journal provided.

General Journal				
Date		Description	Debit	Credit

6. In 20xx, Conejo Coal Company purchased a coal mine for $800,000. It is estimated that 2 million tons of coal can be extracted from the mine. In the space provided, prepare Conejo's adjusting entry for December 31, 20xx, to reflect the extraction and sale of 100,000 tons during the year.

General Journal				
Date		Description	Debit	Credit

Crossword Puzzle
for Chapters 10 and 11

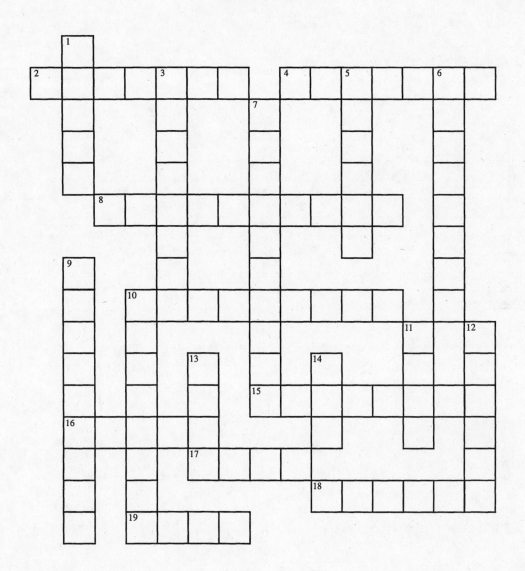

ACROSS

2. Residual (value)
4. Allocate the cost of a natural resource
8. Improvement to plant assets
10. _____-balance method
15. Trade in
16. _____ profit method
17. Just-in-_____ operating environment
18. Inventory estimation technique
19. Inventory method

DOWN

1. Tax depreciation method
3. Allocate the cost of an intangible asset
5. Intangible with a 20-year legal life
6. Possessing physical substance
7. Allocate the cost of plant assets
9. (Goods) sold by one for another
10. Sale, trade-in, or abandonment
11. Asset not subject to allocation process
12. _____ life
13. The "C" of MACRS
14. Inventory valuation rule (abbr.)

CHAPTER 12 CURRENT LIABILITIES

REVIEWING THE CHAPTER

Objective 1: Identify the management issues related to recognition, valuation, classification, and disclosure of current liabilities.

1. **Liabilities** are one of the three major parts of the balance sheet. They are present obligations for either the future payment of assets or the future performance of services that result from past transactions. The primary reason for incurring current liabilities is to meet needs for cash during the operating cycle. Management must carefully manage the cash flows related to current liabilities; the appropriate level of liabilities is critical to business success.

2. Two common measures of the length of time creditors allow for payment are the payables turnover and the average days' payable. **Payables turnover** (measured in "times") shows the relative size of a company's accounts payable, and is calculated as follows:

$$\frac{\text{Cost of Goods Sold} \pm \text{Change in Merchandise Inventory}}{\text{Average Accounts Payable}}$$

Average days' payable, on the other hand, shows the average length of time a company takes to pay its accounts payable. It is computed as follows:

$$\frac{365 \text{ days}}{\text{Payables Turnover}}$$

3. A liability generally should be recorded when an obligation arises, but it is also necessary to make end-of-period adjustments for accrued and esti-

mated liabilities. On the other hand, contracts representing future obligations are not recorded as liabilities until they become current obligations.

4. Liabilities are valued at the actual or estimated amount due, or at the fair market value of goods or services that must be delivered.

5. **Current liabilities** are present obligations that are expected to be satisfied within one year or the normal operating cycle, whichever is longer. Payment is expected to be out of current assets or by taking on another current liability. **Long-term liabilities** are obligations that are not expected to be satisfied within the longer of one year or the normal operating cycle.

6. Supplemental disclosure of liabilities may be required in the notes to the financial statements. An explanation of special credit arrangements, for example, can be very helpful to the financial statement user.

Objective 2: Identify, compute, and record definitely determinable and estimated current liabilities.

7. Current liabilities consist of definitely determinable liabilities and estimated liabilities.

8. **Definitely determinable liabilities** are obligations that can be measured exactly. They include accounts payable, short-term notes payable, accrued liabilities, dividends payable, sales and excise taxes payable, current portions of long-term debt, payroll liabilities, and unearned or deferred revenues.

a. Accounts payable, sometimes called trade accounts payable, are current obligations due to suppliers of goods and services.

b. Companies often obtain a **line of credit** from a bank in order to finance operations. In addition, a company may borrow short-term funds by issuing **commercial paper** (unsecured loans sold to the public).

c. Short-term notes payable are current obligations evidenced by promissory notes. Interest may be either stated separately or included in the face amount. In the latter case, the actual amount borrowed is less than the face amount.

d. Accrued liabilities are actual or estimated liabilities that exist at the balance sheet date but are unrecorded. An end-of-period adjustment is needed to record both the expenses and the accrued liabilities.

e. Dividends payable is an obligation to distribute the earnings of a corporation to its stockholders. It arises only when the board of directors declares a dividend.

f. Most states and many cities levy a sales tax on retail transactions. The federal government also charges an excise tax on some products. The merchant must collect the taxes at the time of the sale and would record both the receipt of cash and the proper tax liabilities.

g. If a portion of long-term debt is due within the next year and is to be paid from current assets, then this amount should be classified as a current liability; the remaining debt should be classified as a long-term liability.

h. Payroll liabilities consist of the employee-related obligations incurred by a business. Not only is the business responsible for paying **wages,** paid at an hourly rate, and **salaries,** paid at a monthly or yearly rate, earned by its employees, it is obligated for such items as social security (FICA) taxes, Medicare, and unemployment taxes. It is also liable for amounts withheld from its employees' gross earnings that must be remitted to government and other agencies.

i. The three general types of liabilities associated with payroll accounting are (a) liabilities for employee compensation, (b) liabilities for employee payroll withholdings, and (c) liabilities for employer payroll taxes. An employee is under the direct supervision and control of the company. An independent contractor (such as a lawyer or a CPA) is not and, therefore, is not accounted for under the payroll system.

j. **Unearned revenues** represent obligations to deliver goods or services in return for advance payment. When delivery takes place, Unearned Revenue is debited and a revenue account is credited.

9. Estimated liabilities are definite obligations. However, the amount of the obligation must be estimated at the balance sheet date because the exact figure will not be known until a future date. Examples of estimated liabilities are income taxes, property taxes, product warranties, and vacation pay.

a. A corporation's income tax depends on its net income, a figure that often is not determined until well after the balance sheet date.

b. Property taxes are taxes levied on real and personal property. Very often a company's accounting period ends before property taxes have been assessed. Therefore, the company must make an estimate. The debit is to Property Tax Expense, and the credit is to Estimated Property Tax Payable.

c. When a company sells its products, many of the warranties will still be in effect during subsequent accounting periods. However, the warranty expense and liability must be recorded in the period of the sale no matter when the company makes good on the warranty. Therefore, at the end of each accounting period, the company should make an estimate of future warranty expense that will apply to the present period's sales.

d. In most companies, employees earn vacation pay for working a certain length of time. Therefore, the company must estimate the vacation pay that applies to each payroll period. The debit is to Vacation Pay Expense, and the credit is to Estimated Liability for Vacation Pay. The liability decreases (is debited) when an employee receives vacation pay.

Objective 3: Define *contingent liability*.

10. A **contingent liability** is a potential liability that may or may not become an actual liability. The uncertainty about its outcome is settled when a future event does or does not occur. Two conditions must be met before a contingency is entered in the accounting records. The liability must be probable and it must be reasonably estimated. Contingent liabilities arise from things like pending lawsuits, tax disputes, and failure to follow government regulations. When a contingent liability does not meet the two above criteria for accrual, it should still be reported in the notes to the financial statements.

Supplemental Objective 4: Compute and record the liabilities associated with payroll accounting.

11. The employer is required by law to withhold certain taxes from the employee's earnings and to remit those taxes to government agencies. The employer also makes other withholdings for the employee's benefit.

    a. Social security and Medicare taxes provide for retirement and disability benefits, survivor's benefits, and medical benefits.

    b. Federal income taxes depend on (1) the amount the employee earns and (2) the number of exemptions claimed on the employee's W-4 form (Employee's Withholding Exemption Certificate). The amount that the employer withholds and remits to the government should be close to the employee's actual federal income tax liability. State income taxes require similar withholding procedures.

    c. Withholdings also are made for pension plans, insurance premiums, union dues, and savings plans.

12. The **payroll register** is a detailed list of the company's total payroll each payday. Each employee's name, regular and overtime hours, gross earnings, deductions, net pay, and payroll classification are listed for that payroll period. The journal entry to record the payroll is based on the column totals of the payroll register.

13. An employee's take-home pay equals his or her gross earnings less total withholdings. To simplify payroll procedures, the company must keep an **employee earnings record** for each employee, listing all payroll data (earnings, deductions, and payment). Each year, the firm must inform the employee of his or her yearly earnings and withholdings on a W-2 form (Wage and Tax Statement). The employee uses this form to complete his or her individual tax return. The employer must send a copy of each W-2 to the IRS.

14. Independent of the employee's taxes, the employer must pay (a) social security taxes, (b) Medicare taxes, (c) federal unemployment insurance taxes (FUTA), and (d) state unemployment insurance taxes. These taxes are considered operating expenses. They require a debit to Payroll Tax Expense and a credit to each of the four tax liabilities.

15. Many companies use a special payroll bank account against which payroll checks are drawn. In addition, monthly or quarterly payments for withholdings must be made to the proper agencies.

Summary of Journal Entries Introduced in Chapter 12

Interest Stated Separately

A. (LO 2)   Cash   XX (amount received)
       Notes Payable   XX (face amount)
         Issued promissory note with interest stated
         separately

B. (LO 2)   Notes Payable   XX (face amount)
       Interest Expense   XX (amount incurred)
         Cash   XX (maturity amount)
         Payment of note with interest stated separately

C. (LO 2)   Interest Expense   XX (amount accrued)
       Interest Payable   XX (amount accrued)
         To record interest expense on note with interest
         stated separately

Interest in Face Amount

D. (LO 2)   Cash   XX (face amount minus interest)
       Discount on Notes Payable   XX (interest in face amount)
         Notes Payable   XX (face amount)
         Issued promissory note with interest included in
         face amount

E. (LO 2)   Notes Payable   XX (face amount)
         Cash   XX (face amount)
         Payment of note with interest included in face
         amount (see also F below)

F. (LO 2)   Interest Expense   XX (amount accrued)
       Discount on Notes Payable   XX (amount accrued)
         To record interest expense on note with interest
         included in face amount

G. (LO 2)   Cash   XX (amount collected)
       Sales   XX (price charged)
       Sales Tax Payable   XX (amount to remit)
       Excise Tax Payable   XX (amount to remit)
         Sale of merchandise and collection of sales and
         excise taxes

H. (LO 2)   Wages Expense   XX (gross amount)
       Employees' Federal Income Taxes Payable   XX (amount withheld)
       Employees' State Income Taxes Payable   XX (amount withheld)
       Social Security Tax Payable   XX (employees' share)
       Medicare Tax Payable   XX (employees' share)
       Medical Insurance Payable   XX (employees' share)
       Pension Contributions Payable   XX (employees' share)
       Wages Payable   XX (take-home pay)
         To record payroll

I.   (LO 2)   Payroll Taxes and Benefits Expense .... XX (total employer payroll taxes)
        Social Security Tax Payable .... XX (employer's share)
        Medicare Tax Payable .... XX (employer's share)
        Medical Insurance Payable .... XX (employer's share)
        Pension Contributions Payable .... XX (employer's share)
        Federal Unemployment Tax Payable .... XX (amount incurred)
        State Unemployment Tax Payable .... XX (amount incurred)
            To record payroll taxes and other costs

J.   (LO 2)   Cash .... XX (amount prepaid)
        Unearned Subscriptions .... XX (amount to earn)
            Receipt of annual subscriptions in advance

K.   (LO 2)   Unearned Subscriptions .... XX (amount earned)
        Subscription Revenues .... XX (amount earned)
            Delivery of monthly magazine issues

L.   (LO 2)   Income Taxes Expense .... XX (amount estimated)
        Estimated Income Taxes Payable .... XX (amount estimated)
            To record estimated federal income taxes

M.   (LO 2)   Property Tax Expense .... XX (amount estimated)
        Estimated Property Tax Payable .... XX (amount estimated)
            To record estimated property tax expense

N.   (LO 2)   Estimated Property Tax Payable .... XX (amount incurred)
        Prepaid Property Tax .... XX (amount to be incurred)
        Cash .... XX (amount paid)
            Payment of property tax

O.   (LO 2)   Product Warranty Expense .... XX (estimated amount)
        Estimated Product Warranty Liability .... XX (estimated amount)
            To record estimated product warranty expense

P.   (LO 2)   Cash .... XX (fee charged)
        Estimated Product Warranty Liability .... XX (cost of part)
        Service Revenue .... XX (fee charged)
        Merchandise Inventory .... XX (cost of part)
            Replacement of part under warranty

Q.   (LO 2)   Vacation Pay Expense .... XX (amount incurred)
        Estimated Liability for Vacation Pay .... XX (amount owed or accrued)
            Estimated vacation pay expense

R.   (LO 2)   Estimated Liability for Vacation Pay .... XX (amount taken)
        Cash (or Wages Payable) .... XX (amount paid or payable)
            Wages of employees on vacation

SELF-TEST

Test your knowledge of the chapter by choosing the best answer for each of the following items.

1. Failure to record a liability will probably
   a. have no effect on net income.
   b. result in overstated net income.
   c. result in overstated total assets.
   d. result in overstated total liabilities and owner's equity.

2. Which of the following is most likely to be a definitely determinable liability?
   a. Property taxes payable
   b. Product warranty liability
   c. Income taxes payable
   d. Interest payable

3. Which of the following is a payroll tax borne by both employee and employer?
   a. Excise tax
   b. Income tax
   c. FUTA tax
   d. Social security and Medicare taxes

4. The amount received by a borrower on a one-year, $3,000, 10 percent note with interest included in the face value is
   a. $3,000.
   b. $2,700.
   c. $3,300.
   d. $2,990.

5. Which of the following is most likely to be an estimated liability?
   a. Deferred revenues
   b. Vacation pay liability
   c. Current portion of long-term debt
   d. Payroll liabilities

6. If product J cost $100 and had a 2 percent failure rate, the estimated warranty expense in a month in which 1,000 units were sold would be
   a. $2,000.
   b. $100.
   c. $20.
   d. $20,000.

7. Of a company's employees, 70 percent typically qualify to receive two weeks' paid vacation per year. The amount of estimated vacation pay liability for a week in which the total payroll is $3,000 is
   a. $2,100.
   b. $42.
   c. $84.
   d. $120.

8. A contingent liability would be recorded in the accounting records if it is
   a. not probable but can be reasonably estimated.
   b. not probable but cannot be estimated.
   c. probable and can be reasonably estimated.
   d. probable but cannot be reasonably estimated.

9. An employee has gross earnings of $500 and withholdings of $31 for social security tax, $7 for Medicare tax, and $60 for income taxes. The employer pays $31 for social security tax, $7 for Medicare tax, and $20 for FUTA. The total cost of the employee to the employer is
   a. $402.
   b. $500.
   c. $558.
   d. $596.

10. Payroll Taxes Expense includes all of the following *except*
   a. federal unemployment tax payable.
   b. social security tax payable.
   c. federal income tax payable.
   d. state unemployment tax payable.

TESTING YOUR KNOWLEDGE

Matching*

Match each term with its definition by writing the appropriate letter in the blank.

_____ 1. Current liabilities

_____ 2. Long-term liabilities

_____ 3. Definitely determinable liabilities

_____ 4. Estimated liabilities

_____ 5. Unearned (deferred) revenues

_____ 6. Vacation pay

_____ 7. Withholdings

_____ 8. Commercial paper

_____ 9. W-2 form

_____ 10. W-4 form

_____ 11. Take-home pay

_____ 12. Employee earnings record

_____ 13. Payroll register

_____ 14. Payroll taxes expense

_____ 15. Contingent liabilities

_____ 16. Wages

_____ 17. Salaries

_____ 18. Line of credit

a. A list of payroll data for all employees for one payday

b. Obligations that are expected to be satisfied within one year or the normal operating cycle, whichever is longer

c. An arrangement with the bank that allows a company to borrow funds when needed

d. Hourly or piecework pay to an employee

e. Obligations that exist but cannot be measured exactly on the balance sheet date

f. Gross earnings less total withholdings

g. Obligations that can be measured exactly

h. A portion of earnings retained by the employer and remitted to the appropriate agencies

i. A statement that lists exemptions claimed

j. Pay received during one's earned time off

k. A yearly statement of earnings and withholdings

l. Unsecured loans sold to the public

m. Social security, Medicare, and unemployment taxes levied on the employer

n. A record containing all payroll data for one employee

o. Obligations to deliver goods or services in return for advance payment

p. Monthly or yearly pay to (usually) a manager or administrator

q. Potential liabilities that may or may not become actual liabilities

r. Obligations that are not expected to be satisfied in the current period

Note to student: The matching quiz might be completed more efficiently by starting with the definition and searching for the corresponding term.

Short Answer

Use the lines provided to answer each item.

1. Current liabilities fall into two principal categories. What are they?

   _____

   _____

2. Provide three examples of contingent liabilities.

   _____

   _____

   _____

3. Provide three examples of estimated liabilities.

   _____

   _____

   _____

4. Provide three examples of definitely determinable liabilities.

   _____

   _____

   _____

5. List four withholdings from an employee's salary that are always or almost always required.

   _____

   _____

   _____

   _____

6. List the four components of payroll taxes expense.

   _____

   _____

   _____

   _____

True-False

Circle T if the statement is true, F if it is false. Please provide explanations for the false answers, using the blank lines at the end of the section.

T F 1. Deferred revenues can be found on the income statement.

T F 2. A contract to purchase goods in the future does not require the recording of a current liability.

T F 3. The failure to record an accrued liability results in an overstatement of net income.

T F 4. The current portion of a long-term debt is a current liability (assume that it is to be satisfied with cash).

T F 5. Sales Tax Payable is an example of an estimated liability.

T F 6. Warranties fall under the category of definitely determinable liabilities.

T F 7. Federal income taxes withheld depend in part on the number of exemptions claimed on the W-4 form.

T F 8. The journal entry to record the payroll is based on the column totals of the payroll register.

T F 9. FUTA is a tax borne by both the employer and the employee.

T F 10. Every contingent liability eventually must become an actual liability or no liability at all.

T F 11. The account Discount on Notes Payable is associated with notes whose interest is stated separately on the face of the note.

T F **12.** Liabilities basically are obligations that result from past transactions.

T F **13.** A CPA is an example of an independent contractor.

T F **14.** If a refrigerator is sold in year 1, and repairs are made in year 2, Product Warranty Expense should be recorded in year 2.

T F **15.** When the payroll is recorded, Wages and Salaries Payable is credited for total take-home pay.

T F **16.** Social security and Medicare taxes are borne by the employee, not the employer.

_____

_____

_____

_____

_____

_____

_____

_____

_____

_____

_____

_____

_____

_____

_____

_____

_____

_____

_____

_____

_____

_____

_____

_____

Multiple Choice

Circle the letter of the best answer.

1. Which of the following is *not* a definitely determinable liability?
   a. Dividends payable
   b. Deferred revenues
   c. Property taxes payable
   d. Excise taxes payable

2. Estimated liabilities do *not* apply to
   a. warranties.
   b. vacation pay.
   c. a corporation's income tax.
   d. pending lawsuits.

3. Which of the following is *not* an employee withholding?
   a. FUTA tax
   b. Union dues
   c. Social security tax
   d. Charitable contributions

4. The amount of federal income tax withheld is recorded as a
   a. payroll expense.
   b. contra account.
   c. current asset.
   d. current liability.

5. When an employee receives vacation pay, the company should debit
   a. Vacation Pay Expense and credit Cash.
   b. Vacation Pay Receivable and credit Cash.
   c. Estimated Liability for Vacation Pay and credit Cash.
   d. Vacation Pay Expense and credit Estimated Liability for Vacation Pay.

6. A company that uses the calendar year receives a property tax bill each March (for that particular calendar year), to be paid by April 10. If entries are made at the end of each month to record property tax expense, the April 10 entry to record payment would include a
   a. debit to Cash.
   b. credit to Estimated Property Tax Payable.
   c. debit to Property Tax Expense.
   d. debit to Prepaid Property Tax.

7. Balboa Engraving, Inc., purchased some equipment by executing a $10,000 non-interest-bearing (interest is included in the face amount) note due in three years. The equipment should be recorded by Balboa at
   a. $10,000 minus the discounted interest on the note.
   b. $10,000 plus the discounted interest on the note.
   c. the amount of the discounted interest on the note.
   d. $10,000.

8. When accounting for a note whose interest is included in its face amount, the account Discount on Notes Payable eventually is converted into
   a. Interest Receivable.
   b. Interest Expense.
   c. Interest Payable.
   d. Interest Income.

APPLYING YOUR KNOWLEDGE

Exercises

1. During 20x1, Pratt's Appliance Store sold 300 washing machines, each with a one-year guarantee. It was estimated that 5 percent of the washing machines eventually will require some type of repair, with an average cost of $35. Prepare the adjusting entry that Pratt's would make concerning the warranty. Also, prepare the entry that the store would make on April 9, 20x2, for one such repair that cost $48.

General Journal				
Date		Description	Debit	Credit

2. Pat Bauer, an office worker who is paid $6.50 per hour, worked 40 hours during the week ended May 7. Social security taxes are 6.20 percent; Medicare taxes are 1.45 percent; union dues are $5; state taxes withheld are $8; and federal income taxes withheld are $52. In addition, Bauer's employer must pay (on the basis of gross earnings) social security taxes of 6.20 percent, Medicare taxes of 1.45 percent, federal unemployment taxes of 0.8 percent, and state unemployment taxes of 5.4 percent. Prepare journal entries that summarize Bauer's earnings for the week and that record the employer's payroll taxes. Round off amounts to the nearest cent.

General Journal				
Date		Description	Debit	Credit

3. Kalfayan Corporation has current assets of $100,000 and current liabilities of $40,000, of which accounts payable are $30,000. Kalfayan's cost of goods sold is $290,000, its merchandise decreased by $15,000, and accounts payable were $20,000 the prior year. In the spaces below, provide the following short-term liquidity measures:

a. Working capital: _____

b. Payables turnover: _____

c. Average days' payable: _____

CHAPTER 13 PARTNERSHIPS

REVIEWING THE CHAPTER

Objective 1: Identify the principal characteristics, advantages, and disadvantages of the partnership form of business.

1. According to the Uniform Partnership Act, a **partnership** is "an association of two or more persons to carry on as co-owners of a business for profit." For accounting purposes, a partnership is treated as a separate entity. Its chief characteristics are as follows:
   a. Voluntary association: Partners choose each other when they form their business.
   b. **Partnership agreement:** Partners have either an oral or a written agreement. A written agreement should contain such specifics as the name, location, and purpose of the business, as well as methods and procedures for income and loss distribution, partner admission and withdrawal, and business liquidation.
   c. **Limited life:** A partnership is dissolved when a partner withdraws, goes bankrupt, becomes incapacitated, retires, or dies. It is also dissolved when a new partner is admitted or when the agreement calls for its dissolution.
   d. **Mutual agency:** Each partner can bind the partnership to outside contracts within the scope of the business.
   e. **Unlimited liability:** Each partner is personally liable for all debts of the partnership.
   f. Co-ownership of partnership property: Business property is owned jointly by all partners.
   g. Participation in partnership income: Each partner shares in the income and losses of the business.

2. A partnership has several advantages. It is easy to form and dissolve, is able to pool capital resources and individual talents, avoids the corporation's tax burden, and allows the partners freedom and flexibility.

3. The disadvantages of a partnership are limited life, mutual agency, unlimited liability, capital limitation, and the difficulty of transferring ownership interest.

4. Under a **limited partnership,** the personal liability of the limited partners cannot exceed the amount of their investment (though the business normally has one or more general partners whose personal liability is unlimited).

5. Under a **joint venture,** two or more entities pool their resources and skills, often for a limited period of time, to achieve a specific goal (such as the production and sale of a new product).

Objective 2: Record partners' investments of cash and other assets when a partnership is formed.

6. The owner's equity section of a partnership's balance sheet is called **partners' equity,** and separate Capital and Withdrawals accounts must be maintained for each partner. When a partner makes an

investment, the assets contributed are debited at their fair market value, and the partner's Capital account is credited.

Objective 3: Compute and record the income or losses that partners share, based on stated ratios, capital balance ratios, and partners' salaries and interest.

7. The method of distributing partnership income and losses should be specified in the partnership agreement. If the agreement does not mention the distribution of income and losses, the law requires that they be shared equally. The most common methods base distribution on (a) a stated ratio only; (b) a capital balance ratio only; or (c) a combination of salaries, interest on each partner's capital, and the stated ratio. Net income is distributed to partners' equity by debiting Income Summary and crediting each partner's Capital account; the reverse is done for a net loss.

8. When income and losses are based on a stated ratio only, partnership income or loss for the period is multiplied by each partner's ratio (stated as a fraction or percentage) to arrive at each partner's share.

9. When income and losses are based on a capital balance ratio only, partnership income or loss for the period is multiplied by each partner's proportion of (a) the capital balance at the beginning of the period or (b) the average capital during the period.

10. When income and losses are based on salaries, interest, and a stated ratio, salaries and interest must be allocated to the partners regardless of the net income figure for the period. Then any net income left over after the salaries and interest must be allocated to the partners in the stated ratio. If salaries and interest are greater than net income, the excess must be deducted from each partner's allocation, in the stated ratio.

Objective 4: Record a person's admission to a partnership.

11. When a partnership is legally dissolved, the partners lose the authority to continue business as a going concern. **Dissolution** of a partnership occurs on (a) the admission of a new partner, (b) the withdrawal of a partner, or (c) the death of a partner.

12. A new partner can be admitted into a partnership by either (a) purchasing an interest in the partnership from one or more of the original partners or (b) investing assets into the partnership.
   a. When a new partner purchases an interest from another partner, the selling partner's capital account is debited and the buying partner's

account credited for the interest sold. The purchase price is ignored in making this entry.
   b. When a new partner invests his or her own assets into the partnership, the contributed assets are debited and the new partner's Capital account is credited. The amount of the debit and credit may or may not equal the value of the assets being contributed. It depends on the value of the business and the method applied. When the partners feel that a share of their business is worth more than the value of the assets being contributed, they generally ask the entering partner to pay them a **bonus.** Under the opposite set of circumstances, a partnership gives the new partner a bonus, or a greater interest in the business than the value of the assets contributed.

Objective 5: Record a person's withdrawal from a partnership.

13. A partner can withdraw from a partnership in one of two ways: (a) by selling his or her interest to new or existing partners or (b) by taking assets from the partnership that are greater than, less than, or equal to his or her capital investment. In addition, when a partner dies, the partnership automatically is dissolved, and immediate steps must be taken to settle with the heirs of the deceased partner.

Objective 6: Compute the distribution of assets to partners when they liquidate their partnership.

14. **Liquidation** of a partnership is the process of ending the business by (a) selling partnership assets, (b) paying off partnership liabilities, and (c) distributing the remaining assets to the partners. The liquidation transactions are summarized in a statement of liquidation.
   a. The sale of partnership assets is recorded by debiting Cash, crediting the assets, and debiting or crediting Gain or Loss from Realization for the difference. The gain or loss then is distributed to the partners in their stated ratio. If a partner's account shows a deficit after the distribution of a loss, he or she must pay personal assets to the business to cover the deficit. If the partner cannot pay, the remaining partners must absorb the deficit in their stated ratio.
   b. The payment of liabilities is recorded by debiting the liabilities and crediting Cash.
   c. The distribution of cash to the partners is recorded by crediting Cash and debiting the partners' Capital accounts for their remaining balances (not in their stated ratio).

A. (LO 2) Cash   XX (amount invested)

             Furniture and Displays   XX (fair market value)

               Jerry Adcock, Capital   XX (total invested)

                  Initial investment of Jerry Adcock in the partnership

B. (LO 2) Cash   XX (amount invested)

             Equipment   XX (fair market value)

               Note Payable   XX (amount to be paid)

               Rose Villa, Capital   XX (difference)

                  Initial investment of Rose Villa in the partnership

C. (LO 3) Income Summary   XX (net income)

             Jerry Adcock, Capital   XX (his share)

             Rose Villa, Capital   XX (her share)

                  Distribution of income for the year to the partners'
Capital accounts

D. (LO 3) Entry C assumes a net income and an increase in both partners'
accounts. However, if the partnership had suffered a net loss,
the debits and credits of the entry would have been reversed.
In addition, it is possible for a partner's account to decrease
even though the company earned a profit, or for it to increase
even though the company suffered a loss.

E. (LO 4) Jerry Adcock, Capital   XX (existing balance)

             Richard Davis, Capital   XX (Adcock's balance)

                  Transfer of Jerry Adcock's equity to Richard Davis
(purchase price ignored)

F. (LO 4) Jerry Adcock, Capital   XX (half of existing balance)

             Rose Villa, Capital   XX (half of existing balance)

               Richard Davis, Capital   XX (half of partners' equity)

                  Transfer of half of Jerry Adcock's and Rose Villa's
equity to Richard Davis

G. (LO 4) Cash   XX (amount invested)

             Richard Davis, Capital   XX (equity interest)

                  Admission of Richard Davis to an interest in the
company; no bonus involved

H. (LO 4) Cash   XX (amount invested)

              Jerry Adcock, Capital   XX (bonus received)

              Rose Villa, Capital   XX (bonus received)

              Richard Davis, Capital   XX (equity interest received)

                  Investment by Richard Davis for an interest in the
firm, and the bonus paid to the original partners

I. (LO 4) Cash .... XX (amount invested)
    Jerry Adcock, Capital .... XX (bonus recorded)
    Rose Villa, Capital .... XX (bonus recorded)
        Richard Davis, Capital .... XX (equity interest received)
            To record the investment by Richard Davis of cash
            and a bonus from Adcock and Villa

J. (LO 5) Rose Villa, Capital .... XX (existing balance)
        Richard Davis, Capital .... XX (Villa's balance)
            Sale of Villa's partnership interest to
            Davis (purchase price ignored)

K. (LO 5) Rose Villa, Capital .... XX (existing balance)
        Judy Jones, Capital .... XX (Villa's balance)
            Sale of Villa's partnership interest to Jones
            (purchase price ignored)

L. (LO 5) Richard Davis, Capital .... XX (existing balance)
        Cash .... XX (amount withdrawn)
        Notes Payable, Richard Davis ..... XX (amount due)
            Withdrawal of Richard Davis from the partnership
            (taking business assets)

M. (LO 5) Entry L assumes that Davis withdraws with an amount
        equal to the balance in his Capital account. If the part-
        ners all agree that he should receive more or less than
        that amount, a bonus to or from the remaining partners
        would have to be incorporated into the entry.

N. (LO 6) Cash .... XX (amount collected)
        Gain or Loss from Realization .... XX (bad debt amount)
            Accounts Receivable .... XX (amount settled)
                Collection of accounts receivable (on liquidation)

O. (LO 6) Cash .... XX (proceeds from sale)
            Merchandise Inventory .... XX (carrying value)
            Gain or Loss from Realization ... XX (amount of gain)
                Sale of inventory (on liquidation)

P. (LO 6) Cash .... XX (proceeds from sale)
            Plant Assets .... XX (carrying value)
                Sale of plant assets (at carrying value, on liquidation)

Q. (LO 6) Accounts Payable (net) .... XX (existing balance)
            Cash .... XX (amount paid)
                Payment of accounts payable (on liquidation)

R. (LO 6) Gain or Loss from Realization .... XX (net realization gain)
            Jerry Adcock, Capital .... XX (share of gain)
            Rose Villa, Capital .... XX (share of gain)
            Richard Davis, Capital .... XX (share of gain)
                Distribution of the gain on assets to the partners
                (on liquidation). (Note: The entry would have
                been the reverse of above if the partnership
                had realized a net loss from realization.)

S. (LO 6) Jerry Adcock, Capital   XX (existing balance)

Rose Villa, Capital   XX (existing balance)

Richard Davis, Capital   XX (existing balance)

    Cash   XX (existing balance)

        Distribution of cash to the partners (on liquidation)

T. (LO 6) Cash   XX (amount invested)

    Richard Davis, Capital   XX (deficit balance)

        Additional investment of Richard Davis to cover

        the negative balance in his Capital account

U. (LO 6) Jerry Adcock, Capital   XX (existing balance)

Rose Villa, Capital   XX (existing balance)

    Cash   XX (existing balance)

        Distribution of (remaining) cash to the partners

        (stated ratios irrelevant)

V. (LO 6) Jerry Adcock, Capital   XX (share absorbed)

Rose Villa, Capital   XX (share absorbed)

    Richard Davis, Capital   XX (deficit balance)

        Transfer of Davis's deficit to Adcock and Villa

SELF-TEST

Test your knowledge of the chapter by choosing the best answer for each of the following items.

1. The ability of a partner to enter into a contract on behalf of all partners is called
   a. unlimited liability.
   b. the partnership agreement.
   c. mutual agency.
   d. voluntary association.

2. Which of the following partnership characteristics is considered a disadvantage?
   a. Voluntary association
   b. Participation in partnership income
   c. Mutual agency
   d. Co-ownership of partnership property

3. A partner invests in a partnership a building with an $80,000 carrying value and a $100,000 fair market value. The related mortgage payable of $45,000 is assumed by the partnership. As a result of the investment, the partner's Capital account should be credited
   a. $35,000.
   b. $55,000.
   c. $80,000.
   d. $100,000.

4. Partner X has a January 1 capital balance of $24,000 and withdraws $9,000 on May 1. What is her average capital balance for the calendar year?
   a. $16,500
   b. $18,000
   c. $21,500
   d. $33,000

5. MyLahn and Jeffrey are partners in a business. MyLahn's original capital was $40,000 and Jeffrey's was $60,000. They agreed to share profits and losses as follows:

	MyLahn	Jeffrey
Salaries	$14,000	$20,000
Interest on original capital	10%	10%
Remaining income or loss	40%	60%

   If income for the year was $80,000, how much of that income would MyLahn receive?
   a. $14,400
   b. $18,000
   c. $21,600
   d. $32,400

6. Assuming the same facts as in 5, if income for the year was $40,000, how much of that income would Jeffrey receive?
   a. $20,000
   b. $22,000
   c. $23,600
   d. $26,000

7. Assuming the same facts as in 5, if the net loss for the year was $10,000, what share of the loss would MyLahn receive?
   a. $15,000
   b. $26,000
   c. ($3,600)
   d. ($6,400)

8. O and P are partners who share profits and losses in the ratio of 3:2 and have the following capital balances on December 31, 20xx:

O, Capital	P, Capital
$500,000	$200,000

   Assume that the partners agree to let Q into the partnership if he invests $300,000 for a one-fourth interest. Q's capital balance would be
   a. $250,000.
   b. $300,000.
   c. $500,000.
   d. $1,000,000.

9. Assuming the same facts as in 8, assume that P withdraws from the partnership by selling her interest in the partnership to Q for $300,000. Q's capital balance in the partnership would be
   a. $500,000.
   b. $300,000.
   c. $200,000.
   d. $100,000.

10. In a partnership liquidation,
    a. the last journal entry credits the partners' Capital accounts.
    b. gains and losses on the sale of assets are allocated to the partners based on their current capital balances.
    c. the distribution of remaining assets to the partners is based on their stated ratios.
    d. creditors must be paid before partners.

TESTING YOUR KNOWLEDGE

Matching*

Match each term with its definition by writing the appropriate letter in the blank.

_____ 1. Partnership

_____ 2. Voluntary association

_____ 3. Partnership agreement

_____ 4. Limited life

_____ 5. Mutual agency

_____ 6. Unlimited liability

_____ 7. Stated ratio

_____ 8. Dissolution

_____ 9. Liquidation

_____ 10. Bonus

_____ 11. Partners' equity

_____ 12. Statement of liquidation

_____ 13. Joint venture

a. The sale of partnership assets and payment to creditors and owners

b. The fact that any change in the partners' original association causes the business to dissolve

c. The power of each partner to enter into contracts that are within the normal scope of the business

d. The balance sheet section that lists the partners' capital accounts

e. An association of two or more entities to achieve a specific goal

f. A formula that can be used to compute the allocation of net income or loss to the partners

g. A summary of liquidation transactions

h. The claim to the partners' personal assets by creditors if the partnership cannot pay its debts

i. The end of a partnership as a going concern

j. The specifics of how a partnership will operate

k. The partners' consent to join one another in forming a partnership

l. An amount credited to a new partner's Capital account for more or less than the value of the assets contributed

m. An association of two or more persons to carry on as co-owners of a business for profit

Short Answer

Use the lines provided to answer each item.

1. List seven events that dissolve a partnership.

_____

_____

_____

_____

_____

_____

2. List the three steps involved in liquidating a partnership.

_____

_____

_____

Note to student: The matching quiz might be completed more efficiently by starting with the definition and searching for the corresponding term.

3. List four advantages of the partnership form of business.

_____

_____

_____

_____

4. List five disadvantages of the partnership form of business.

_____

_____

_____

_____

_____

True-False

Circle T if the statement is true, F if it is false. Please provide explanations for the false answers, using the blank lines at the end of the section.

T F **1.** A partnership agreement is not legal unless it is in writing.

T F **2.** One way in which a partnership can be dissolved is by the admission of a new partner.

T F **3.** If a partner in the restaurant business signs a contract to purchase a tractor for the partnership, without the other partners' knowledge, the contract probably would not be binding on the partnership.

T F **4.** If Partners A and B share income in a 3:2 ratio but no stipulation has been made for sharing losses, losses should be shared equally.

T F **5.** When salary and interest allocations for the partners exceed net income for the period, a net loss has occurred.

T F **6.** When a partner invests property into a partnership, the property ceases to belong to the partner.

T F **7.** It is possible for a partnership to incur a net loss for the period and actually increase one or more of the owners' accounts at the time that the loss is allocated.

T F **8.** If Partner C sells her $20,000 interest in the partnership to D for $25,000, D's Capital account is credited for $25,000.

T F **9.** When an entering partner pays a bonus for an interest in a partnership, the original partners' Capital accounts are unchanged.

T F **10.** When the original partners allow the entering partner a bonus for a certain interest in the partnership, the original partners' Capital accounts are unchanged.

T F **11.** If a partner withdraws from a partnership for less than his or her capital investment, the remaining partners receive the remainder in the stated ratio.

T F **12.** The last step in a liquidation is to pay the partners in the stated ratio.

T F **13.** When the partners are paid at the conclusion of a liquidation, their Capital accounts are debited.

T F **14.** Upon liquidation, when a partner cannot eliminate a deficit in his or her account by contributing personal assets, the remaining partners must contribute their personal assets.

T F **15.** In a limited partnership, the personal liability of a general partner is unlimited.

_____

_____

_____

_____

_____

_____

_____

_____

_____
_____
_____
_____
_____
_____
_____
_____

_____
_____
_____
_____
_____
_____
_____
_____

Multiple Choice

Circle the letter of the best answer.

1. A partnership's income and losses can be distributed using all of the following *except*
   a. a stated ratio only.
   b. a salary and interest allowance only.
   c. average capital balances only.
   d. beginning capital balances only.

2. Partners A and B receive salary allowances of $8,000 and $2,000, respectively, and share the remainder equally. If the company earned $5,000 during the period, what is the effect on A's Capital account?
   a. A $4,000 increase
   b. A $5,000 increase
   c. A $5,500 increase
   d. A $2,500 decrease

3. A partnership has $60,000 in equity. L contributes $45,000 for a one-third interest. How much should L's account be credited under the bonus method?
   a. $15,000
   b. $20,000
   c. $35,000
   d. $45,000

4. Partners M and N have capital balances of $20,000 and $30,000, respectively, and share income and losses in a 3:2 ratio. P contributes $10,000 for a one-fourth interest under the bonus method. What is the new balance in M's account?
   a. $17,000
   b. $17,500
   c. $18,000
   d. $20,000

5. Partners R, S, and T share income and losses equally and have capital balances of $10,000, $20,000, and $30,000, respectively. Because S wants to withdraw from the partnership, the assets are revalued and are found to be undervalued by $6,000. How much should S be allowed to take on withdrawal from the partnership?
   a. $18,000
   b. $20,000
   c. $22,000
   d. $26,000

6. Partners W, X, and Y have beginning capital balances of $5,000, $8,000, and $7,000, respectively. If income and losses are allocated on the basis of beginning capital balances, how much of 20xx's net income of $60,000 should be allocated to Y?
   a. $7,000
   b. $20,000
   c. $21,000
   d. $27,000

7. Gains and losses from assets sold on liquidation of a partnership are
   a. ignored in the statement of liquidation.
   b. divided equally among the partners.
   c. divided among the partners in proportion to their existing capital balances.
   d. divided among the partners in the stated ratio.

8. A partnership
   a. must allow all interested parties to become partners.
   b. is not subject to a corporate tax burden.
   c. agreement is required to be in writing.
   d. is bound by all outside contracts entered into by its partners.

Partnerships

APPLYING YOUR KNOWLEDGE

Exercises

1. Partners A, B, and C each receive a $10,000 salary, as well as a 5 percent interest on their respective capital balances of $60,000, $40,000, and $50,000. If they share income and losses in a 3:2:1 ratio, how much net income or loss would be allocated to each under the following circumstances?

   a. A net income of $40,500

      A = $_____

      B = $_____

      C = $_____

   b. A net income of $25,500

      A = $_____

      B = $_____

      C = $_____

   c. A net loss of $4,500

      A = $_____

      B = $_____

      C = $_____

2. Partners D, E, and F have capital balances of $7,000, $15,000, and $20,000, respectively, before liquidation. Assets total $65,000, and liabilities total $23,000. If the assets are sold for $45,000, and the partners' stated ratio is 5:3:2, how much would each partner receive as a result of liquidation (if deficits are absorbed by the other partners)?

      D = $_____

      E = $_____

      F = $_____

3. Partners G, H, and I have capital balances of $10,000 each, and share income and losses in a 2:2:1 ratio. They agree to allow J to purchase a one-third interest in the business. They use the bonus method to record the transaction. Provide the proper journal entry under each of the following assumptions:

   a. J contributes $12,000 in cash.
   b. J contributes $15,000 in cash.
   c. J contributes $21,000 in cash.

General Journal				
Date		Description	Debit	Credit

CHAPTER 14 CONTRIBUTED CAPITAL

REVIEWING THE CHAPTER

Objective 1: Identify and explain the management issues related to contributed capital.

1. A **corporation** is a business organization authorized by the state to conduct business and is a separate legal entity from its owners. It is the dominant form of American business because it is able to gather large amounts of capital.

2. The management of contributed capital, critical to the financing of a corporation, includes the issues of (a) managing under the corporate form of business, (b) using equity financing, (c) determining dividend policies, and (d) evaluating performance using return on equity. These issues will be addressed in the paragraphs to follow.

3. Before a corporation can do business, it must apply for and receive a charter from the state. The state must approve the **articles of incorporation,** which describe the basic purpose and structure of the proposed corporation.

4. Beginning capital is raised through the issue of shares of stock to investors, known as stockholders. The stockholders usually meet once a year to elect directors and to carry on other important business. Each **share of stock,** or unit of ownership in a corporation, entitles its owner to one vote.

5. The corporate structure includes the board of directors, which sets corporate policy, and the operating officers, who carry on the daily operations. The board is elected by the stockholders, and the managers (operating officers) are appointed by the board.

6. Some specific duties of the board of directors are to declare **dividends,** which are distributions of resources, generally in the form of cash, to the stockholders; authorize contracts; decide on executive salaries; and arrange major loans with banks. It is also common for the board to appoint an **audit committee,** one of whose functions is to engage the independent auditors, to serve as a channel of communication between the corporation and its independent auditor. The audit committee is made up of outside directors and helps ensure the board's objectivity in judging management's performance. Management's main means of reporting the corporation's financial position and results of operations is its annual report.

7. The corporate form of business has several advantages over the sole proprietorship and partnership. It is a separate legal entity and offers limited liability to the owners. It also offers ease of capital generation and ease of transfer of ownership. Other advantages are the lack of mutual agency in a corporation and its continuous existence. In addition, a corporate form of business allows centralized authority and responsibility and professional management.

8. The corporate form of business also has several disadvantages when compared with the sole proprietorship and partnership. It is subject to greater government regulation and **double taxation** (the corporation's income is subject to income taxes and its stockholders are taxed on any dividends). The limited liability of the owners can limit the

amount a small corporation can borrow. In addition, separation of ownership and control may allow management to make harmful decisions.

9. Ownership in a corporation is evidenced by a document called a **stock certificate.** A stockholder sells stock by endorsing the stock certificate and sending it to the corporation's secretary. The secretary (assisted by independent registrars and transfer agents) is responsible for transferring the corporation's stock, maintaining stockholders' records, and preparing a list of stockholders for stockholders' meetings and for the payment of dividends.

10. The articles of incorporation (of a corporate charter) specify the **authorized stock,** or the maximum number of shares that the corporation is allowed to issue. **Par value** (also specified in the corporate charter) is the legal value of a share of stock. **Legal capital** equals the number of shares issued times the par value; it is the minimum amount that can be reported as contributed capital.

11. Corporations often hire an **underwriter,** an intermediary between the corporation and the investing public, to help in their **initial public offering (IPO)** of capital stock. A corporation in this instance is said to be "going public." The underwriter charges a fee for this service, whereby it guarantees the sale of the corporation's stock.

12. Dividends are usually stated as a specified dollar amount per share of stock and are declared by the board of directors (with the advice of senior management).

13. One may evaluate the amount of dividends received by referring to the **dividends yield,** which is calculated as follows:

$$\frac{\text{Dividends per Share}}{\text{Market Price per Share}}$$

Expressed as a percentage, the dividends yield measures the return, in terms of dividends, per share of stock.

14. The **price/earnings (P/E) ratio,** on the other hand, measures investors' confidence in the company's future. It is calculated as follows:

$$\frac{\text{Market Price per Share}}{\text{Earnings per Share}}$$

A price/earnings ratio of 15 times, for example, means that investors are confident enough in the company to pay $15 per share of stock for every dollar of earnings accruing to one share.

15. A number of factors affect the decision to pay dividends. Such factors include the extent of profitable operations, the expected volatility of earnings, and the actual amount of cash available for dividend payments.

16. One measure of management's performance is the **return on equity,** calculated as follows:

$$\frac{\text{Net Income}}{\text{Average Stockholders' Equity}}$$

Expressed as a percentage, the return on equity is affected by such management decisions as the issuance of stock and the acquisition of treasury stock.

Objective 2: Define *start-up and organization costs* and state their effects on financial reporting.

17. The costs of forming a corporation, called **start-up and organization costs,** include incorporation fees, attorneys' fees, stock-printing costs, accountants' fees, and other costs necessary for corporate formation. Such costs must be expensed when incurred.

Objective 3: Identify the components of stockholders' equity.

18. In a corporation's balance sheet, the owners' claims to the business are called stockholders' equity. The stockholders' equity section is divided into two parts: contributed capital (the stockholders' investments) and retained earnings (earnings that have remained in the business).

19. When only one type of stock is issued, it is called **common stock.** A second type of stock, called preferred stock, also can be issued. Because common stockholders' claim to assets on liquidation ranks behind that of creditors and preferred stockholders, common stock is considered the **residual equity** of a corporation.

20. **Issued stock** consists of shares that have been sold or otherwise transferred to stockholders. **Outstanding stock** consists of shares that have been issued, but not repurchased, by the issuing corporation. Treasury stock consists of shares bought back and being held by the corporation.

Objective 4: Account for cash dividends.

21. Dividends usually are stated as a specified dollar amount per share of stock and are declared by the board of directors. The **date of declaration** is the date the board of directors formally declares a dividend, specifying that the owners of the stock on

the **date of record** will receive the dividends on the **date of payment.** After the date of record, stock is said to be **ex-dividend** (without dividend rights). A **liquidating dividend** is the return of contributed capital to the stockholders. It normally is paid when a company is going out of business or is reducing its operations.

22. When cash dividends are declared, Cash Dividends Declared is debited and Cash Dividends Payable is credited; when they are paid, Cash Dividends Payable is debited and Cash is credited. The Cash Dividends Declared account is closed to Retained Earnings at the end of the year. No journal entry is made on the date of record.

Objective 5: Identify the characteristics of preferred stock, including the effect on distribution of dividends.

23. Holders of **preferred stock** are given preference over common shareholders on dividend declaration and liquidation. Each share of preferred stock entitles its owner to a dividend each year. This dividend is a specific dollar amount or percentage of par value. Preferred stockholders receive their dividends before common stockholders receive anything. Once the preferred stockholders have received the annual dividends to which they are entitled, however, the common stockholders generally receive the remainder.

24. In addition, preferred stock can be (a) cumulative or noncumulative, (b) convertible or nonconvertible, and (c) callable. It usually has no voting rights.
    a. If the stock is **cumulative preferred stock** and the preferred stockholders do not receive the full amount of their annual dividend, the unpaid amount is carried over to the next year. Unpaid back dividends are called **dividends in arrears** and should be disclosed either on the balance sheet or in a note to the financial statements. When the stock is **noncumulative preferred stock,** unpaid dividends are not carried over to the next period.
    b. An owner of **convertible preferred stock** has the option to exchange each share of preferred stock for a set number of shares of common stock.
    c. Most preferred stock is **callable preferred stock,** which means that the corporation has the right to buy the stock back at a specified call or redemption price. If the owner so desires, convertible preferred stock could alternatively be converted to common stock.

Objective 6: Account for the issuance of stock for cash and other assets.

25. Capital stock may or may not have a par value, depending on the specifications in the charter. When par value stock is issued, the Capital Stock account is credited for the legal capital (par value), and any excess is recorded as Paid-in Capital in Excess of Par Value. In the stockholders' equity section of the balance sheet, the entire amount is labeled Total Contributed Capital. On rare occasions, stock is issued at a discount (less than par value), requiring a debit to Discount on Capital Stock.

26. **No-par stock** is stock for which a par value has not been established. It can be issued with or without a stated value. **Stated value,** which is established by the board of directors, is the legal capital for a share of no-par stock. The total stated value is recorded in the Capital Stock account. Any amount received in excess of stated value is recorded as Paid-in Capital in Excess of Stated Value. If no stated value is set, the entire amount received is legal capital and is credited to Capital Stock.

27. Sometimes stock is issued in exchange for assets or for services received. This kind of transaction should be recorded at the fair market value of the stock. If the stock's fair market value cannot be determined, the fair market value of the assets or services received should be used.

Objective 7: Account for treasury stock.

28. **Treasury stock** is common or preferred stock that has been issued and reacquired by the issuing company. That is, it is issued but no longer outstanding. Treasury stock is purchased (a) to distribute to employees through stock option plans, (b) to maintain a favorable market for the company's stock, (c) to increase earnings per share, (d) to use in purchasing other companies, and (e) to prevent a hostile takeover of the company.

29. Treasury stock can be held indefinitely, reissued, or canceled, and has no rights until it is reissued. Treasury stock, the last item in the stockholders' equity section of the balance sheet, appears as a deduction from the total of contributed capital and retained earnings.

30. When treasury stock is purchased, its account is debited for the purchase cost. It may be reissued at cost, above cost, or below cost. When cash received from a reissue exceeds the cost, the difference is credited to Paid-in Capital, Treasury Stock. When cash received is less than cost, the difference is debited to Paid-in Capital, Treasury

Stock (and Retained Earnings if needed). In no case should a gain or loss be recorded.

31. When treasury stock is retired, all the contributed capital associated with the retired shares must be removed from the accounts. When less was paid on reacquisition than was contributed originally, the difference is credited to Paid-in Capital, Retirement of Stock. When more is paid, the difference is debited to Retained Earnings.

Objective 8: Account for the exercise of stock options.

32. A **stock option plan** is an agreement whereby corporate employees can purchase a certain quantity of the company's stock at a certain price for a certain period of time. If the plan allows virtually all employees to purchase stock at the existing market price, then the journal entry on issue resembles the entry made when stock is sold to outsiders. However, if only certain employees (usually management) are allowed to purchase the corporation's stock in the future at a fixed price, the plan is said to be compensatory.

33. On the grant date, the amount by which the estimated fair value of the options (covered in a more advanced course) exceeds the option price is either (a) recorded as compensation expense over the grant period, or (b) reported in the notes to the financial statements. Most companies choose the latter approach, which also requires disclosure of the impact on income and earnings per share of not recording compensation expense.

A. (LO 4) Cash Dividends Declared   XX (amount declared)
            Cash Dividends Payable   XX (amount to be paid)
                Declared cash dividend to common or preferred
                stockholders

B. (LO 4) Cash Dividends Payable   XX (amount paid)
            Cash   XX (amount paid)
                Paid cash dividends declared in A above

C. (LO 6) Cash   XX (amount invested)
            Common Stock   XX (legal capital amount)
                Issued par value common stock for par value

D. (LO 6) Cash   XX (amount invested)
            Common Stock   XX (legal capital amount)
            Paid-in Capital in Excess of Par Value, Common   XX (excess of par)
                Issued par value common stock for amount in excess
                of par value

E. (LO 6) Cash   XX (amount invested)
            Common Stock   XX (legal capital amount)
                Issued no-par common stock (no stated value
                established)

F. (LO 6) Cash   XX (amount invested)
            Common Stock   XX (legal capital amount)
            Paid-in Capital in Excess of Stated Value, Common XX (excess of stated value)
                Issued no-par common stock with stated value for
                amount in excess of stated value

G. (LO 6) Start-up and Organization Expense   XX (fair market value of services)
            Common Stock   XX (par value)
            Paid-in Capital in Excess of Par Value, Common   XX (excess of par)
                Issued par value common stock for incorporation
                services

H. (LO 6) Land   XX (fair market value of stock)
            Common Stock   XX (par value)
            Paid-in Capital in Excess of Par Value, Common   XX (excess of par)
                Issued par value common stock with a market value
                in excess of par value for a piece of land

I. (LO 7) Treasury Stock, Common   XX (cost)
            Cash   XX (amount paid)
                Acquired shares of the company's common stock

J. (LO 7) Cash   XX (amount received)
            Treasury Stock, Common   XX (cost)
                Reissued shares of treasury stock at cost

K. (LO 7) Cash   XX (amount received)
    Treasury Stock, Common   XX (cost)
    Paid-in Capital, Treasury Stock   XX ("gain")
        Sold shares of treasury stock at amount above cost

L. (LO 7) Cash   XX (amount received)
    Paid-in Capital, Treasury Stock   XX ("loss")
    Retained Earnings (only if needed)   XX ("loss")
        Treasury Stock, Common   XX (cost)
        Sold shares of treasury stock at amount below cost

M. (LO 7) Common Stock   XX (par value)
    Paid-in Capital in Excess of Par Value, Common   XX (excess of par)
    Retained Earnings (only if needed)   XX (premium paid)
        Treasury Stock, Common   XX (cost)
        Retired treasury stock; cost exceeded original
        investment amount

N. (LO 7) If the treasury stock in M had been retired for an amount
less than the original investment amount, then instead of
Retained Earnings being debited for the excess paid,
Paid-in Capital, Retirement of Stock would be
credited for the difference.

O. (LO 8) Cash   XX (amount invested)
    Common Stock   XX (par value)
    Paid-in Capital in Excess of Par Value, Common   XX (excess of par)
        Issued par value common stock under employee
        stock option plan

SELF-TEST

Test your knowledge of the chapter by choosing the best answer for each of the following items.

1. One disadvantage of the corporate form of business is
   a. government regulation.
   b. centralized authority and responsibility.
   c. the corporation being a separate legal entity.
   d. continuous existence.

2. The start-up and organization costs of a corporation should
   a. be recorded and maintained as an intangible asset for the life of the corporation.
   b. be recorded as an intangible asset and amortized over a reasonable length of time.
   c. be written off as an expense when incurred.
   d. not be incurred before the state grants the corporation its charter.

3. All of the following normally are found in the stockholders' equity section of a corporate balance sheet *except*
   a. paid-in capital in excess of par value.
   b. retained earnings.
   c. cash dividends payable.
   d. common stock.

4. The board of directors of the Wong Corporation declared a cash dividend on January 18, 20x8, to be paid on February 18, 20x8, to shareholders holding stock on February 2, 20x8. Given these facts, February 2, 20x8 is the
   a. date of declaration.
   b. date of record.
   c. payment date.
   d. ex-dividend date.

5. The journal entry to record the declaration of a cash dividend
   a. reduces assets.
   b. increases liabilities.
   c. increases total stockholders' equity.
   d. does not affect total stockholders' equity.

6. Dividends in arrears are dividends on
   a. noncumulative preferred stock that have not been declared for some specific period of time.
   b. cumulative preferred stock that have been declared but have not been paid.
   c. cumulative preferred stock that have not been declared for some specific period of time.
   d. common stock that can never be declared.

7. The par value of common stock represents the
   a. amount entered into the corporation's Common Stock account when shares are issued.
   b. exact amount the corporation receives when the stock is issued.
   c. liquidation value of the stock.
   d. stock's market value.

8. The Paid-in Capital in Excess of Stated Value account is used when
   a. the par value of capital stock is greater than the stated value.
   b. capital stock is sold at an amount greater than stated value.
   c. the market value of the stock rises above its stated value.
   d. the number of shares issued exceeds the stock's stated value.

9. Which of the following is properly deducted from stockholders' equity?
   a. Treasury stock
   b. Retained earnings
   c. Dividends in arrears
   d. Paid-in capital in excess of par value

10. A plan under which employees are allowed to purchase shares of stock in a company at a specified price is called a stock
    a. option plan.
    b. subscription plan.
    c. dividend plan.
    d. compensation plan.

TESTING YOUR KNOWLEDGE

*Matching**

Match each term with its definition by writing the appropriate letter in the blank.

_____ 1. Corporation

_____ 2. Start-up and organization costs

_____ 3. Issued stock

_____ 4. Authorized stock

_____ 5. Outstanding stock

_____ 6. Common stock

_____ 7. Preferred stock

_____ 8. Dividends in arrears

_____ 9. Par value

_____ 10. No-par stock

_____ 11. Stated value

_____ 12. Treasury stock

_____ 13. Ex-dividend

_____ 14. Liquidating dividend

_____ 15. Convertible preferred stock

_____ 16. Callable preferred stock

_____ 17. Cumulative preferred stock

_____ 18. Stock option plan

_____ 19. Stock certificate

_____ 20. Residual equity

a. Unpaid back dividends

b. Descriptive of common stockholders' ownership in a corporation

c. Without dividend rights

d. The amount of legal capital of a share of no-par stock

e. Stock that is presently held by stockholders

f. The dominant form of business in the United States

g. The type of stock whose holders have prior claim over common stockholders to dividends

h. Issued stock that has been reacquired by the corporation

i. Stock whose unpaid dividends "carry over" to future years until paid

j. Proof of ownership in a corporation

k. Expenditures necessary to form a corporation

l. The maximum amount of stock that a corporation may issue

m. The name of the stock when only one type of stock has been issued

n. Stock that may or may not have a stated value

o. The legal value for stock that is stated in the charter

p. Stock that has been sold to stockholders and may or may not have been bought back by the corporation

q. Stock that may be bought back at the option of the issuing corporation

r. An agreement whereby certain employees may purchase stock at a fixed price

s. The return of contributed capital to a corporation's stockholders

t. Preferred stock that an investor may exchange for common stock

---

Note to student: The matching quiz might be completed more efficiently by starting with the definition and searching for the corresponding term.

Short Answer

Use the lines provided to answer each item.

1. List eight advantages of the corporate form of business.

_____

_____

_____

_____

_____

_____

2. List four disadvantages of the corporate form of business.

_____

_____

_____

3. Name the two major portions of the stockholders' equity section of a balance sheet.

_____

_____

4. Preferred shareholders are given preference over common shareholders under what two circumstances?

_____

_____

5. Under what circumstance would a corporation have more shares of stock issued than outstanding?

_____

_____

6. What is the difference between treasury stock and unissued stock?

_____

_____

_____

True-False

Circle T if the statement is true, F if it is false. Please provide explanations for the false answers, using the blank lines at the end of the section.

T F 1. Corporate income is taxed twice, at the corporate level and at the individual level (when it is distributed as dividends).

T F 2. The concept of legal capital was established to protect the corporation's stockholders.

T F 3. Ordinarily, creditors cannot attach the personal assets of the corporation's stockholders.

T F 4. Start-up and organization costs must be charged as expenses in the year the corporation is formed.

T F 5. Contributed capital consists of capital stock plus paid-in capital in excess of par (stated) value.

T F 6. A transfer agent keeps records of stock transactions.

T F   7. Preferred stock cannot be both convertible and cumulative.

T F   8. Dividends in arrears do not exist when preferred stock is noncumulative.

T F   9. The worth of a share of stock can be measured by its par value.

T F 10. The purchase of treasury stock reduces total assets and total stockholders' equity.

T F 11. Preferred stockholders are guaranteed annual dividends; common stockholders are not.

T F 12. Preferred stock is considered the residual equity of a corporation.

T F 13. The amount of compensation in connection with a stock option plan is measured on the date the option is exercised.

T F 14. On the date a dividend is paid, total assets and total stockholders' equity decrease.

T F 15. Dividends in arrears should appear as a liability on the balance sheet.

T F 16. Treasury Stock is listed on the balance sheet as an asset.

T F 17. When a corporation sells stock to the investing public, it often engages the services of an underwriter.

T F 18. When treasury stock is sold at more than its cost, Gain on Sale of Treasury Stock is credited.

T F 19. The higher the market price per share of stock, the lower the dividends yield.

T F 20. The purchase of treasury stock by a corporation will decrease its return on equity.

T F 21. The higher the price/earnings ratio, the higher is investors' confidence in a company's future.

Circle the letter of the best answer.

1. When treasury stock is reissued below cost, all of the following may be true *except*
   a. Retained Earnings is debited.
   b. Treasury Stock is credited.
   c. Paid-in Capital, Treasury Stock is debited.
   d. Loss on Reissue of Treasury Stock is debited.

2. The purchase of treasury stock does *not* affect
   a. the amount of stock outstanding.
   b. the amount of stock issued.
   c. total assets.
   d. total stockholders' equity.

3. Which of the following statements is true?
   a. Outstanding shares plus issued shares equal authorized shares.
   b. Unissued shares plus outstanding shares equal authorized shares.
   c. Authorized shares minus unissued shares equal issued shares.
   d. Unissued shares minus issued shares equal outstanding shares.

4. Rooney Corporation has outstanding 1,000 shares of $100 par value, 7 percent noncumulative preferred stock, and 20,000 shares of $10 par value common stock. Last year, the company paid no dividends; this year, it distributed $40,000 in dividends. What portion of this $40,000 should common stockholders receive?
   a. $0
   b. $2,800
   c. $26,000
   d. $33,000

5. Which of the following is *not* a characteristic of corporations in general?
   a. Separation of ownership and management
   b. Ease of transfer of ownership
   c. Double taxation
   d. Unlimited liability of stockholders

6. On which of the following dates is a journal entry made?
   a. Date of record
   b. Date of payment
   c. Date of declaration
   d. Both **b** and **c**

7. Stock is said to be "ex-dividend" after
   a. it has been sold to another party.
   b. the date of record.
   c. the date of payment.
   d. the date of declaration.

8. When callable preferred stock is called and surrendered, the stockholder is *not* entitled to
   a. a call premium.
   b. the par value of the stock.
   c. any dividends in arrears.
   d. the market value of the stock.

APPLYING YOUR KNOWLEDGE

Exercises

1. In the journal provided, prepare the entries for the following transactions.

Jan. 1 Paid $8,000 in legal and incorporation fees to form Gambino Corporation.

Feb. 9 Issued 5,000 shares of $100 par value common stock at $115 per share.

Apr. 12 Exchanged 2,000 shares of 4 percent, no-par preferred stock, which had a stated value of $100 per share, for a building with a market value of $240,000. The market value of the stock cannot be determined.

June 23 Declared a $4 per share dividend on the preferred stock, to be paid on July 8. The date of record is July 1.

July 8 Paid the dividend declared on June 23.

Dec. 20 The corporation's president exercised her option to purchase 200 shares of $100 par value common stock at $110 per share. The market price on that date was $130 per share.

	General Journal		
Date	**Description**	**Debit**	**Credit**

2. Goldman Corporation began operation on August 10, 20x1, by issuing 50,000 shares of $10 par value common stock at $50 per share. As of January 1, 20x3, its capital structure was the same. For each of the following sets of facts for January 20x3, prepare the proper entry in the journal provided. In all cases, assume sufficient cash and retained earnings.

Jan. 12 The corporation purchases 5,000 shares of stock from the stockholders at $60 per share.

20 The corporation reissues 2,000 shares of treasury stock at $65 per share.

27 The corporation reissues another 2,000 shares of treasury stock at $58 per share.

31 The corporation retires the remaining 1,000 treasury shares.

General Journal				
Date		Description	Debit	Credit

3. Westridge Corporation paid no dividends in its first two years of operations. In its third year, it paid $51,000 in dividends. For all three years, there have been 1,000 shares of 6 percent, $100 par value cumulative preferred stock, and 5,000 shares of $10 par value common stock outstanding. How much of the $51,000 in dividends goes to

a. preferred stockholders? $ _____

b. common stockholders? $ _____

4. Assume the same facts as in Exercise **3** at the left, except that Westridge's preferred stock is *noncumulative*. How much of the $51,000 in dividends goes to

a. preferred stockholders? $ _____

b. common stockholders? $ _____

Crossword Puzzle
for Chapters 12, 13, and 14

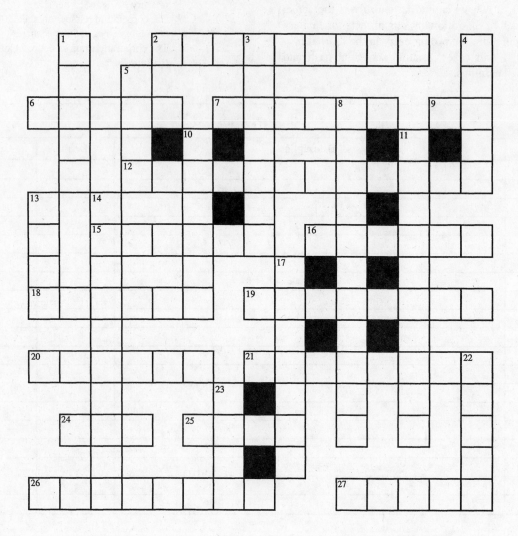

ACROSS

2. Like partnership liability
6. Stock designation (hyphenated)
7. _____ credit (2 words)
9. _____-dividend
12. Partnership conclusions
15. _____ security tax
16. Value assigned to no-par stock
18. Mutual _____
19. Employee _____ record
20. Sold, as stock
21. Liquidating _____
24. Protector of the investing public (abbr.)
25. Abbreviation for 15-Across
26. _____ Earnings (corporate)
27. Extra paid for admission of new partner

DOWN

1. Earnings before deductions
3. Part of "IPO"
4. Payroll _____ Expense
5. Buy back, as stock
8. In circulation, as stock
10. Common stock is a corporation's residual _____
11. Possible, as a liability
13. Unemployment tax initials
14. Property tax determination
17. Contributed _____
22. Liabilities
23. Limited _____ of partnerships

CHAPTER 15 THE CORPORATE INCOME STATEMENT AND THE STATEMENT OF STOCKHOLDERS' EQUITY

REVIEWING THE CHAPTER

Objective 1: Identify the issues related to evaluating the quality of a company's earnings.

1. The most commonly used predictors of a company's performance are expected changes in earnings per share and in return on equity. Because net income is a component of both these ratios, the **quality of earnings** must be good if the measure is to be valid. The quality of earnings, or the substance and sustainability of earnings, is affected by (a) the accounting methods and estimates the company's management chooses and (b) the nature of nonoperating items on the income statement.

2. A different net income figure results, for example, when different estimates and methods for dealing with uncollectible accounts, inventory, depreciation, depletion, and amortization are chosen. In general, the method that produces a lower, or more conservative, figure also produces a better quality of earnings. In addition, nonoperating and nonrecurring items, such as discontinued operations, extraordinary gains and losses, and the effects of accounting changes, can impair comparability if the financial analyst refers only to the bottom-line figure. Fortunately, generally accepted accounting principles require that the significant accounting policies are both explained (in the notes to the financial statements) and applied consistently wherever possible.

Objective 2: Prepare a corporate income statement.

3. Corporate financial statements should present **comprehensive income**—the change in a company's equity during a period from sources other than owners and includes net income, change in unrealized investment gains and losses, and other items affecting equity. This approach to the measurement of income has resulted in several items being added to the income statement—discontinued operations, extraordinary items, and accounting changes. In addition, earnings per share figures must be disclosed.

4. Comprehensive income is most commonly reported in the statement of stockholders' equity. It is sometimes reported on a separate statement of comprehensive income, and on rare occasions it is reported on the income statement.

Objective 3: Show the relationships among income taxes expense, deferred income taxes, and net of taxes.

5. Corporate taxable income is determined by subtracting allowable business deductions from includable gross income. Tax rates currently range from a 15 percent to a 39 percent marginal rate.

6. Computing income taxes for financial reporting differs from computing income taxes due the government for the same accounting period. This

difference is caused by the fact that financial reporting income is governed by generally accepted accounting principles, whereas taxable income is governed by the Internal Revenue Code.

7. When income for financial reporting differs from taxable income, the **income tax allocation** technique should be used. Under this method, the difference between the current tax expense and income tax expense is debited or credited to an account called **Deferred Income Taxes.** Adjustments to this account must be made in light of legislated changes in income tax laws and regulations.

8. Deferred income taxes are the result of temporary differences in the treatment of certain items (such as depreciation) for tax and financial reporting purposes. They are classified as current or noncurrent, depending upon the classification of the related asset or liability that created the temporary difference.

9. Certain income statement items must be reported **net of taxes,** or after considering applicable tax effects, to avoid distorting net operating income. These items are discontinued operations, extraordinary gains and losses, and accounting changes.

Objective 4: Describe the disclosure on the income statement of discontinued operations, extraordinary items, and accounting changes.

10. The results of operations for the period and any gains or losses from the **discontinued operations** of a segment of a business should be disclosed (net of taxes) after income from continuing operations. A **segment** is defined as a separate major line of business or class of customer.

11. An **extraordinary item** is an event that is unusual and occurs infrequently. Extraordinary items that are material in amount should be disclosed separately on the income statement (net of taxes) after discontinued operations.

12. Extraordinary gains and losses arise from such events as natural disasters, theft, the passage of a new law, the takeover of property by a foreign government, and the early retirement of debt.

13. A company can change from one accounting principle to another (e.g., from FIFO to LIFO) only if it can justify the new method as better accounting practice. The change must be disclosed in the financial statements. The **cumulative effect of an accounting change** on prior years (net of taxes) should appear on the income statement after extraordinary items.

Objective 5: Compute earnings per share.

14. Readers of financial statements use the earnings per share figure to judge a company's performance, to estimate its future earnings, and to compare it with other companies. Earnings per share figures should be disclosed for (a) income from continuing operations, (b) income before extraordinary items and the cumulative effect of accounting changes, (c) the cumulative effect of accounting changes, and (d) net income. These figures should appear on the face of the income statement.

15. A company that has issued no securities that are convertible into common stock has a **simple capital structure.** In this case, only **basic earnings per share** would be presented, the calculation of which is

$$\frac{\text{Net Income} - \text{Nonconvertible Preferred Dividends}}{\text{Weighted-Average Common Shares Outstanding}}$$

16. A company that has issued securities that can be converted into common stock has a **complex capital structure. Potentially dilutive securities,** such as stock options and convertible preferred stocks or bonds, are so-named because they have the potential to decrease earnings per share. In this case, a dual presentation of basic and **diluted earnings per share** is required. The latter figure shows the maximum potential effect of dilution on the common stockholders' ownership position.

Objective 6: Prepare a statement of stockholders' equity.

17. The **statement of stockholders' equity** can be used in place of the statement of retained earnings. It is a labeled computation of the changes in the stockholders' equity accounts during the accounting period. It contains all the components of the statement of retained earnings, a summary of the period's stock transactions, and accumulated other comprehensive income (such as foreign currency translation adjustments).

18. **Retained earnings** are the profits that a corporation has earned since its beginning, minus any losses, dividends declared, or transfers to contributed capital. Ordinarily, Retained Earnings has a credit balance. When a debit balance exists, the corporation is said to have a **deficit.** Retained earnings are not the same as cash or any other asset, but simply an intangible representation of earnings "plowed back into the business."

19. Retained earnings can be unrestricted or restricted. Unrestricted retained earnings dictate the asset amount (if available) that can be distributed to stockholders as dividends. A **restriction on retained earnings** dictates the asset amount that must be retained in the business for other purposes. Retained earnings are restricted for contractual or legal reasons, or by voluntary actions of the board of directors. Restrictions on retained earnings are disclosed most commonly in the notes to the financial statements.

Objective 7: Account for stock dividends and stock splits.

20. A **stock dividend** is a proportional distribution of shares of stock to a corporation's stockholders. Stock dividends are declared to (a) give evidence of the company's success without paying a cash dividend, (b) reduce a stock's market price, (c) allow a nontaxable distribution, and (d) increase the company's permanent capital. The result of a stock dividend is the transfer of a part of retained earnings to contributed capital. For a small stock dividend (less than 20 to 25 percent), the market value of the shares distributed is transferred from retained earnings. For a large stock dividend (greater than 20 to 25 percent), the par or stated value is transferred. A stock dividend does not change total stockholders' equity or any individual's proportionate equity in the company.

21. A **stock split** is an increase in the number of shares of stock outstanding, with a corresponding decrease in the par or stated value of the stock. For example, a 3-for-1 split on 40,000 shares of $30 par value would result in the distribution of 80,000 additional shares. (That is, someone who owned one share now would own three shares.) The par value would be reduced to $10. A stock split does not increase the number of shares authorized, nor does it affect the balances in stockholders' equity.

22. The purpose of a stock split is to improve the stock's marketability by pushing its market price down. In the example above, if the stock was selling for $180 per share, a 3-for-1 split probably would cause the market price to fall to about $60 per share. A memorandum entry should be made for a stock split, disclosing the decrease in par or stated value as well as the increase in the number of shares of stock outstanding.

Objective 8: Calculate book value per share.

23. The **book value** of a share of stock equals the net assets represented by one share of a company's stock. If the company has common stock only, the book value per share is arrived at by dividing stockholders' equity by the number of outstanding and distributable shares. When the company also has preferred stock, the call value of the preferred stock plus any dividends in arrears are deducted from stockholders' equity in computing the **book value per share** of common stock.

Summary of Journal Entries Introduced in Chapter 15

A. (LO 3) Income Taxes Expense   XX (amount per GAAP)
      Income Taxes Payable   XX (currently payable)
      Deferred Income Taxes   XX (eventually payable)
          To record estimated current and deferred income taxes

B. (LO 7) Stock Dividends Declared   XX (amount transferred)
      Common Stock Distributable   XX (par value amount)
      Paid-in Capital in Excess of Par Value, Common   XX (excess of par)
          Declared a stock dividend on common stock

C. (LO 7) Common Stock Distributable   XX (par value amount)
      Common Stock   XX (par value amount)
          Distributed a stock dividend

SELF-TEST

Test your knowledge of the chapter by choosing the best answer for each of the following items.

1. The balance of the Retained Earnings account represents
   a. an excess of revenues over expenses for the most current operating period.
   b. the profits of a company since its inception, less any losses, dividends to stockholders, or transfers to contributed capital.
   c. cash set aside for specific future uses.
   d. cash available for daily operations.

2. A corporation should account for the declaration of a 3 percent stock dividend by
   a. transferring from retained earnings to contributed capital an amount equal to the market value of the dividend shares.
   b. transferring from retained earnings to contributed capital an amount equal to the legal capital represented by the dividend shares.
   c. making only a memorandum entry in the general journal.
   d. transferring from retained earnings to contributed capital whatever amount the board of directors deems appropriate.

3. Which of the following increases the number of shares of common stock outstanding?
   a. A stock split
   b. A restriction on retained earnings
   c. Treasury stock
   d. A cash dividend

4. When retained earnings are restricted, total retained earnings
   a. increase.
   b. decrease.
   c. may increase or decrease.
   d. are unaffected.

5. The purpose of a statement of stockholders' equity is to
   a. summarize the changes in the components of stockholders' equity over the accounting period.
   b. disclose the computation of book value per share of stock.
   c. budget for the transactions expected to occur during the forthcoming period.
   d. replace the statement of retained earnings.

6. All of the following elements of a corporation's common stock can be determined from the accounting records *except*
   a. par value.
   b. stated value.
   c. book value.
   d. market value.

7. Which of the following items appears on the corporate income statement before income from continuing operations?
   a. Income from operations of a discontinued segment
   b. Income taxes expense
   c. The cumulative effect of a change in accounting principle
   d. An extraordinary gain

8. When there is a difference in the timing of revenues and expenses for accounting and for income tax purposes, it is usually necessary to
   a. prepare an adjusting entry.
   b. adjust figures on the corporate tax return.
   c. perform income tax allocation procedures.
   d. do nothing because the difference is a result of two different sets of rules.

9. A loss due to discontinued operations should be reported on the income statement
   a. before both extraordinary items and the cumulative effect of an accounting change.
   b. before the cumulative effect of an accounting change and after extraordinary items.
   c. after both extraordinary items and the cumulative effect of an accounting change.
   d. after the cumulative effect of an accounting change and before extraordinary items.

10. Which of the following would be involved in the computation of earnings per common share for a company with a simple capital structure?
    a. Common shares authorized
    b. Dividends declared on nonconvertible preferred stock
    c. The shares of nonconvertible preferred stock outstanding
    d. Treasury shares

TESTING YOUR KNOWLEDGE

*Matching**

Match each term with its definition by writing the appropriate letter in the blank.

_____ 1. Retained earnings

_____ 2. Deficit

_____ 3. Statement of stockholders' equity

_____ 4. Income tax allocation

_____ 5. Simple capital structure

_____ 6. Complex capital structure

_____ 7. Discontinued operations

_____ 8. Comprehensive income

_____ 9. Stock dividend

_____ 10. Stock split

_____ 11. Restricted retained earnings

_____ 12. Segments

_____ 13. Potentially dilutive securities

_____ 14. Extraordinary item

_____ 15. Earnings per share

_____ 16. Accounting change

_____ 17. Book value per share

a. An unusual and infrequent gain or loss

b. The makeup of a corporation that has issued convertible securities

c. A negative figure for retained earnings

d. Distinct parts of business operations

e. A summary of the changes in stockholders' equity accounts during the period

f. The net assets represented by one share of a company's stock

g. The change in a company's equity during a period from sources other than owners, including net income, change in unrealized investment gains and losses, and other items affecting equity

h. Use of a different but more appropriate accounting method

i. A proportional distribution of stock to a corporation's stockholders

j. The profits that a corporation has earned since its inception, minus any losses, dividends declared, or transfers to contributed capital

k. A measure of net income earned for each share of common stock

l. A corporate stock maneuver in which par or stated value is changed

m. The makeup of a corporation that has not issued convertible securities

n. The income statement section immediately before extraordinary gains or losses

o. The technique to reconcile accounting income and taxable income

p. The quantity of assets that are not available for dividends

q. Options and convertible preferred stocks that could lower the earnings per share figure

---

Note to student: The matching quiz might be completed more efficiently by starting with the definition and searching for the corresponding term.

Short Answer

Use the lines provided to answer each item.

1. List three ways in which the Retained Earnings account can be reduced.

   _____

   _____

   _____

2. What are the two major distinctions between a stock dividend and a stock split?

   _____

   _____

   _____

   _____

3. What two conditions must be met for an item to qualify as extraordinary?

   _____

   _____

4. Number the following items to indicate their order of appearance on an income statement:

   _____ Cumulative Effect of Accounting Change

   _____ Revenues

   _____ Extraordinary Gains and Losses

   _____ Net Income

   _____ Discontinued Operations

   _____ Income from Continuing Operations

5. What are the three means of reporting comprehensive income used by corporations?

   _____

   _____

   _____

True-False

Circle T if the statement is true, F if it is false. Please provide explanations for the false answers, using the blank lines at the end of the section.

T F 1. If an extraordinary gain of $20,000 has occurred, it should be reported net of taxes at more than $20,000.

T F 2. A restriction on retained earnings represents cash set aside for a special purpose.

T F 3. The book value of a share of common stock decreases when dividends are declared.

T F 4. After a stock dividend is distributed, each stockholder owns a greater percentage of the corporation.

T F 5. The market value of a stock on the date a small stock dividend is declared has no bearing on the journal entry.

T F 6. The main purpose of a stock split is to reduce the stock's par value.

T F 7. A gain on the sale of a plant asset qualifies as an extraordinary item.

T F 8. Extraordinary items should appear on the statement of stockholders' equity.

T F 9. The effect of a change from straight-line depreciation to accelerated depreciation should be reported on the income statement immediately after extraordinary items.

T F 10. Common Stock Distributable is a current liability on the balance sheet.

T F 11. Both basic and diluted earnings per share data should be provided for a corporation with a complex capital structure.

T F **12.** If taxable income always equaled accounting income, there would be no need for income tax allocation.

T F **13.** The quality of earnings is affected by the existence of an extraordinary item on the income statement.

T F **14.** Potentially dilutive securities are included in the calculation of basic earnings per share.

T F **15.** Stock Dividends Declared is closed to Retained Earnings at the end of the accounting period.

_____

_____

_____

_____

_____

_____

_____

_____

_____

_____

_____

_____

_____

_____

_____

_____

_____

_____

Multiple Choice

Circle the letter of the best answer.

1. Which of the following has no effect on retained earnings?
   a. Stock split
   b. Stock dividend
   c. Cash dividend
   d. Net loss

2. A company with 10,000 shares of common stock outstanding distributed a 10 percent stock dividend and then split its stock 4 for 1. How many shares are now outstanding?
   a. 2,750
   b. 41,000
   c. 44,000
   d. 55,000

3. When retained earnings are restricted, which of the following statements is true?
   a. Total retained earnings increase.
   b. The company is no longer limited in the amount of dividends it can pay.
   c. Total retained earnings are reduced.
   d. Total stockholders' equity remains the same.

4. On the date that a stock dividend is distributed,
   a. Common Stock Distributable is credited.
   b. Cash is credited.
   c. Retained Earnings remains the same.
   d. no entry is made.

5. The effect of an accounting change should appear on
   a. the income statement.
   b. the balance sheet.
   c. the statement of stockholders' equity.
   d. no financial statement.

6. Cohen Corporation had 60,000 shares of common stock outstanding from January 1 to October 1, and 40,000 shares outstanding from October 1 to December 31. What is the weighted-average number of shares used to calculate earnings per share?
   a. 45,000 shares
   b. 50,000 shares
   c. 55,000 shares
   d. 100,000 shares

7. If retained earnings were $70,000 on January 1, 20xx, and $100,000 on December 31, 20xx, and if cash dividends of $15,000 were declared and paid during the year, net income for the year must have been
   a. $30,000.
   b. $45,000.
   c. $55,000.
   d. $85,000.

8. Which of the following would *not* appear on a statement of stockholders' equity?
   a. Conversion of preferred stock into common stock
   b. Dividends declared
   c. Discontinued operations
   d. Accumulated other comprehensive income

9. A corporation has issued only one type of stock and wants to compute book value per share. It needs all the information below *except*
   a. retained earnings.
   b. the current year's dividends.
   c. total contributed capital.
   d. total shares outstanding and distributable.

10. Retained earnings
    a. are the same as cash.
    b. are the amount invested by stockholders in a corporation.
    c. equal cumulative profits, less losses and dividends declared and transfers to contributed capital.
    d. are not affected by revenues and expenses.

11. The quality of a company's earnings may be affected by the
    a. countries in which the company operates.
    b. choice of independent auditors.
    c. industry in which the company operates.
    d. accounting methods used by the company.

APPLYING YOUR KNOWLEDGE

Exercises

1. For each of the following sets of facts, prepare the proper entry in the journal provided.

 Sept. 1 Tinsley Corporation begins operations by issuing 10,000 shares of $100 par value common stock at $120 per share.

 Mar. 7 A 5 percent stock dividend is declared. The market price of the stock is $130 per share on March 7.

 30 This is the date of record for the stock dividend.

 Apr. 13 The stock dividend is distributed.

General Journal				
Date		Description	Debit	Credit

2. A company has $100,000 in operating income before taxes. It also had an extraordinary loss of $30,000 when lightning struck one of its warehouses. The company must pay a 40 percent tax on all items. Complete the partial income statement in good form.

Operating Income Before Taxes	$100,000

3. Hammond Corporation had taxable income of $40,000, $40,000, and $80,000 in 20x1, 20x2, and 20x3, respectively. Its income for accounting purposes was $60,000, $30,000, and $70,000 for 20x1, 20x2, and 20x3, respectively. The difference between taxable income and accounting income was due to $30,000 in expenses that were deductible in full for tax purposes in 20x1 but were expensed one-third per year for accounting purposes. Make the correct journal entry to record income taxes in each of the three years. Assume a 40 percent tax rate.

General Journal				
Date		Description	Debit	Credit

4. Gledhill Corporation's balance sheet as of December 31, 20xx, includes the following information regarding stockholders' equity:

Contributed Capital		
Preferred Stock, $50 par value, 7% cumulative, 4,000 shares authorized, issued, and outstanding		$200,000
Common Stock, no-par, 30,000 shares authorized, issued, and outstanding		360,000
Paid-in Capital in Excess of Par Value, Preferred		40,000
Total Contributed Capital		$600,000
Retained Earnings		80,000
Total Stockholders' Equity		$680,000

Dividends in arrears total $28,000.

In the space that follows, compute the book value per share of both preferred stock and common stock.

5. Throughout 20xx, Reseda Corporation had 10,000 shares of common stock outstanding, as well as 30,000 shares of nonconvertible preferred stock. Net income for the year was $50,000, preferred dividends totaled $20,000, and common dividends totaled $5,000. In the space below, calculate basic earnings per share.

CHAPTER 16 LONG-TERM LIABILITIES

REVIEWING THE CHAPTER

Objective 1: Identify the management issues related to issuing long-term debt.

1. Long-term liabilities are obligations that are expected to be settled beyond one year or the normal operating cycle, whichever is longer. Exactly how management finances its operations is vital to a business's survival. The management issues related to issuing long-term debt are (a) whether or not to have long-term debt, (b) how much long-term debt to have, and (c) what types of long-term debt to have.

2. To finance long-term assets, research and development, and other activities of long-run benefit, corporations must obtain funds that can be used for many years. This may be accomplished by issuing stock or by issuing long-term debt in the form of bonds, notes, mortgages, and leases. There are both advantages and disadvantages to issuing long-term debt, as explained below.

3. One advantage of issuing long-term debt is that common stockholders retain their level of control, since bondholders and other creditors do not have voting rights. Another advantage is that interest on debt is tax-deductible to the issuing corporation, thus lowering the tax burden. A third advantage is the **financial leverage** or *trading on the equity* that results from issuing debt. That is, if earnings on the funds obtained exceed the interest incurred, then earnings (and earnings per share) that accrue to the common stockholders will increase.

4. There are some disadvantages to issuing long-term debt, however. First, the more debt that is issued, the more periodic interest that must be paid. Similarly, the principal amount *must* be paid at maturity. Default on either interest or principal could force the business into bankruptcy. Another disadvantage is that if the interest incurred on the funds obtained exceeds the related earnings, then the attempt at financial leverage has backfired.

5. The use of debt financing varies widely across industries. One common measure of the risk (of default) undertaken by a company issuing debt is the **interest coverage ratio,** which is calculated as follows:

$$\frac{\text{Income Before Taxes} + \text{Interest Expense}}{\text{Interest Expense}}$$

The higher the interest coverage ratio (measured in "times"), the lower the company's risk of default on interest payments.

Objective 2: Identify and contrast the major characteristics of bonds.

6. A **bond** is a security, usually long-term, that represents money borrowed from the investing public by a corporation (or government). Bondholders are considered creditors (not owners) of the issuing corporation, who are entitled to periodic interest, plus the principal of the debt on some specified date. As is true for all corporate creditors, their

claims for interest and principal take priority over stockholders' claims.

7. When bonds are issued, the corporation executes a contract with the bondholders called a **bond indenture.** In addition, the company issues bond certificates or registration numbers as evidence of its debt to the bondholders. A **bond issue** is made up of the total value of bonds issued at one time. Bonds are usually issued with a face value that is some multiple of $1,000, and carry a variety of features.

   a. **Secured bonds** give the bondholders a claim to certain assets of the company upon default. **Unsecured bonds** (also called *debenture bonds*) are issued on the general credit of the company.

   b. When all the bonds of an issue mature on the same date, they are called **term bonds.** When the bonds mature over several maturity dates, they are called **serial bonds.**

   c. Bond prices are expressed as a percentage of face value. For example, when bonds with a face value of $100,000 are issued at 97, the company receives $97,000.

Objective 3: Record the issuance of bonds at face value and at a discount or premium.

8. Bonds payable (along with any unamortized discounts or premiums) usually appear with the long-term liabilities section of the balance sheet. However, bonds that will mature within one year, and which will be retired with the use of current assets, are classified as current liabilities. In addition, the important provisions of the bond indentures are disclosed in the notes to the financial statements.

9. When the **face interest rate** (or the rate paid on specific bonds) equals the **market interest rate** (also called the *effective interest rate,* the rate paid on bonds of similar risk) for similar bonds on the issue date, the corporation will probably receive face value for the bonds.

10. Regardless of the issue price, bondholders are entitled to interest, which is based on the face amount. Interest for a period of time is computed by this formula:

$$\text{Interest} = \text{Principal} \times \text{Rate} \times \text{Time}$$

11. When the face interest rate is less than the market interest rate for similar bonds on the issue date, the bonds will probably sell at a **discount** (less than face value).

12. Unamortized Bond Discount appears on the balance sheet as a contra-liability to Bonds Payable. The difference between the two amounts is called the *carrying value* or *present value.* The carrying value increases as the discount is amortized and equals the face value of the bonds at maturity.

13. When the face interest rate is greater than the market interest rate for similar bonds on the issue date, the bonds usually sell at a **premium** (greater than face value). Unamortized Bond Premium is added to Bonds Payable on the balance sheet to produce the carrying value.

14. A separate account should be established for bond issue costs. These costs are spread over the life of the bonds, often through the amortization of a discount (which would be raised) or a premium (which would be lowered).

Objective 4: Use present values to determine the value of bonds.

15. Theoretically, the value of a bond is equal to the sum of the present values of (a) the periodic interest payments and (b) the single payment of principal at maturity. The discount rate used is based on the current market rate of interest.

Objective 5: Use the straight-line and effective interest methods to amortize bond discounts and premiums.

16. When bonds are issued at a discount or premium, the interest payments do *not* equal the (true) total interest cost. Instead, total interest cost equals (a) interest payments over the life of the bond plus (b) the original discount amount, or minus (c) the original premium amount.

17. A **zero coupon bond** is a promise to pay a fixed amount at maturity, with no periodic interest payments. Investor earnings consist of the large discount upon issue, which in turn is amortized by the issuing corporation over the life of the bond.

18. A discount on bonds payable is considered an interest charge that must be amortized (spread out) over the life of the bond. Amortization is generally recorded on the interest payment dates, using either the straight-line method or the effective interest method.

19. Under the **straight-line method** of amortization, the amount to be amortized each interest period equals the bond discount divided by the number of interest payments during the life of the bond.

20. The effective interest method of amortization is more difficult to apply than the straight-line method but must be used instead when the results differ significantly.

21. To apply the **effective interest method** when a discount is involved, the market rate or effective rate of interest for similar securities when the bonds were issued must first be determined. This interest rate (halved for semiannual interest) is multiplied by the existing carrying value of the bonds for each interest period to obtain the bond interest expense to be recorded. The actual interest paid is then subtracted from the bond interest expense recorded to obtain the discount amortization for the period. Because the unamortized discount is now less, the carrying value is now greater. This new carrying value is applied to the next period, and the same amortization procedure is repeated.

22. Amortization of a premium acts as an offset against interest paid in determining the interest expense to be recorded. Under the straight-line method, the premium to be amortized in each period equals the bond premium divided by the number of interest payments during the life of the bond.

23. The effective interest method is applied to bond premiums in the same way that it is applied to bond discounts. The only difference is that the amortization for the period is computed by subtracting the bond interest expense recorded from actual interest paid (the reverse is done for amortizing a discount).

Objective 6: Account for bonds issued between interest dates and make year-end adjustments.

24. When bonds are issued between interest dates, the interest that has accrued since the last interest date is collected from the investor upon issue. It is then returned to the investor (along with the interest earned) on the next interest date.

25. When the accounting period ends between interest dates, the accrued interest and the proportionate discount or premium amortization must be recorded.

Objective 7: Account for the retirement of bonds and the conversion of bonds into stock.

26. **Callable bonds** are bonds that may be retired by the corporation before the maturity date. The action of retiring a bond issue before its maturity date is called **early extinguishment of debt**. When the market rate for bond interest drops, a company may want to call its bonds and substitute debt with a lower interest rate. When bonds are called (for whatever reason), an entry is needed to eliminate Bonds Payable and any unamortized premium or discount, and to record the payment of cash at the **call price**. In addition, an extraordinary gain or loss on the retirement of the bonds would be recorded. (Extraordinary items were explained fully in Chapter 15.)

27. **Convertible bonds** are bonds that can be exchanged for other securities (usually common stock) at the option of the bondholder. When a bondholder converts his or her bonds into common stock, the common stock is recorded by the company at the carrying value of the bonds. Specifically, the entry eliminates Bonds Payable and any unamortized discount or premium, and records common stock and paid-in capital in excess of par value. No gain or loss is recorded.

28. A corporation might issue convertible bonds (a) because investors, as a result, will accept a lower rate of interest, (b) to avoid a shift in control, since bondholders do not have voting rights, (c) to benefit from the tax-deductibility of the bond interest, (d) in the hopes that the resultant earnings will exceed the interest cost, and (e) to achieve a certain financial flexibility.

Objective 8: Explain the basic features of mortgages payable, installment notes payable, long-term leases, and pensions and other postretirement benefits as long-term liabilities.

29. A **mortgage** is a long-term debt secured by real property, usually payable in equal monthly installments. Upon payment of an installment, both Mortgage Payable and Mortgage Interest Expense are debited, and Cash is credited. Each month, the interest portion of the payment decreases, while the principal portion of the payment increases.

30. The principal and interest on long-term notes are either payable on one maturity date or due in periodic payments. The latter notes are known as **installment notes payable** and are commonly used by businesses to finance the purchase of equipment. The installment payments can be structured to include either (a) accrued interest plus equal amounts of principal or (b) accrued interest plus increasing amounts of principal. The former method results in decreasing payments, whereas the latter method produces equal payments. The effective interest calculation would be applied in either case.

31. A lease is a contract that allows a business or individual to use an asset for a specific length of time in return for periodic payments. The parties involved in a lease are the **lessor,** who owns the lease asset, and the **lessee,** who pays rent to the lessor for use of the leased asset. A **capital lease** is so much like a sale (as determined by certain criteria) that it should be recorded by the lessee as an asset (to be depreciated) and a related liability. An **operating lease** is a lease that does not meet the criteria for capital leases; each monthly lease payment should be charged to Rent Expense.

32. A **pension plan** is a contract whereby a company agrees to pay benefits to its employees after they retire. Benefits to retirees are usually paid out of a **pension fund.** Pension plans are classified as defined contribution plans or defined benefit plans. **Other postretirement benefits,** such as health care, should be estimated and accrued while the employee is still working (in accordance with the matching rule).

A. (LO 3) Cash   XX (amount received)
        Bonds Payable   XX (face value)
        Sold bonds at face value

B. (LO 3) Bond Interest Expense   XX (amount incurred)
        Cash (or Interest Payable)   XX (amount paid or due)
        Paid (or accrued) interest to bondholders

C. (LO 3) Cash   XX (amount received)
        Unamortized Bond Discount   XX (amount of discount)
        Bonds Payable   XX (face value)
        Sold bonds at a discount

D. (LO 3) Cash   XX (amount received)
        Unamortized Bond Premium   XX (amount of premium)
        Bonds Payable   XX (face value)
        Sold bonds at a premium

E. (LO 5) Bond Interest Expense   XX (amount incurred)
        Unamortized Bond Discount   XX (amount amortized)
        Cash (or Interest Payable)   XX (amount paid or due)
        Paid (or accrued) interest to bondholders and
        amortized the discount

F. (LO 5) Bond Interest Expense   XX (amount incurred)
        Unamortized Bond Premium   XX (amount amortized)
        Cash (or Interest Payable)   XX (amount paid or due)
        Paid (or accrued) interest to bondholders and
        amortized the premium

G. (LO 6) Cash   XX (amount received)
        Bond Interest Expense   XX (accrued amount)
        Bonds Payable   XX (face value)
        Sold bonds at face value plus accrued interest
        (see entry H)

H. (LO 6) Bond Interest Expense   XX (six months' amount)
        Cash (or Interest Payable)   XX (amount paid or due)
        Paid (or accrued) semiannual interest on bonds issued
        in G

I. (LO 6) The year-end accrual for bond interest expense is identical
        to entry E for discounts and entry F for premiums, except that
        in both cases Interest Payable is credited instead of Cash.

J. (LO 6) Bond Interest Expense   XX (amount incurred)
        Interest Payable   XX (amount accrued)
        Unamortized Bond Premium   XX (amount amortized)
        Cash   XX (amount paid)
        Paid semiannual interest including interest
        previously accrued, and amortized the
        premium for the period since the end of
        the fiscal year

K. (LO 7) Bonds Payable   XX (face value)
         Unamortized Bond Premium   XX (current credit balance)
         Loss on Retirement of Bonds (Extraordinary)   XX (see explanation)
             Cash   XX (amount paid)
                 Retired bonds at a loss; the loss equals the excess of
                 the call price over the carrying value

L. (LO 7) Bonds Payable   XX (face value)
         Unamortized Bond Premium   XX (current credit balance)
             Cash   XX (amount paid)
             Gain on Retirement of Bonds (Extraordinary)   XX (see explanation)
                 Retired bonds at a gain; the gain equals
                 the excess of the carrying value over the
                 call price

M. (LO 7) Bonds Payable   XX (face value)
         Unamortized Bond Premium   XX (current credit balance)
             Common Stock   XX (par value)
             Paid-in Capital in Excess of Par Value, Common   XX (excess of par)
                 Converted bonds payable into common stock
                 (Note: No gain or loss recorded; also, an unamortized
                 bond discount would have been credited in the entry,
                 if appropriate.)

N. (LO 8) Mortgage Payable   XX (principal)
         Mortgage Interest Expense   XX (interest)
             Cash   XX (monthly payment)
                 Made monthly mortgage payment

O. (LO 8) Cash   XX (amount received)
             Notes Payable   XX (amount borrowed)
                 Borrowed on a long-term installment note

P. (LO 8) Notes Payable   XX (principal)
         Interest Expense   XX (interest)
             Cash   XX (installment payment)
                 Installment payment on note

Q. (LO 8) Equipment Under Capital Lease   XX (present value)
             Obligations Under Capital Lease   XX (present value)
                 To record capital lease contract

R. (LO 8) Depreciation Expense, Equipment Under
             Capital Lease   XX (amount allocated)
             Accumulated Depreciation, Equipment Under
                 Capital Lease   XX (amount allocated)
                 To record depreciation expense on capital lease

S. (LO 8) Interest Expense   XX (amount incurred)
         Obligations Under Capital Lease   XX (amount reduced)
             Cash   XX (amount paid)
                 Made payment on capital lease

SELF-TEST

Test your knowledge of the chapter by choosing the best answer for each of the following items.

1. It is advantageous for a company to use financial leverage when
   a. it can earn more in assets than it pays in interest.
   b. it can earn less in assets than it pays in interest.
   c. its debt to equity ratio is very high.
   d. it needs to conserve cash.

2. A bond indenture is a(n)
   a. bond on which interest payments are past due.
   b. bond that is secured by specific assets of the issuing corporation.
   c. agreement between the issuing corporation and the bondholders.
   d. bond that is unsecured.

3. If the market rate of interest is lower than the face interest rate on the date of issuance, the bonds will
   a. sell at a discount.
   b. sell at a premium.
   c. sell at face value.
   d. not sell until the face interest rate is adjusted.

4. The current value of a bond can be determined by calculating the present value of the
   a. face value of the bond.
   b. interest payments.
   c. interest payments plus any discount or minus any premium.
   d. interest payments plus the face value of the bond.

5. When the straight-line method is used to amortize a bond discount, the interest expense for an interest period is calculated by
   a. deducting the amount of discount amortized for the period from the amount of cash paid for interest during the period.
   b. adding the amount of discount amortized for the period to the amount of cash paid for interest during the period.
   c. multiplying the face value of the bonds by the face interest rate.
   d. multiplying the carrying value of the bonds by the effective interest rate.

6. The total interest cost on a ten-year, 9 percent, $1,000 bond that is issued at 95 is
   a. $50.
   b. $140.
   c. $900.
   d. $950.

7. Metis Corporation issued a ten-year, 10 percent bond payable in 20x4 at a premium. During 20x5, the company's accountant failed to amortize any of the bond premium. The omission of the premium amortizaton
   a. does not affect the net income reported for 20x5.
   b. causes the net income for 20x5 to be overstated.
   c. causes the net income for 20x5 to be understated.
   d. causes retained earnings at the end of 20x5 to be overstated.

8. The Wang Corporation has authorized a bond issue with interest payment dates of January 1 and July 1. If the bonds are sold at the face amount on March 1, the cash Wang receives is equal to the face amount of the bonds
   a. plus the interest accrued from March 1 to July 1.
   b. plus the interest accrued from January 1 to March 1.
   c. minus the interest accrued from March 1 to July 1.
   d. minus the interest accrued from January 1 to March 1.

9. Bonds that contain a provision that allows the holders to exchange the bonds for other securities of the issuing corporation are called
   a. secured bonds.
   b. callable bonds.
   c. debenture bonds.
   d. convertible bonds.

10. Which of the following is most likely a capital lease?
    a. A five-year lease on a new building
    b. A two-year lease on a truck with an option to renew for one more year
    c. A five-year lease on a computer with an option to buy for a small amount at the end of the lease
    d. A monthly lease on a building that can be canceled with 90 days' notice

TESTING YOUR KNOWLEDGE

Matching*

Match each term with its definition by writing the appropriate letter in the blank.

_____ 1. Bonds

_____ 2. Bond indenture

_____ 3. Secured bonds

_____ 4. Debentures

_____ 5. Term bonds

_____ 6. Serial bonds

_____ 7. Zero coupon bonds

_____ 8. Financial leverage (trading on the equity)

_____ 9. Callable bonds

_____ 10. Bond discount

_____ 11. Bond premium

_____ 12. Effective interest method

_____ 13. Capital lease

_____ 14. Operating lease

_____ 15. Convertible bonds

_____ 16. Pension plan

_____ 17. Pension fund

_____ 18. Bond certificate

_____ 19. Early extinguishment of debt

a. Unsecured bonds
b. A lease that amounts to a sale
c. Bonds that may be retired by the company before maturity
d. Borrowing for the financial benefit of stockholders
e. The difference between face value and a lower amount paid for bonds
f. Bonds whose holders receive no periodic interest, but that are issued at a large discount
g. A true lease, recorded with debits to Rent Expense
h. Proof of a company's debt to a bondholder
i. Long-term debt instruments
j. The contract between the bondholder and the corporation
k. The retirement of bonds prior to maturity
l. The amortization method based on carrying value
m. The difference between face value and a greater amount paid for bonds
n. A program whereby a company agrees to pay benefits to its employees when they retire
o. Bonds that mature on one specific date
p. The source of benefits that are paid to retirees
q. Bonds that are backed by certain assets
r. Bonds that may be exchanged for common stock
s. Bonds that mature in installments

---

*Note to student: The matching quiz might be completed more efficiently by starting with the definition and searching for the corresponding term.

Short Answer

Use the lines provided to answer each item.

1. Distinguish between the terms *debenture* and *indenture*.

   _____

   _____

   _____

   _____

2. Under what circumstances would a premium probably be received on a bond issue?

   _____

   _____

   _____

   _____

3. What is the formula for computing interest for a period of time?

   _____

   _____

4. When valuing a bond, what two components are added together to determine the present value of the bond?

   _____

   _____

5. State three advantages of issuing long-term debt rather than common stock.

   _____

   _____

   _____

   _____

   _____

   _____

True-False

Circle T if the statement is true, F if it is false. Please provide explanations for the false answers, using the blank lines at the end of the section.

T F 1. Bondholders are owners of a corporation.

T F 2. Financial leverage is also known as trading on the equity.

T F 3. Bond interest can be paid only when declared by the board of directors.

T F 4. Bonds with a lower interest rate than the market rate (for similar bonds) will probably sell at a discount.

T F 5. When a bond premium is amortized, the bond interest expense recorded is greater than the cash paid.

T F 6. When the effective interest method is used to amortize a bond discount, the amount amortized increases each year.

T F 7. When bonds are issued between interest dates, Bond Interest Expense is debited for accrued interest since the last interest date.

T F 8. As a bond premium is amortized, the carrying value of bonds payable decreases.

T F 9. When bonds are issued at a discount, the total interest cost to the issuing corporation equals the interest payments minus the bond discount.

T F 10. When bonds are retired, all of the premium or discount associated with the bonds must be canceled.

T F **11.** When the effective interest method is used to amortize a premium on bonds payable, the premium amortized decreases each year.

T F **12.** When bonds are issued at a premium, the total interest cost to the issuing corporation equals the interest payments minus the bond premium.

T F **13.** Under operating leases, assets should be recorded at the present value of future lease payments.

T F **14.** Pension expense is usually difficult to measure because it is based on many estimates, such as employee life expectancy and employee turnover.

T F **15.** When bonds are converted into stock, a gain or loss should be recorded.

T F **16.** Bond issue costs should be amortized over the life of the bonds.

T F **17.** Postretirement health care benefits should be expensed while the employee is still working.

T F **18.** A disadvantage of issuing long-term debt is the increased risk of default.

T F **19.** A low interest coverage ratio indicates a low risk of default on interest payments.

_____

_____

_____

_____

_____

_____

_____

_____

_____

_____

_____

_____

_____

_____

_____

_____

_____

_____

Multiple Choice

Circle the letter of the best answer.

1. Assume that $900,000 of 5 percent bonds are issued (at face value) two months before the next semiannual interest date. Which of the following statements correctly describes the journal entry?
   a. Cash is debited for $900,000.
   b. Cash is debited for $907,500.
   c. Bond Interest Expense is credited for $7,500.
   d. Bond Interest Expense is credited for $15,000.

2. As a mortgage is paid off, the
   a. principal portion of the fixed payment increases.
   b. interest portion of the fixed payment increases.
   c. principal and interest portions do not change each interest period.
   d. monthly payments increase.

3. Unamortized Bond Premium is presented on the balance sheet as a(n)
   a. long-term asset.
   b. stockholders' equity account.
   c. deduction from Bonds Payable.
   d. addition to Bonds Payable.

4. When the interest dates on a bond issue are May 1 and November 1, the adjusting entry to record bond interest expense on December 31 might include a
   a. debit to Interest Payable.
   b. credit to Cash.
   c. credit to Unamortized Bond Discount.
   d. credit to Bond Interest Expense.

5. Under the effective interest method, as a discount is amortized each period, the
   a. amount amortized decreases.
   b. interest expense recorded increases.
   c. interest paid to bondholders increases.
   d. bonds' carrying value decreases.

6. Which of the following would probably be considered an operating lease?
   a. A six-year lease on equipment with an option to renew for another six years
   b. A five-year lease on machinery, cancelable at the end of the lease period by the lessor
   c. A 40-year lease on a building, equal to its useful life
   d. A seven-year lease on a company vehicle with an option to buy the vehicle for $1 at the end of the lease period

7. A $200,000 bond issue with a carrying value of $195,000 is called at 102 and retired. Which of the following statements about the journal entry prepared is true?
   a. An extraordinary gain of $5,000 is recorded.
   b. An extraordinary loss of $4,000 is recorded.
   c. An extraordinary loss of $9,000 is recorded.
   d. No gain or loss is recorded.

8. A company has $600,000 in bonds payable with an unamortized premium of $12,000. If one-third of the bonds are converted to common stock, the carrying value of the bonds payable will decrease by
   a. $196,000.
   b. $200,000.
   c. $204,000.
   d. $208,000.

APPLYING YOUR KNOWLEDGE

Exercises

1. A corporation issues $600,000 of ten-year, 7 percent bonds at 98½ on one of its semiannual interest dates. Assuming straight-line amortization, answer each of the following questions.
   a. What is the amount of the bond discount? $_____

   b. How much interest is paid on the next interest date? $_____

   c. How much bond interest expense is recorded on the next interest date? $_____

   d. After 3 years, what is the carrying value of the bonds? $_____

2. A corporation issues $500,000 of 20-year, 7 percent bonds at 110. Interest is paid semiannually, and the effective interest method is used for amortization. Assume that the market rate for similar investments is 6 percent and that the bonds are issued on an interest date.
   a. What amount was received for the bonds? $_____

   b. How much interest is paid each interest period? $_____

   c. How much bond interest expense is recorded on the first interest date? $_____

   d. How much of the premium is amortized on the first interest date? $_____

   e. What is the carrying value of the bonds after the first interest date? $_____

3. A corporation issued $600,000 of ten-year, 8 percent bonds at 106. In the space provided, calculate the total interest cost.

4. On December 31, 20x1, Buratti Company borrows $50,000 on a 10 percent installment note, to be paid annually over five years. In the journal provided on the next page, prepare the entry to record the note, as well as the December 31, 20x2, and December 31, 20x3, entries to record the first two annual payments. Assume that the principal is paid in equal installments and that the interest on the unpaid balance accrues annually.

General Journal

Date		Description	Debit	Credit

5. Assume the same facts and requirements as in Exercise 4 on page 204, except that payments are made in equal installments of $13,189.

	General Journal		
Date	Description	Debit	Credit

Crossword Puzzle
for Chapters 15 and 16

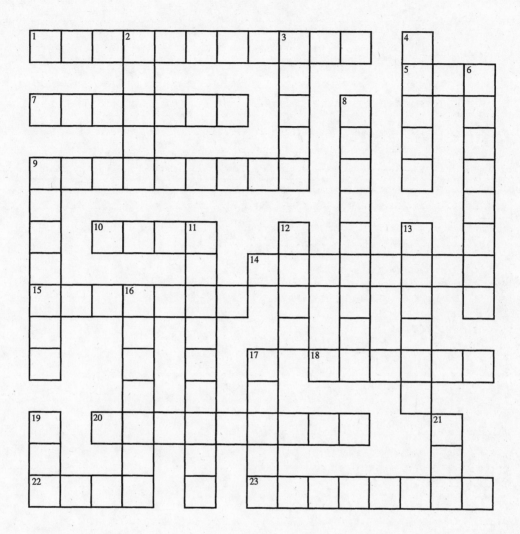

ACROSS

1. Arrangement for retirement income (2 words)
5. Face value (of bonds)
7. Bonds _____ (liability account)
9. Unsecured bond
10. _____ coupon bonds
14. Debt secured by property
15. Type of capital structure
18. Buy back and retire bonds
20. Deduction in statement of stockholders' equity
22. Bonds with one maturity date
23. Stock bought back by a corporation

DOWN

2. Diluted earnings per _____
3. Use another's property for a fee
4. Corporate move to lower the market price of stock
6. _____ earnings
8. Bond contract
9. 6-Down, when negative
11. Type of lease
12. _____ value per share
13. True value of stock
16. Opposite of bond discount
17. Example of extraordinary loss
19. _____ of taxes
21. Amount transferred to contributed capital for large stock dividend

CHAPTER 17 THE STATEMENT OF CASH FLOWS

REVIEWING THE CHAPTER

Objective 1: Describe the statement of cash flows, and define *cash* and *cash equivalents*.

1. The **statement of cash flows** is considered a major financial statement, as are the income statement, balance sheet, and statement of stockholders' equity. The statement of cash flows, however, provides much information and answers certain questions that the other three statements do not. Its presentation is required by the FASB.

2. The statement of cash flows shows the effect on **cash** and cash equivalents of the operating, investing, and financing activities of a company for an accounting period. **Cash equivalents** are short-term, highly liquid investments such as money market accounts, commercial paper (short-term notes), and U.S. Treasury bills. Short-term investments (marketable securities) are *not* considered cash equivalents.

Objective 2: State the principal purposes and uses of the statement of cash flows.

3. The principal purpose of the statement of cash flows is to provide information about a company's cash receipts and cash payments during an accounting period. The statement of cash flows' secondary purpose is to provide information about a company's operating, investing, and financing activities during the period.

4. Investors and creditors can use the statement of cash flows to assess such things as the company's ability to generate positive future cash flows, ability to pay its liabilities, ability to pay dividends, and need for additional financing. In addition, management can use the statement of cash flows (among other things) to assess the debt-paying ability of the business, determine dividend policy, and plan for investing and financing needs.

Objective 3: Identify the principal components of the classifications of cash flows, and state the significance of noncash investing and financing transactions.

5. The statement of cash flows categorizes cash receipts and cash payments as operating, investing, and financing activities.
   a. **Operating activities** include receiving cash from customers from the sale of goods and services, receiving interest and dividends on loans and investments, receiving cash from the sale of trading securities, and making cash payments for wages, goods and services, interest, taxes, and purchases of trading securities.
   b. **Investing activities** include purchasing and selling long-term assets and marketable securities (other than trading securities or cash equivalents) as well as making and collecting on loans to other entities.
   c. **Financing activities** include issuing and buying back capital stock as well as borrowing and repaying loans on a short- or long-term basis (i.e., issuing bonds and notes). Dividends paid would also be included in this category, but repayment of accounts payable or accrued liabilities would not.

6. The statement of cash flows should include a separate schedule of **noncash investing and financing transactions,** involving only long-term assets, long-term liabilities, or stockholders' equity. Transactions such as the issuance of a mortgage for land or the conversion of bonds into stock represent simultaneous investing and financing activities that do not, however, result in an inflow or outflow of cash.

Objective 4: Analyze the statement of cash flows.

7. The statement of cash flows can be analyzed by examining certain relationships. Two such cash-flow relationships, or measures, are cash-generating efficiency and free cash flow.

8. **Cash-generating efficiency,** which focuses on net cash flows from operating activities, is the ability of a company to generate cash from its current or continuing operations. It may be expressed in terms of the following three ratios: cash flow yield, cash flows to sales, and cash flows to assets.
   a. **Cash flow yield** equals net cash flows from operating activities divided by net income (or income from continuing operations). A cash flow yield of 2.0 times, for example, means that operating activities have generated twice as much cash flow as net income.
   b. **Cash flows to sales** equals net cash flows from operating activities divided by net sales. A ratio of 5.7 percent, for example, means that operating cash flows of 5.7 cents have been generated for every dollar of net sales.
   c. **Cash flows to assets** equals net cash flows from operating activities divided by average total assets. A ratio of 4.8 percent, for example, means that operating cash flows of 4.8 cents have been generated for every dollar of average total assets.

9. **Free cash flow** is a measure of cash remaining from operating activities after providing for certain commitments. It equals net cash flows from operating activities minus dividends minus net capital expenditures (purchases minus sales of plant assets). A *positive* free cash flow means that the company has met its cash commitments and has cash remaining to reduce debt or expand further. A *negative* free cash flow means that the company will have to sell investments, borrow money, or issue stock to continue at its planned levels.

10. As is true with all financial statement ratios, the trends in the cash-generating efficiency and free cash flow over several years should be examined to analyze a company's cash flows.

Objective 5: Use the indirect method to determine cash flows from operating activities.

11. In the formal statement of cash flows, individual cash inflows from operating, investing, and financing activities are shown separately in their respective categories. To prepare the statement, one needs to examine a comparative balance sheet, the current income statement, and additional information about transactions affecting noncurrent accounts during the period. The four steps in statement preparation are (1) determining cash flows from operating activities, (2) determining cash flows from investing activities, (3) determining cash flows from financing activities, and (4) presenting the information obtained in the first three steps in the form of a statement of cash flows.

12. Cash flows from operating activities result from converting accrual-basis net income to a cash basis and may be determined using either the **direct method** (explained in paragraphs 20 and 21 below) or the more common **indirect method.**

13. Under the indirect method, the net cash flows from operating activities is determined by taking net income and adding or deducting items that do not affect cash flow from operations. Items to add include depreciation expense, amortization expense, depletion expense, losses, decreases in certain current assets (accounts receivable, inventory, and prepaid expenses), and increases in certain current liabilities (accounts payable, accrued liabilities, and income taxes payable). Items to deduct include gains, increases in certain current assets (see above), and decreases in certain current liabilities (see above).

14. The direct and indirect methods produce the same results and are both considered GAAP. The FASB, however, recommends use of the direct method accompanied by a required separate schedule (the indirect method) reconciling net income to net cash flows.

Objective 6: Determine cash flows from investing activities and financing activities.

15. When determining cash flows from investing and financing activities, the objective is to explain the change in the appropriate account balances from one year to the next. As previously stated, investing activities focus on the purchase and sale of long-term assets and short-term investments (other than trading securities or cash equivalents).
   a. Under the indirect approach, gains and losses from the sale of the above assets should be

deducted from and added back to, respectively, net income to arrive at net cash flows from operating activities.

b. Under the direct approach, gains and losses are simply ignored in determining net cash flows from operating activities.

c. Under both approaches, the full cash proceeds are entered into the Cash Flows from Investing Activities section of the statement of cash flows.

16. Financing activities focus on certain liability and stockholders' equity accounts and include short- and long-term borrowing (notes and bonds) and repayment, issuance and repurchase of capital stock, and payment of dividends. Changes in the Retained Earnings account are explained in the statement of cash flows, for the most part, through analyses of net income and dividends declared.

Objective 7: Use the indirect method to prepare a statement of cash flows.

17. Exhibit 4 of your textbook presents a completed statement of cash flows using the indirect method. As already explained, the essence of the indirect approach is the conversion of net income into net cash flows from operating activities.

Supplemental Objective 8: Prepare a work sheet for the statement of cash flows.

18. A work sheet for preparing the statement of cash flows is especially useful in complex situations. Using the indirect approach, it essentially allows for the systematic analysis of all changes in the balance sheet accounts.

19. Exhibit 5 of your textbook presents the format of a completed work sheet. In preparing the work sheet, five steps should be followed.

a. Enter all balance sheet accounts into the Description column, listing all debit accounts before credit accounts.

b. Enter all end-of-prior-period amounts and end-of-current-period amounts in the designated columns, and foot. The total debits should equal the total credits in each column.

c. In the bottom portion of the work sheet, write the captions Cash Flows from Operating Activities, Cash Flows from Investing Activities, and Cash Flows from Financing Activities, leaving sufficient space between sections to enter data.

d. Analyze the change in each balance sheet account, using the income statement and information on other transactions that affect noncurrent accounts during the period. Then enter the resulting debits and credits in the Analysis of Transactions columns, labeling each entry with a key letter corresponding to a reference list of changes.

e. Foot the top and bottom portions of the Analysis of Transactions columns. The top portion should balance immediately, but the bottom portion should balance only when the net increase or decrease in cash is entered (credited for an increase or debited for a decrease). The changes in cash entered into the top and bottom of the work sheet must equal each other and should be labeled with the same key letter.

Supplemental Objective 9: Use the direct method to determine cash flows from operating activities and prepare a statement of cash flows.

20. Under the direct method, the net cash flows from operating activities is determined by taking cash receipts from sales, adding interest and dividends received, and deducting cash payments for purchases, operating expenses, interest, and income taxes. The only difference between the direct and indirect methods of preparing a statement of cash flows is in the structure of the Cash Flows from Operating Activities section. (See the table on page 212.)

21. Exhibit 7 of your textbook presents a completed statement of cash flows that has incorporated the direct method. When the direct method is used, a schedule explaining the difference between reported net income and cash flows from operating activities must be provided.

Formulas to Determine Cash Flows from Operating Activities under the Direct Method

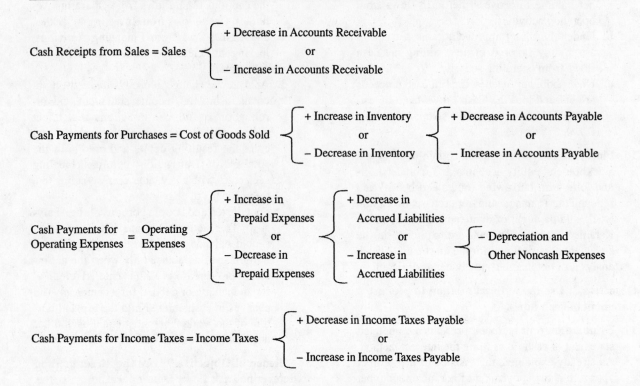

SELF-TEST

Test your knowledge of the chapter by choosing the best answer for each of the following items.

1. Cash equivalents include
   a. three-month Treasury bills.
   b. short-term investments.
   c. accounts receivable.
   d. long-term investments.

2. The primary purpose of the statement of cash flows is to provide information
   a. regarding the results of operations for a period of time.
   b. regarding the financial position of a company as of the end of an accounting period.
   c. about a company's operating, investing, and financing activities during an accounting period.
   d. about a company's cash receipts and cash payments during an accounting period.

3. Which of the following is supplemental to the statement of cash flows?
   a. Operating activities
   b. Investing activities
   c. Significant noncash transactions
   d. Financing activities

4. Which of the following would be classified as an operating activity on the statement of cash flows?
   a. Declared and paid a cash dividend
   b. Issued long-term notes for plant assets
   c. Paid interest on a long-term note
   d. Purchased a patent

5. Which of the following would be classified as an investing activity on the statement of cash flows?
   a. Declared and paid a cash dividend
   b. Issued long-term notes for plant assets
   c. Paid interest on a long-term note
   d. Purchased a patent

6. Which of the following would be classified as a financing activity on the statement of cash flows?
   a. Declared and paid a cash dividend
   b. Issued long-term notes for plant assets
   c. Paid interest on a long-term note
   d. Purchased a patent

7. On the statement of cash flows, the net amount of the major components of cash flow will equal the increase or decrease in
   a. cash and accounts receivable.
   b. working capital.
   c. cash and cash equivalents.
   d. very short-term investments.

8. Cash flow yield is expressed in terms of
   a. dollars.
   b. times.
   c. a percentage.
   d. days.

9. A basic feature of the work sheet approach to preparing the statement of cash flows is that entries are made on the work sheet to
   a. be used for reference for later entry in the general journal.
   b. adjust the cash amount to an accrual basis.
   c. explain the changes in income statement accounts.
   d. explain the changes in balance sheet accounts.

10. The direct method of preparing the operating activities section of the statement of cash flows differs from the indirect method in that it
    a. starts with the net income figure.
    b. lists the changes in current asset accounts in the operating section.
    c. begins with cash from customers, which is revenues adjusted for the change in accounts receivable.
    d. lists significant noncash transactions.

TESTING YOUR KNOWLEDGE

Matching*

Match each term with its definition by writing the appropriate letter in the blank.

_____ 1. Statement of cash flows

_____ 2. Cash equivalents

_____ 3. Operating activities

_____ 4. Investing activities

_____ 5. Financing activities

_____ 6. Noncash investing and financing transactions

_____ 7. Direct method

_____ 8. Indirect method

_____ 9. Cash-generating efficiency

_____ 10. Free cash flow

a. The items placed at the bottom of the statement of cash flows in a separate schedule

b. Net cash flows from operating activities minus dividends minus net capital expenditures

c. In determining cash flows from operations, the procedure that starts with the figure for net income

d. A measure expressed as cash flow yield, cash flows to sales, or cash flows to assets

e. The statement of cash flows section that deals mainly with stockholders' equity accounts and borrowing

f. The financial report that explains the change in cash during the period

g. The statement of cash flows section that deals with long-term assets and marketable securities other than trading securities or cash equivalents

h. In determining cash flows from operations, the procedure that adjusts each income statement item from an accrual basis to a cash basis

i. The statement of cash flows section that most closely relates to net income (loss)

j. Short-term, highly liquid investments

Short Answer

Use the lines provided to answer each item.

1. Give two examples of noncash investing and financing transactions.

   _____

   _____

   _____

   _____

2. When the statement of cash flows is prepared under the indirect method, why are depreciation, amortization, and depletion expense added back to net income to determine cash flows from operating activities?

   _____

   _____

   _____

   _____

Note to student: The matching quiz might be completed more efficiently by starting with the definition and searching for the corresponding term.

3. Which sections of the statement of cash flows are prepared identically under the direct and indirect methods?

_____

_____

_____

_____

4. List three examples of cash equivalents.

_____

_____

_____

True-False

Circle T if the statement is true, F if it is false. Please provide explanations for the false answers, using the blank lines at the end of the section.

T F   **1.** The statement of cash flows is a major financial statement required by the FASB.

T F   **2.** Payment on an account payable is considered a financing activity.

T F   **3.** The proceeds from the sale of available-for-sale securities would be considered an investing activity, whether the investments are classified as short-term or long-term.

T F   **4.** To calculate cash payments for purchases, the cost of goods sold must be known, along with the changes in inventory and accounts payable during the period.

T F   **5.** Under the indirect method, a decrease in prepaid expenses would be added to net income in determining net cash flows from operating activities.

T F   **6.** The schedule of noncash investing and financing transactions might include line items for depreciation, depletion, and amortization recorded during the period.

T F   **7.** In the Analysis of Transactions columns of the bottom portion of a statement of cash flows work sheet, Retained Earnings is credited and Dividends Paid debited for dividends paid during the period.

T F   **8.** In the Cash Flows from Operating Activities section of a statement of cash flows work sheet, the items that are credited in the Analysis of Transactions columns must be deducted from net income in the statement of cash flows.

T F   **9.** A net positive figure for cash flows from investing activities implies that the business is generally expanding.

T F   **10.** The issuance of common stock for cash would be disclosed in the financing activities section of the statement of cash flows.

T F   **11.** Under the indirect method, a loss on the sale of buildings would be deducted from net income in the operating activities section of the statement of cash flows.

T F   **12.** To calculate cash payments for operating expenses, operating expenses must be modified by (among other items) depreciation, which is treated as an add-back.

T F   **13.** Cash obtained by borrowing is considered a financing activity, whether the debt is classified as short-term or long-term.

T F   **14.** The purchase of land in exchange for the issuance of common stock in effect represents simultaneous investing and financing activities.

T F   **15.** It is possible for the direct and indirect methods to produce different net-change-in-cash figures on a statement of cash flows.

T F   **16.** Free cash flow does not include a deduction for dividends because dividend payment is never required.

_____

_____

_____

_____

_____

_____

_____

_____

_____

_____

_____

_____

_____

Multiple Choice

Circle the letter of the best answer.

1. How would interest and dividends received be included on a statement of cash flows that employs the indirect method?
   a. Included as components of net income in the operating activities section
   b. Deducted from net income in the operating activities section
   c. Included in the investing activities section
   d. Included in the financing activities section
   e. Included in the schedule of noncash investing and financing transactions

2. How would a gain on the sale of investments be disclosed on a statement of cash flows that employs the indirect method?
   a. Added to net income in the operating activities section
   b. Deducted from net income in the operating activities section
   c. Included in the investing activities section
   d. Included in the financing activities section
   e. Included in the schedule of noncash investing and financing transactions

3. How would an increase in accounts payable be disclosed on a statement of cash flows that employs the indirect method?
   a. Added to net income in the operating activities section
   b. Deducted from net income in the operating activities section
   c. Included in the investing activities section
   d. Included in the financing activities section
   e. Included in the schedule of noncash investing and financing transactions

4. How would the purchase of a building by incurring a mortgage payable be disclosed on a statement of cash flows that employs the indirect method?
   a. Added to net income in the operating activities section
   b. Deducted from net income in the operating activities section
   c. Included in the investing activities section
   d. Included in the financing activities section
   e. Included in the schedule of noncash investing and financing transactions

5. How would dividends paid be disclosed on a statement of cash flows that employs the indirect method?
   a. Added to net income in the operating activities section
   b. Deducted from net income in the operating activities section
   c. Included in the investing activities section
   d. Included in the financing activities section
   e. Included in the schedule of noncash investing and financing transactions

6. How would an increase in inventory be disclosed on a statement of cash flows that employs the indirect method?
   a. Added to net income in the operating activities section
   b. Deducted from net income in the operating activities section
   c. Included in the investing activities section
   d. Included in the financing activities section
   e. Included in the schedule of noncash investing and financing transactions

7. All of the following represent cash flows from operating activities *except* cash
   a. payments for income taxes.
   b. receipts from sales.
   c. receipts from the issuance of stock.
   d. payments for purchases.

8. When net income is recorded (debited) in the Analysis of Transactions columns of a statement of cash flows work sheet, which item is credited?
   a. Cash
   b. Income summary
   c. Net increase in cash
   d. Retained earnings

9. Brooks Corporation had cash sales of $30,000 and credit sales of $70,000 during the year, and the Accounts Receivable account increased by $14,000. Cash receipts from sales totaled
   a. $70,000.
   b. $86,000.
   c. $100,000.
   d. $114,000.

10. The calculations of cash flow yield, cash flows to sales, and cash flows to assets are all based upon
    a. net cash flows from financing activities.
    b. net increase or decrease in cash.
    c. net cash flows from operating activities.
    d. net cash flows from investing activities.

APPLYING YOUR KNOWLEDGE

Exercises

1. Use the following information to calculate the items below.

Accounts Payable, Jan. 1, 20xx	$ 47,000
Accounts Payable, Dec. 31, 20xx	54,000
Accounts Receivable, Jan. 1, 20xx	32,000
Accounts Receivable, Dec. 31, 20xx	22,000
Accrued Liabilities, Jan. 1, 20xx	17,000
Accrued Liabilities, Dec. 31, 20xx	11,000
Cost of Goods Sold for 20xx	240,000
Depreciation Expense for 20xx	20,000
Income Taxes Expense for 20xx	33,000
Income Taxes Payable, Jan. 1, 20xx	4,000
Income Taxes Payable, Dec. 31, 20xx	6,000
Inventory, Jan. 1, 20xx	86,000
Inventory, Dec. 31, 20xx	74,000
Operating Expenses for 20xx	70,000
Prepaid Expenses, Jan. 1, 20xx	2,000
Prepaid Expenses, Dec. 31, 20xx	3,000
Sales for 20xx	350,000

a. Cash payments for operating expenses =

   $ _____

b. Cash receipts from sales =

   $ _____

c. Cash payments for income taxes =

   $ _____

d. Cash payments for purchases =

   $ _____

e. Net cash flows from operating activities =

   $ _____

2. For 20x7, Canoga Corporation had average total assets of $800,000, net sales of $900,000, net income of $60,000, net cash flows from operating activities of $120,000, dividend payments of $30,000, purchases of plant assets of $75,000, and sales of plant assets of $40,000. Using this information, compute the following cash flow measures.

a. Cash flow yield = _____ times

b. Cash flows to sales = _____ %

c. Cash flows to assets = _____ %

d. Free cash flow = $_____

3. Use the following information to complete Madera Corporation's statement of cash flows work sheet on the next page for the year ended December 31, 20x9. Make sure to use the key letters in the Analysis of Transactions columns to refer to the following explanation list:

a. Net income for 20x9 was $22,000.

b–d. These key letters record changes in current assets and current liabilities.

e. Sold plant assets that cost $30,000 with accumulated depreciation of $10,000, for $24,000.

f. Purchased plant assets for $62,000.

g. Recorded depreciation expense of $26,000 for 20x9.

h. Converted bonds payable with a $10,000 face amount into common stock.

i. Declared and paid dividends of $12,000.

x. This key letter codes the change in cash.

<table>
<tr><td colspan="5" align="center">**Madera Corporation**
Work Sheet for the Statement of Cash Flows
For the Year Ended December 31, 20x9</td></tr>
<tr><td></td><td>**Account Balances 12/31/x8**</td><td colspan="2">**Analysis of Transactions for 20x9**</td><td>**Account Balance 12/31/x9**</td></tr>
<tr><td></td><td></td><td>**Debit**</td><td>**Credit**</td><td></td></tr>
<tr><td>**Debits**</td><td></td><td></td><td></td><td></td></tr>
<tr><td>Cash</td><td>35,000</td><td></td><td></td><td>29,000</td></tr>
<tr><td>Accounts Receivable</td><td>18,000</td><td></td><td></td><td>21,000</td></tr>
<tr><td>Inventory</td><td>83,000</td><td></td><td></td><td>72,000</td></tr>
<tr><td>Plant Assets</td><td>200,000</td><td></td><td></td><td>232,000</td></tr>
<tr><td>Total Debits</td><td>336,000</td><td></td><td></td><td>354,000</td></tr>
<tr><td>**Credits**</td><td></td><td></td><td></td><td></td></tr>
<tr><td>Accumulated Depreciation</td><td>40,000</td><td></td><td></td><td>56,000</td></tr>
<tr><td>Accounts Payable</td><td>27,000</td><td></td><td></td><td>19,000</td></tr>
<tr><td>Bonds Payable</td><td>100,000</td><td></td><td></td><td>90,000</td></tr>
<tr><td>Common Stock</td><td>150,000</td><td></td><td></td><td>160,000</td></tr>
<tr><td>Retained Earnings</td><td>19,000</td><td></td><td></td><td>29,000</td></tr>
<tr><td>Total Credits</td><td>336,000</td><td></td><td></td><td>354,000</td></tr>
<tr><td>**Cash Flows from Operating Activities**</td><td></td><td></td><td></td><td></td></tr>
<tr><td>**Cash Flows from Investing Activities**</td><td></td><td></td><td></td><td></td></tr>
<tr><td>**Cash Flows from Financing Activities**</td><td></td><td></td><td></td><td></td></tr>
<tr><td>**Net Decrease in Cash**</td><td></td><td></td><td></td><td></td></tr>
</table>

CHAPTER 18 FINANCIAL PERFORMANCE EVALUATION

REVIEWING THE CHAPTER

Objective 1: Describe and discuss financial performance evaluation by internal and external users.

1. **Financial performance evaluation** (also called *financial statement analysis*) comprises all the techniques employed by users of financial statements to show important relationships in the financial statements and to relate them to important business financial objectives.

2. The users of financial statements are classified as either internal or external. The primary internal user is management, which sets financial performance objectives. A comprehensive financial plan should contain performance objectives in the areas of liquidity, profitability, long-term solvency, cash flow adequacy, and market strength. Management's main responsibilities are to develop and carry out plans to accomplish its financial performance objectives and to monitor key financial performance measures.

3. The main external users of financial statements are creditors and investors. Both creditors and investors will probably acquire a **portfolio,** or group of loans or investments, which allows the creditors and investors to average both the returns and the risks.

4. Creditors and investors use financial performance evaluation (a) to assess past performance and current position and (b) to assess future potential and the risk related. Information about the past and present is very helpful in making projections about the future. Moreover, the easier it is to predict future performance, the less risk is involved. The lower risk means that the investor or creditor will require a lower expected rate of return.

Objective 2: Describe and discuss the standards for financial performance evaluation.

5. Decision makers assess performance by means of (a) rule-of-thumb measures, (b) analysis of past performance of the company, and (c) comparison with industry norms.
   a. Rule-of-thumb measures for key financial ratios are helpful but should not be the only basis for making a decision. For example, a company may report high earnings per share but may lack sufficient current assets to pay current debts.
   b. The past performance of a company can help show trends. The skill lies in the analyst's ability to predict whether a trend will continue or will reverse itself.
   c. Comparing a company's performance with the performance of other companies in the same industry is helpful, but there are three limitations to using industry norms as standards. First, no two companies are exactly the same. Second, many companies, called **diversified companies,** or *conglomerates,* operate in many unrelated industries, so that comparison is hard. (However, the FASB requirement to report financial information by segments has been somewhat helpful.) Third, different companies may use different acceptable accounting procedures for recording similar items.

Objective 3: State the sources of information for financial performance evaluation.

6. The chief sources of information about publicly held corporations are reports published by the company, SEC reports, business periodicals, and credit and investment advisory services.

   a. A corporation's annual report provides useful financial information. It includes the following sections: (1) management's analysis of the past year's operations, (2) the financial statements, (3) the notes to the statements, including the company's principal accounting procedures, (4) the auditors' report, and (5) a five- or ten-year summary of operations.

   b. **Interim financial statements** may indicate significant changes in a company's earnings trend. They consist of limited financial information, not subject to a full audit, that covers less than a year (usually quarterly or monthly).

   c. Publicly held corporations are required to file with the SEC an annual report (Form 10-K), a quarterly report (Form 10-Q), and a current report of significant events (Form 8-K). These reports are available to the public and are a valuable source of financial information.

   d. Financial analysts obtain information from such sources as *The Wall Street Journal, Forbes, Barron's, Fortune,* the *Financial Times,* Moody's, Standard & Poor's, Dun & Bradstreet, Mergent's, and Robert Morris Associates.

Objective 4: Apply horizontal analysis, trend analysis, and vertical analysis to financial statements.

7. The most common tools and techniques of financial performance evaluation are horizontal analysis, trend analysis, vertical analysis, and ratio analysis.

   a. Comparative financial statements show the current and prior year's information side by side to aid in financial statement analysis. In **horizontal analysis,** absolute and percentage changes in specific items from one year to the next are shown. The first of the two years being considered is called the **base year,** and the percentage change is computed by dividing the amount of the change by the base-year amount.

   b. **Trend analysis** is the same as horizontal analysis, except that percentage changes are calculated for several consecutive years. For percentage changes to be shown over several years, **index numbers** must be used against which changes in related items are measured. The index is obtained by dividing the index year amount by the base year amount, and then multiplying the result by 100.

   c. In **vertical analysis,** the percentage relationship of individual items on the statement to a total within the statement (e.g., cost of goods sold as a percentage of net sales) is presented. The result is a **common-size statement.** On a common-size balance sheet, total assets and total liabilities and stockholders' equity would both be labeled 100 percent. On a common-size income statement, sales or revenues would be labeled 100 percent. Common-size statements may be presented in comparative form to show information both within the period and between periods and to make comparisons between companies.

8. In **ratio analysis,** which is a technique to evaluate financial performance, certain relationships (ratios) between financial statement components are determined and then compared with those of prior years or other companies. Ratios provide information about a company's liquidity, profitability, long-term solvency, cash flow adequacy, and market strength.

Objective 5: Apply ratio analysis to financial statements in a comprehensive evaluation of a company's financial performance.

9. The most common ratios are shown in the table on the next page.

Ratio	Components	Use or Meaning
Liquidity Ratios		
Current ratio	$\dfrac{\text{Current Assets}}{\text{Current Liabilities}}$	Measure of short-term debt-paying ability
Quick ratio	$\dfrac{\text{Cash + Marketable Securities + Receivables}}{\text{Current Liabilities}}$	Measure of short-term debt-paying ability
Receivable turnover	$\dfrac{\text{Net Sales}}{\text{Average Accounts Receivable}}$	Measure of relative size of accounts receivable and effectiveness of credit policies
Average days' sales uncollected	$\dfrac{\text{Days in Year}}{\text{Receivable Turnover}}$	Measure of average days taken to collect receivables
Inventory turnover	$\dfrac{\text{Cost of Goods Sold}}{\text{Average Inventory}}$	Measure of relative size of inventory
Average days' inventory on hand	$\dfrac{\text{Days in Year}}{\text{Inventory Turnover}}$	Measure of average days taken to sell inventory
Payables turnover	$\dfrac{\text{Cost of Goods Sold} \pm \text{Change in Inventory}}{\text{Average Accounts Payable}}$	Measure of relative size of accounts payable
Average days' payable	$\dfrac{\text{Days in Year}}{\text{Payables Turnover}}$	Measure of average days taken to pay accounts payable

(**Note:** The term **operating cycle** means the time it takes to sell and collect for products sold. It equals average days' inventory on hand plus average days' sales uncollected.)

Ratio	Components	Use or Meaning
Profitability Ratios		
Profit margin	$\dfrac{\text{Net Income}}{\text{Net Sales}}$	Measure of net income produced by each dollar of sales
Asset turnover	$\dfrac{\text{Net Sales}}{\text{Average Total Assets}}$	Measure of how efficiently assets are used to produce sales
Return on assets	$\dfrac{\text{Net Income}}{\text{Average Total Assets}}$	Measure of overall earning power or profitability
Return on equity	$\dfrac{\text{Net Income}}{\text{Average Stockholders' Equity}}$	Measure of profitability of stockholders' investments
Long-Term Solvency Ratios		
Debt to equity ratio	$\dfrac{\text{Total Liabilities}}{\text{Stockholders' Equity}}$	Measure of capital structure and leverage
Interest coverage ratio	$\dfrac{\text{Income Before Income Taxes + Interest Expense}}{\text{Interest Expense}}$	Measure of creditors' protection from default on interest payments
Cash Flow Adequacy Ratios		
Cash flow yield	$\dfrac{\text{Net Cash Flows from Operating Activities}}{\text{Net Income}}$	Measure of ability to generate operating cash flows in relation to net income
Cash flows to sales	$\dfrac{\text{Net Cash Flows from Operating Activities}}{\text{Net Sales}}$	Measure of ability of sales to generate operating cash flows
Cash flows to assets	$\dfrac{\text{Net Cash Flows from Operating Activities}}{\text{Average Total Assets}}$	Measure of ability of assets to generate operating cash flows
Free cash flow	Net Cash Flows from Operating Activities – Dividends – Net Capital Expenditures	Measure of cash generated or cash deficiency after providing for commitments
Market Strength Ratios		
Price/earnings (P/E) ratio	$\dfrac{\text{Market Price per Share}}{\text{Earnings per Share}}$	Measure of investor confidence in a company
Dividends yield	$\dfrac{\text{Dividends per Share}}{\text{Market Price per Share}}$	Measure of current return to an investor in a stock

SELF-TEST

Test your knowledge of the chapter by choosing the best answer for each of the following items.

1. A general rule in choosing among alternative investments is the greater the risk taken, the
   a. greater the return required.
   b. lower the profits expected.
   c. lower the potential expected.
   d. greater the price of the investment.

2. Which of the following is the most useful in evaluating whether a company has improved its position in relation to its competitors?
   a. Rule-of-thumb measures
   b. Past performance of the company
   c. Past and current performances of the company
   d. Industry averages

3. One of the best places to look for early signals of change in a company's profitability is the
   a. interim financial statements.
   b. year-end financial statements.
   c. annual report sent to stockholders.
   d. annual report sent to the SEC.

4. Cash flow yield equals net cash flows from operating activities divided by
   a. average stockholders' equity.
   b. net income.
   c. average total assets.
   d. net sales.

5. In trend analysis, each item is expressed as a percentage of the
   a. net income figure.
   b. retained earnings figure.
   c. base year figure.
   d. total assets figure.

6. In a common-size balance sheet for a wholesale company, the 100 percent figure is
   a. merchandise inventory.
   b. total current assets.
   c. total property, plant, and equipment.
   d. total assets.

7. The best way to study the changes in financial statements between two years is to prepare
   a. common-size statements.
   b. a trend analysis.
   c. a horizontal analysis.
   d. a ratio analysis.

8. A common measure of liquidity is
   a. return on assets.
   b. profit margin.
   c. inventory turnover.
   d. interest coverage.

9. Asset turnover is most closely related to
   a. profit margin and return on assets.
   b. profit margin and debt to equity.
   c. interest coverage and debt to equity.
   d. earnings per share and profit margin.

10. Which of the following describes the computation of the interest coverage ratio?
   a. Net income minus interest expense divided by interest expense
   b. Net income plus interest expense divided by interest expense
   c. Income before income taxes plus interest expense divided by interest expense
   d. Net income divided by interest expense

TESTING YOUR KNOWLEDGE

*Matching**

Match each term with its definition by writing the appropriate letter in the blank.

_____ 1. Financial performance evaluation

_____ 2. Portfolio

_____ 3. Diversified companies (conglomerates)

_____ 4. Interim financial statements

_____ 5. Horizontal analysis

_____ 6. Base year

_____ 7. Trend analysis

_____ 8. Index number

_____ 9. Vertical analysis

_____ 10. Common-size statement

_____ 11. Ratio analysis

_____ 12. Operating cycle

a. The time it takes to sell and collect for products sold

b. A group of investments or loans

c. The determination of certain relationships between financial statement components

d. A financial statement expressed in terms of percentages, the result of vertical analysis

e. Limited financial information for less than a year (usually quarterly or monthly)

f. The first year being considered when horizontal analysis is used

g. Techniques used to show important relationships in financial statements

h. A presentation of the percentage change in specific items over several years

i. A number used in trend analysis to show change in related items from one year to another

j. A presentation of absolute and percentage changes in specific items from one year to the next

k. A presentation of the percentage relationships of individual items on a statement to a total within the statement

l. Companies that operate in many unrelated industries

Short Answer

Use the lines provided to answer each item.

1. List four ratios that measure profitability.

_____

_____

_____

_____

2. Briefly distinguish between horizontal and vertical analysis.

_____

_____

_____

_____

_____

Note to student: The matching quiz might be completed more efficiently by starting with the definition and searching for the corresponding term.

3. List the three methods by which decision makers assess performance.

_____

_____

_____

4. Why is it wiser to acquire a portfolio of small investments rather than one large investment?

_____

_____

_____

5. List four measures of cash flow adequacy.

_____

_____

_____

_____

True-False

Circle T if the statement is true, F if it is false. Please provide explanations for the false answers, using the blank lines at the end of the section.

T F **1.** Horizontal analysis is possible for both an income statement and a balance sheet.

T F **2.** Common-size financial statements show dollar changes in specific items from one year to the next.

T F **3.** A company with a 2.0 current ratio will experience a decline in the current ratio when a short-term liability is paid.

T F **4.** Inventory is not included in computing the quick ratio.

T F **5.** Inventory turnover equals average inventory divided by cost of goods sold.

T F **6.** The price/earnings ratio must be computed before earnings per share can be determined.

T F **7.** When computing the return on equity, interest expense must be added back to net income.

T F **8.** When a company has no debt, its return on assets equals its return on equity.

T F **9.** The lower the debt to equity ratio, the riskier the situation.

T F **10.** Receivable turnover measures the time it takes to collect an average receivable.

T F **11.** A low interest coverage would be cause for concern for a company's bondholders.

T F **12.** Average days' inventory on hand is a liquidity ratio.

T F **13.** Dividends yield is a profitability ratio.

T F **14.** On a common-size income statement, net income is given a label of 100 percent.

T F **15.** Interim financial statements may serve as an early signal of significant changes in a company's earning trend.

T F **16.** Probably the best source of financial news is _The Wall Street Journal_.

T F **17.** Return on assets equals the profit margin times asset turnover.

T F **18.** The higher the payables turnover, the longer the average days' payable.

T F **19.** The annual report filed with the SEC is known as Form 10-K.

_____

_____

_____

_____

_____

_____

_____

_____

_____ _____
_____ _____
_____ _____
_____ _____
_____ _____
_____ _____
_____ _____
_____ _____

Multiple Choice

Circle the letter of the best answer.

1. Which of the following is a measure of long-term solvency?
   a. Current ratio
   b. Interest coverage
   c. Asset turnover
   d. Profit margin

2. Short-term creditors would probably be *most* interested in which of the following ratios?
   a. Current ratio
   b. Average days' inventory on hand
   c. Debt to equity ratio
   d. Quick ratio

3. Net income is irrelevant in computing which of the following ratios?
   a. Cash flow yield
   b. Return on assets
   c. Asset turnover
   d. Return on equity

4. A high price/earnings ratio indicates
   a. investor confidence in high future earnings.
   b. that the stock is probably overvalued.
   c. that the stock is probably undervalued.
   d. little investor confidence in high future earnings.

5. Index numbers are used in
   a. trend analysis.
   b. ratio analysis.
   c. vertical analysis.
   d. common-size statements.

6. The main internal user of financial statements is
   a. the SEC.
   b. management.
   c. investors.
   d. creditors.

7. Comparing performance with industry norms is complicated by
   a. the existence of diversified companies.
   b. the use of different accounting procedures by different companies.
   c. the fact that companies in the same industry usually differ in some respect.
   d. all of the above.

8. A low receivable turnover indicates that
   a. few customers are defaulting on their debts.
   b. the company's inventory is moving very slowly.
   c. the company is making collections from its customers very slowly.
   d. a small proportion of the company's sales are credit sales.

9. In a common-size income statement, net income is labeled
   a. 0 percent.
   b. the percentage that net income is in relation to sales.
   c. the percentage that net income is in relation to operating expenses.
   d. 100 percent.

10. Which of the following measures equals cash generated or cash deficiency after providing for commitments?
    a. Cash flows to assets
    b. Cash flow yield
    c. Free cash flow
    d. Cash flows to sales

APPLYING YOUR KNOWLEDGE

Exercises

1. Complete the horizontal analysis for the comparative income statements shown here. Round percentages to the nearest tenth of a percent.

	20x2	20x1	Increase (Decrease) Amount	Percentage
Sales	$250,000	$200,000		
Cost of Goods Sold	144,000	120,000		
Gross Margin	$106,000	$ 80,000		
Operating Expenses	62,000	50,000		
Income Before Income Taxes	$ 44,000	$ 30,000		
Income Taxes	16,000	8,000		
Net Income	$ 28,000	$ 22,000		

2. The following is financial information for Evans Corporation for 20xx. Current assets consist of cash, accounts receivable, marketable securities, and inventory. Assume no change in inventory.

Average accounts receivable	$100,000
Average (and ending) inventory	180,000
Cost of goods sold	350,000
Current assets, Dec. 31	500,000
Current liabilities, Dec. 31	250,000
Market price, Dec. 31, on 21,200 shares	40/share
Net income	106,000
Net sales	600,000
Average stockholders' equity	480,000
Average total assets	880,000
Net cash flows from operating activities	75,000
(Average) accounts payable	50,000

Compute the following ratios as of December 31. Round off to the nearest tenth of a whole number for **a–l** and **o–p,** to the nearest hundredth of a whole number in **m** and **n.**

a. Current ratio = _____

b. Quick ratio = _____

c. Inventory turnover = _____

d. Average days' inventory on hand = _____

e. Return on assets = _____

f. Return on equity = _____

g. Receivable turnover = _____

h. Average days' sales uncollected = _____

i. Profit margin = _____

j. Cash flow yield = _____

k. Cash flows to sales = _____

l. Cash flows to assets = _____

m. Asset turnover = _____

n. Price/earnings ratio = _____

o. Payables turnover = _____

p. Average days' payable = _____

Crossword Puzzle
for Chapters 17 and 18

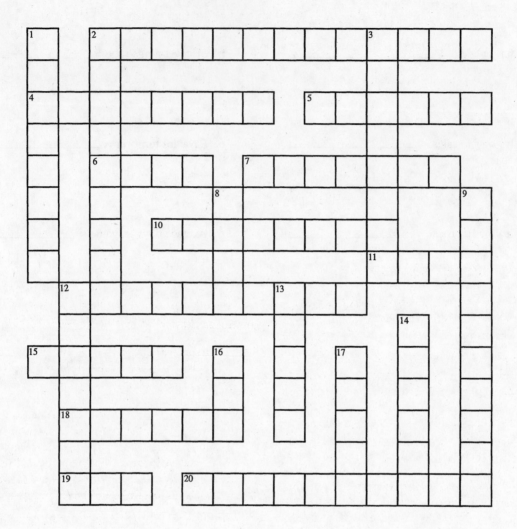

ACROSS

2. Ratio indicating investor confidence in a company (2 words)

4. Analysis resulting in 12-Across

5. _____ on assets (measure of profitability)

6. Free cash _____

7. Quarterly financial statement, e.g.

10. Financial statement examination

11. 1-Down is a long-_____ solvency ratio

12. Statement showing percentage relationships (hyphenated)

15. _____ analysis, a variation of horizontal analysis

18. Return on _____ (measure of profitability)

19. An operating-activity outflow

20. Analysis involving dollar and percentage changes

DOWN

1. Interest _____ ratio

2. Group of investments or loans

3. An operating-activity inflow or outflow

8. Indirect-method "minus" adjustment

9. _____ paper (short-term notes)

12. With 17-Down, a measure of liquidity

13. Number used in 15-Across

14. Statement of cash flows method

16. Dun & Bradstreet's *Industry Norms and _____ Business Ratios*

17. See 12-Down

CHAPTER 19   A MANAGER'S PERSPECTIVE: THE CHANGING BUSINESS ENVIRONMENT

REVIEWING THE CHAPTER

Objective 1: Define *management accounting* and distinguish between management accounting and financial accounting.

1. **Management accounting** is the process of identifying, measuring, accumulating, analyzing, preparing, interpreting, and communicating information used by management to plan, evaluate, and control within the organization and to ensure that its resources are used and accounted for appropriately. The information that management accounting provides should be timely and accurate and support management decisions regarding pricing, planning, operating and other types of decisions. Management accounting helps all sizes and types of organizations make better decisions.

2. Management accounting provides essential information for management planning, control, performance measurement, and decision making that may either be historical or future oriented. Financial accounting conveys economic information primarily to external parties that is historical in nature and in compliance with GAAP. Management accounting can be distinguished from financial accounting by looking at (a) report(s) format, (b) purpose of reports, (c) primary users, (d) units of measure, (e) nature of information, and (f) frequency of reports.

Objective 2: Explain the management cycle and its connection to management accounting.

3. The management cycle involves four stages: (1) planning, (2) executing, (3) reviewing, and (4) reporting. The management accounting activities— (a) developing plans and analyzing alternatives, (b) communicating plans to key personnel, (c) evaluating performance, (d) reporting the results of activities, and (e) accumulating, maintaining, and processing the financial and nonfinancial information of the organization—complement the management cycle. Management accounting can provide an ongoing stream of relevant information that can assist managers in developing a business plan, communicating that plan to interested parties, evaluating performance, and reporting the result of operating activities for a period of time.

Objective 3: Identify the management philosophies of continuous improvement and discuss the role of management accounting in implementing those philosophies.

4. Several management philosophies have been developed to assist firms in competing in an expanding global market: just-in-time (JIT) operating techniques, total quality management (TQM), activity-based management (ABM), and the theory of constraints (TOC).
   a. A **just-in-time (JIT) operating philosophy** requires that all resources, including materials, personnel, and facilities, be acquired and used only as needed. Its objectives are to improve productivity and eliminate waste.
   b. **Total quality management (TQM)** describes an environment in which all functions work together to build quality into a firm's products or services. Managers use accounting information

about the magnitude and classification of costs of quality to help achieve their goals. The **costs of quality** include both the costs of achieving quality and the costs of poor quality in the manufacture of a product or the delivery of a service.

   c. **Activity-based management (ABM)** entails the identification of all major operating activities, the determination of what resources are consumed by each activity, the identification of what causes resource usage of each activity, and the categorization of which activities are value-adding and which are not. ABM includes **activity-based costing (ABC),** a management accounting practice that identifies all of an organization's major operating activities (both production and non-production), traces costs to those activities, and then determines which products or services use the resources and services supplied by those activities. Activities that add value to a product or service, as perceived by the customer, are known as **value-adding activities.** Such activities are enhanced to improve product or service quality and customer satisfaction. All other activities are called **non-value-adding activities.**

   d. The **theory of constraints (TOC)** contends that there are limiting factors, or bottlenecks, during the production of any product or service. TOC helps managers set priorities for how they spend their time and other resources. After identifying limitations or constraints, it focuses resources on efforts that will produce the most effective improvements.

5. A goal of JIT, TQM, ABM, and TOC is perfection by means of **continuous improvement.** That is, management should never be satisfied with the status quo. Instead, it should seek better methods, products, processes, and resources.

Objective 4: Define *performance measures,* **recognize the uses of those measures in the management cycle, and prepare an analysis of nonfinancial data.**

6. **Performance measures** may be financial or nonfinancial and may be viewed as quantitative tools that an organization uses to gauge if its processes or tasks have achieved its goals. Management uses performance measures in each stage of the management cycle to provide incentives for improvement.

7. Examples of financial performance measures include return on investment, net income as a percentage of sales, costs of poor quality as a percentage of sales, etc. Each of these examples utilizes monetary measures to determine the performance of various units of an organization.

8. Examples of nonfinancial performance measures can include the number of times an object (product, service, or activity) occurs, the time to perform a task, the number of customer complaints, the time it takes to fill an order, the number of orders shipped the same day, or the hours of inspection. Each of these nonfinancial performance measurements are used by management to enable the firm to better compete in today's tough global market.

9. The **balanced scorecard** helps an organization to measure and evaluate itself from a variety of viewpoints. It links the perspective of the organization's stakeholder groups—investors, employees, internal business process groups, and customers—with the organization's mission and vision, performance measures, strategic plan, and resources. The balanced scorecard analyzes both financial and nonfinancial performance measures.

Objective 5: Identify the important questions a manager must consider before requesting or preparing a management report.

10. An internal report's format and structure are determined by the manager generating the report, based upon the type of information needed and the time constraints of the project. A successful report is one that has considered the four W's: Why? Who? What? and When?

   a. The preparer (manager) should address the question, "*Why* is this report being prepared?" That is, the report should be focused and should fulfill a particular need.

   b. An additional consideration is, "To *whom* will the report be distributed?" A widely distributed report, for example, normally contains concise, summarized information.

   c. The preparer should decide *what* information will satisfy the need and *what* form of presentation will be most effective.

   d. An equally important consideration is, "*When* is the report due?" The tradeoff between timeliness and accuracy is especially evident when a report must be prepared at almost a moment's notice.

Objective 6: Compare accounting for inventories and cost of goods sold in service, merchandising, and manufacturing organizations.

11. Service organizations, merchandising organizations, and manufacturing organizations provide financial statements to outside parties. Service

businesses sell only services, do not have inventory, and determine the cost of sales. The cost of sales is equal to net cost of services sold. Merchandising and manufacturing businesses maintain levels of inventory and calculate gross margin using sales and cost of goods sold information. However, there are several differences between these two types of organizations that result in manufacturing organizations having more complexities. These complexities arise because a merchandising organization buys goods that are already complete and ready for resale whereas a manufacturing organization must design and manufacture goods before they are ready for sale. A merchandising organization typically maintains only one inventory account on the balance sheet, whereas a manufacturing organization has three inventory accounts (Materials, Work in Process, and Finished Goods) on the balance sheet. Whereas a merchandising organization includes the cost of purchases in the calculation of cost of goods sold, a manufacturing organization must determine the cost of goods manufactured to include in the calculation of cost of goods sold.

12. A service organization calculates its cost of sales using the following equation:

    Cost of Sales = Net Cost of Services Sold

13. A merchandising organization determines the cost of goods sold based on the following model:

    Cost of Goods Sold = Beginning Merchandise Inventory + Net Cost of Purchases – Ending Merchandise Inventory

14. A manufacturing organization uses materials, labor, and manufacturing overhead in the production process. After materials are purchased, the Materials Inventory account shows the balance of the cost of unused materials. During production, the costs of manufacturing the product accumulate in the Work in Process Inventory. Once the product is completed, the cost of the goods manufactured is shown in the Finished Goods Inventory

account. When the completed product is sold, the manufacturing organization calculates the cost of goods sold using the following model:

Cost of Goods Sold = Beginning Finished Goods Inventory + Cost of Goods Manufactured – Ending Finished Goods Inventory

15. The *cost of goods available for sale* for a merchandising organization is the total of the beginning Merchandise Inventory balance plus the net cost of purchases. Once a determination as to the amount of ending Merchandise Inventory is made, then the difference between cost of goods available for sale and the ending Merchandise Inventory balance represents Cost of Goods Sold for the period. For a manufacturing organization, the sum of the beginning Finished Goods Inventory balance plus the cost of goods manufactured represents the cost of goods available for sale. Once a determination as to the amount of unsold products in the Finished Goods Inventory is made, then the difference between cost of goods available for sale and the ending Finished Goods Inventory balance represents Cost of Goods Sold for the period.

Objective 7: Identify the standards of ethical conduct for management accountants.

16. Management accountants are often confronted by ethical challenges. These challenges may result from both internal and external pressures. Management accountants and financial managers have the responsibility to help management balance the needs of various external parties. Throughout their careers, they have an obligation to the public, their profession, the organization they serve, and themselves to maintain the highest standards of ethical conduct. Standards of ethical conduct have been formally adopted by the Institute of Management Accountants. These standards cover the management accountant's responsibility in the area of competence, confidentiality, integrity, and objectivity.

Test your knowledge of the chapter by choosing the best answer for each of the following items.

1. A management accounting system is a necessary component for
   a. manufacturing companies only.
   b. service organizations only.
   c. not-for-profit organizations only.
   d. all types of organizations.

2. When applied collectively to a company's financial, production, and distribution data, internal management accounting procedures will
   a. guarantee the generation of a profit.
   b. satisfy requirements of the Internal Revenue Service.
   c. satisfy management's information needs.
   d. represent the union's basic collective bargaining agreement.

3. Which of the following statements is false?
   a. Management is responsible for preparing a company's annual financial statements, but this information is disclosed primarily for external users.
   b. Management accountants are not restricted to using the historical dollar and can employ any unit of measure useful in a situation.
   c. Financial accounting has only one restrictive guideline: The accounting practice or technique used must produce useful information.
   d. Typically, financial accounting records and reports information on the assets, liabilities, equities, and net income of a company as a whole.

4. Which of the following is *not* a stage in the management cycle?
   a. Planning
   b. Executing
   c. Financial statement preparation
   d. Reviewing

5. Which of the following management philosophies have evolved to assist firms competing in a global market?
   a. Just-in-time operating philosophy
   b. Total quality management
   c. Activity-based management
   d. All of the above

6. The primary difference between a manufacturing organization and a merchandising organization is that
   a. a manufacturing organization makes a product to sell, whereas a merchandising organization buys a product ready for resale.
   b. a merchandising organization does not need a management accounting system, but a manufacturing organization relies heavily on such a system.
   c. a merchandising organization makes a product to sell, whereas a manufacturing organization buys a product ready for resale.
   d. a manufacturing organization does not need a management accounting system, but a merchandising organization relies heavily on such a system.

7. Performance measures may be either financial or nonfinancial in nature. Which of the following is *not* a financial performance measure that may be used by a business enterprise?
   a. Number of customer complaints
   b. Return on equity
   c. Sales for the month
   d. Total costs of production

8. The cost of goods available for sale for a merchandising organization is
   a. cost of goods manufactured and cost of purchases.
   b. ending Merchandise Inventory balance plus cost of purchases.
   c. beginning Merchandise Inventory balance plus net cost of purchases.
   d. none of the above.

9. Which of the following statements is *false* about service organizations?
   a. Service organizations do not maintain inventory levels.
   b. Service organizations use management information to make better decisions.
   c. The income statement prepared for a service organization reports cost of sales instead of cost of goods sold.
   d. The balance sheet prepared for a service organization includes an inventory account called Cost of Service.

10. Management accountants often face ethical dilemmas during their careers. The Institute of Management Accountants has adopted standards of ethical conduct that address different areas of responsibility that a management accountant has to the following entities *except* the
   a. Internal Revenue Service.
   b. public.
   c. profession.
   d. organization they serve.

TESTING YOUR KNOWLEDGE

Matching*

Match each term with its definition by writing the appropriate letter in the blank.

_____ 1. Theory of constraints (TOC)

_____ 2. Value-adding activity

_____ 3. Activity-based management (ABM)

_____ 4. Total quality management (TQM)

_____ 5. Continuous improvement

_____ 6. Management accounting

_____ 7. Balanced scorecard

_____ 8. Nonvalue-adding activity

_____ 9. Just-in-time (JIT) operating philosophy

_____ 10. Activity-based costing (ABC)

a. A framework of both financial and nonfinancial performance measures that links the perspectives of different shareholder groups

b. Something that increases both product cost and desirability

c. Management approach that identifies and analyzes all major operating activities in hopes of eliminating those that have no value

d. System in which personnel are hired and materials purchased only as needed

e. Constant steps taken to move closer to perfection

f. A management approach that helps managers identify limitations or constraints and helps to set priorities on time and resources

g. Coordinated effort to achieve product or service excellence

h. System that identifies and analyzes both production and nonproduction operating activities

i. The field involved with providing useful information to managers for decision-making purposes

j. Something that increases product cost but does not enhance product desirability

Short Answer

Use the lines provided to answer each item.

1. What are the four traditional stages of an organization's management cycle?

_____

_____

_____

_____

2. Briefly explain what is meant by a just-in-time operating philosophy.

_____

_____

_____

_____

Note to student: The matching quiz might be completed more efficiently by starting with the definition and searching for the corresponding term.

3. Management accountants must adhere to what four facets of ethical conduct?

_____

_____

_____

_____

4. Identify the "four W's" of preparing a management report.

_____

_____

_____

_____

5. Compare and contrast the cost of sales and the cost of goods sold.

_____

_____

_____

_____

True-False

Circle T if the statement is true, F if it is false. Please provide explanations for the false answers, using the blank lines at the end of the section.

T F **1.** A merchandiser's goods that are for sale are called _finished goods inventory._

T F **2.** The function of the management accountant is to make important decisions for the company.

T F **3.** Management accounting exists primarily for the benefit of people inside the company.

T F **4.** A management accountant for a company or government organization relies more on financial accounting principles than on management accounting rules.

T F **5.** The business entity as a whole is the focal point of analysis in financial accounting.

T F **6.** The data that support management accounting reports often are subjective.

T F **7.** Financial accounting reports may be prepared monthly, quarterly, and/or annually on a regular basis, or they may be requested daily or on an irregular basis.

T F **8.** Computing ending inventory values is more complex for a merchandising organization than for a manufacturing organization.

T F **9.** Avoiding conflicts of interest relates most closely to the ethical standard of confidentiality.

T F **10.** Enhancing one's professional skills relates most closely to the ethical standard of objectivity.

T F **11.** The just-in-time operating philosophy emphasizes the elimination of waste.

T F **12.** Performance measures may be either financial or nonfinancial measures.

T F **13.** Nonvalue-adding activities should be considered prime targets for elimination.

T F **14.** Management accountants often prepare analyses expressed in nonfinancial units.

T F **15.** Planning is the second stage in the traditional management cycle.

T F **16.** Activity-based management identifies activities as being value-adding or nonvalue-adding.

T F **17.** Activities that add value to a product or service, as perceived by the manufacturer, are known as value-adding activities.

_____

_____

_____
_____
_____
_____
_____
_____
_____
_____
_____
_____
_____
_____

_____
_____
_____
_____
_____
_____
_____
_____
_____
_____
_____
_____

Multiple Choice

Circle the letter of the best answer.

1. Developing skills on an ongoing basis relates most closely to which of the following standards of ethical conduct?
   a. Integrity
   b. Objectivity
   c. Confidentiality
   d. Competence

2. Refusing a gift that might influence one's actions relates most closely to which of the following standards of ethical conduct?
   a. Integrity
   b. Objectivity
   c. Confidentiality
   d. Competence

3. Management accounting and financial accounting do *not* differ with respect to
   a. the primary users of information.
   b. the timeliness of data.
   c. restrictive guides.
   d. unit of measurement.

4. Continuous improvement has, as its goal, perfection. Which of the following contributes to a firm achieving this goal?
   a. Just-in-time operating philosophy
   b. Total quality management
   c. Activity-based management
   d. All of the above

5. Management accounting rules and procedures normally rely on
   a. the double-entry system.
   b. generally accepted accounting principles.
   c. their usefulness as a guide.
   d. the historical dollar.

6. Management accounting reports and analyses are usually heavily subjective, which means that
   a. much of the data have been estimated.
   b. the reports ignore inflation.
   c. the data are verifiable.
   d. the reports use historical-dollar information.

7. Managers often compare actual performance to the expected performance at which stage in the management cycle?
   a. Planning
   b. Executing
   c. Reviewing
   d. Reporting

8. Which of the following is *not* based on nonfinancial data?
   a. Analysis of deliveries
   b. Operating budgets
   c. Survey of customers served
   d. Analysis of labor hours worked

APPLYING YOUR KNOWLEDGE

Exercises

1. Complete the chart at the bottom of the page by writing the appropriate letter in the blanks under each column. (*Hint:* First determine if Financial or Management Accounting; then select the appropriate line.)

   a. Business entity as a whole
   b. No guides or restrictions; only criterion is usefulness
   c. Various levels of internal management
   d. Demands objectivity; historical in nature
   e. Persons and organizations outside the business entity
   f. Whenever needed; might not be on a regular basis
   g. Double-entry system
   h. Various segments of the business entity
   i. Historical dollar
   j. Heavily subjective for planning purposes, but objective data are used when relevant; futuristic in nature
   k. Periodically on a regular basis
   l. Not restricted to double-entry system; any useful system
   m. Adherence to generally accepted accounting principles
   n. Any useful monetary or physical measurement, such as labor hour or machine hour; if dollars are used, may be historical or future dollars

	Financial Accounting	*Management Accounting*
1. Primary users of information	_____	_____
2. Types of accounting systems	_____	_____
3. Restrictive guidelines	_____	_____
4. Units of measurement	_____	_____
5. Focal point of analysis	_____	_____
6. Frequency of reporting	_____	_____
7. Degree of objectivity	_____	_____

2. Dom Lucia is the owner of Dom's Pizza Palace in upstate New York. The restaurant is always very busy. Over the years, Dom has developed measures of efficiency for his employees.

During March, the following labor-hour information was generated for the month's servers:

Number of Pizzas Served per Hour	Employee Rating
Over 20	Excellent
17–19	Good
14–16	Average
10–13	Lazy
Under 10	The Pits

Employee	Hours Worked	Number of Pizzas Served
P. Sanchez	130	2,860
S. Wang	140	2,520
R. Scotti	145	1,885
E. Butterfield	136	2,176
B. Jolita	168	3,192
B. Warner	154	2,310
G. Cohen	150	1,350

Evaluate the performance of these employees.

3. The Sun Factory is implementing a total quality management philosophy in their organization. They have found the following costs that have an impact on their profits. Identify the following as **a** (Costs of Achieving Quality) or **b** (Cost of Poor Quality):

1. Rework   _____

2. Warranty Repairs   _____

3. Employee Training   _____

4. Material Inspection Costs   _____

5. Customer Complaints   _____

CHAPTER 20 COST CONCEPTS AND COST ALLOCATION

REVIEWING THE CHAPTER

Objective 1: State how managers use information about costs in the management cycle.

1. Because costs affect the profitability of the organization, managers are concerned with receiving accurate and up-to-date cost information. Whether an organization is a manufacturer, merchandiser, or service organization, operating cost information is very important. This cost information is used in the management cycle functions of planning, executing, reviewing, and reporting.
   a. In the planning stage, managers may use operating cost information to develop budgets and to estimate selling prices for their goods or services.
   b. In the executing stage, managers may use cost information to estimate profitability of a given product or service, decide whether to drop a product line or service, or determine a selling price for a product or service.
   c. In the reviewing stage, managers like to know if there were significant variances between estimated costs and the actual costs. Such variances help managers to ascertain the reasons for cost overruns and enable them to avoid such problems in the future.
   d. In the reporting stage, managers expect to see financial statements that include actual costs and performance reports that summarize variance analyses.

Objective 2: Identify various approaches managers use to classify costs.

2. Cost classification is very important for the long-term success of businesses. An individual cost item can be classified in different ways depending on the objective of the analysis. The text discusses four general ways costs may be classified: (a) cost traceability, (b) cost behavior, (c) value-adding versus nonvalue-adding costs, and (d) costs for financial reporting.

3. Cost traceability allows managers to trace the costs related to a particular product or cost object. Such cost tracing gives managers a better idea of the actual costs to better support pricing and resource allocation decisions.
   a. Costs that can be conveniently or economically traced to a specific product or cost object are known as **direct costs.** For example, the wages of production workers may be directly traced to an individual product.
   b. **Indirect costs** are costs that cannot be conveniently or economically traced to a particular product or cost object. Examples of indirect costs include rivets used in the production of airplanes and glue used in the production of furniture. Although indirect costs may be difficult to trace, they must be included in the cost of a product. Therefore, management

accountants typically use some type of formula to assign indirect costs to the product or cost object.

4. Cost behavior concerns the way various costs change (or do not change) in relation to volume or activity of the business. Costs are typically classified as either variable costs or fixed costs. A **variable cost** is a cost that changes in direct proportion to a change in production output (or any other measure of volume). A **fixed cost** is a cost that remains constant within a defined range of activity or time period.

5. Value-adding versus nonvalue-adding costs involve managers' attempts to identify those costs that either add value to a product or service or do not add value. Such a classification can better enable managers to achieve continuous improvement in their activities. To determine if a cost is a value-adding cost, managers must be able to identify what customers value in a particular product or service. A **value-adding cost** is the cost of an activity that increases the market value of a good or service. An example of a value-adding cost would be the use of a higher quality material to increase the value in the eyes of the customer. A **nonvalue-adding cost** is the cost of an activity that adds cost to the product or service but does not increase its market value. For example, the accounting department is necessary for the operation of the business but does not add value to the product or service.

6. For financial reporting purposes, costs are classified as either product costs or period costs.
   a. **Product costs** (also called *inventoriable costs*) include the three elements of manufacturing cost—direct materials, direct labor, and manufacturing overhead. A product cost can be inventoried and remain an asset as part of the materials, work in process, or finished goods inventories. Product costs appear on the income statement as cost of goods sold or on the balance sheet as finished goods inventory.
   b. **Period costs** (also called *noninventoriable costs*) do not benefit future periods, so they are classified as expenses in the period in which they are incurred. In other words, any costs that cannot be inventoried, such as selling and administrative costs, are considered period costs and appear as operating expenses on the income statement.

Objective 3: Define and give examples of the three elements of product cost and compute a product unit cost for a manufacturing organization.

7. Manufacturing costs are classified as direct materials, direct labor, or manufacturing overhead costs (indirect manufacturing costs).
   a. **Direct materials costs** are costs of materials that can be conveniently and economically traced to specific products. Direct materials used in producing a desk are the wood used as legs, drawers, and desk top.
   b. **Direct labor costs** are the costs of labor to complete activities in the production process that can be conveniently and economically traced to specific units of product.
   c. **Manufacturing overhead costs** are production-related costs that cannot be practically or conveniently traced directly to the end product. They are also called *factory overhead, factory burden,* or *indirect manufacturing costs.* Two common components of manufacturing overhead are indirect materials and indirect labor costs.
      • **Indirect materials costs** are materials that are too insignificant to assign as part of its direct materials, such as the cost of nails, rivets, lubricants, and small tools.
      • **Indirect labor costs** are labor costs for production-related activities that cannot be conveniently traced to a product. These costs of labor include maintenance, inspection, engineering design, supervision, materials handling, and machine handling.
      • Other indirect manufacturing costs include building maintenance, machinery and tool maintenance, property taxes, property insurance, pension fund, depreciation on plant and equipment, rent, and utilities expense.

8. A **product unit cost** is made up of direct materials, direct labor, and manufacturing overhead costs. To compute a unit cost either 1) divide the total cost of direct materials, direct labor, and manufacturing overhead by the total number of units produced or 2) determine the cost per unit for each element of the product cost and add those per-unit costs. This unit cost is used for inventory pricing of finished goods inventory and as a basis for determining the price of the product. Management accountants can calculate the product unit cost using actual, normal, or standard costing methods.

a. **Actual costing** uses the *actual* costs of direct materials, direct labor, and manufacturing overhead to calculate the actual product unit cost at the end of the accounting period, when actual costs are known.

b. **Normal costing** combines the *actual* direct materials and direct labor costs and *estimated* manufacturing overhead costs in calculating a normal product unit cost. Estimated manufacturing overhead costs are *applied* to the product at a predetermined rate. Normal costing may be used at a point in time when the actual manufacturing overhead costs are not yet known.

c. **Standard costing** allows managers to use estimates (standards) of direct materials, direct labor, and manufacturing overhead costs to determine the standard product unit cost. Such standard costs are also useful to managers as a benchmark for pricing decisions and for controlling product costs.

Objective 4: Describe the flow of product-related activities, documents, and costs through the Materials Inventory, Work in Process Inventory, and Finished Goods Inventory accounts.

9. The manufacturer maintains three separate inventory accounts: **Materials Inventory, Work in Process Inventory,** and **Finished Goods Inventory.** The Materials Inventory account balance represents costs of all purchased but unused direct materials. The Work in Process Inventory account balance contains costs attached to partially completed products. The Finished Goods Inventory account balance represents the cost of products completed but not yet sold.

10. There are a number of source documents that flow through the production process in order for accountants to properly track costs and provide managers with the information they require. These documents are often used to support changes in account balances.

11. **Prime costs** are those costs that are typically the primary costs of production. These costs represent the total costs of direct materials and direct labor for a given product. **Conversion costs** are the costs of converting raw materials into finished goods, which include direct labor and manufacturing overhead costs.

12. The following represents some of the common source documents that flow through a production firm and the activities that are affected by them:

a. The purchasing starts with a *purchase request* for specific quantities of materials needed in the manufacturing process. If the materials are not on hand then the purchasing department will prepare a *purchase order* and send it to their suppliers. When the firm receives the materials they will prepare a *receiving report* confirming the accuracy of the shipment. Subsequent to the receipt of the goods received, a *vendor's invoice* is received requesting payment for the materials purchased. The cost of such materials are added to the balance in the Materials Inventory account.

b. As production begins, the storeroom clerk will receive a properly authorized *materials request form* specifying which materials should be sent to the production area. The cost of direct materials increases the balance of the Work in Process Inventory account and decreases the balance of the Materials Inventory account. Indirect materials transferred will increase the balance of the Manufacturing Overhead account and decrease the balance of the Materials Inventory account. *Time cards* are kept for production employees and the cost of their labor increases the Work in Process Inventory account. A *job order cost card* is used to record all costs incurred as the products move through production.

c. When production is completed, the balance of the Finished Goods Inventory is increased and the Work in Process Inventory is decreased. When a product is sold, a *sales invoice* is prepared while a customer's order is filled. A *shipping document* is then prepared showing the quantity and description of the goods shipped to the customer. As products are sold, the balance in the Cost of Goods Sold account increases and the balance in the Finished Goods Inventory account decreases.

13. **Manufacturing cost flow** is the flow of manufacturing costs (direct materials, direct labor, and manufacturing overhead) from their incurrence through the Materials Inventory, Work in Process Inventory, and Finished Goods Inventory accounts into the Cost of Goods Sold account. Manufacturing costs flow first into the Materials Inventory account, which is used to record the

costs of materials when they are received and again when they are issued for use in a production process. All manufacturing-related costs (direct materials, direct labor, and manufacturing overhead) are recorded in the Work in Process Inventory account as the production process begins. These total costs of direct materials, direct labor, and manufacturing overhead incurred and charged to production during an accounting period are called **total manufacturing costs.** When products are completed, the cost of all units completed and moved to the finished goods storage is the **cost of goods manufactured.** As the goods are finished, the cost of all units completed and moved to the finished goods storage is the the cost of goods manufactured. The costs of the finished goods move to the Finished Goods Inventory account from the Work in Process Inventory account.

Objective 5: Prepare a statement of cost of goods manufactured and an income statement for a manufacturing organization.

14. The manufacturer's income statement is much like that of the merchandiser. The two differences are that the manufacturer uses the heading Cost of Goods Manufactured instead of Purchases, and Finished Goods Inventory instead of Merchandise Inventory.

15. The manufacturer prepares a **statement of cost of goods manufactured** so that the cost of goods sold can be summarized in the income statement. Three steps are involved in preparing this statement, as follows:

   a. First, the cost of direct materials used must be found. (Arbitrary numbers are used here to aid understanding.)

Beginning Balance, Materials Inventory	$100
Add Direct Materials Purchases (net)	350
Cost of Direct Materials Available for Use	$450
Less Ending Balance, Materials Inventory	200
Cost of Direct Materials Used	$250 (1)

   b. Second, total manufacturing costs must be computed.

Cost of Direct Materials Used (computed in section **a**)	$ 250 (1)
Add Direct Labor Costs	900
Add Total Manufacturing Overhead Costs	750
Total Manufacturing Costs	$1,900 (2)

   c. Third, the cost of goods manufactured must be computed.

Total Manufacturing Costs (computed in section **b**)	$1,900 (2)
Add Beginning Balance, Work in Process Inventory	400
Total Cost of Work in Process During the Period	$2,300
Less Ending Balance, Work in Process Inventory	700
Cost of Goods Manufactured	$1,600 (3)

16. When the figure for the cost of goods manufactured has been computed, it can be transferred to the cost of goods sold section of the income statement, as follows:

Beginning Balance, Finished Goods Inventory	$1,250
Add Cost of Goods Manufactured (computed in section **c**)	1,600 (3)
Total Cost of Finished Goods Available for Sale	$2,850
Less Ending Balance, Finished Goods Inventory	300
Cost of Goods Sold	$2,550

17. As previously stated, a manufacturer's income statement is identical to that of a merchandiser's, with the exception of the way cost of goods sold is calculated.

Objective 6: Define *cost allocation* and explain how cost objects, cost pools, and cost drivers are used to apply manufacturing overhead.

18. Manufacturing overhead costs are indirect costs that must be collected and then applied. The process of assigning indirect costs is known as **cost allocation.** These costs are assigned to various cost objects using an allocation base that represents a major function of the business. A **cost object** is the destination of an assigned or allocated cost. In manufacturing organizations cost objects are the products being manufactured.

19. A **cost pool** is a collection of overhead costs related to a cost object (a production-related activity). A **cost driver** is an activity that causes the cost pool to increase in amount as the cost driver increases in volume.

20. The process of allocating manufacturing overhead involves the four stages of the management cycle. Step one is planning, wherein management accountants calculate a predetermined overhead rate (in traditional settings) or an activity pool rate (in activity-based costing settings). The second step (executing) applies the *estimated* manufacturing overhead costs to the product's costs as units are manufactured. In step three (reviewing), the actual manufacturing overhead costs are recorded. Step four (reporting) is a reconciliation step, whereby management accountants calculate the difference between actual manufacturing overhead costs and applied manufacturing overhead.

21. Overapplied overhead arises when applied overhead is greater than the actual overhead costs. The situation where applied overhead is less than actual overhead costs is known as underapplied overhead. The amount of overapplied (underapplied) overhead would result in the accountant decreasing (increasing) the Cost of Goods Sold account and increasing the Manufacturing Overhead control account, if the amount is not material. If the amount is material then the accountant would adjust not only the Cost of Goods Sold account but also the Work in Process Inventory and Finished Goods Inventory accounts.

22. Special care must be taken to calculate predetermined overhead rates that are as accurate as possible since managers will use them in both pricing decisions and in controlling costs. The successful allocation of manufacturing overhead costs depends on two factors—a careful estimate of the total manufacturing overhead costs and a good forecast of the activity used as the cost driver.

Objective 7: Calculate product unit cost using the traditional allocation of manufacturing overhead costs.

23. In a traditional allocation environment, one predetermined overhead rate is used to apply manufacturing overhead to a product cost. The total manufacturing overhead costs represent one cost pool, and a traditional activity base, such as direct labor hours, direct labor costs, machine hours, or units of production, becomes the cost driver.

24. The first step in calculating the product unit cost in the traditional allocation method is to compute a predetermined overhead rate. The second step is to apply manufacturing overhead to the products using the rate calculated in step one and multiplying by the cost driver (e.g., direct labor hours, direct labor costs, etc.).

25. For example, assume the following: We estimate total manufacturing overhead to be $100,000 and our cost driver (direct labor hours) is estimated to be 5,000 hours. Actual direct labor hours total 4,500 with 2,000 related to the production of Product A and 2,500 to Product B. We produced a total of 6,000 units of Product A and 7,000 of Product B.

   a. Our predetermined overhead rate would be:

   $$\frac{\$100,000}{5,000} = \$20 \text{ per Direct Labor Hour}$$

   b. The next step is to apply manufacturing overhead to both products:

A: 2,000 D.L. Hours × $20 Rate	=	$40,000
B: 2,500 D.L. Hours × $20 Rate	=	50,000
Total Applied		$90,000

   Thus, applied overhead is:

   $$A: \frac{\$40,000 \text{ Applied}}{6,000 \text{ Units}} = \$6.67 \text{ per Unit}$$

   $$B: \frac{\$50,000 \text{ Applied}}{7,000 \text{ Units}} = \$7.14 \text{ per Unit}$$

   c. If actual manufacturing overhead were indeed $100,000, we would have $10,000 underapplied manufacturing overhead ($100,000 actual minus $90,000 applied).

Objective 8: Calculate product unit cost using activity-based costing to assign manufacturing overhead costs.

26. **Activity-based costing (ABC)** is a method of assigning costs that calculates a more accurate product cost by categorizing all indirect costs by activity, tracing the indirect costs to those activities, and assigning activity costs to products using a cost driver that is related to the cause of the cost. The first step in calculating product unit cost using activity-based costing is to estimate the total manufacturing overhead costs and then group these costs in appropriate activity pools related to specific activities. After identifying the appropriate number of activity pools and a cost driver, estimated activity pool amounts and estimated cost driver levels must be determined. The next step is to calculate an activity cost rate for each activity pool. The cost pool rate is the estimated activity

pool amount divided by the estimated cost driver level. Manufacturing overhead costs are then applied to the products by using the cost driver (activity) levels for each cost driver multiplied by the appropriate rate.

27. Step 1: Calculate the overhead activity cost rates as shown in the first table on this page.

28. Step 2: Apply manufacturing overhead costs to production as shown in the second table on this page.

29. The example shown in the second table at the bottom of this page shows that the manufacturing overhead cost for Product B was lower than that for Product A. The reason for this difference primarily relates to the larger number of setups and inspections required for Product A compared to Product B. As a result of this costing method, management may want to investigate why Product A requires so many more setups and inspections compared to B. This method provides a more accurate product unit cost.

Objective 9: Apply costing concepts to a service organization.

30. When you shift from a manufacturing environment to a service-oriented environment, the only major difference is that you are no longer dealing with a product that can be assembled, stored, and valued. Services are rendered and cannot be stored up or placed in inventory. Of the three manufacturing cost elements, direct materials cost is no longer applicable to the pricing mechanism. Service costing consists of direct labor and service overhead costs. For the most part, service costing is for cost control and pricing purposes.

Activity Pool	Estimated Activity Pool Amount	Cost Driver	Cost Driver Level	Activity Cost Rate
Setup	$10,000	Number of setups	100 setups	$100 per setup
Inspection	8,000	Number of inspections	400 inspections	$20 per inspection
Building	7,000	Machine hours	3,500 machine hours	$2 per machine hour
Packaging	5,000 $30,000	Packaging hours	1,000 packaging hours	$5 per packaging hour

			Product A	Product B	
Activity Pool	Activity Cost Rate	Cost Driver Level	Cost Applied	Cost Driver Level	Cost Applied
Setup	$100	70	$ 7,000	30	$ 3,000
Inspection	20	250	5,000	150	3,000
Building	2	1,500	3,000	2,000	4,000
Packaging	5	300	1,500	700	3,500
Total			$16,500		$13,500
÷ by Number of Units			1,000		2,000
= Manufacturing Overhead Cost per Unit			$16.50		$6.75

SELF-TEST

Test your knowledge of the chapter by choosing the best answer for each of the following items.

1. Manufacturing overhead costs include all of the following *except*
   a. direct labor.
   b. indirect labor.
   c. indirect materials.
   d. other indirect manufacturing costs.

2. Total product cost would include
   a. direct labor.
   b. indirect labor.
   c. manufacturing overhead.
   d. all of the above.

3. Which of the following documents is *not* used to account for the cost of materials?
   a. Receiving report
   b. Purchase order
   c. Job card
   d. Purchase request

4. Which of the following documents starts the purchasing process?
   a. Purchase order
   b. Purchase request
   c. Materials request
   d. Vendor's invoice

5. All manufacturing costs incurred and assigned to products currently being produced are classified as
   a. work in process inventory costs.
   b. materials inventory costs.
   c. finished goods inventory costs.
   d. costs of goods sold.

6. Given estimated total manufacturing overhead costs of $100,000, estimated total direct labor hours (cost driver) of 10,000, and units produced of 6,000, the predetermined overhead rate under the traditional approach to allocating overhead is
   a. 10 percent.
   b. 6 percent.
   c. $6.
   d. $10.

7. If the beginning Materials Inventory account balance was $4,200, the ending balance was $3,940, and $21,560 of materials were used during the month, what was the cost of the materials purchased during this time period?
   a. $21,600
   b. $21,820
   c. $21,790
   d. $21,300

8. At Price Company, the month-end cost of goods sold was $393,910, the beginning finished goods inventory was $40,410, and the ending finished goods inventory was $42,900. What was the total cost of completed goods transferred to finished goods inventory during the month?
   a. $396,400
   b. $391,120
   c. $391,420
   d. $393,400

9. Underapplied manufacturing overhead would result if
   a. actual manufacturing overhead is less than estimated manufacturing overhead.
   b. applied overhead is less than actual manufacturing overhead.
   c. applied overhead is greater than actual manufacturing overhead.
   d. the cost of indirect materials is less than estimated.

10. One of the key differences between activity-based costing (ABC) and traditional costing is that
    a. traditional costing methods use multiple activity pools.
    b. ABC uses multiple activity pools.
    c. ABC uses a single activity pool.
    d. ABC uses a single cost driver.

TESTING YOUR KNOWLEDGE

Matching*

Match each term with its definition by writing the appropriate letter in the blank.

_____ 1. Time card

_____ 2. Manufacturing overhead

_____ 3. Direct materials

_____ 4. Indirect materials

_____ 5. Direct labor

_____ 6. Indirect labor

_____ 7. Cost driver

_____ 8. Cost pool

_____ 9. Standard costing

_____ 10. Total product costs

_____ 11. Work in Process Inventory account

_____ 12. Finished Goods Inventory account

_____ 13. Cost of goods manufactured

_____ 14. Total manufacturing costs

_____ 15. Cost allocation

a. Materials that cannot be conveniently and economically traced to specific products

b. Materials that can be conveniently and economically traced to specific products

c. All indirect manufacturing costs

d. Wages, salaries, and related costs that cannot be conveniently and economically traced to specific products

e. Total costs charged to completed units during the period

f. Direct labor, direct materials, manufacturing overhead

g. Wages, salaries, and related costs that can be conveniently and economically traced to specific products

h. A record of the number of hours worked by an employee

i. The assignment of a specific cost to a specific cost objective

j. An activity that causes the activity pool to increase in amount

k. A collection of overhead costs or other indirect costs related to a cost object

l. Holds the costs assigned to all completed units that haven't been sold

m. A method of cost measurement that uses the estimated costs of direct materials, direct labor, and manufacturing overhead to calculate a product unit cost

n. Total costs charged to production during the period

o. Records all manufacturing costs incurred and assigned to partially completed units of product

Short Answer

Use the lines provided to answer each item.

1. Manufacturers have three types of inventory. Name them.

_____

_____

_____

2. What are the three chief components of manufacturing costs?

_____

_____

_____

_____

Note to student: The matching quiz might be completed more efficiently by starting with the definition and searching for the corresponding term.

3. When is a materials cost considered to be a direct materials cost?

_____

_____

4. State four ways that managers use product costing information.

_____

_____

_____

_____

5. Show how cost of direct materials used is computed.

_____

+ _____

= _____

− _____

= _____

6. Show how total manufacturing costs are computed.

_____

+ _____

+ _____

= _____

7. Show how cost of goods manufactured is computed.

_____

+ _____

= _____

− _____

= _____

8. Explain how a predetermined overhead rate is computed.

_____

_____

_____

_____

9. What is overapplied manufacturing overhead?

_____

_____

_____

_____

10. What is cost of goods manufactured?

_____

_____

_____

_____

True-False

Circle T if the statement is true, F if it is false. Please provide explanations for the false answers, using the blank lines at the end of the section.

T F **1.** A product cost should not appear in the income statement until the period in which the product is sold.

T F **2.** The Work in Process Inventory account does not contain any period costs (expenses).

T F **3.** Activity-based costing uses multiple cost pools.

T F **4.** Factory burden is another term for manufacturing overhead.

T F **5.** The Materials Inventory account decreases as materials are used in production.

T F **6.** Most costs incurred by a manufacturer and called product costs are also incurred by a service organization.

T F **7.** An example of a cost driver used in ABC is number of inspections.

T F **8.** A purchase order is prepared before the purchase request.

T F   9. Factory supervisory costs are classified as direct labor.

T F 10. The statement of cost of goods manufactured must be prepared after the income statement.

T F 11. For the manufacturer to compute cost of goods sold, the beginning finished goods amount must be known.

T F 12. Cost of goods manufactured minus total manufacturing costs equals the change in Work in Process Inventory during the period.

T F 13. Cost of goods manufactured must be computed before total manufacturing costs.

T F 14. Cost of materials used must be computed before cost of goods manufactured.

T F 15. Activity-based costing calculates a more accurate product cost than traditional costing methods.

T F 16. An increase in the amount of an activity pool indicates that the cost driver has increased.

T F 17. As cost objects become smaller, manufacturing costs are more easily traceable to those objects.

T F 18. Depreciation on plant and equipment is a direct cost.

Circle the letter of the best answer.

1. Which of the following is considered a direct materials cost?
   a. The cost of glue used in making a bookcase
   b. The janitor's salary
   c. The cost of legs used in making a chair
   d. The cost of rags used in cleaning a machine

2. Documents relating to materials must be processed in a specific order. Which of the following lists those documents in their proper order?
   a. Materials request, purchase request, purchase order, receiving report
   b. Purchase order, purchase request, receiving report, materials request
   c. Purchase request, purchase order, receiving report, materials request
   d. Receiving report, purchase order, materials request, purchase request

3. Which of the following would probably be considered a period cost?
   a. Salaries paid to the salespeople
   b. Wages paid to an assembly-line worker
   c. Freight in
   d. Materials used in the manufacture of a product

4. A document sent to the vendor to buy goods is a
   a. purchase request.
   b. materials request.
   c. receiving report.
   d. purchase order.

5. Before materials can be issued into production, which form should be presented to the storeroom clerk?
   a. Materials request
   b. Purchase request
   c. Job card
   d. Purchase order

6. "Activities" in activity-based costing are analogous to
   a. cost objects.
   b. activity pools.
   c. cost drivers.
   d. manufacturing overhead.

7. Activity pools in activity-based costing are
   a. usually fewer in number than in traditional costing systems.
   b. used to accumulate costs.
   c. the products being manufactured.
   d. the same as overapplied manufacturing overhead.

8. In traditional costing systems, how many cost drivers are typically used?
   a. 1
   b. 2
   c. 3
   d. 4

9. Managers use product cost information in which of the management cycle steps?
   a. Planning
   b. Executing
   c. Reviewing
   d. All of the above

APPLYING YOUR KNOWLEDGE

Exercises

1. Katori Corporation has provided the following data for 20xx:

Cost of Goods Manufactured	$450,000
Finished Goods, Jan. 1	75,000
Finished Goods, Dec. 31	80,000
Direct materials, Jan. 1	92,000
Direct materials, Dec. 31	70,000
Work in Process, Jan. 1	55,000
Work in Process, Dec. 31	64,000

In the space provided at right, compute Cost of Goods Sold.

2. Given the data below, calculate the activity pool rates, total costs applied, costs applied to Product A and Product B, and the overhead cost per unit.

Activity Pool	Estimated Activity Pool Amount	Cost Driver	Cost Driver Level	Activity Cost Rate
Setup	$10,000	Number of setups	200 setups	$
Inspection	6,000	Number of inspections	300 inspections	
Building	8,000	Machine hours	4,000 machine hours	
Packaging	4,000 $28,000	Packaging hours	1,000 packaging hours	$

		Product A		Product B	
Activity Pool	Activity Cost Rate	Cost Driver Level	Cost Applied	Cost Driver Level	Cost Applied
Setup	$	70	$	30	$
Inspection		250		150	
Building		1,500		2,000	
Packaging		300	_____	700	_____
Total			$		$
÷ by Number of Units			1,000		2,000
= Manufacturing Overhead Cost per Unit			$		$

3. Given the following accounting data, complete the statement of cost of goods manufactured for Spencer Company in the form provided below.

Depreciation, Factory Building and Equipment	$ 31,800
Direct Labor	142,900
Factory Insurance	2,300
Factory Utilities Expense	26,000
Finished Goods Inventory, Jan. 1	82,400
Finished Goods Inventory, Dec. 31	71,000
General and Administrative Expenses	163,000
Indirect Labor	42,800
Net Sales	855,100
Other Factory Costs	12,600
Materials Inventory, Jan. 1	8,700
Materials Inventory, Dec. 31	32,600
Materials Purchased (net)	168,300
Selling Expenses	88,500
Work in Process Inventory, Jan. 1	34,200
Work in Process Inventory, Dec. 31	28,700

Spencer Company
Statement of Cost of Goods Manufactured
For the Year Ended December 31, 20xx

4. Classify each of the following costs as direct materials, direct labor, or manufacturing overhead by using the letters DM, DL, or OH.

_____ **a.** Sandpaper

_____ **b.** Worker who assembles the product

_____ **c.** Worker who cleans and sets up machinery

_____ **d.** Steel plates used in production

_____ **e.** Glue and nails

_____ **f.** Worker who sands product before painting

_____ **g.** Wheels attached to product

_____ **h.** Depreciation of machinery

_____ **i.** Paint used to touch up finished product

Crossword Puzzle
for Chapters 19 and 20

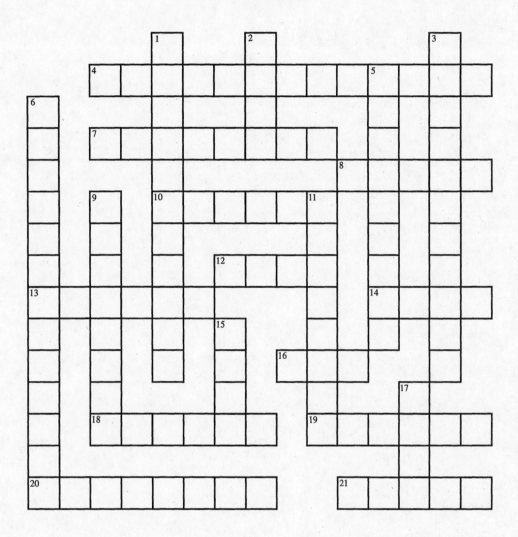

ACROSS

4. Document sent to a supplier (2 words)
7. Not traceable to specific products
8. Normal inventory account balance
10. _____ goods manufactured (2 words)
12. Begin the management cycle
13. Noninventoriable (cost)
14. Indirect material item
16. Management report audience
18. Activity that increases cost pool
19. Traceable to specific products
20. Allowable product unit cost
21. The "T" of "TQM"

DOWN

1. Expenditure traceable to goods (2 words)
2. Predetermined overhead _____
3. Materials request
5. _____ report (prepared when goods arrive)
6. Goods partially complete (3 words)
9. Indirect manufacturing costs
11. _____ goods (ready-for-sale inventory)
15. Employee _____ cards
17. Example of 9-Down

CHAPTER 21 COSTING SYSTEMS: JOB ORDER AND PROCESS COSTING

REVIEWING THE CHAPTER

Objective 1: Discuss the role information about costs plays in the management cycle and explain why product unit cost is important.

1. The role of the management accountant is to develop a management information system that provides managers with the information they need.

2. Costing information is used in each stage of the management cycle. During the planning stage, managers use information about costs to set performance expectations, estimate service or product costs, and set selling prices in both manufacturing and service organizations. During the executing stage, managers use information about costs in controlling costs, managing the company's activity volume, assuring quality, and negotiating prices. During the reviewing stage, managers watch for changes in cost or quality by comparing actual and targeted total and unit costs and by monitoring price and volume information. During the reporting stage, actual and targeted total and unit costs are compared and performance is evaluated for future planning and decision-making strategies.

Objective 2: Distinguish between the different types of product costing systems and identify the information each provides.

3. A **product costing system** is a set of procedures used to account for an organization's product costs and provide timely and accurate unit cost information for pricing, cost planning and control, inventory valuation, and financial statement preparation. Two basic approaches to cost accounting systems are job order costing and process costing.

4. A **job order costing system** is used in companies that manufacture large, one-of-a-kind, or special-order products, such as ships, wedding invitations, or bridges. Under a job order system, direct materials, direct labor, and manufacturing overhead are traced to specific job orders or batches of products. A **job order** is a customer order for a specific number of specially designed, made-to-order products.

5. A **process costing system** is used when a large number of similar products are being manufactured, typically by continuous production flow. Companies producing paint, automobiles, or breakfast cereal would probably use some form of a process costing system. Under such a system, direct materials, direct labor, and manufacturing overhead are first traced to processes or work cells and then assigned to the products produced by those processes or work cells. A separate Work in Process Inventory account is used for each process, department or work cell.

6. Few actual production processes match a job order costing or process costing system exactly. As a result, most product costing systems combine parts of both job order costing and process costing.

7. In recent years, new approaches have evolved regarding product costing. These approaches emphasize the elimination of waste, the importance

of quality, value-added processing, and increased customer satisfaction.

Objective 3: Explain the cost flow in a job order costing system for a manufacturing company.

8. In a job order costing system, there is a specific procedure for recording materials, labor, and manufacturing overhead. This costing system is designed to gather costs for a specific order or batch of products. The costs are connected with specific jobs by means of **job order cost cards.** One job order cost card is maintained for each job to accumulate its costs. The job order cost cards for all uncompleted jobs make up the subsidiary ledger for the Work in Process Inventory account.

9. It is important to understand how the various costs are incurred, recorded, and transferred within the system. This cost flow, along with the job order cost cards and the subsidiary ledgers for materials and finished goods inventories, forms the core of the job order costing system, as illustrated below.

   a. The purchase of materials or supplies is recorded by increasing Materials Inventory and decreasing Cash or increasing Accounts Payable.

   b. When materials or supplies are issued into production, Work in Process Inventory is increased for the direct materials portion, Manufacturing Overhead is increased for the indirect materials portion, and Materials Inventory is reduced.

   c. The total cost of wages earned during the period by all production employees increases the Factory Payroll account and increases the Wages Payable account. The factory payroll is distributed to the production accounts by increasing the Work in Process Inventory for direct labor, increasing Manufacturing Overhead for indirect labor, and decreasing Factory Payroll for the total amount.

   d. Manufacturing overhead costs, other than indirect materials and indirect labor, increase Manufacturing Overhead and decrease an appropriate account, such as Cash or Accounts Payable.

   e. Manufacturing overhead is applied to specific jobs by increasing the Work in Process Inventory account and reducing the Manufacturing Overhead account.

   f. Upon the completion of a specific job, Finished Goods Inventory is increased and Work in Process Inventory is decreased.

   g. When the finished goods are sold, there are two effects. First, the sale is recorded by increasing Cash or Accounts Receivable and increasing Sales for the total sales price. Second, Cost of Goods Sold is recognized and Finished Goods Inventory is reduced for the cost attached to the goods sold.

   h. At the end of the period, an adjustment must be made for under- or overapplied overhead.

Objective 4: Prepare a job order cost card and compute a job order's product unit cost.

10. Each job has a job cost card, which becomes part of the subsidiary ledger to support the Work in Process Inventory account. The job cost card includes the costs of direct materials used, direct labor, and manufacturing overhead assigned to the job. When the job is completed, the product unit cost is computed by dividing the total costs for the job by the number of goods units produced.

11. Many service organizations use job order costing to compute the cost of providing their services. Because service organizations do not manufacture products, they have little or no cost for materials.

12. Job order cost cards are used to track the costs of labor, materials and supplies, and service overhead for a job. Many times service jobs are based on **cost-plus contracts** that require the customer to pay all costs plus a predetermined amount of profit.

13. At the completion of a job, the costs on the completed job order cost card become the cost of services. The cost of services is adjusted at the end of the accounting period for the difference between the applied service overhead costs and the actual service overhead costs.

Objective 5: Explain the product flow and cost flow in a process costing system.

14. Before a product is completed, it usually must go through several departments. For example, a bookcase might go through the cutting, assembling, and staining departments. In a process cost system, a separate Work in Process Inventory account is maintained for each department. Each Work in Process Inventory account contains costs of direct materials (if any), direct labor, and manufacturing overhead for that department plus any costs that have been transferred in from the previous department.

15. When goods are mass-produced, they normally flow in a first-in, first-out (FIFO) manner. Although the assumption of cost flows may be FIFO based, an average costing method can be used instead for a process costing system.

16. The **FIFO costing method** is more widely used and more accurate than average costing. Under this method, the cost flow follows the logical flow of production. The costs assigned to the first materials processed in a department are the first costs transferred out when those materials flow to the next department.

Objective 6: Prepare a process cost report.

17. A **process cost report** is a three-part report managers use to track and analyze costs in a process costing system. The process cost report consists of the schedule of equivalent production, the unit cost analysis schedule, and the cost summary schedule.

18. **Equivalent production** (also called *equivalent units*) is a measure of the number of equivalent whole units produced during a given period of time. Under the FIFO costing method, equivalent production equals the sum of (a) the number of units started and completed during the period and (b) the number of equivalent whole units produced from both beginning and ending work in process inventory. In the latter computation, a "percentage of completion" factor must be applied to partially completed units.

19. Equivalent production must be computed separately for direct materials and conversion costs. **Conversion costs,** which are the combined total costs of direct labor and manufacturing overhead, are often incurred uniformly throughout the production process. Direct materials are usually added to the production process at the beginning of the process; therefore, equivalent units for materials typically reflect 100 percent completion.

20. The computation of equivalent production for conversion costs consists of three components: the cost to finish the beginning work in process, the cost to begin and finish the completed units, and the cost to begin work on the units in the ending work in process inventory.

21. A **schedule of equivalent production** is used to compute a period's equivalent production for both direct materials costs and conversion costs.

22. The purposes of a **unit cost analysis schedule** are to (a) accumulate all costs charged to the Work in Process Inventory account of each department, production process, or work cell and (b) compute the cost per equivalent unit for both direct materials and conversion costs. The schedule is divided into a Total Cost Analysis section and a Computation of Equivalent Unit Costs section.
   a. The total cost analysis consists of beginning inventory costs plus current period costs for both direct materials and conversion costs. The result is total costs to be accounted for.
   b. Equivalent unit costs equal the current period's direct materials and conversion costs divided by equivalent units for direct materials and conversion costs from the schedule of equivalent production.

23. The **cost summary schedule** distributes total costs accumulated during the period to units in ending work in process inventory or to units completed and transferred out of the department. Information for the cost summary schedule is taken from the schedule of equivalent production and the unit cost analysis schedule. When figures for the cost of ending work in process inventory and the cost of goods transferred out of the department are determined, they are totaled and compared with the total costs to be accounted for in the unit cost analysis schedule.
   a. The cost of goods transferred out of the department is arrived at as follows: (1) Determine the cost connected to units in beginning work in process inventory (same as the ending work in process inventory of the preceding period). (2) Figure the costs necessary to complete the units in beginning inventory by using unit cost and equivalent unit figures. (3) Multiply units started and completed by the total unit cost as computed in the unit cost analysis schedule. (4) Add the amounts together. When there are no units in beginning work in process inventory, the cost of goods transferred out of the department consists entirely of the cost of units started and completed during the period.
   b. The cost of ending work in process inventory is arrived at as follows: (1) Multiply equivalent units for materials in ending work in process inventory by the unit cost as computed in the unit cost analysis schedule. (2) Multiply equivalent units for conversion costs in ending work in process inventory by the unit cost as

computed in the unit cost analysis schedule. (3) Add the two amounts together.

Objective 7: Evaluate operating performance using information about product cost.

24. Job order and process costing systems provide managers with useful information regarding operating performance. Both systems provide the following measurements that help managers analyze operating efficiency: (a) cost trends, (b) units produced per period, (c) materials usage per unit produced, (d) labor cost per unit, (e) special order needs of customers, and (f) comparisons of the cost-effectiveness of changing to a more advanced production process.

25. Such cost information can assist managers in making decisions such as: (a) pricing decisions, (b) reporting amounts on financial statements, (c) cost reduction, and (d) to change technology employed in the production process.

SELF-TEST

Test your knowledge of the chapter by choosing the best answer for each of the following items.

1. Which of the following industries is most likely to use the job order costing system?
   a. Jet aircraft company
   b. Paint producing company
   c. Soft drink producing company
   d. Oil refining company

2. An approach to product costing that assigns all types of manufacturing costs to a specific order or batch of products is known as
   a. job order costing.
   b. process costing.
   c. total costing.
   d. absorption costing.

3. Which of the following industries is most likely to use a process costing system?
   a. Bridge-building company
   b. Oil-refining company
   c. Highway construction company
   d. Made-to-order boat company

4. How many Work in Process Inventory accounts will a company using a process costing system have in its product costing process?
   a. Depends on the number of products produced
   b. Only one
   c. One for each department or process
   d. Always three

5. If a department using a FIFO process costing system had 1,400 units in beginning Work in Process Inventory 40 percent complete, started and completed 4,900 units, and had 1,200 units in ending Work in Process Inventory 60 percent complete, what is the number of equivalent units for materials costs, assuming materials are added at the beginning of the process?
   a. 6,100
   b. 7,500
   c. 6,300
   d. 4,900

6. Assuming the same facts as in **5**, what is the number of equivalent units for conversion costs when those costs are incurred uniformly throughout the process?
   a. 6,180
   b. 7,120
   c. 6,460
   d. 7,500

7. The key document used for tracking product costs in a job order cost system is a job order
   a. materials receiving report.
   b. cost card.
   c. requisition form.
   d. materials requisition card.

8. Melnor Products, Inc., produces deluxe office desks. During January, the following costs were incurred to complete Job ACA 12: direct materials, $12,210; supplies, $1,440; direct labor, $3,460; and indirect labor, $5,200. Manufacturing overhead was applied at a rate of $35 per machine hour, and the job required 670 machine hours. If the job called for 96 deluxe desks, how much did each desk cost to produce?
   a. $694.06
   b. $476.66
   c. $232.40
   d. $407.50

9. The Hood Corporation had the following information generated for May:

   Beginning work in process inventory: 1,000 units, 50 percent complete; direct materials cost, $14,700; conversion costs, $13,550

   Units started and completed: 8,000

   Ending work in process inventory: 640 units, 80 percent complete

   Current period costs: direct materials, $127,872; conversion, $243,324

   Equivalent units: direct materials costs, 8,640 units; conversion costs, 9,012 units

   Direct materials added at the beginning of the process and conversion costs incurred uniformly throughout the process

   If the corporation uses the FIFO process costing approach, what is the unit cost for materials for May?
   a. $27.10
   b. $27.00
   c. $14.70
   d. $14.80

10. Assuming the same facts as in **9**, what is the unit cost for conversion costs for May?
    a. $27.10
    b. $27.00
    c. $14.70
    d. $14.80

TESTING YOUR KNOWLEDGE

Matching*

Match each term with its definition by writing the appropriate letter in the blank.

_____ 1. Process costing system

_____ 2. Schedule of equivalent production

_____ 3. Unit cost analysis schedule

_____ 4. Conversion costs

_____ 5. Job order costing system

_____ 6. Job order cost cards

_____ 7. Job order

_____ 8. Manufacturing Overhead account

_____ 9. Equivalent production (equivalent units)

a. An accounting record that contains indirect factory costs incurred and applied

b. The accounting method used by a manufacturer of one-of-a-kind or special order products

c. The accounting method used when large quantities of identical products are being produced

d. Records of the accumulation of job costs

e. A customer order for a specific number of special-order products

f. The combined total of direct labor and manufacturing overhead costs incurred by a department

g. The schedule that computes a cost-per-unit figure

h. Whole units produced, taking into consideration partially completed units

i. The schedule in which equivalent unit production is computed

Short Answer

Use the lines provided to answer each item.

1. What three schedules are prepared in a process costing system? List them in their order of preparation.

   _____

   _____

   _____

2. Show the computation for equivalent units, under the FIFO costing approach.

   _____

   + _____

   + _____

   = _____

3. What two items are computed in the cost summary schedule?

   _____

   _____

4. List three examples of products for which a job order cost system should be used.

   _____

   _____

   _____

Note to student: The matching quiz might be completed more efficiently by starting with the definition and searching for the corresponding term.

Circle T if the statement is true, F if it is false. Please provide explanations for the false answers, using the blank lines at the end of the section.

T F 1. The factory payroll is distributed to production by increasing Work in Process Inventory (for direct labor), reducing Manufacturing Overhead (for indirect labor), and reducing Factory Payroll.

T F 2. When overhead costs are applied to specific jobs, Work in Process Inventory is increased and Manufacturing Overhead is decreased.

T F 3. When goods are shipped to the customer, Cost of Goods Sold should be increased and Work in Process Inventory decreased.

T F 4. A manufacturer of custom-made clothing would probably use a job order costing system.

T F 5. A job order costing system normally uses a periodic inventory system.

T F 6. The cost information needed in computing product unit cost may be found on the completed job order cost cards.

T F 7. Because process costing is used where large quantities of identical items are being produced, only one Work in Process Inventory account is ever needed.

T F 8. Manufacturing overhead must be applied to production for the period.

T F 9. The unit cost analysis schedule must be prepared before the cost summary schedule.

T F 10. In a process costing system, ending Work in Process Inventory is determined by multiplying total units by total cost per unit.

T F 11. When goods are completed in Department 1 and transferred to Department 2, Finished Goods Inventory is debited and Work in Process—Department 1 is credited.

T F 12. Units completed minus units in beginning inventory equal units started and completed (assuming that all units in beginning inventory have been completed).

T F 13. The computational check for total costs to be accounted for is made in the unit cost analysis schedule.

_____

_____

_____

_____

_____

_____

_____

_____

_____

_____

_____

Multiple Choice

Circle the letter of the best answer.

1. A certain department started and completed 10,000 units during the period. Beginning inventory of 5,000 units was 60 percent complete for conversion costs, and ending inventory of 7,000 units was 30 percent complete for conversion costs. What is equivalent production for conversion costs for the period, under the FIFO costing method?
   a. 4,000 units
   b. 14,100 units
   c. 15,000 units
   d. 17,100 units

2. Which of the following is *not* a schedule prepared under a process costing system?
   a. Cost summary schedule
   b. Schedule of equivalent production
   c. Schedule of conversion costs
   d. Unit cost analysis schedule

3. Which of the following is *not* a component of cost of goods transferred out of the department in the cost summary schedule?
   a. Costs necessary to complete units in beginning inventory
   b. Costs attached to units in beginning inventory
   c. Costs of units started and completed
   d. Costs necessary to complete units in ending inventory

4. Unit costs will not appear on which of the following schedules?
   a. Schedule of equivalent production
   b. Unit cost analysis schedule
   c. Cost summary schedule
   d. Unit costs appear in each of these schedules.

5. A job order costing system would most likely be used by the manufacturer of which of the following?
   a. Paper clips
   b. Gasoline
   c. Supersonic jets
   d. Electric typewriters

6. A process costing system does *not*
   a. contain several Work in Process Inventory accounts.
   b. accumulate manufacturing costs by job or batch of products.
   c. base costing on weekly or monthly time periods.
   d. apply to continuous production flow situations.

7. A job order costing system
   a. accumulates manufacturing costs and assigns them to specific jobs.
   b. measures costs for each completed job.
   c. uses one Work in Process Inventory account.
   d. has all of the above characteristics.

8. A process costing system
   a. collects manufacturing costs and groups them by department, work center, or work cell.
   b. accumulates manufacturing costs and assigns them to specific jobs.
   c. measures costs for each completed job.
   d. uses one Work in Process Inventory account.

9. Which of the following product costing measurements can help managers analyze operating efficiency?
   a. Cost trend of a product
   b. Materials usage per unit
   c. Labor cost per unit
   d. All of the above will assist managers.

10. A process costing system would be used by companies that produce all of the following *except*
    a. beverages.
    b. computers.
    c. specialty suits.
    d. vacuum cleaners.

APPLYING YOUR KNOWLEDGE

Exercises

1. Data for Department 1 of the Morris Manufacturing Company for the month of May are as follows:

   Beginning Work in Process Inventory
   Units = 2,000
   Direct materials = 100% complete
   Conversion costs = 30% complete
   Direct materials costs = $12,000
   Conversion costs = $3,000

   Ending Work in Process Inventory
   Direct materials = 100% complete
   Conversion costs = 30% complete

   Operations for May
   Units started = 24,000
   Direct materials costs = $114,000
   Conversion costs = $30,750
   Units completed and transferred to the next department = 19,000

   Assuming a FIFO costing method, complete the three schedules that follow. Round off unit cost computations to three decimal places.

		Equivalent Units	
Units—Stage of Completion	Units to Be Accounted For	Materials Costs	Conversion Costs

Morris Manufacturing Company
Schedule of Equivalent Production
For the Month Ended May 31, 20xx

Morris Manufacturing Company
Unit Cost Analysis Schedule
For the Month Ended May 31, 20xx

	Total Costs			Equivalent Unit Costs	
	Costs from Beginning Inventory	Costs from Current Period	Total Costs to Be Accounted For	Equivalent Units	Cost per Equivalent Unit
Direct materials costs					
Conversion costs					
Totals					

Morris Manufacturing Company
Cost Summary Schedule
For the Month Ended May 31, 20xx

	Cost of Goods Transferred to Next Department	Cost of Ending Work in Process Inventory
Beginning inventory		
Units started and completed		
Ending inventory		
Computational check:		

2. Brockton Shoe Company manufactures shoes of unusual lengths and widths on special order. For each of the following sets of facts, enter increases and decreases in the T-accounts provided below. Assume that the company uses a job order costing system.

Dec. 23 Purchased (on credit) materials costing $2,950.
26 Issued materials costing $850 into production. Of this amount, $50 was for indirect materials.
26 Paid the following bills:

Utilities	$350
Rent	$700
Telephone	$150

27 The week's gross payroll of $1,500 was distributed to production accounts. Of this amount, 80 percent represents direct labor. (Do not prepare the entries when the payroll is *paid*.)

27 The week's overhead costs are applied to production based on direct labor dollars. Estimated overhead for the year is $165,000, and estimated direct labor dollars are $55,000.
29 Goods costing $3,900 were completed.
30 Finished goods costing $2,000 were shipped to a customer. The selling price was 70 percent greater than the cost, and payment for the goods is expected next month.
31 Applied overhead for the year was $132,500, and actual overhead was $130,000. The difference is closed into Cost of Goods Sold.

Materials Inventory

Accounts Payable

Work In Process Inventory

Manufacturing Overhead

Factory Payroll

Cash

Finished Goods Inventory

Cost of Goods Sold

Sales

Accounts Receivable

Crossword Puzzle
for Chapter 21

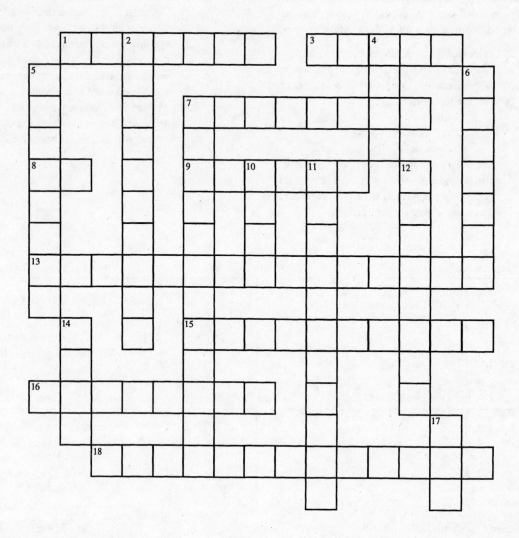

ACROSS

1. _____ Payroll account
3. Management process divided into stages
7. Outlay per manufactured item (2 words)
8. Cost _____ goods sold
9. Cost that can be traced to a specific job or product
13. Productive output of 6-Down (2 words)
15. Manufacturing output
16. First stage of 3-Across
18. With 10-Down, used in applying overhead to jobs

DOWN

2. Direct labor and factory overhead costs
4. _____-plus contract
5. Costing system for batches of products (2 words)
6. Costing system for mass production
7. Actual overhead exceeding allocated overhead
10. See 18-Across
11. Schedule used in 6-Down (2 words)
12. Manufacturing task or function
14. Work center
17. For each, as in cost for each unit

CHAPTER 22 ACTIVITY-BASED SYSTEMS: ACTIVITY-BASED MANAGEMENT AND JUST-IN-TIME

REVIEWING THE CHAPTER

Objective 1: Explain the role of activity-based systems in the management cycle.

1. Activity-based systems are information systems that provide quantitative information about activities in an organization and that improve the cost information supplied to managers. They enable managers to improve operating processes and make better pricing decisions.

2. Activity-based systems provide useful information to managers in each stage of the management cycle. In the planning stage, activity-based systems assist managers in identifying value-adding activities, determining the required resources for such activities, and estimating service costs. In the executing and reviewing stages, activity-based systems assist managers in determining the **full product cost** (which includes not only the costs of direct materials and direct labor but also the costs of all production and nonproduction activities), identifying actions that may reduce costs, and determining if cost reduction goals were achieved. In the reporting stage, managers receive information regarding cost of inventory and the degree to which product goals were achieved.

Objective 2: Define *activity-based management (ABM)* and discuss its relationship with the supply network and the value chain.

3. **Activity-based management** (ABM) is an approach to managing an organization that identifies all major operating activities, determines what resources are consumed by each activity, identifies how resources are consumed by each activity, and categorizes the activities as either adding value to a product or service or not adding value.

4. Activity-based management, which focuses on the reduction or elimination of nonvalue-adding activities, is helpful for both strategic planning and operational decision making because it provides financial and operational performance information at the activity level that is useful for making decisions about business segments, such as product lines, market segments, and customer groups. It also helps managers eliminate waste and inefficiencies and redirect resources to activities that add value to the product or service.

5. Managers utilize two tools of ABM: supply networks and value chains. A **supply network** is an interdependent web of organizations that supply materials, products, or services to a customer. If managers better understand their product's or service's supply network, they can better understand their organization's role in providing services or products to their customers. A **value chain** is a related sequence of value-creating activities within an organization. The value chain differs from company to company depending on a number of variables, including the size of the company and the types of products or services sold. A company can increase its profitability by understanding not only its value chain, but also how its value-adding activities fit into its suppliers' and customers' value chains.

Objective 3: Distinguish between value-adding and nonvalue-adding activities, and describe process value analysis.

6. A **value-adding activity** is an activity that adds value to a product or service from the customer's perspective. Examples include assembling a car, painting a car, and installing brakes on a car. A **nonvalue-adding activity** is an activity that adds cost to a product or service but does not increase its market value. Examples include moving materials and storing materials. By identifying nonvalue-adding activities, organizations can reduce costs and redirect resources to value-adding activities.

7. **Process value analysis (PVA)** is an analytical method of identifying all activities and relating them to the events that cause or drive the need for the activities and the resources consumed. PVA analysis forces managers to look critically at all phases of their operations and can assist managers in reducing nonvalue-adding activities and costs and improve cost traceability.

Objective 4: Define *activity-based costing*, and explain how a cost hierarchy and a bill of activities are used.

8. **Activity-based costing (ABC)** is a method of assigning costs that calculates a more accurate product cost by identifying all of an organization's major operating activities, tracing the indirect costs to those activities, and assigning activity costs to products using a cost driver that is related to the cause of the cost. The implementation of ABC involves five steps:
   a. Identify and classify each activity
   b. Estimate the cost of resources for each activity
   c. Identify a cost driver for each activity and estimate the quantity of each cost driver
   d. Calculate an activity cost rate
   e. Assign costs to cost objects based on the level of activity required to make the product or provide the service

9. Two tools that help organizations implement ABC are a cost hierarchy and a bill of activities. A **cost hierarchy** is a framework for classifying activities according to the level at which their costs are incurred. Typically, to create a cost hierarchy, production activities are identified and classified into four levels. **Unit-level activities** are those activities performed each time a unit is produced. **Batch-level activities** are those activities performed each time a batch of goods is produced. **Product-level activities** are those performed to support the diversity of products in a manufacturing plant. **Facility-level activities** are activities performed to support a facility's general manufacturing process. The frequency of activities varies across levels and both value-adding and nonvalue-adding activities are included in the cost hierarchy. Service organizations can also use a cost hierarchy to group activities.

10. After the cost hierarchy is created, a summary of these activities is prepared in the form of the bill of activities. The **bill of activities** is a list of activities and related costs that is used to compute the costs assigned to activities and the product unit cost. A bill of activities may be used as the primary document or as a supporting schedule to calculate the product unit cost in job order or process costing. It may also be used in a service organization.

Objective 5: Define the *just-in-time (JIT) operating philosophy* and identify the elements of a JIT operating environment.

11. Organizations are facing pressures to reinvent themselves and rethink their organizational processes and basic operating methods. One of management's operating philosophies for the new manufacturing environment is JIT. The **just-in-time (JIT) operating philosophy** requires that all resources, including materials, personnel, and facilities, be acquired and used only as needed, thereby reducing or eliminating waste. The objectives of the JIT operating philosophy require management to redesign its operating systems, plant layout, and basic management methods to conform to several basic concepts.

12. Elements that support the JIT philosophy are (a) maintaining minimum inventory levels; (b) developing **pull-through production,** a system design in which production is triggered by a customer order (traditional systems utilize the **push-through method,** which is a production system in which products are manufactured in long production runs and stored in anticipation of customers' orders); (c) purchasing materials and producing products as needed, in smaller lot sizes; (d) performing simple, inexpensive machine setups; (e) creating flexible manufacturing **work cells,** autonomous production lines that can efficiently and continuously perform all required operations; (f) developing a multiskilled work force; (g) maintaining high levels of product quality; (h) enforcing a system of effective preventive maintenance; and (i) encouraging continuous work environment improvement.

Objective 6: Identify the changes in product costing that result when a firm adopts a JIT operating environment.

13. The traditional operating environment divides the production process into five parts: (1) processing time, (2) inspection time, (3) moving time, (4) queue time, and (5) storage time.
    a. **Processing time** is the time required to work on a product.
    b. **Inspection time** is the time spent to detect product flaws or to rework defective units.
    c. **Moving time** is the time needed to transfer a product from one operation or department to another.
    d. **Queue time** is the time a product waits to be worked on once it reaches the next operation or department.
    e. **Storage time** is the time a product spends in materials storage, work in process inventory, or finished goods inventory.

14. In product costing under JIT, costs associated with processing time are categorized as either direct materials costs or conversion costs. **Conversion costs** include the total of direct labor costs and manufacturing overhead costs incurred by a production department, JIT work cell, or other work center. Under JIT, product costs associated with inspection, moving, queue, and storage time should be reduced or eliminated because they do not add value to the product.

15. The key measure in a JIT operating environment is **throughput time,** the time it takes to move a product through the entire production process. Measures of product movement are used to apply conversion costs to products.

16. With the help of computer monitoring of the JIT production cell, several costs that used to be treated as indirect costs are treated and traced as direct costs of a work cell. Only costs associated with building occupancy, insurance, and property taxes remain indirect costs of work cells.

Objective 7: Define and apply *backflush costing,* and compare the cost flows in traditional and backflush costing.

17. In a just-in-time environment, managers continuously seek ways to reduce wasted resources and time. So far, this chapter has focused on how waste can be reduced from production operations, but waste can also be reduced in other areas. This may be done, for example, by simplifying the cost flow through the accounting records. First, since labor costs are reduced in a JIT environment, the accounting system adds direct labor costs and allocated manufacturing costs into the Work in Process Inventory account. Second, because direct materials arrive just in time to be used in the production process, there is little reason to maintain a separate Materials Inventory account.

18. A JIT organization can also streamline its accounting process by using backflush costing. When **backflush costing** is used, all product costs are first accumulated in the Cost of Goods Sold account. Then, at period end, the costs are "flushed back" into the appropriate inventory accounts. The objective is to save recording time by having all product costs flow straight to a final destination and then, at period end, working backward to determine the proper balances for Work in Process Inventory and Finished Goods Inventory accounts.

19. In a traditional costing system, when direct materials arrive at the factory, their costs flow into the Materials Inventory account. Then, when the direct materials are requisitioned into production, their costs flow into the Work in Process Inventory account. When direct labor is used, its costs are added to the Work in Process Inventory account. Manufacturing overhead is then applied and is added to the other costs in the Work in Process Inventory account. At the end of the manufacturing process, the costs are transferred to the Finished Goods Inventory account. When the units are sold, their costs are transferred to Cost of Goods Sold.

20. In a JIT environment where backflush costing is used, the direct materials costs and the conversion costs (direct labor and manufacturing overhead) are immediately charged to the Cost of Goods Sold account. At the end of the period, the costs of goods in work in process inventory and in finished goods inventory are determined, and those costs are flushed back to the Work in Process Inventory account and the Finished Goods Inventory account. Once these costs have been flushed back, the Cost of Goods Sold account contains only the costs of units completed and sold during the period.

Objective 8: Compare ABM and JIT as activity-based systems.

21. ABM and JIT are similar in that as activity-based systems, they both analyze processes and identify

value-adding and nonvalue-adding activities to improve product or service quality, reduce costs, and improve the organization's efficiency and productivity. The end result is to improve the quality of information given to managers to use to make decisions.

22. ABM and JIT differ in their methods of costing and cost assignment. Using ABC, ABM helps calculate product costs by using cost drivers to allocate the indirect manufacturing overhead costs to cost objects. ABC is used with job order and process costing systems.

23. JIT reorganizes activities so that they are performed within work cells. The costs of those activities become direct costs to the work cell. The total production costs within the work cell can then be assigned using simple cost drivers such as process hours or direct materials cost. This approach focuses on the output at the end of the production process and simplifies the accounting system.

SELF-TEST

Test your knowledge of the chapter by choosing the best answer for each of the following items.

1. Which of the following is *not* a basic concept underlying just-in-time operations?
   a. An emphasis on quality and continuous improvement
   b. Producing goods only as they are needed
   c. Maintaining inventory levels to support probable demand
   d. The belief that simple is better

2. The move to a just-in-time operating environment is facilitated by
   a. creating production work cells that comprise several different types of operations.
   b. enhancing the storage functions within a factory.
   c. concentrating on areas of possible cost reduction rather than on the reduction of processing time.
   d. increasing inventories so that customers' demands can always be met.

3. Pull-through production means that
   a. the size of production runs is determined by how much can be pulled through the production process.
   b. production processes rely on long production runs to reduce the number of machine setups.
   c. it is very difficult to pull products through the production process.
   d. a customer order triggers the purchase of materials and the scheduling of production for the required products.

4. An activity that adds costs to the product or service but does not increase its market value is known as a
   a. cost-adding activity.
   b. cost driver.
   c. nonvalue-adding activity.
   d. value-adding activity.

5. Activity-based systems are used in which stage of the management cycle?
   a. Executing
   b. Planning
   c. Reviewing
   d. All of the above

6. In a backflush costing system, all product costs are first charged to the
   a. Materials Inventory account.
   b. Finished Goods Inventory account.
   c. Cost of Goods Sold account.
   d. Work in Process Inventory account.

7. Which of the following would most likely be a value-adding cost in the production of a table?
   a. Salary of job foreman
   b. Electric utility cost
   c. Cost of mahogany versus pine
   d. Depreciation of factory building

8. Which of the following is *not* an activity level in a cost hierarchy?
   a. Cost level
   b. Batch level
   c. Unit level
   d. Product level

9. *Processing time* may be defined as the time
   a. spent to detect product flaws.
   b. required to work on a product.
   c. a product waits to be worked on once it reaches the next operation or department
   d. a product spends in materials storage, work in process inventory, or finished goods inventory.

10. In a traditional costing system, direct materials that arrive at the factory flow first into the
    a. Cost of Goods Sold account.
    b. Finished Goods Inventory account.
    c. Materials Inventory account.
    d. Work in Process Inventory account.

TESTING YOUR KNOWLEDGE

Matching*

Match each term with its definition by writing the appropriate letter in the blank.

———— 1. Conversion costs

———— 2. Inspection time

———— 3. Activity-based system

———— 4. Just-in-time (JIT) operating philosophy

———— 5. Value chain

———— 6. Pull-through production

———— 7. Supply network

———— 8. Nonvalue-adding activity

———— 9. Work cell

———— 10. Cost hierarchy

———— 11. Push-through method

———— 12. Bill of activities

———— 13. Unit-level activities

a. The time spent either looking for product flaws or reworking defective units

b. An overall operating concept of management in which all resources, including materials, personnel, and facilities, are used in a just-in-time manner

c. An activity that adds costs to the product but does not increase its market value

d. A related sequence of value-creating activities within an organization

e. An interdependent web of organizations that supplies materials, products, or services to a customer

f. A customer order triggers the purchase of materials and the scheduling of production for the required products

g. An information system that provides quantitative information about activities in an organization

h. An autonomous production line that can perform all required operations efficiently and continuously

i. Direct labor and manufacturing overhead costs incurred by a department, work cell, or other work center

j. A framework for classifying activities to the level at which their costs are incurred

k. A production system in which products are manufactured in long production runs and stored in anticipation of customers' orders

l. Activities performed each time a unit is produced

m. A list of activities and related costs that is used to compute the costs allocated to activities and the product unit cost

———

Note to student: The matching quiz might be completed more efficiently by starting with the definition and searching for the corresponding term.

Short Answer

Use the lines provided to complete each item.

1. Briefly define the just-in-time operating philosophy.

_____

_____

_____

_____

_____

_____

_____

2. What are the five steps in implementing an activity-based costing system?

1. _____

2. _____

3. _____

4. _____

5. _____

3. Define *process value analysis (PVA)* and explain how it can be helpful to managers.

_____

_____

_____

_____

_____

_____

4. Just-in-time is not an inventory system. Explain.

_____

_____

_____

_____

_____

_____

_____

True-False

Circle T if the statement is true, F if it is false. Please provide explanations for the false answers, using the blank lines at the end of the section.

T F **1.** Activity-based management and just-in-time have different primary goals.

T F **2.** Eliminating waste is a key ingredient of the just-in-time operating philosophy.

T F **3.** In a JIT environment, materials and other resources are acquired and used only as needed in order to eliminate waste.

T F **4.** Pull-through production means that a customer order triggers the purchase of materials and the scheduling of production for a product.

T F **5.** A primary goal of the JIT operating philosophy is to cut the processing time of a product.

T F **6.** Product inspections are not performed in a just-in-time operating environment.

T F **7.** Queue time is the time spent moving a product from one operation or department to another.

T F **8.** Processing time is the actual time that a product spends being worked on.

T F **9.** Service organizations can also use a cost hierarchy to group activities.

T F **10.** The cost hierarchy for a service organization includes only unit level and batch level activities.

T F 11. A bill of activities is used in traditional costing systems.

T F 12. When an organization uses a backflush costing system, it backs costs out of the Cost of Goods Sold account.

T F 13. A nonvalue-adding activity adds costs to the product but does not increase its market value.

T F 14. Installing an airbag in an automobile is an example of a value-adding activity.

T F 15. Activity-based management can be used in all stages of the management cycle.

_____

_____

_____

_____

_____

_____

_____

_____

Multiple Choice

Circle the letter of the best answer.

1. Which of the following activities would *not* be a batch-level activity?
   a. Production-line setup
   b. Production-line inspection
   c. Installation of vehicle engine
   d. Scheduling

2. Which of the following is *not* an element of the just-in-time operating philosophy?
   a. Maintaining minimum inventory levels
   b. Developing a multiskilled labor force
   c. Increasing emphasis on direct labor variance analysis
   d. Encouraging continuous improvement in the work environment

3. Pull-through production planning and scheduling means that
   a. automated trucks pull the products through the production process.
   b. a customer order triggers the purchase of materials and the scheduling of production.
   c. a customer complaint triggers the scheduling of rework on the defective product.
   d. the production and scheduling processes are not functioning properly and that a special pull device must be adapted to correct the situation.

4. Maintaining minimum inventory levels is a goal of JIT because
   a. carrying inventory is a waste of working capital.
   b. carrying inventory maximizes the use of factory floor space.
   c. customer needs are no longer a major consideration.
   d. the company's current ratio is increased.

5. Unit costs within a JIT operating environment are minimized by
   a. using very inexpensive materials and supplies.
   b. performing quick, inexpensive machine setups.
   c. sacrificing quality for high-speed processes.
   d. using unskilled labor wherever possible.

6. Which of the following is *not* part of the traditional production process?
   a. Storage time
   b. Processing time
   c. Queue time
   d. Decision time

7. Which of the following would be a nonvalue-adding activity for a pizzeria?
   a. Home delivery
   b. Buying fresh pepperoni
   c. Recording daily cash receipts
   d. Preparing thick pizza dough

8. Which of the following costs would *not* initially flow into the Cost of Goods Sold account when a backflush costing system is used in a JIT environment?
   a. Sales salaries
   b. Applied manufacturing overhead
   c. Direct materials
   d. Direct labor

9. In the planning stage of the management cycle, an activity-based management system can provide useful information to help managers
   a. estimate product costs.
   b. attain production goals.
   c. determine inventory cost on the balance sheet.
   d. do all of the above.

10. Processing time is
    a. the time spent either looking for product flaws or reworking defective units.
    b. the actual amount of time spent working on a product.
    c. the amount of time a product spends waiting to be worked on.
    d. none of the above.

APPLYING YOUR KNOWLEDGE

Exercises

1. The Puffy Corporation produces ten types of bicycles. The fully suspended titanium model is the most expensive and the most difficult to produce. The rigid-frame steel model is the easiest to produce and is the leading seller for the company. The other models range from a fully suspended aluminum frame to a front-suspension steel frame and get more complex as suspension is added and frame materials change. Bikes Incorporated recently ordered 350 of the front-suspended aluminum bikes. Paula Jas, the controller of Puffy Corporation, decides to test the activity-based costing approach to product costing on this order. Costs directly traceable to the Bikes Incorporated order are as follows:

Direct materials	$28,645
Purchased parts	$38,205
Direct labor hours	660
Average direct labor pay rate per hour	$7.00

Other operating cost data:
Traditional costing approach:
   Manufacturing overhead costs were assigned at a rate of 160 percent of direct labor dollars.

a. Use a traditional costing approach to compute the total cost and the product unit cost of the Bikes Incorporated order.

b. Using an activity-based costing approach, compute the total cost and the product unit cost of the Bikes Incorporated order.

Activity-based costing approach:

Activity	Activity Cost Rate	Cost Driver Level
Unit level:		
Parts production	$19 per machine hour	190 machine hours
Assembly	$9.50 per direct labor hour	42 direct labor hours
Packaging/ shipping	$13 per unit	350 units
Batch level:		
Work cell setup	$45 per setup	8 setups
Product level:		
Product design	$31 per engineering hour	38 engineering hours
Product simulation	$45 per testing hour	14 testing hours
Facility level:		
Building occupancy	125% of direct labor costs	$4,620 direct labor costs

2. Listed below are several commonly incurred costs in a manufacturing environment:

Direct labor	Operating supplies
Depreciation, machinery	Fire insurance, plant
Raw materials	Setup labor
Product design costs	Rework costs
President's salary	Supervisory salaries
Small tools	Utilities costs, machinery

Identify each type of cost as being either direct or indirect, assuming the cost is incurred in (a) a traditional manufacturing setting and (b) a JIT operating environment.

Explain your reasons for any classification changes.

3. Kim Lazar is converting the accounting system of the UCF Manufacturing Company to account for costs related to the company's new JIT environment. The Work in Process Inventory account has been installed. The following transactions took place last week:

Dec. 22 Metal brackets for Jobs 213 and 216 were ordered and received, $4,890.

23 Steel castings for the product's body were received, $13,300.

23 Work began on both jobs.

24 Both jobs completed, total costs: Job 213, $14,870; Job 216, $17,880.

26 Job 216 shipped to customer (the company prices its products using a 60 percent markup over cost).

Using the following T accounts, record the above transactions.

Work in Process Inventory	Finished Goods Inventory	Cost of Goods Sold

Accounts Payable	Accounts Receivable	Sales

CHAPTER 23 COST BEHAVIOR ANALYSIS

REVIEWING THE CHAPTER

Objective 1: Define *cost behavior* and explain how managers use this concept in the management cycle.

1. **Cost behavior,** the way costs respond to changes in activity or volume, affects many decisions managers make during the planning, executing, and reporting stages of the management cycle.

2. In the planning stage, managers want to know how many units must be sold to cover all costs or to generate a targeted amount of profits or operating income. During the executing stage, managers must understand cost behavior to determine the impact of its decision on income. In the reporting stage, managers may use reports on cost behavior to analyze how changes in cost and sales affect various areas of the business, as well as to make decisions about whether to eliminate a particular product, accept a special order, or outsource certain activities.

Objective 2: Identify specific types of variable and fixed cost behavior, and discuss how operating capacity and relevant range relate to cost behavior.

3. Total costs that change in direct proportion to changes in productive output (or some other measure of activity) are called **variable costs.** Since variable costs change with volume or output, it is essential to know an organization's operating capacity. **Operating capacity** is the upper limit of an organization's productive output given its existing resources. There are three common measures of operating capacity:

a. **Theoretical (ideal) capacity** is the maximum productive output for a given time period, assuming that all machinery are operating at optimum speed and without interruption.

b. **Practical capacity** is theoretical capacity reduced by normal and expected work stoppages.

c. **Normal capacity** is the average annual level of operating capacity needed to meet expected sales demand. It is a realistic measure of what an organization is likely to produce, not what it *can* produce. Most organizations do not operate at either theoretical or practical capacity. Both measures include **excess capacity,** machinery and equipment kept on standby.

4. The traditional view of variable costs assumes that there is a linear relationship between costs and levels of activities. However, many variable costs behave in a nonlinear fashion. For example, an additional hourly rental rate for computer usage may be higher than the previous hour's rental rate.

5. **Fixed costs** are costs that remain constant within a relevant range of volume or activity. The **relevant range** is the range of volume or activity in which actual operations are likely to occur. Depreciation expense, salaries, and annual property taxes are examples of fixed costs. If production exceeds the relevant range, then fixed costs may indeed change.

6. a. Unit fixed costs change as volume increases or decreases. Unit fixed costs vary inversely with activity or volume. If more units are produced

than anticipated, the fixed costs are spread over more units, thus decreasing the fixed cost per unit. If fewer units are produced than anticipated, the fixed costs are spread over fewer units, thus increasing the fixed cost per unit.

b. One should be careful when working with fixed costs per unit because their use is limited. Usually fixed costs are considered as a total rather than on a per unit basis.

Objective 3: Define *mixed cost,* and use the high-low method to separate the variable and fixed components of a mixed cost.

7. **Mixed costs** are a combination of fixed and variable cost components. For example, mixed costs would be found in an account like Telephone and Gas & Electricity.

8. It is important to be able to break mixed costs down into their fixed and variable components. Two cost separation techniques commonly applied are the scatter diagram technique and the high-low method.

a. A **scatter diagram** is a graph containing plotted points that represent the relationship between the cost item and the related activity measure. If a somewhat linear relationship appears to exist, a cost line can be drawn through the points to approximately represent their relationship.

b. The **high-low method** is a mathematical technique used to calculate a formula to estimate the total costs (fixed and variable) within the relevant range.

Objective 4: Define *cost-volume-profit analysis* and discuss how managers use this analysis.

9. **Cost-volume-profit (C-V-P) analysis** is an examination of the cost behavior patterns that underlie the relationships among cost, volume of output, and profit. C-V-P analysis is used primarily as a planning and control tool. Among the uses of C-V-P analysis are projecting profit at different activity levels, measuring the performance of a department within a company, and assisting in the analysis of decision alternatives. Based on the notion of cost behavior, C-V-P analysis helps management by making use of a number of techniques and problem-solving procedures. It can also be applied to measure the effects of alternative choices, such as changes in variable and fixed costs, selling prices, or sales volume. Other applications include assistance in product pricing, product mix analysis, adding or dropping a product line, and accepting special orders.

Objective 5: Compute a breakeven point in units of output and in sales dollars, and prepare a breakeven graph.

10. The **breakeven point** is the point at which sales revenues equal the sum of all variable and fixed costs. A company can earn a profit only by surpassing the breakeven point. The breakeven equation is $S = VC + FC$. In this equation, S represents sales, VC represents variable costs, and FC represents fixed costs.

11. A standard breakeven graph has five parts: (a) a horizontal axis representing volume, (b) a vertical axis representing dollars of cost or revenue, (c) a horizontal fixed-cost line, (d) a sloping line beginning at the point that the fixed-cost line crosses the vertical axis representing total cost, and (e) a sloping line beginning at the origin representing total revenue. At the point where the total revenue line crosses the total cost line, revenues equal total costs.

Objective 6: Define *contribution margin* and use the concept to determine a company's breakeven point for a single product and for multiple products.

12. **Contribution margin** is the amount that remains after total variable costs are subtracted from sales. A product line's contribution margin represents its net contribution to paying off fixed costs and earning a profit.

13. Contribution margin may be viewed as:

$$S - VC = CM$$
and
$$CM - FC = P$$

Where: S = Sales Revenue
VC = Variable Costs
CM = Contribution Margin
FC = Fixed Costs
P = Profit (Loss)

14. Using the contribution margin, the breakeven point (BE) can be expressed as the point at which contribution margin minus total fixed costs equals zero. Stated another way, the BE is at the point where the contribution margin equals total fixed costs.

15. The breakeven point for multiple products can be computed in three steps:

a. Compute the weighted-average contribution margin by multiplying the contribution margin for each product by its percentage of the sales mix. The **sales mix** is the proportion of each product's unit sales relative to the organization's total unit sales.

b. Calculate the weighted-average breakeven point by dividing total fixed costs by the weighted-average contribution margin.

c. Calculate the breakeven point for each product by multiplying the weighted-average breakeven point by each product's percentage of the sales mix.

Objective 7: Apply cost-volume-profit analysis to estimated levels of future sales and to changes in costs and selling prices.

16. The primary goal of a business venture is to generate a profit, not merely to break even. A targeted profit can be factored into the cost-volume-profit (C-V-P) analysis to estimate the profitability of a new venture. This use of C-V-P analysis is:

$$S = VC + FC + P$$

P in this situation is the targeted profit; solve for the number of unit sales needed to achieve the desired profit.

17. The contribution margin approach is very useful for planning purposes. For example, it can be used to calculate projected operating income given a change in one or more of the income statement components. Changes in production costs, selling and administrative costs, variable costs, fixed costs, product demand, and selling price can drastically alter projected operating income.

18. To make use of C-V-P analysis, six assumptions must be made.

a. The behavior of variable and fixed costs can be measured accurately.

b. Costs and revenues have a close linear relationship.

c. Efficiency and productivity hold steady within the relevant range of activity.

d. Cost and price variables hold steady during the period being planned.

e. The sales mix does not change during the period being planned.

f. Production and sales volume will be about equal.

Objective 8: Apply cost-volume-profit analysis to a service business.

19. Service concerns, as well as manufacturers and merchandisers, need to account for and control costs. In a service business, however, no physical product is manufactured. Instead, services are rendered for a fee.

20. The application of C-V-P analysis to a service business involves four decisions:

a. Estimating service overhead costs. The steps in estimating service overhead costs are (1) calculate the variable service overhead cost per service, (2) calculate the total fixed service overhead costs, (3) state the formula for total service overhead costs, and (4) calculate the total service overhead costs assuming a given level of estimated services.

b. Determining the breakeven point, where $Sx = VCx + FC$. Solve for x where x = number of services (e.g., tax returns prepared by an accountant).

c. Determining the effect of a change in operating costs. If fixed or variable costs change, what would be the effect on profitability?

d. Achieving a target profit. Target profit can be computed after the three preceding steps by using the following formula for a given number of services:

$$Sx = VCx + FC + P$$

Where: x = Target Sales in Units

SELF-TEST

Test your knowledge of the chapter by choosing the best answer for each of the following items.

1. "The way that costs respond to changes in volume or activity" is the definition of
   a. cost flow.
   b. cost behavior.
   c. period costs.
   d. product costs.

2. The maximum productive output of an operating unit for a given period, assuming all machinery and equipment are operating at optimum speed without any interruptions, reduced by normal and expected work stoppages is called
   a. theoretical capacity.
   b. excess capacity.
   c. practical capacity.
   d. normal capacity.

3. The records of Technology Company reveal the following data about electrical costs:

Month	Activity Level	Cost
April	960 machine hours	$ 8,978
May	940 machine hours	8,842
June	1,120 machine hours	10,066

Using the high-low method, the variable cost per machine hour for the quarter was
   a. $6.80.
   b. $8.60.
   c. $7.40.
   d. $4.70.

4. Assuming the same facts as in **3**, the monthly fixed costs were
   a. $2,230.
   b. $2,450.
   c. $2,540.
   d. $1,890.

5. Product AB has a suggested selling price of $27 per unit and a projected variable cost per unit of $15. It is expected to increase fixed costs by $197,040 per month. The breakeven point in sales units per month is
   a. 16,240.
   b. 11,590.
   c. 11,950.
   d. 16,420.

6. Assuming the same facts as in **5**, the breakeven point in sales dollars per month is
   a. $443,340.
   b. $322,650.
   c. $312,930.
   d. $438,480.

7. Assuming the same facts as in **5**, how many units must be sold each month to earn a profit of $6,000 per month?
   a. 12,450
   b. 16,740
   c. 16,920
   d. 12,090

8. Assuming the same facts as in **5**, how many units must be sold each month to support an additional fixed monthly cost of $15,000 in advertising plus earn a profit of $9,000 per month?
   a. 18,240
   b. 18,420
   c. 13,590
   d. 13,950

9. Products A, B, and C have contribution margins of $3, $5, and $4 per unit, respectively. Granada Company intends to manufacture one of the products and expects sales to be $30,000 regardless of which product it manufactures. Which product will result in the highest profit for Granada, assuming that the same machinery and workers would be used to produce each?
   a. A
   b. B
   c. C
   d. More information is needed.

10. Which of the following statements is true regarding fixed costs?
   a. Fixed costs will vary within the relevant range.
   b. Fixed costs vary directly with activity levels.
   c. Per unit fixed costs vary inversely with activity.
   d. Per unit fixed costs are constant in the relevant range.

TESTING YOUR KNOWLEDGE

*Matching**

Match each term with its definition by writing the appropriate letter in the blank.

_____ 1. Cost behavior

_____ 2. Variable costs

_____ 3. Fixed costs

_____ 4. Relevant range

_____ 5. Mixed costs

_____ 6. Theoretical (ideal) capacity

_____ 7. Practical capacity

_____ 8. Normal capacity

_____ 9. Cost-volume-profit (C-V-P) analysis

_____ 10. Breakeven point

_____ 11. Contribution margin

a. The operating level needed to satisfy expected sales demand
b. The maximum productive output possible over a given period of time
c. The sales volume at which overall profit is zero
d. How costs change in relation to volume
e. Sales minus total variable costs
f. A method of determining profit at different levels of volume
g. Costs that vary in direct proportion to volume
h. Costs that remain constant within the relevant range of volume
i. Ideal capacity minus normal work stoppages
j. Costs with both fixed and variable elements
k. The volume range within which actual operations are likely to occur

Short Answer

Use the lines provided to answer each item.

1. What is the breakeven formula?

_____

2. Give three examples of mixed costs.

_____

_____

_____

3. Briefly explain the purpose of the high-low method.

_____

_____

_____

_____

_____

4. Distinguish between the concepts of sales and contribution margin.

_____

_____

_____

_____

_____

5. On the five lines below, show how profit is calculated using the contribution margin format.

_____

− _____

= _____

− _____

= _____

Note to student: The matching quiz might be completed more efficiently by starting with the definition and searching for the corresponding term.

6. What are the four decisions that must be made using
   C-V-P analysis in a service business?

_____   _____

_____   _____

_____   _____

_____   _____

_____   _____

True-False

Circle T if the statement is true, F if it is false. Please
provide explanations for the false answers, using the
blank lines at the end of the section.

T F **1.** On a per unit basis, variable costs remain
         constant with changes in volume.

T F **2.** On a breakeven graph, fixed costs are rep-
         resented by a horizontal line.

T F **3.** A fixed cost may change when it is out-
         side the relevant range.

T F **4.** Factory insurance is an example of a vari-
         able cost.

T F **5.** The most realistic plant capacity measure
         is practical capacity.

T F **6.** At the breakeven point, sales equal total
         costs.

T F **7.** A contribution margin cannot be realized
         until the breakeven point has been sur-
         passed.

T F **8.** The breakeven point in dollars can be de-
         termined by multiplying breakeven units
         by the selling price.

T F **9.** Property taxes are an example of a fixed
         cost.

T F **10.** An assumption of C-V-P analysis is that
         the sales mix does not change during the
         period being planned.

T F **11.** A mixed cost is one in which both variable
         and fixed cost components are combined.

T F **12.** On a breakeven graph, the horizontal axis
         represents dollars of cost or revenue.

T F **13.** At the breakeven point, the total contribu-
         tion margin equals fixed costs.

T F **14.** A reduction in sales dollars also reduces
         the contribution margin per unit.

T F **15.** At the point where the total revenue line
         crosses the total cost line on a breakeven
         graph, revenues equal total costs.

T F **16.** C-V-P analysis does not apply to service
         industries.

_____   _____

_____   _____

_____   _____

_____   _____

_____   _____

_____   _____

_____ _____
_____ _____
_____ _____
_____ _____
_____ _____
_____ _____
_____ _____
_____ _____

Multiple Choice

Circle the letter of the best answer.

1. Taxi fares with a certain base price plus a mileage charge would be an example of a
   a. fixed cost.
   b. variable cost.
   c. mixed cost.
   d. standard cost.

2. When fixed costs are $10,000, variable cost is $8 per unit, and selling price is $10 per unit, the breakeven point is
   a. 1,000 units.
   b. 1,250 units.
   c. 5,000 units.
   d. 10,000 units.

3. When volume equals zero units,
   a. fixed cost equals $0.
   b. variable cost equals $0.
   c. total cost equals $0.
   d. net income equals $0.

4. At the breakeven point,
   a. total contribution margin equals fixed cost.
   b. sales equal variable cost.
   c. total cost equals contribution margin.
   d. profit equals total cost.

5. In graph form, the breakeven point is at the intersection of the
   a. total-revenue and variable-cost lines.
   b. total-cost line and vertical axis.
   c. variable-cost and fixed-cost lines.
   d. total-cost and total-revenue lines.

6. The operating capacity that is required to satisfy anticipated sales demand is
   a. normal capacity.
   b. excess capacity.
   c. practical capacity.
   d. theoretical capacity.

7. As volume decreases,
   a. variable cost per unit decreases.
   b. fixed cost in total decreases.
   c. variable cost in total remains the same.
   d. fixed cost per unit increases.

8. When both the selling price and the variable cost per unit are increased by $5,
   a. more units need to be sold to break even.
   b. fewer units need to be sold to break even.
   c. the contribution margin per unit also increases by $5.
   d. the breakeven point remains the same.

9. Product X has a selling price of $50 and a variable cost per unit of 70 percent of the selling price. If fixed costs total $30,000, how many units must be sold to earn a profit of $45,000?
   a. 900
   b. 1,500
   c. 2,143
   d. 5,000

10. Product Y has a variable cost per unit of $10 and requires a fixed investment of $40,000. If sales are anticipated at 10,000 units, what selling price must be established to earn a profit of $26,000?
    a. $16.60
    b. $14.00
    c. $12.60
    d. $6.60

11. When calculating the breakeven point for multiple products, a weighted-average contribution margin must be calculated. This calculation is
    a. variable costs of each product times units of each product.
    b. contribution margin for each product times each product's percentage of sales mix.
    c. total number of units of each product times sales price for each product.
    d. the sum total fixed costs and total variable costs for each product.

12. Which of the following is a step in calculating the breakeven point for a service business?
    a. Estimating service overhead costs
    b. Computing variable overhead cost per service
    c. Computing total overhead cost, based on an estimated number of services
    d. All of the above are steps used by service businesses.

APPLYING YOUR KNOWLEDGE

Exercises

1. Leisure Manufacturing Company is planning to introduce a new line of bowling balls. Annual fixed costs are estimated to be $80,000. Each ball will be sold to retailers for $13 and requires $9 of variable costs.

    a. The breakeven point in units is

    _____.

    b. The breakeven point in dollars is

    _____.

    c. If 12,000 balls are sold per year, the overall profit or loss will be

    _____.

    d. The number of balls that must be sold for an annual profit of $50,000 is

    _____.

3. The following company-vehicle repair figures were assembled for Chess Cab Company for the first four months of 20x1:

Month	Activity Level	Cost
January	10,000 miles	$3,400
February	12,400	3,900
March	11,200	3,550
April	9,600	3,200

    a. Using the high-low method, produce a total cost formula for the company that describes its cost behavior for vehicle repairs.

    b. Using the answer to **a** above, approximately what repair cost would the company expect to have at an activity level of 16,000 miles?

2.

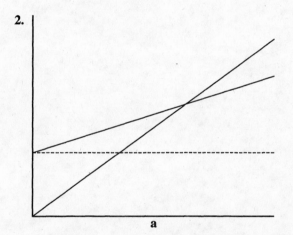

a

Using the letters that correspond with the labels listed below, identify the elements on this break-even graph. "Volume" has already been indicated.

    a. Volume
    b. Cost or revenue
    c. Breakeven point
    d. Profit area
    e. Loss area
    f. Fixed cost
    g. Total cost
    h. Contribution margin
    i. Sales

4. Evans Corporation sold 20,000 units of Product Z last year. Each unit sold for $40 and had a variable cost of $26. Annual fixed costs totaled $300,000. This year, management is thinking of reducing the selling price by 15 percent, purchasing less expensive material to save $2 per unit, and spending $50,000 more on advertising. It is expected that sales will double with the proposed changes.

a. What was the company's profit or loss last year?

$_____

b. What would the corporation's per-unit contribution margin be after the proposed changes are made?

c. If the projections are accurate, what would the corporation's profit be after the changes are made?

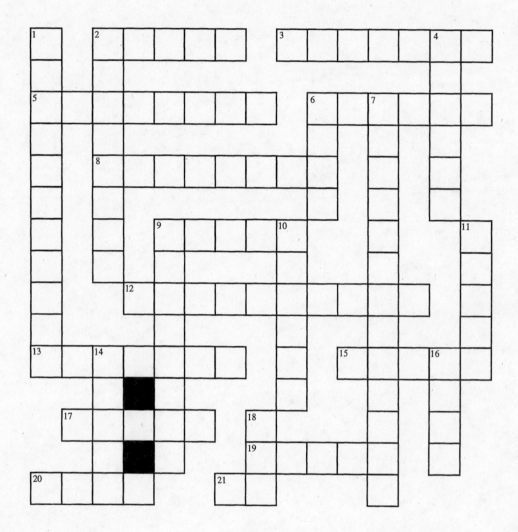

ACROSS

2. See 2-Down
3. _____ value analysis (PVA)
5. Product combination analysis (2 words)
6. _____ capacity (standby equipment)
8. Cost affected by volume change
9. Cost not affected by volume change
12. Value-adding and nonvalue-adding, for example
13. Method to separate mixed costs (hyphenated)
15. _____ chain
17. Conversion and full product, for example
19. _____-level activities (by job)
20. The "J" of JIT
21. S – VC = _____

DOWN

1. Method of long production runs (hyphenated)
2. With 2-Across, expected span of activity
4. Activity-based _____ (such as JIT or ABM)
6. Break _____
7. Activity classification by levels (2 words)
9. _____-level activities (by plant)
10. Cost causer
11. _____ (waiting) time
14. _____ margin
16. _____-level activities (by item)
18. Kin to JIT, for short

CHAPTER 24 THE BUDGETING PROCESS

REVIEWING THE CHAPTER

Objective 1: Define *budgeting* **and explain its role in the management cycle.**

1. **Budgeting** is the process of identifying, gathering, summarizing, and communicating financial and nonfinancial information about an organization's future activities. Budgeting is used in all types of organizations and is synonymous with managing an organization.

2. A **budget** is a plan of action that forecasts future financial and nonfinancial transactions, activities, and events. A budget can show planned activities to meet certain requirements or standards established during the planning stage.

3. Unlike many of the areas studied in accounting, there is no standard form or structure for a budget. A budget's structure depends on what is being budgeted, the size of the organization preparing the budget, the degree to which the budgeting process is integrated into the financial structure of the enterprise, and the amount of training the budget preparer has in his or her background.

4. The key to a successful budgeting process is **participative budgeting.** This is a process in which personnel at all levels of the organization take an active and meaningful part in the creation of the budget.

5. During the planning stage of the management cycle, budgeting helps managers to (a) relate an organization's long-term goals to its short-term activities, (b) distribute resources and workloads, (c) communicate responsibilities, (d) select performance measures, and (e) set goals for bonuses and rewards.

6. During the executing stage of the management cycle, budgeting helps managers to (a) communicate expectations, (b) challenge and motivate others, (c) coordinate activities, (d) benchmark, and (e) recognize problems.

7. During the reviewing stage of the management cycle, budgeting helps managers to (a) calculate variances, (b) evaluate performance, (c) determine timeliness, and (d) create solutions for continuous improvement.

8. During the reporting stage of the management cycle, budgeting helps managers to continuously communicate budget information and provide continuous feedback about the organization's operating, investing, and financing activities.

Objective 2: Describe the master budget process for different types of organizations, and list the guidelines for preparing budgets.

9. A **master budget** is a set of budgets that consolidates an organization's financial information into budgeted financial statements for a future period of time. Regardless of the type of organization, master budgets provide helpful information for planning, executing, reviewing, and reporting. Master budgets help new organizations obtain financing and help existing organizations plan future operating, investing, and financing activities.

10. A master budget includes a set of operating budgets that support a budgeted income statement. Additionally, a master budget presents a set of financial budgets that include a budgeted balance sheet, a cash budget, and a capital expenditures budget.

11. There are some similarities between the master budgets of manufacturing, retail, and service organizations. Each type of organization needs a set of operating budgets to support the budgeted income statement. In all three types of organizations, the budget information from the operating budgets and the capital expenditures budget affects the cash budget and the budgeted balance sheet. The cash budget also provides information for the budgeted balance sheet.

12. The main difference in the master budget process for the three different types of organizations involves the preparation of operating budgets for the budgeted income statement.
   a. For a manufacturing organization, the operating budgets include budgets for sales, production, direct materials purchases, direct labor, manufacturing overhead, cost of goods manufactured, and selling and administrative expenses.
   b. For a retail organization, the operating budgets include a sales budget, a purchases budget, a cost of goods sold budget, and a selling and administrative expense budget. The sales budget is prepared first because it is used to estimate sales volume and revenues. Once this is known, then managers can develop operating budgets to achieve these sales goals and generate profits on those sales.
   c. A service organization's operating budgets include budgets for service revenue, labor, services overhead, and selling and administrative expenses. The labor budget reflects the estimated labor hours and labor rates to provide the services.

13. The following guidelines are helpful when preparing a budget:
   a. Know the purpose of the budget.
   b. Identify the user group and their information needs.
   c. Begin the budget with a clearly stated title or heading.
   d. Identify the format for the budget, and use appropriate formulas and calculations to derive the quantitative information.
   e. Label the budget's components, and list the unit and financial data in an orderly manner.
   f. Know the sources of budget information.
   g. Revise the budget until all planning decisions are included.

Objective 3: Prepare a budgeted income statement and supporting operating budgets.

14. The starting point for preparing a master budget is the **sales budget.** A sales budget is a detailed plan, expressed in both units and dollars, that identifies expected product (or service) sales for a future period. The sales budget represents the total budgeted sales using the following equation:

$$\begin{matrix} \text{Total} \\ \text{Budgeted} \\ \text{Sales} \end{matrix} = \begin{matrix} \text{Estimated} \\ \text{Selling Price} \\ \text{per Unit} \end{matrix} \times \begin{matrix} \text{Estimated} \\ \text{Sales in} \\ \text{Units} \end{matrix}$$

15. The estimated sales volume is very important in the budget process because it will affect the level of operating activities and the amount of resources necessary to operate. A sales forecast can help in this process. A **sales forecast** is a projection of sales demand (the estimated sales in units) based upon an analysis of external and internal factors.

16. After the preparation of the sales budget, a production budget is prepared. A **production budget** identifies the products or services that must be produced or provided to meet sales and inventory needs. The production budget is based on the following formula:

$$\begin{matrix} \text{Total} \\ \text{Production} \\ \text{Units} \end{matrix} = \begin{matrix} \text{Budgeted} \\ \text{Sales in} \\ \text{Units} \end{matrix} + \begin{matrix} \text{Desired} \\ \text{Units of} \\ \text{Ending} \\ \text{Finished} \\ \text{Goods} \\ \text{Inventory} \end{matrix} - \begin{matrix} \text{Desired} \\ \text{Units of} \\ \text{Beginning} \\ \text{Finished} \\ \text{Goods} \\ \text{Inventory} \end{matrix}$$

17. Once the production budget is prepared, the **direct materials purchases budget** can be prepared. This budget provides a detailed schedule that identifies the purchases required for budgeted production and inventory needs and the costs associated with those purchases. The direct materials purchases budget is based on three steps. First, calculate the total production needs in units. Second, use the following formula to create the direct materials purchases in units for each accounting period in the budget:

$$\begin{matrix} \text{Total} \\ \text{Units of} \\ \text{Direct} \\ \text{Materials} \\ \text{to Be} \\ \text{Purchased} \end{matrix} = \begin{matrix} \text{Total} \\ \text{Production} \\ \text{Needs in} \\ \text{Units of} \\ \text{Direct} \\ \text{Materials} \end{matrix} + \begin{matrix} \text{Desired} \\ \text{Units of} \\ \text{Ending} \\ \text{Direct} \\ \text{Materials} \\ \text{Inventory} \end{matrix} - \begin{matrix} \text{Desired} \\ \text{Units of} \\ \text{Beginning} \\ \text{Direct} \\ \text{Materials} \\ \text{Inventory} \end{matrix}$$

Third, calculate the cost of the direct materials purchases by multiplying the total unit purchases of direct materials by the direct materials cost per unit.

18. The **direct labor budget** is a detailed schedule that identifies the direct labor needs for a future period and the labor costs associated with those needs. The steps in preparing the direct labor budget are: (a) estimate the total direct labor hours by multiplying the estimated direct labor hours per unit by the anticipated units of production, and (b) calculate the total budgeted direct labor cost by multiplying the estimated total direct labor hours by the estimated direct labor cost per hour.

19. The **manufacturing overhead budget** is a detailed schedule of anticipated manufacturing costs, other than direct materials and direct labor costs, that must be incurred to meet the production expectations of a future period. It has two purposes: (a) to integrate the overhead cost budgets from the production and production-related departments and (b) to group information for the calculation of manufacturing overhead rates for the upcoming accounting period.

20. A **selling and administrative expense budget** is a detailed plan of operating expenses, other than those of the production function, needed to support the sales and overall operations of the organization for a future period.

21. The **cost of goods manufactured budget** is a detailed schedule that summarizes the costs of production for a future period. The sources of information for this budget are the budgets for direct materials, direct labor, and manufacturing overhead. Review Exhibit 7 in the text for a detailed example of a cost of goods manufactured budget.

22. After the operating budgets have been prepared, the budgeted income statement can be prepared. A **budgeted income statement** projects net income based on the estimated revenues and expenses for a future period. Data related to projected sales and costs come from the previously prepared operating budgets.

23. A **capital expenditures budget** is a detailed plan pertaining to the amount and timing of anticipated capital expenditures for a future period. Buying equipment or building a new facility are examples of capital expenditures that would require this budget.

Objective 4: Prepare a cash budget.

24. A **cash budget** is a summary of all planned cash transactions found in the detailed operating budgets and in the forecasted income statement. For example, cash receipts may be predicted mainly from the sales budget. The main objectives of a cash budget are to (a) show the projected ending cash balance and (b) allow management to anticipate periods of high or low cash availability. An expected period of low cash availability, for example, would alert management that short-term borrowing may be necessary. Care must be taken to include only cash inflows and outflows that are likely during the period.

25. The cash budget consists of (projected) cash receipts, cash disbursements, beginning cash balance, and ending cash balance.

Estimated Ending Cash Balance	=	Total Estimated Cash Receipts	−	Total Estimated Cash Payments	+	Estimated Beginning Cash Balance

Objective 5: Prepare a budgeted balance sheet.

26. The final step in developing the master budget is to prepare a budgeted balance sheet. A **budgeted balance sheet** projects the financial position of an organization for a future period. The budgeted balance sheet takes data from a number of previously prepared budgets. A thorough review of Exhibit 12 in the text is necessary to see all the different data sources.

SELF-TEST

Test your knowledge of the chapter by choosing the best answer for each of the following items.

1. Which of the following is *not* a guideline for budgeting preparation?
   a. Know the purpose of the budget.
   b. Identify the user group and their information needs.
   c. Begin the budget with a clearly stated heading.
   d. All of the above are budget guidelines.

2. Participative budgeting is the key to a successful budgeting process because
   a. senior executives dictate targets and goals and expect all employees to implement them.
   b. the budget director prepares the master budget and its supporting budgets.
   c. only middle managers prepare the budgets; upper management gets involved only with strategic budgeting.
   d. personnel at all levels of the organization take a meaningful and active part in the creation of the budget.

3. Assume that Costabile Enterprises uses three gallons of material 2D, two gallons of material 4R, five gallons of material 6T, and ten gallons of material 8K to make each twenty-gallon barrel of plant food. Expected costs per gallon are: 2D, $2.40; 4R, $1.80; 6T, $10.50; and 8K, $3.30. The production budget indicates that 12,400 barrels will be produced in April, 10,800 barrels in May, and 9,800 barrels in June. Materials are purchased one month ahead of production. What is the total dollar value of budgeted materials purchases in April?
   a. $1,040,040
   b. $1,194,120
   c. $549,040
   d. $449,620

4. The cash budget must be prepared before which of the following documents can be developed?
   a. Capital expenditures budget
   b. Sales budget
   c. Forecasted balance sheet
   d. Forecasted income statement

5. Which of the following variables are needed to prepare a cash budget?
   a. Total estimated cash receipts
   b. Total estimated cash payments
   c. Estimated beginning cash balance
   d. All of the above

6. A retail organization would *not* have which of the following operating budgets?
   a. Direct materials purchases budget
   b. Sales budget
   c. Cost of goods sold budget
   d. Selling and administrative expense budget

7. The initial step in preparing a master budget is the preparation of the
   a. cash budget.
   b. capital expenditures budget.
   c. cost of goods sold budget.
   d. sales budget.

8. Which of the following budgets would have inputs from essentially all other budgets?
   a. Sales budget
   b. Direct materials purchases budget
   c. Budgeted balance sheet
   d. Production budget

9. Using budgets to evaluate performance is usually done in which stage of the management cycle?
   a. Reviewing
   b. Planning
   c. Reporting
   d. None of the above

10. Which of the following details the costs of production for a future period?
    a. Direct materials purchases budget
    b. Cost of goods manufactured budget
    c. Budgeted balance sheet
    d. Manufacturing overhead budget

TESTING YOUR KNOWLEDGE

Matching*

Match each term with its definition by writing the appropriate letter in the blank.

_____ 1. Budgetary control

_____ 2. Master budget

_____ 3. Cash budget

_____ 4. Sales budget

_____ 5. Budget director (controller)

_____ 6. Production budget

_____ 7. Budgeted income statement

_____ 8. Cost of goods manufactured budget

_____ 9. Sales forecast

_____ 10. Direct materials purchases budget

_____ 11. Budgeted balance sheet

a. A statement that projects the financial position of an organization for a future period

b. A projection of sales demand based on an analysis of both internal and external factors

c. A detailed schedule that summarizes the costs of production for a future period

d. Projects net income based on estimated revenues and expenses for a future period

e. A detailed schedule that identifies the purchases required for budgeted production

f. The basis for all other operating budgets

g. A combined set of departmental or functional period budgets that have been consolidated into forecasted financial statements for the whole company

h. The basis for the materials, labor, and overhead budgets

i. The person in charge of the budgeting process

j. The budget prepared after all period budgets and the forecasted income statement

k. The planning of, and control over, future company activities

Short Answer

Use the lines provided to answer each item.

1. Briefly define *budgeting*.

_____

_____

_____

_____

_____

2. Describe a master budget and list the other supporting budgets.

_____

_____

_____

_____

Note to student: The matching quiz might be completed more efficiently by starting with the definition and searching for the corresponding term.

3. What are the two main objectives of a cash budget?

_____

_____

_____

_____

_____

_____

4. What are the three steps in preparing a direct materials purchases budget?

_____

_____

_____

_____

_____

True-False

Circle T if the statement is true, F if it is false. Please provide explanations for the false answers, using the blank lines at the end of the section.

T F **1.** A long-term plan is called a master budget.

T F **2.** A master budget refers to planned activities for a segment of the business only.

T F **3.** A projection of sales must be made before the production budget can be devised.

T F **4.** A service organization would not have a direct materials budget.

T F **5.** Depreciation expense would be listed as a cash disbursement in the cash budget.

T F **6.** Establishing long-range goals should go before establishing short-range goals.

T F **7.** The capital expenditures budget concerns purchases of facilities and equipment.

T F **8.** Total sales for a period would be included in that period's cash budget as part of cash receipts.

T F **9.** Information must be provided from the cash budget in order to prepare the selling and administrative expense budget.

T F **10.** The first step in preparing a direct labor budget is to calculate the estimated total direct labor hours for the period.

T F **11.** When preparing a sales budget, external factors have no influence on the sales forecast.

T F **12.** Once the sales budget is prepared, then the production budget can be prepared.

T F **13.** The first step in developing the master budget is to prepare a budgeted balance sheet.

_____

_____

_____

_____

_____

_____

_____

_____

_____

_____

_____

_____

_____

_____

_____

_____

_____

_____

_____

_____

Multiple Choice

Circle the letter of the best answer.

1. The first step in preparing a master budget is preparing
   a. a forecasted income statement.
   b. a general operating budget.
   c. a forecasted balance sheet.
   d. detailed operating budgets.

2. Which of the following components of the master budget must be prepared before the others?
   a. Direct labor budget
   b. Manufacturing overhead budget
   c. Production budget
   d. Direct materials purchases budget

3. The cash budget is prepared
   a. before all operating budgets are prepared.
   b. after the forecasted income statement but before the forecasted balance sheet.
   c. as the last step in the master budget.
   d. only if the company has doubts about its debt-paying ability.

4. Which of the following data would *not* be found on a direct labor budget?
   a. Direct labor hours per unit
   b. Total budgeted direct labor
   c. Estimated total direct labor hours
   d. Forecasted sales in dollars

5. Which of the following budgets would *not* be a source of cash payments in the cash budget?
   a. Sales budget
   b. Capital expenditures budget
   c. Selling cost budget
   d. Direct labor budget

6. The cash budget consists of
   a. projected cash receipts.
   b. the ending cash balance.
   c. projected cash disbursements.
   d. all of the above.

7. The following budget information is provided for Woodley Company:

Quarter	1	2	3
Production in units	23,000	24,000	21,000

   Each finished unit requires three pounds of material. The inventory of material at the end of each quarter should equal 10 percent of the following quarter's production needs. How many pounds of material should be purchased for the second quarter?
   a. 71,100 pounds
   b. 72,000 pounds
   c. 74,400 pounds
   d. 75,000 pounds

8. A service organization would prepare all of the following budgets except the
   a. direct labor budget.
   b. services overhead budget.
   c. cash budget.
   d. direct materials budget.

9. Timbo Company typically pays 40 percent of its purchases on account in the month of purchase and 60 percent in the month following purchase. Given the following direct material projections, what would be the expected cash payments for March 20x0?

	Purchases on Account	Cash Purchases
February 20x0	$10,000	$ 5,000
March 20x0	15,000	20,000
April 20x0	4,000	8,000

a. $35,000
b. $30,000
c. $32,000
d. $20,000

10. In order to determine total budgeted direct labor costs, estimated direct labor cost per hour must be multiplied by the
a. predetermined manufacturing overhead rate.
b. unit sales projection.
c. total estimated units of production.
d. estimated total direct labor hours.

APPLYING YOUR KNOWLEDGE

Exercises

1. Donlevy Company produces and sells a single product. Expected sales for the next four months are:

Month	Units
April	10,000
May	12,000
June	15,000
July	9,000

The company needs a *production budget* for the second quarter. Experience indicates that end-of-month finished goods inventory must equal 10 percent of the following month's sales in units. At the end of March, 1,000 units were on hand. Compute production needs for the second quarter by preparing a production budget.

Donlevy Company
Production Budget
For the Quarter Ended June 30, 20xx

2. Monahan Enterprises needs a cash budget for the month of June. The following information is available:

   a. The cash balance on June 1 is $7,000.
   b. Sales for May and June are $80,000 and $60,000, respectively. Cash collections on sales are 30 percent in the month of the sale, 65 percent in the following month, and 5 percent uncollectible.
   c. General and administrative expenses are budgeted at $24,000 for June. Depreciation represents $2,000 of this amount.
   d. Inventory purchases will total $30,000 in June and totaled $40,000 in May. Half of inventory purchases are always paid for in the month of the purchase. The remainder are paid for in the following month.
   e. Office furniture costing $3,000 will be purchased for cash in June, and selling expenses (exclusive of $2,000 in depreciation) are budgeted at $14,000.
   f. The company must maintain a minimum ending cash balance of $4,000 and can borrow from the bank in multiples of $100. All loans are repaid after 60 days.

   In the space provided, prepare a cash budget for Monahan Enterprises for the month of June.

Monahan Enterprises
Cash Budget
For the Month Ended June 30, 20xx

---

3. Jeppo Titanium Company manufactures three products in a single plant with two departments: Bending and Welding. The company has estimated costs for products X and Y and is currently analyzing direct labor hour requirements for the budget year 20x1. The department data are:

Estimated hours per unit	Bending	Welding
Product X	1	2
Product Y	.6	3
Hourly labor rate	$10	$15

Budgeted unit production in 20x1 of Product X is 10,000 and of Product Y, 20,000. Prepare a direct labor budget for 20x1 that shows the budgeted direct labor costs for each department and for the company as a whole.

Jeppo Titanium Company
Direct Labor Budget
For the Year Ended December 31, 20x1

4. Explain the role of budgeting in each of the stages of the management cycle.

_____   _____

_____   _____

_____   _____

_____   _____

_____   _____

_____   _____

_____   _____

_____   _____

_____   _____

_____   _____

_____   _____

_____   _____

_____   _____

_____   _____

_____   _____

_____   _____

CHAPTER 25 PERFORMANCE MEASUREMENT USING STANDARD COSTING

REVIEWING THE CHAPTER

Objective 1: Define *standard costs* and describe how managers use standard costs in the management cycle.

1. **Standard costs** are realistically predetermined costs that are developed from analyses of both past and projected future costs and operating conditions. **Standard costing** is a budgetary control technique whereby standard costs for direct materials, direct labor, and manufacturing overhead flow through the inventory accounts and eventually into the Cost of Goods Sold account. Instead of using actual costs for product costing purposes, standard costs are used.

2. During the planning stage, standard costs can be used to estimate costs for direct materials, direct labor, and variable manufacturing overhead. These estimated costs serve as goals for product costing and can also be used in product distribution and pricing.

3. Standard costs are used in the executing stage of the management cycle to apply dollar, time, and quantity standards to work being performed.

4. During the reviewing stage, actual costs incurred are compared with standard costs, and the **variances** are computed. Variances provide measures of performance that can be used to control costs.

5. During the reporting stage of the management cycle, standard costs are used to report on operations and managerial performance. A variance report may be tailored to a manager's responsibilities to provide useful information about how well operations are proceeding and how well the manager is controlling them.

6. Standard costs can be used in all types of organizations. However, in a service organization, there would be no standards for direct materials.

Objective 2: Identify the six elements of, and compute, a standard unit cost.

7. A standard unit cost contains the following six parts: (a) direct materials price standard, (b) direct materials quantity standard, (c) direct labor time standard, (d) direct labor rate standard, (e) standard variable manufacturing overhead rate, and (f) standard fixed manufacturing overhead rate.

8. The standard cost per unit of output is the result of the following standard amounts:
   a. **Standard Direct Materials Cost** = Direct Materials Price Standard × Direct Materials Quantity Standard
      (1) The **direct materials price standard** is the estimated cost of a specific direct material to be used in the next accounting period.
      (2) The **direct materials quantity standard** is the estimated amount of direct materials expected to be used.
   b. **Standard Direct Labor Cost** = Direct Labor Rate Standard × Direct Labor Time Standard
      (1) The **direct labor rate standard** is the expected hourly direct labor cost for each function or job classification to prevail in the next accounting period.

(2) The **direct labor time standard** is the expected time required for each department, machine, or process to complete the production of one unit or one batch of output.

c. **Standard Manufacturing Overhead Cost =** (Standard Variable Manufacturing Overhead Rate + Standard Fixed Manufacturing Overhead Rate)

(1) The **standard variable manufacturing overhead rate** is the total budgeted variable manufacturing overhead costs divided by an expected standard basis (such as machine hours or direct labor hours).

(2) The **standard fixed manufacturing overhead rate** is the total budgeted fixed manufacturing overhead costs divided by a number or an expected standard basis (such as machine hours or direct labor hours).

9. A product's standard unit cost is determined by adding the standard direct materials cost, the standard direct labor cost, and the standard manufacturing overhead cost. Under a standard cost system, costs flow through accounts in a way similar to that discussed in prior chapters for a manufacturer's inventory system. However, direct materials, direct labor, and manufacturing overhead are entered into Work in Process Inventory at standard (not actual) cost.

Objective 3: Describe how to control costs through variance analysis.

10. **Variance analysis** is the process of computing the differences between standard (or budgeted) costs and actual costs and identifying the causes of those differences. Variances between standard and actual costs are usually determined for direct materials, direct labor, and manufacturing overhead. When standard costs exceed actual costs, the variance is favorable (F). When the reverse is true, the variance is unfavorable (U).

11. Variance analysis helps managers to locate areas of operating efficiency or inefficiency so that corrective action can be taken, if necessary. The mere computation of a variance is important; however, identifying the *reason* for a variance is critical if corrective actions are to be taken.

Objective 4: Compute and analyze direct materials variances.

12. The **total direct materials cost variance** is the difference between the standard cost of direct materials and the actual costs incurred. The total direct materials cost variance is broken down into direct materials price variance and direct materials quantity variance.

a. The **direct materials price variance** is the difference between the standard price and the actual price, multiplied by the actual quantity purchased, where:

(1) Direct Materials Price Variance = (Standard Price − Actual Price) × Actual Quantity

b. The **direct materials quantity variance** is the difference between the standard quantity and the actual quantity of material used, multiplied by the standard price, where:

(1) Direct Materials Quantity Variance = Standard Price × (Standard Quantity − Actual Quantity)

Objective 5: Compute and analyze direct labor variances.

13. The **total direct labor cost variance** consists of the direct labor rate variance plus the direct labor efficiency variance.

a. The **direct labor rate variance** is the difference between the standard direct labor rate and the actual direct labor rate, multiplied by the actual direct labor hours worked, where:

(1) Direct Labor Rate Variance = (Standard Rate − Actual Rate) × Actual Hours

b. The **direct labor efficiency variance** is the difference between the standard direct labor hours allowed for the good units produced and the actual direct labor hours worked, multiplied by the standard direct labor rate, where:

(1) Direct Labor Efficiency Variance = Standard Rate × (Standard Hours Allowed − Actual Hours)

Objective 6: Define and prepare a flexible budget.

14. A **flexible budget** (sometimes referred to as a *variable budget*) is a summary of expected costs for various levels of output or activity. For each level, budgeted fixed and variable costs and their totals are presented. Also presented is the budgeted variable cost per unit, which of course is the same for all levels of output. Once prepared, the flexible budget is used to determine the **flexible budget formula.** The flexible budget formula is (Variable Cost per Unit × Number of Units Produced) + Budgeted Fixed Costs. This formula can then be applied to any level of output to figure its budgeted total cost. The budgeted total cost can be compared with actual costs to measure the performance of individuals and departments.

Objective 7: Compute and analyze manufacturing overhead variances.

15. The basic approach to computing the manufacturing overhead variance is to compute the **total manufacturing overhead variance,** which is the difference between the actual manufacturing overhead costs incurred and the standard manufacturing overhead costs applied to production using the standard variable and fixed manufacturing overhead rates. The total standard manufacturing overhead rate consists of two parts: (1) the variable rate and (2) the fixed rate which is calculated by dividing budgeted fixed manufacturing overhead by normal capacity. The manufacturing overhead variance is then divided into two parts: the controllable total manufacturing overhead variance and the manufacturing overhead volume variance.

    a. The **controllable manufacturing overhead variance** is the difference between the actual manufacturing overhead costs incurred and the manufacturing overhead costs budgeted for the level of production reached. This variance focuses on the amount of good units produced and examines the difference between actual manufacturing overhead incurred and standard overhead allowed at the actual level of production attained.

    b. The **manufacturing overhead volume variance** is the difference between the manufacturing overhead budgeted for the level of production achieved and the manufacturing overhead allocated to production using the standard variable and fixed manufacturing overhead rates. Since this variance gauges the use of existing facilities and capacity, a volume variance will occur if more or less capacity than normal is used.

Objective 8: Explain how variances are used to evaluate managers' performance.

16. The management should establish policies and procedures for (1) preparing operational plans, (2) assigning responsibility for performance, (3) communicating operational plans to key personnel, (4) evaluating each area of responsibility, (5) identifying the causes of significant variances, and (6) taking corrective action to eliminate problems.

17. The key to preparing a performance report based on standard costs and related variances is to (1) identify those responsible for each variance, (2) determine the causes for each variance, and (3) develop a reporting format suited to the task.

Test your knowledge of the chapter by choosing the best answer for each of the following items.

1. Standard costing analysis can be used in which of the following stages of the management cycle?
   a. Planning
   b. Reviewing
   c. Executing
   d. All of the above

2. The direct labor efficiency variance is the difference between standard direct labor hours allowed for the good units produced and the
   a. standard hours allowed and standard rate per hour.
   b. actual direct labor hours worked, multiplied by the standard direct labor rate.
   c. direct labor rate per hour.
   d. none of the above.

3. An unfavorable manufacturing overhead volume variance will exist when
   a. budgeted manufacturing overhead for the level of production is less than manufacturing overhead applied.
   b. total manufacturing overhead is less than the predetermined overhead rate.
   c. budgeted manufacturing overhead for the level of production exceeds standard manufacturing overhead applied.
   d. none of the above obtain.

4. Which of the following is the correct formula to determine the direct materials price variance?
   a. (Standard Price ÷ Actual Price) × Actual Quantity
   b. (Standard Price – Actual Price) × Standard Quantity
   c. (Standard Price – Actual Price) × Actual Quantity
   d. (Standard Quantity – Actual Quantity) × Actual Price

5. Which of the following is *not* an element of a standard unit cost?
   a. Direct materials price standard
   b. Actual direct labor costs
   c. Direct labor rate standard
   d. All of the above are included in a standard unit cost.

6. Product engineering specifications, the quality of direct materials, and the age and productivity of machinery influence the direct
   a. materials quantity standard.
   b. labor rate standard.
   c. materials price standard.
   d. labor time standard.

7. To compute the standard fixed manufacturing overhead rate, total budgeted fixed manufacturing overhead is divided by the
   a. flexible budget formula.
   b. actual hours worked.
   c. standard hours allowed.
   d. normal capacity.

8. The Sahlen Company uses a standard cost accounting system in its glass division. The standard cost of making one glass windshield is:

Direct materials (60 lb @ $1/lb)	$ 60.00
Direct labor (3 hr @ $10/hr)	30.00
Manufacturing overhead (3 hr @ $8/hr)	24.00
Total standard unit cost	$114.00

The current variable manufacturing overhead rate is $3 per labor hour and the budgeted fixed manufacturing overhead is $27,000. During January, the division produced 1,650 windshields compared to normal capacity of 1,800 windshields. The actual cost per windshield was:

Direct materials (58 lb @ $1.10/lb)	$ 63.80
Direct labor (3.1 hr @ $10/hr)	31.00
Manufacturing overhead	
$39,930/1,650 products)	24.20
Total actual unit cost	$119.00

The total direct materials quantity variance for January is
   a. $9,570 (U).
   b. $9,570 (F).
   c. $3,300 (F).
   d. $3,300 (U).

9. Assuming the same facts as in **8,** the labor rate variance for January is
   a. 0.
   b. $1,650 (U).
   c. $1,920 (F).
   d. $1,650 (F).

10. In the flexible budget formula for a department, the variable portion of the formula states that the variable cost per unit is multiplied by the
   a. standard hours worked.
   b. number of units produced.
   c. standard hours allowed.
   d. number of units planned.

TESTING YOUR KNOWLEDGE

Matching*

Match each term with its definition by writing the appropriate letter in the blank.

_____ 1. Controllable manufacturing overhead variance

_____ 2. Variance

_____ 3. Direct materials price standard

_____ 4. Variance analysis

_____ 5. Standard costs

_____ 6. Favorable variance

_____ 7. Unfavorable variance

_____ 8. Direct materials price variance

_____ 9. Direct materials quantity variance

_____ 10. Direct labor rate variance

_____ 11. Direct labor efficiency variance

_____ 12. Performance report

_____ 13. Flexible budget

a. The difference between the standard direct labor rate and the actual direct labor rate, times actual direct labor hours worked

b. Actual costs exceeding standard costs

c. Expected costs for various levels of anticipated production

d. The difference between standard price and actual price, times actual quantity of material purchased

e. A written comparison between actual costs and budgeted costs for a segment of the business

f. The difference between standard quantity and quantity of material used, times standard price

g. Standard costs exceeding actual costs

h. The difference between standard direct labor hours allowed and actual direct labor hours worked, times standard direct labor rate

i. Predetermined costs that are expressed as a cost per unit of finished product

j. The difference between actual manufacturing overhead incurred and the manufacturing overhead budgeted for the level of production reached

k. The difference between a standard cost and an actual cost

l. A careful estimate of the cost of a specific direct material in the next accounting period

m. The process of computing the difference between standard costs and actual costs and identifying the causes of those differences

---

Note to student: The matching quiz might be completed more efficiently by starting with the definition and searching for the corresponding term.

Short Answer

Use the lines provided to answer each item.

1. Discuss how standard costing can be used in each stage of the management cycle.

_____

_____

_____

_____

_____

2. When does a favorable manufacturing overhead volume variance exist?

_____

_____

_____

_____

3. What are the six standards used to compute total standard unit cost?

_____

_____

_____

_____

_____

_____

4. When does a favorable direct materials quantity variance exist?

_____

_____

5. When does an unfavorable direct labor rate variance exist?

_____

_____

True-False

Circle T if the statement is true, F if it is false. Please provide explanations for the false answers, using the blank lines at the end of the section.

T F 1. Time and motion studies of workers are used in establishing direct labor rate standards.

T F 2. Under a standard costing system, all costs that flow through the inventory accounts are at standard.

T F 3. Computing variances is an essential part of the planning function of budgetary control.

T F 4. It is impossible to have unfavorable direct materials price and direct materials quantity variances and have a favorable total direct materials cost variance.

T F 5. The flexible budget includes both budgeted fixed costs and budgeted variable costs for each level of anticipated activity.

T F 6. The total direct labor cost variance consists of the direct labor rate variance plus the direct labor efficiency variance.

T F 7. The total standard manufacturing overhead rate consists of only the standard variable rate.

T F 8. Computing the total direct labor cost variance is more important than computing the direct labor rate and direct labor efficiency variances.

T F 9. Performance reports should contain only those cost items controllable by the manager receiving the report.

T F 10. A flexible budget is also known as a fixed budget.

T F **11.** It is possible to have an unfavorable manufacturing overhead volume variance and have a favorable total manufacturing overhead variance.

T F **12.** Once an unfavorable variance has been calculated, it is unnecessary to determine the underlying cause.

T F **13.** The flexible budget formula is an equation that determines the correct budgeted cost for any level of productive activity.

_____

_____

_____

_____

_____

_____

_____

_____

_____

_____

_____

_____

_____

_____

_____

_____

_____

_____

_____

_____

_____

_____

_____

_____

Multiple Choice

Circle the letter of the best answer.

1. Workers' wages paid during a period are all that is needed to compute the
   a. actual direct labor cost.
   b. direct labor rate standard.
   c. standard direct labor cost.
   d. direct labor cost variance.

2. Which of the following would *not* be a possible cause of a direct materials price variance?
   a. Changes in vendors' prices, either up or down
   b. Inaccurate direct materials price standards
   c. Differences in anticipated versus actual quantity discounts received
   d. All of the above could be a cause.

3. If an organization is not using a flexible budget that adjusts with changes in activity, it is probably using a
   a. master budget.
   b. production budget.
   c. cash disbursements budget.
   d. static budget.

4. If actual manufacturing overhead was $140,000 and the standard manufacturing overhead applied to good units produced was $100,000, then the organization had a(n)
   a. unfavorable variance of $40,000.
   b. favorable variance of $40,000.
   c. error in calculation.
   d. none of the above.

5. Given the following information, what would be the total budgeted costs at 10,000 units of output?

Variable costs:	
Direct materials	$4.00 per unit
Direct labor	1.00 per unit
Variable manufacturing overhead	3.00 per unit
Fixed manufacturing overhead	$20,000

   a. $80,000
   b. $100,000
   c. $40,000
   d. Undeterminable given the data provided

6. Assuming the same facts as in 5, what would be the total budgeted costs at a production level of 20,000 units?
   a. $180,000
   b. $160,000
   c. $20,000
   d. Undeterminable given the data provided

7. Which of the following variances would be used to evaluate the performance of the purchasing manager?
   a. Direct materials price variance
   b. Direct labor rate variance
   c. Direct labor efficiency variance
   d. Direct materials quantity variance

8. If employees take more time to achieve a given level of production than the standard allows, there will be a(n)
   a. favorable direct labor rate variance.
   b. unfavorable direct labor rate variance.
   c. favorable direct labor efficiency variance.
   d. unfavorable direct labor efficiency variance.

9. In a flexible budget, which total costs would *not* change, given different levels of production?
   a. Fixed manufacturing overhead
   b. Variable manufacturing overhead
   c. Direct labor costs
   d. Direct materials costs

10. Standard costing can be used by managers for
    a. evaluating performance.
    b. identifying inefficiencies.
    c. product pricing.
    d. all of the above.

APPLYING YOUR KNOWLEDGE

Exercises

1. Goethe Company employs a standard costing system in the manufacture of expensive handpainted dishes. The standards for the current year are:

   Direct materials price standards
Porcelain	$.80/lb.
Red paint	$1.00/tube
Blue paint	$1.00/tube

   Direct materials quantity standards
Porcelain	½ lb./dish
Red paint	1 tube/20 dishes
Blue paint	1 tube/50 dishes

   Direct labor time standards
Molding department	.03 hour/dish
Painting department	.05 hour/dish

   Direct labor rate standards
Molding department	$4.00/hour
Painting department	$6.00/hour

   Standard manufacturing overhead rates
Standard variable manu-facturing overhead rate	$3.00/direct labor hour
Standard fixed manu-facturing overhead rate	$2.00/direct labor hour

   Compute the standard manufacturing cost per dish for direct materials, direct labor, and overhead.

Porcelain	$_____
Red paint	_____
Blue paint	_____
Molding department wages	_____
Painting department wages	_____
Variable manufacturing overhead	_____
Fixed manufacturing overhead	_____
Standard cost of one dish	$_____

2. Sturchio Company expects fixed manufacturing overhead to total $50,000 for 20xx. In addition, variable costs per unit are expected to be: direct labor, $4.50; direct materials, $1.25; and variable manufacturing overhead, $2.75. Using these data, prepare a flexible budget for a 10,000-unit, 15,000-unit, and 20,000-unit volume. In addition, determine the flexible budget formula.

Sturchio Company
Flexible Budget
For the Year Ended December 31, 20xx

---

3. Mississippi Sporting Goods Company uses a standard costing system for producing 10-pound steel dumbbells. The standard cost for steel is $.60 per pound, and each dumbbell should require .3 standard direct labor hours at a standard rate of $4.50 per hour. During the month of March, 65,000 dumbbells were actually produced. During the period, 657,000 pounds of steel were used and purchased, at a cost of $381,060. Direct labor hours numbered 22,100 at an expense of $100,555. Using the data above, compute the following variances for the month of March. Indicate whether each variance is favorable or unfavorable by writing F or U after each amount.

a. Direct materials price variance =

$ _____

b. Direct materials quantity variance =

$ _____

c. Direct labor rate variance =

$ _____

d. Direct labor efficiency variance =

$ _____

Crossword Puzzle
for Chapters 24 and 25

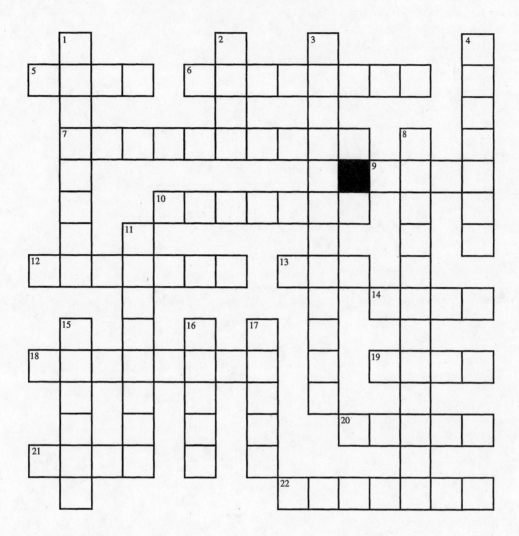

ACROSS

5. Budget disclosing receipts and payments
6. Direct materials variance
7. Idle-cash purchase
9. Item in 5-Across
10. _____ expenditures budget
12. _____ and administrative expense budget
13. Opposite of "less" in a budget
14. Budget objective
18. Operating, investing, or financing
19. Cash _____ forecast
20. Budget expressed in hours and dollars
21. Direct labor _____ standard
22. Formal business plans

DOWN

1. Standard minus actual
2. Part of "JIT"
3. Predetermined amount for materials, etc. (2 words)
4. Budgeted _____ sheet
8. Cost that can be influenced
11. Budget covering a range of volumes
15. Performance report column
16. Static, as some budgets
17. Management process, in four stages

CHAPTER 26 PERFORMANCE MANAGEMENT AND EVALUATION

REVIEWING THE CHAPTER

Objective 1: Describe how the balanced scorecard aligns performance with organizational goals and explain the balanced scorecard's role in the management cycle.

1. The **balanced scorecard** is a framework that links the perspectives of an organization's four basic stakeholder groups with the organization's mission and vision, performance measures, strategic plan, and resources. The four groups are investors, employees, internal business processes, and customers. An organization will determine each group's objectives and translate them into performance measures that have specific quantifiable targets.

2. During the planning stage, the balanced scorecard provides a framework that enables managers to translate their organization's vision and strategy into operational terms and objectives. Once the objectives are set, managers can select performance measures and set performance targets.

3. During the executing stage, managers use the objectives for the organization as the basis for decision making within their individual areas of responsibility.

4. During the reviewing stage, managers will review financial and nonfinancial results to evaluate their strategies in meeting the objectives and performance targets set during the planning stage and compare the targets with actual results.

5. The reporting stage of the management cycle requires the preparation of a variety of reports to enable managers to monitor and evaluate performance measures that add value for the stakeholder groups.

Objective 2: Discuss performance measurement and state the issues that affect management's ability to measure performance.

6. A **performance management and evaluation system** is a set of procedures that account for and report on both financial and nonfinancial performance, so that a company can identify how well it is doing, where it is going, and what improvements will make it more profitable.

7. **Performance measurement** is the use of quantitative tools to gauge an organization's performance in relation to a specific goal or an expected outcome. Each organization must develop a unique set of performance measures appropriate to its specific situation that will help managers to distinguish between what is being measured and the actual measures used to monitor performance.

Objective 3: Define *responsibility accounting* and describe the role responsibility centers play in performance management and evaluation.

8. **Responsibility accounting** is an information system that classifies data according to areas of responsibility and reports each area's activities by including only the revenue, cost, and resource categories that the assigned manager can control. The system is used to prepare budgets by responsibility area and to report the actual results of each responsibility center. Costs and revenues

that a manager can be held responsible for are called **controllable costs and revenues** because they result from a manager's actions, influence, or decisions.

9. A **responsibility center** is an organizational unit whose manager has been assigned the responsibility of managing a portion of the organization's resources. The five types of responsibility centers are as follows:

   a. A **cost center** is a responsibility center whose manager is accountable only for controllable costs that have well-defined relationships between the center's resources and products or services.

   b. A **discretionary cost center** is a responsibility center whose manager is accountable only for costs in which the relationship between resources and products or service produced is not well defined. These centers, like cost centers, have approved budgets that set spending limits.

   c. A **revenue center** is accountable primarily for revenue; its success is based on its ability to generate revenue.

   d. A **profit center** is a responsibility center whose manager is accountable for both revenue and costs and for the resulting operating income.

   e. An **investment center** is a responsibility center whose manager is accountable for profit generation; the manager can also make significant decisions about the resources the center uses. The manager can control revenues, costs, and the investments of assets to achieve the organization's goals.

10. An **organization chart** is a visual representation of an organization's hierarchy of responsibility for the purposes of management control.

Objective 4: Prepare performance reports for the various types of responsibility centers, including reports based on flexible budgets for cost centers and variable costing for profit centers.

11. Performance reports should contain costs, revenues, and resources that are controllable by individual managers to compare actual performance and budget expectations.

12. Flexible budgeting is a cost control tool used to evaluate performance and is derived by multiplying actual unit output by the standard unit costs. By using standard costing to compare with actual costs, specific variances for direct materials, direct labor, and manufacturing overhead can be computed.

13. **Variable costing** is a method of preparing profit center performance reports that classifies a manager's controllable costs as either variable or fixed. To evaluate profit center performance, the variable cost of goods sold and the variable selling and administrative expenses are subtracted from sales to arrive at the contribution margin for the center. All controllable fixed manufacturing, selling, or administrative costs are subtracted from the contribution margin to determine the operating income.

14. In the traditional income statement, all manufacturing costs are assigned to cost of goods sold. A variable costing income statement uses the same format as the contribution income statement and includes only direct materials, direct labor, and variable manufacturing overhead to compute variable cost of goods sold. Fixed manufacturing overhead is considered a cost of the current accounting period and is listed with fixed selling expenses.

Objective 5: Use the traditional performance measures of return on investment and residual income to evaluate investment centers.

15. **Return on investment** is the performance measure that takes into account both operating income and the assets invested to earn that income. Return on investment is computed as follows:

$$\text{Return on Investment (ROI)} = \frac{\text{Operating Income}}{\text{Assets Invested}}$$

(Note: Assets invested is the average of the beginning and ending asset balances for the period.)

16. **Profit margin** is the ratio of operating income to sales, which represents the percentage of each sales dollar that results in profit.

17. **Asset turnover** is the ratio of sales to average assets invested. It indicates the productivity of assets or the number of sales dollars generated by each dollar invested in assets.

18. Return on investment is equal to profit margin multiplied by asset turnover:

$$\text{ROI} = \text{Profit Margin} \times \text{Asset Turnover}$$

or

$$\text{ROI} = \frac{\text{Operating Income}}{\text{Sales}} \times \frac{\text{Sales}}{\text{Assets Invested}} = \frac{\text{Operating Income}}{\text{Assets Invested}}$$

19. **Residual income** is the operating income that an investment center earns above the minimum

desired return on invested assets. The formula for computing the residual income of an investment is:

$$\text{Residual Income} = \text{Operating Income} - (\text{Desired ROI} \times \text{Assets Invested})$$

Objective 6: Use economic value added to evaluate investment centers.

20. **Economic value added** is an indicator of performance that measures the shareholder wealth created by an investment center. The formula is:

$$\text{Economic Value Added} = \text{After-Tax Operating Income} - \text{Cost of Capital in Dollars}$$

or

$$\text{Economic Value Added} = \text{After-Tax Operating Income} - [\text{Cost of Capital} \times (\text{Total Assets} - \text{Current Liabilities})]$$

Cost of capital is the minimum desired rate of return on an investment.

Objective 7: Explain how properly linked performance incentives and measures add value for all stakeholders in performance management and evaluation.

21. Linking goals to measurable objectives and performance targets are necessary to measure the effectiveness of the performance of a center, a manager, and the entire company. **Performance-based pay** is tying appropriate compensation incentives to the achievement of measurable performance targets. Some examples may include cash bonuses, trips, profit sharing, and company stock options.

Test your knowledge of the chapter by choosing the best answer for each of the following items.

1. During the planning stage, the balanced scorecard provides
   a. reports to enable managers to monitor performance measures.
   b. financial and nonfinancial results to evaluate managers' strategies.
   c. a framework that enables managers to translate their organization's vision and strategy into operational terms and objectives.
   d. managers with objectives as a basis for decision making.

2. The responsibility center whose manager is accountable for both revenues and costs and for the resulting operating income is the
   a. investment center.
   b. profit center.
   c. cost center.
   d. discretionary center.

3. The difference between a variable costing income statement and a traditional income statement is that in a variable statement
   a. all expenses are included in calculating cost of goods sold.
   b. only fixed costs are included in cost of goods sold.
   c. all variable costs including variable selling and administrative costs are included in cost of goods sold.
   d. both statements are prepared the same.

4. Operating income divided by assets invested represents which of the following performance measures?
   a. Return on investment
   b. Residual income
   c. Economic value added
   d. Cost of capital

5. In a flexible budget formula for a department, the variable portion of the formula states that the standard variable cost per unit is multiplied by the
   a. standard hours worked.
   b. number of units produced.
   c. standard hours allowed.
   d. number of units planned.

6. What type of responsibility center are accounting, personnel, and legal departments?
   a. Discretionary center
   b. Cost center
   c. Profit center
   d. Investment center

7. The standard cost for producing a bottle of mustard is as follows:

Direct materials	$.35
Direct labor	$.10
Variable overhead	$.05
Total fixed overhead	$3,000

The company estimated producing 10,000 bottles for the month of April. The actual number of bottles produced was 11,000. The flexible budget will equal
   a. $5,000.
   b. $3,000.
   c. $8,000.
   d. $8,500.

8. Which of the following is *not* included as a variable cost in the flexible budget of a candy maker?
   a. Sugar
   b. Depreciation expense
   c. Candy wrappers
   d. Sales commissions

9. The minimum desired rate of return on an investment is known as
   a. cost of capital.
   b. return on investment.
   c. operating income.
   d. profit margin.

10. The objective of performance-based pay is to
    a. give all employees a Christmas bonus.
    b. guarantee that all employees get a pay raise each year.
    c. link compensation to the measurable performance targets of an employee.
    d. link an employee's overtime with the production for a given period.

TESTING YOUR KNOWLEDGE

Matching*

Match each term with its definition by writing the appropriate letter in the blank.

_____ 1. Profit center

_____ 2. Organization chart

_____ 3. Residual income

_____ 4. Cost center

_____ 5. Balanced scorecard

_____ 6. Cost of capital

_____ 7. Profit margin

_____ 8. Asset turnover

_____ 9. Performance-based pay

_____ 10. Economic value added

a. Minimum desired rate of return on an investment

b. A framework that links the perspectives of an organization's four basic stakeholder groups with the organization's mission and vision, performance measures, strategic plan, and resources

c. The ratio of operating income to sales

d. An indicator of performance that measures the shareholder wealth created by an investment center

e. A responsibility center that has well-defined relationships between its resources and products or services and has only controllable costs

f. The operating income that an investment center earns above a minimum desired return on invested assets

g. A responsibility center whose manager is accountable for both revenue and costs and for the resulting operating income

h. A visual representation of an organization's hierarchy of responsibility for the purposes of management control

i. The ratio of sales to average assets invested

j. Tying appropriate compensation incentives to the achievement of measurable performance targets

Short Answer

Use the lines provided to answer each item.

1. What is the formula for economic value added?

_____

_____

_____

2. What are the five responsibility centers?

_____

_____

_____

_____

3. Explain the difference between a variable costing income statement and a traditional income statement.

_____

_____

_____

4. What is the purpose of a balanced scorecard?

_____

_____

_____

Note to student: The matching quiz might be completed more efficiently by starting with the definition and searching for the corresponding term.

Circle T if the statement is true, F if it is false. Please provide explanations for the false answers, using the blank lines at the end of the section.

T F   **1.** Responsibility accounting is an information system that classifies data according to areas of responsibility.

T F   **2.** A discretionary center is a responsibility center whose manager is accountable for controllable costs of a center that has its resources and products well defined.

T F   **3.** Return on investment is equal to profit margin divided by asset turnover.

T F   **4.** The flexible budget formula is an equation that determines the correct budgeted cost for any level of production activity.

T F   **5.** Performance reports should contain all costs, revenues, and resources regardless of whether managers can control them or not.

T F   **6.** The traditional income statement, the variable income statement, and the contribution margin income statement will produce the same net income.

T F   **7.** The four basic stakeholder groups are investors, customers, employees, and creditors.

T F   **8.** The asset turnover ratio is the ratio of sales to current assets.

T F   **9.** An investment center is a responsibility center whose manager is accountable for profit generation and whose manager can make significant decisions about the resources the center uses.

T F   **10.** During the reporting stage of the management cycle, the accounting department should prepare a standard set of reports to enable managers to compare their performance with other departments.

_____

_____

_____

_____

_____

_____

_____

_____

_____

_____

_____

_____

Multiple Choice

Circle the letter of the best answer.

1. In a flexible budget, which total costs would *not* change, given different levels of production?
   a. Fixed manufacturing overhead
   b. Variable manufacturing overhead
   c. Direct labor costs
   d. Direct materials costs

2. Given the following information, what would be the total flexible budget at 20,000 units of output?

   Variable costs:
Direct materials	$4 per unit
Direct labor	1 per unit
Variable overhead	3 per unit

   Fixed manufacturing overhead $20,000

   a. $160,000
   b. $20,000
   c. $180,000
   d. $80,000

3. The four basic stakeholder groups are
   a. investors, employees, internal business processes, and customers.
   b. employees, creditors, customers, and management.
   c. investors, employees, creditors, and customers.
   d. investors, tax authorities, employees, and customers.

4. To compute return on investment, the following equation would be used:
   a. Operating Income ÷ Assets Invested
   b. Operating Income − (Desired ROI × Assets Invested)
   c. Operating Income × Assets Invested
   d. Operating Income + (Desired ROI × Assets Invested)

5. Which of the following ratios represents the percentage of each sales dollar that results in profit?
   a. Cost of capital
   b. Profit margin
   c. Net sales
   d. Net income after taxes

6. Which of the following centers is accountable primarily for revenue and its success judged on its ability to generate revenue?
   a. Profit center
   b. Investment center
   c. Revenue center
   d. Discretionary center

7. A variable income statement would include which of the following costs as part of the cost of goods sold?
   a. Direct materials, direct labor, and all manufacturing overhead
   b. Direct materials, direct labor, and only fixed manufacturing overhead
   c. Direct materials, direct labor, and only variable manufacturing overhead
   d. Only manufacturing overhead

8. All of the following are responsibility centers *except*
   a. cost centers.
   b. operating centers.
   c. profit centers.
   d. investment centers.

9. Using reports to evaluate performance is usually done in which stage of the management cycle?
   a. Reviewing
   b. Planning
   c. Reporting
   d. Evaluating

10. Managers use the asset turnover ratio to determine the
    a. productivity of assets or the number of sales dollars generated by each dollar invested in assets.
    b. productivity of liabilities or the number of sales dollars generated by each dollar owed.
    c. productivity of sales by the number of asset dollars generated by each dollar of sales.
    d. None of the above

APPLYING YOUR KNOWLEDGE

Exercises

1. The Corwin Company manufactures scented candles. For the year ended December 31, 2002, the company expects its fixed manufacturing overhead to equal $135,000. Variable costs to produce their candles are as follows: direct materials, $1.80; direct labor, $.35; and variable manufacturing overhead, $.60. Using these data, prepare a flexible budget assuming the production of 350,000 candles.

Corwin Company
Flexible Budget
For the Year Ended December 31, 2002

---

2. The December 31, 20xx, Budget Versus Actual Report for the Cazuelas Company was prepared as follows:

Cazuelas Company
Budget Versus Actual Report
For the Year Ended December 31, 20xx

	Budget	Actual	Variance
Sales	120,000	125,000	5,000
COGS	70,000	79,000	(9,000)
Gross margin	50,000	46,000	(4,000)
Operating expenses	30,000	28,000	2,000
Net income	20,000	18,000	(2,000)

Additional information: Each unit is sold for $100. The standard cost per unit is $62.50.

What is the amount of variance that each of the following responsibility centers would be accountable for?

a. Revenue center

b. Profit center

c. Cost center (Production Department)

CHAPTER 27 ANALYSIS FOR DECISION MAKING

REVIEWING THE CHAPTER

Objective 1: Explain how managers make short-run decisions during the management cycle, and identify the steps in the management decision cycle.

1. Managers make many decisions that will affect their organization's activities in the short run. They need historical and estimated quantitative information that is both financial and nonfinancial in nature. Such information will help managers answer the question, What will happen if we choose one alternative over another?

2. **Short-run decision analysis** is an important component of the management cycle. In the planning stage, managers use the analysis to estimate costs and revenue information; in the executing stage, managers make and implement short-run decisions to improve their organization's profitability and liquidity; in the reviewing stage, managers can use such analysis to determine if the decision's results met expectations and, if necessary, identify and prescribe corrective action; and in the reporting stage, reports are continuously provided, supported by relevant quantitative and qualitative information.

3. Managers must identify and assess the importance of all relevant factors when making short-run decisions. They must also make sure that the decision is compatible with their organization's strategic plan.

4. The **management decision cycle** covers (a) discovering the problem or need, (b) identifying the alternative courses of action, (c) analyzing the effects of each alternative on business operations, (d) selecting the best alternative, and (e) judging the success of the decision through a postdecision audit.

Objective 2: Define and explain incremental analysis and its related concepts.

5. **Incremental analysis** (also referred to as *differential analysis*) helps managers compare cost and revenue data of alternative courses of action. Only data that are different for the different alternatives are included in the analysis. According to the incremental-analysis method, the alternative that results in the highest increase in net income or cost savings is the best alternative.

6. The first step in the incremental analysis is to eliminate any irrelevant revenues and costs. Irrelevant costs include sunk costs and costs that will not differ between the alternatives. A **sunk cost** is a cost that was incurred because of a previous decision and cannot be recovered through the current decision.

7. Once irrelevant revenues and costs are identified, the incremental analysis may be prepared using only projected revenues and expenses that will differ between the alternatives, allowing managers to evaluate and choose the best course of action.

8. When analyzing short-run decisions, managers must consider the effects of **opportunity costs,** which are the revenues that are forfeited or lost when one decision is chosen over another.

9. Special decision reports are necessary when qualitative information supports or replaces the quantitative analysis. These reports do not have a "correct" format. Rather, experienced accountants prepare reports to fit the individual situation.

Objective 3: Prepare evaluations of alternatives for make-or-buy decisions, special order decisions, product mix decisions, and sell or process-further decisions.

10. Management must continually carry out **make-or-buy analysis** about parts that go into product assembly. Probably the best method to employ is incremental analysis, in which only the relevant costs are compared. All other things being equal, the alternative resulting in the lowest incremental cost (the most profitable) is the one that should be chosen. Information needed about the making of the product is (a) what is the need for additional equipment, (b) what are the variable costs of making the item, and (c) what are the incremental fixed costs. Information needed about the buying of the product is (a) what is the purchase price of the item, (b) will rent or net cash flows be generated from any vacated space in the factory, and (c) what is the residual value of unused machinery.

11. Management often must decide whether to accept or reject special product orders at prices below normal market prices. **Special order analysis** is used to help managers decide whether to accept or reject a special order. A company should only consider a special order if unused capacity exists, which would keep fixed costs unchanged and irrelevant to the decision. The only costs affected by the order are variable or relevant costs.

12. **Product mix analysis** is used to find the most profitable combination of product sales when the company is producing more than one product. Generally, the strategy is first to figure the contribution margin for each product. Then the ratio of contribution margin to capital equipment should be figured for each to see whether some products are more profitable than others. If extra demand exists for more profitable products, then production should be shifted to those products.

13. Sometimes two or more products or services are created simultaneously from a common raw material or input. Such products, known as **joint products,** cannot be identified as separate products during some or all of the production process. Only at a specific point, called the **split-off point,** do joint products become separate and identifiable. For example, in the petroleum industry when crude oil is refined, it is only after the split-off point that gasoline, kerosene, and motor oils become identifiable as separate products.
    a. Some products may be sold at the split-off point and others may be processed further. Extra processing adds value to the product but normally also increases costs. **Sell or process-further**

analysis helps managers determine whether to sell a joint product at the split-off point or process it further. This technique enables managers to analyze the incremental costs and revenues of the two possible courses of action to see whether the increase in total revenue will exceed the additional costs of processing. Joint costs incurred before split-off do not affect the decision. Such an analysis involves selecting the course of action that will maximize operating income.

    b. Measuring incremental costs for processing beyond the split-off point can create problems. The costs of direct materials, direct labor, and variable manufacturing overhead are indeed incremental. However, fixed costs are not incremental since they will be incurred regardless of the decision. Therefore, fixed manufacturing overhead costs common to other production activity must be excluded from a sell or process-further analysis.

Objective 4: Identify the types of projected costs and revenues used to evaluate alternatives for capital investment.

14. Decisions about when and how much to spend on capital facilities and other long-term projects are referred to as **capital investment decisions.** **Capital investment analysis** (also called *capital budgeting*) is the process of (a) identifying the need for an investment, (b) analyzing different courses of action, (c) preparing reports for management, (d) choosing the best alternative, and (e) rationing capital investment funds among competing resource needs. Because capital budgeting is probably the largest and most complicated decision analysis facing management, it requires the aid of all functional areas of the business.

15. When evaluating a proposed capital expenditure, some of the various measures of costs and revenues used are:
    a. Net Income and Net Cash Inflows—**Net cash inflow,** the balance of increases in cash receipts over increases in cash payments resulting from a capital expenditure, is used in evaluating capital projects when either the payback period or the net present value method is employed. **Cost savings** measure the benefits from proposed capital investments.
    b. Equal Versus Unequal Cash Flows—Projected cash flows may be the same for each year or they may vary from year to year. Unequal cash flows are common and must be analyzed for each year of an asset's life.
    c. Carrying Value of Assets—**Carrying value** is the undepreciated portion of the original cost

of a long-term asset. For evaluating purposes, carrying value of an old asset is irrelevant but net proceeds from the asset's sale or disposal are relevant.

d. **Depreciation Expense and Income Taxes—** Depreciation is a noncash expense requiring no cash outlay during the period. It can, however, affect cash flows because of its effects on income taxes, so it is assumed in this chapter that those effects have been taken into consideration in computing cash flows.

e. **Disposal or Residual Values—**Projected disposal or residual values of replacement equipment are relevant to evaluating a proposed capital expenditure because they represent future cash inflows and usually differ among alternatives.

Objective 5: Apply the concept of the time value of money.

16. An organization will analyze cash flows of long-term capital investment in terms of the time value of money. The **time value of money** is the concept that cash flows of equal dollar amounts separated by a time interval have different present values because of the effects of compound interest. The notions of interest, present value, and future value are all related to the value of money.

17. **Interest** is the cost associated with the use of money for a specific period of time. **Simple interest** is the interest cost of one or more periods when the amount on which the interest is computed stays the same. **Compound interest** is the interest cost for two or more periods when the amount on which the interest is computed changes each period to include all interest paid in previous periods.

18. **Present value** is the amount that must be invested at a given rate of compound interest to produce a given future value.

19. **Future value** is the amount an investment will be worth at a future date if invested at compound interest.

20. An **ordinary annuity** is a series of equal payments or receipts that will begin one time period from the current date. Computing the present value of an ordinary annuity is equal to the present value of equal amounts equally spaced over a period of time.

Objective 6: Analyze capital investment proposals using the net present value method.

21. The **net present value method** evaluates a capital investment by discounting its future cash flows to their present values and subtracting the amount

of the initial investment from the sum of those amounts. (The discount multiplier is based on the minimum desired rate of return and the discount period.) If the net present value of all of the future cash flows exceeds the cost of the asset to be purchased, the expenditure is justified.

22. If the yearly net cash flows incurred over the life of the asset are equal in amount, a factor from Table 4 in Appendix D at the back of the text (corresponding to the required rate of return and the number of years the asset will be used) is multiplied by the yearly cash flow amount. If the yearly net cash flows incurred over the life of the asset are unequal in amount, then each year's net cash flow is multiplied by the correct factor on Table 3 and the discounted amounts are added together to determine the present value. The advantages of the net present value method are that the time value of money is incorporated, and the measurement of total cash flows over the life of the investment brings profitability into the analysis. The disadvantage of the net present value method is its complexity; some managers prefer the simpler computations of the payback period method or accounting rate-of-return method.

Objective 7: Analyze capital investment proposals using the accounting rate-of-return method and the payback period method.

23. The **accounting rate-of-return method** is designed to measure the benefit of a potential capital investment. It is calculated as:

$$\frac{\text{Project's Average Annual Net Income}}{\text{Average Investment Cost}}$$

The average investment cost is calculated as:

$$\left(\frac{\text{Total Investment} - \text{Residual Value}}{2}\right) + \text{Residual Value}$$

If this method is used, management should think seriously about the investment if the rate of return is higher than the minimum desired rate.

24. The **payback period method** is a tool for finding the minimum length of time it would take to recover an initial investment. When a choice must be made between investment alternatives, the one with the shortest payback period is best under this method. The payback period is computed as follows:

$$\text{Payback Period} = \frac{\text{Cost of Investment}}{\text{Annual Net Cash Inflows}}$$

SELF-TEST

Test your knowledge of the chapter by choosing the best answer for each of the following items.

1. Which of the following is *not* considered to be a short-run decision?
   a. Make-or-buy decisions
   b. Capital investment decisions
   c. Special order decisions
   d. Sell or process-further decisions

2. An approach to decision analysis that concentrates on only those revenue and cost items that differ between decision alternatives is known as
   a. contribution margin analysis.
   b. incremental analysis.
   c. make-or-buy analysis.
   d. special order analysis.

3. A management decision to accept or reject a sizable but unusual order that generally has a reduced price is known as a
   a. make-or-buy decision.
   b. sell or process-further decision.
   c. special order decision.
   d. segment elimination decision.

4. Which of the following pieces of information is *not* relevant when evaluating a capital investment decision?
   a. Book value of the capital asset being replaced
   b. Carrying value of the capital asset being replaced
   c. Net cash flows from the proposal
   d. Cost savings from the proposal

5. Mecca Enterprises is contemplating a major investment in a new flexible manufacturing system (FMS). The company's minimum desired accounting rate of return is 16 percent. The total investment is $2,500,000 with a 10 percent residual value at the end of its eight-year expected life. The company uses straight-line depreciation. The FMS should produce $1,400,000 of additional cash revenue annually. Annual cash operating costs are expected to be $600,000. The company is in the 34 percent tax bracket. Using the accounting rate-of-return method, what is the expected after-tax rate of return from the proposed FMS project?
   a. 38.4%
   b. 26.6%
   c. 24.9%
   d. 19.2%

6. Assuming the same facts as in question **5**, and using the payback period method, what is the expected payback period for the proposed FMS project (ignoring taxes)?
   a. 3.625 years
   b. 3.125 years
   c. 3.954 years
   d. 4.009 years

7. The time value of money is the concept that cash flows of equal dollar amounts in different intervals of time have different present values because of
   a. future values.
   b. compound interest.
   c. simple interest.
   d. cost savings.

8. Which of the following may be a reason for a proposed new machine having a projected net cash flow greater than projected net income?
   a. Depreciation expense
   b. Operating machine at capacity
   c. Erroneous sales forecasts
   d. None of the above

9. Which of the following variables is included in calculating the accounting rate of return?
   a. Noncash expenses
   b. Cash expenses
   c. Average investment cost
   d. All of the above

10. If the present value of annual cash outflows is greater than the present value of the annual cash inflows, then the net present value is
    a. negative.
    b. positive.
    c. zero.
    d. None of the above

TESTING YOUR KNOWLEDGE

Matching*

Match each term with its definition by writing the appropriate letter in the blank.

_____ 1. Incremental analysis

_____ 2. Capital investment analysis

_____ 3. Management decision cycle

_____ 4. Accounting rate-of-return method

_____ 5. Payback period method

_____ 6. Net present value method

_____ 7. Product mix analysis

_____ 8. Capital investment decision

_____ 9. Time value of money

a. The capital budgeting method that determines the minimum length of time it would take to recover the initial investment in an asset

b. The process of identifying the need for a facility, analyzing different actions, preparing reports, choosing the best alternative, and rationing available funds among competing needs

c. Determining the most profitable combination of product sales or services

d. The concept ignored by the accounting rate-of-return and payback period methods

e. The capital budgeting method that divides a proposed project's net income by the average investment cost

f. The capital budgeting method that discounts all net cash inflows to the present

g. The comparison of cost and revenue data that differ among alternatives

h. Determining when and how much to spend on capital facilities

i. The five steps managers take in making decisions and following up on them.

Short Answer

Use the lines provided to answer each item.

1. List the five steps in the management decision cycle.

_____

_____

_____

_____

_____

2. What are the five steps involved in capital investment analysis?

_____

_____

_____

_____

_____

Note to student: The matching quiz might be completed more efficiently by starting with the definition and searching for the corresponding term.

3. Distinguish between relevant and irrelevant information.

_____

_____

_____

4. List three methods frequently used to evaluate capital investment proposals.

_____

_____

_____

5. What three factors are needed in make-or-buy analysis for a "buy" decision?

_____

_____

_____

True-False

Circle T if the statement is true, F if it is false. Please provide explanations for the false answers, using the blank lines at the end of the section.

T F **1.** The future value is the amount an investment will be worth at a future date if invested at compound interest.

T F **2.** When incremental analysis is used, the main concern is with each alternative's net income projection.

T F **3.** Capital budgeting involves the various methods of obtaining cash for business operations.

T F **4.** The simplest method to apply in evaluating a capital investment proposal is the net present value method.

T F **5.** The time value of money is ignored in both the accounting rate-of-return and the payback period methods.

T F **6.** The payback period is the maximum length of time it should take to recover the cost of an investment.

T F **7.** The payback period equals the cost of the capital investment divided by the annual net cash inflow.

T F **8.** Under the net present value method, there is no need for a minimum desired rate of return.

T F **9.** Under the net present value method, a negative net present value means that the project proposal should probably be rejected.

T F **10.** Incremental analysis is very useful for make-or-buy decisions.

T F **11.** For special order analysis, the only relevant costs are costs that vary because of this decision.

T F **12.** When a product mix analysis is being performed, the product with the highest contribution margin per unit of a scarce resource is always the one that is most beneficial to the company.

T F **13.** In the reviewing stage of the management cycle, determinations are made about whether a decision met expectations.

T F **14.** Managers use only internally generated information in decision analysis.

T F **15.** Often decision making involves selecting among many alternatives.

T F **16.** Opportunity costs are revenues that are expected to be reached when an alternative is chosen.

_____
_____
_____
_____
_____
_____
_____
_____
_____
_____

_____
_____
_____
_____
_____
_____
_____
_____
_____
_____

Multiple Choice

Circle the letter of the best answer.

1. Under the accounting rate-of-return method, which of the following elements is irrelevant?
   a. The residual value of an asset
   b. Annual net cash inflow
   c. The cost of an asset
   d. The project's average annual net income

2. Probably the best method to use in deciding to make or buy a part for a product is
   a. direct costing.
   b. the payback period method.
   c. incremental analysis.
   d. the net present value method.

3. The contribution approach would probably *not* be used when
   a. deciding whether to discontinue a particular product line.
   b. performing product mix analysis.
   c. deciding which of two machines to purchase.
   d. deciding whether to accept a special order.

4. Products A, B, and C have contribution margins of $3, $5, and $4 per unit, respectively. Granada Company intends to manufacture one of the products and expects sales to be $30,000 regardless of which product it manufactures. Which product will result in the highest net income for Granada, assuming that the same machinery and workers would be used to produce each?
   a. A
   b. B
   c. C
   d. More information is needed.

5. Periodic depreciation of equipment is a
   a. cash expense.
   b. noncash expense.
   c. noncash revenue.
   d. None of the above.

6. When using the net present value method, which of the following net cash inflows will result in the highest amount when discounted to the present period (20x1) at a 10 percent discount rate? (Use the tables in Appendix B of your text.)
   a. $755 in 20x1
   b. $815 in 20x2
   c. $880 in 20x3
   d. $1,000 in 20x4

7. Depreciation produces
   a. a cash inflow equal to the related tax savings.
   b. a cash outflow equal to the depreciation charged.
   c. a cash outflow equal to the related tax savings.
   d. no cash inflow or outflow.

8. Special decision reports are always
   a. in contribution margin format.
   b. a set structure.
   c. prepared by accountants to fit the needs of the decision maker or the manager.
   d. None of the above.

APPLYING YOUR KNOWLEDGE

Exercises

1. A company is considering the purchase of a machine to produce the plastic chin protectors used in hockey. The machine costs $70,000 and would have a 5-year life (no residual value). The machine is expected to produce $8,000 per year in net income (after depreciation). Assume that the company uses straight-line depreciation, and that the maximum payback period is 3 years (ignore any tax effects).

   a. Using the payback period approach, determine whether or not the company should invest in the machine. Show all your work.

   b. Determine the accounting rate of return.

2. A machine that costs $20,000 will produce a net cash inflow of $5,000 in the first year of operations and $6,000 in each of the remaining 4 years of use. Present value information for the 16 percent rate of return is as follows:

   Present value of $1 due in 1 year   = .862
   Present value of $1 due in 2 years = .743
   Present value of $1 due in 3 years = .641
   Present value of $1 due in 4 years = .552
   Present value of $1 due in 5 years = .476

   Using the net present value method, determine whether the company should purchase the machine.

3. On June 30, 20x1, Omni Books, Unltd., had 100,000 unsold 20x1 calendars. Direct materials cost is $3 per calendar, direct labor is $2 per calendar, variable overhead is $.50 per calendar, and fixed overhead (based on a production volume of 300,000 calendars) is $1 per calendar. Shipping and packaging (paid by the company) is $1.75 per calendar. The normal selling price is $12 per calendar. What is the *minimum* special price that the company could set for the unsold calendars?

4. Snoball Donut Company is considering the acquisition of a new automatic donut dropper machine that will cost $400,000. The machine will have a life of five years and will produce a cash savings from operations of $160,000 per year. The asset is to be depreciated using the straight-line method and will have no residual value. The company's income tax rate is 34 percent and management expects a 10 percent minimum after-tax rate of return on all investments.

Write the letter of the best answer below.

_____ 1. The depreciation per year on the machine will be
   a. $40,000.
   b. $48,000.
   c. $60,000.
   d. $80,000.

_____ 2. The tax benefit (increase in cash flow) resulting from the annual depreciation charge will be
   a. $16,000.
   b. $24,000.
   c. $27,200.
   d. $32,000.

_____ 3. The accounting rate of return on the machine is
   a. 26.4 percent.
   b. 52.8 percent.
   c. 41.2 percent.
   d. 17.7 percent.

_____ 4. The payback period will be
   a. 2 years.
   b. 3 years.
   c. 4 years.
   d. 5 years.

_____ 5. The present value of future net after-tax cash inflows is
   a. $503,445.
   b. $303,280.
   c. $406,395.
   d. $606,560.

_____ 6. After considering the results in 3–5 above, the company
   a. should invest in the machine.
   b. should not invest in the machine.

Crossword Puzzle
for Chapters 26 and 27

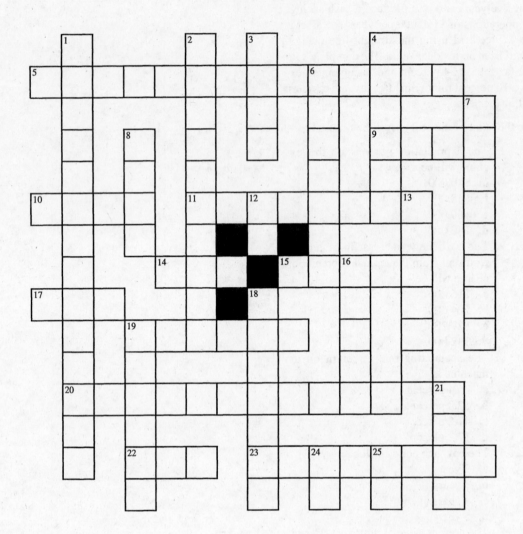

ACROSS

5. Word with accounting or center
9. Begin the management cycle
10. Cost that cannot be recovered
11. See 15-Across
14. _____ present value method
15. With 11-Across, sales divided by resources invested
17. Combination of products or services
19. Accounting _____-return method (2 words)
20. _____ cost (revenue forfeited)
22. Short-_____ decision analysis
23. _____ valued added (EVA)

DOWN

1. Earnings above a minimum desired level (2 words)
2. The "I" of ROI
3. _____ value of money
4. Interest that does not compound
6. Cash receipts
7. The cost of using money
8. _____-or-buy decision
12. 1-Down, for short
13. The "R" of ROI
16. _____-off point
18. Performance incentives
19. Performance document
21. Single item produced or sold
24. The "O" of ROI
25. Cost _____ capital

APPENDIX A INTERNATIONAL ACCOUNTING

REVIEWING THE APPENDIX

1. When businesses expand internationally (called *multinational* or *transnational corporations*), two accounting problems arise: (a) The financial statements of foreign subsidiaries involve different currencies. These must be translated into domestic currency by means of an *exchange rate*. (b) The foreign financial statements are not necessarily prepared in accordance with domestic financial accounting standards.

2. Purchases and sales with foreign countries pose no accounting problem for the domestic company when the domestic currency is being used. However, when the transaction involves foreign currency, the domestic company will probably realize and record an *exchange gain or loss*. This exchange gain or loss reflects the change in the exchange rate from the transaction date to the date of payment.

3. When financial statements are prepared between the transaction date and the date of payment, GAAP requires that an unrealized gain or loss must be recorded if the exchange rate has changed.

4. A foreign subsidiary that a parent company controls should be included in the parent company's consolidated financial statements. The subsidiary's financial statements must therefore be restated into the parent's *reporting currency*. The method of *restatement* depends on the foreign subsidiary's *functional currency*—that is, the currency with which it transacts most of its business.

5. There are two basic types of foreign operations. Type I subsidiaries are self-contained within a foreign country. Their financial statements must be restated from the functional currency (local currency in this case) to the reporting currency. Type II subsidiaries are simply an extension of the parent's operations. Their financial statements must be restated from the local currency to the functional currency (which in this case is the same as the reporting currency).

6. When a Type I subsidiary operates in a country where there is hyperinflation (more than 100 percent cumulative inflation over three years), it is treated as a Type II subsidiary, with the functional currency being the U.S. dollar.

Summary of Journal Entries Introduced in Appendix A

A.   Accounts Receivable, foreign company   XX (amount billed)
       Sales   XX (amount billed)
           Credit sale made, fixed amount billed in foreign currency,
           recorded in U.S. dollars

B.   Cash   XX (amount received)
       Exchange Gain or Loss   XX (the difference)
           Accounts Receivable, foreign company   XX (amount billed)
               Received payment in foreign currency, exchange loss
               arose from weakening of foreign currency in relation
               to U.S. dollar

C.   Purchases   XX (amount billed)
           Accounts Payable, foreign company   XX (amount billed)
               Credit purchase made, fixed amount billed in foreign
               currency

D.   Accounts Payable, foreign company   XX (amount billed)
       Exchange Gain or Loss   XX (the difference)
       Cash   XX (amount paid)
           Made payment in foreign currency, exchange gain
               arose from weakening of foreign currency in relation
               to U.S. dollar

E.   Accounts Payable, foreign company   XX (amount of gain)
       Exchange Gain or Loss   XX (amount of gain)
           Made adjusting entry to record unrealized exchange
              gain on outstanding payable to be settled in a foreign
              currency

F.   Note: When a U.S. company transacts business entirely in U.S.
     dollars, no exchange gain or loss will occur. Those simple journal
     entries illustrated in your textbook are not duplicated here.

TESTING YOUR KNOWLEDGE

Matching*

Match each term with its definition by writing the appropriate letter in the blank.

_____ **1.** Restatement

_____ **2.** Exchange rate

_____ **3.** Reporting currency

_____ **4.** Functional currency

_____ **5.** Multinational (transnational) corporation

a. A business that operates in more than one country

b. The type of money in which a given set of consolidated financial statements is presented

c. The expressing of one currency in terms of another

d. The type of money with which a company transacts most of its business

e. The value of one currency in terms of another

Note to student: The matching quiz might be completed more efficiently by starting with the definition and searching for the corresponding term.

APPLYING YOUR KNOWLEDGE

Exercise

1. Ison Corporation, an American company, sold merchandise on credit to a Mexican company for 100,000 pesos. On the sale date, the exchange rate was $.05 per peso. On the date of receipt, the value of the peso had declined to $.045. Prepare the entries in the journal to record Ison Corporation's sale and receipt of payment. Leave the date column empty, as no dates have been specified.

General Journal				
Date		Description	Debit	Credit

APPENDIX B LONG-TERM INVESTMENTS

REVIEWING THE APPENDIX

1. Long-term investments in bonds are recorded at cost including commissions. When the bonds are purchased between interest dates, the investor must also pay for the accrued interest (which will be returned to the investor on the next interest payment date).

2. Most long-term bond investments are classified as *available-for-sale securities* because investors usually sell before the securities mature. Such securities are valued at fair (market) value. Long-term bond investments are classified as *held-to-maturity securities* when an early sale is *not* intended. Such securities are valued at cost, adjusted by discount or premium amortization.

3. All long-term investments in the stock of other companies are recorded at cost. After purchase, the accounting treatment depends on the extent of influence exercised by the investing company. If the investing company can affect the operating and financing policies of the investee, even though it owns 50 percent or less of the investee's voting stock, it has *significant influence*. If the investing company can decide the operating and financing policies of the investee because it owns more than 50 percent of the investee's voting stock, it has *control*.

4. The extent of influence exercised over another company is often difficult to measure accurately. However, unless there is evidence to the contrary, long-term investments in stock are classified as (a) noninfluential and noncontrolling (generally less than 20 percent ownership), (b) influential but non-controlling (generally 20 to 50 percent ownership), and (c) controlling (over 50 percent ownership).

5. The cost adjusted to market method should be used in accounting for noninfluential and noncontrolling investments. The equity method should be used in accounting for all other (that is, influential or controlling) investments. In addition, consolidated financial statements should usually be prepared when a controlling relationship exists.

   a. Under the *cost adjusted to market method,* the investor credits Dividend Income as dividends are received. In addition, the securities are recorded on the balance sheet and in comprehensive income disclosures at the lower of cost or market. Unrealized Loss on Long-Term Investments is debited and Allowance to Adjust Long-Term Investments to Market is credited for the excess of total cost over total market. For available-for-sale equity securities, the Unrealized Loss on Long-Term Investments appears in the stockholders' equity section of the balance sheet as a negative amount (and as a component of other comprehensive income), and the Allowance to Adjust Long-Term Investments to Market appears in the asset section as a contra account to Long-Term Investments. An adjusting entry opposite to the one described above would be made when market value relative to cost has increased.

b. Under the *equity method,* the investor records investment income as a debit to the Investment account and a credit to an Investment Income account. The amount recorded is the investee's periodic net income times the investor's ownership percentage. When the investor receives a cash dividend, the Cash account is debited and the Investment account is credited. All long-term investments in stock are initially recorded at cost, regardless of the method to account for subsequent transactions.

6. When a company has a controlling interest in another company, the investor is called the *parent company* and the investee is called the *subsidiary.* Companies in such a relationship must prepare *consolidated financial statements* (combined statements of the parent and its subsidiaries).

Summary of Journal Entries Introduced in Appendix B

A. Long-Term Investments   XX (purchase price)
   Cash   XX (purchase price)
     Purchased long-term investment in stock

B. Unrealized Loss on Long-Term Investments   XX (amount of decline)
   Allowance to Adjust Long-Term Investments to Market   XX (amount of decline)
     Recorded reduction of long-term investment to market

C. Cash   XX (amount received)
   Loss on Sale of Investments   XX (the difference)
     Long-Term Investments   XX (purchase price)
     Sold shares of stock (Note: Had a gain on sale arisen,
     Gain on Sale of Investment would have been credited.)

D. Cash   XX (amount received)
   Dividend Income   XX (amount received)
     Received cash dividend; cost adjusted to market
     method assumed

E. Allowance to Adjust Long-Term Investments to Market   XX (amount of recovery)
   Unrealized Loss on Long-Term Investments   XX (amount of recovery)
     Recorded the adjustment in long-term investment so it is
     reported at market (market still below cost)

F. Investment in XYZ Corporation   XX (amount paid)
   Cash   XX (amount paid)
     Invested in XYZ Corporation common stock

G. Investment in XYZ Corporation   XX (equity percentage of income)
   Income, XYZ Corporation Investment   XX (equity percentage of income)
     Recognized percentage of income reported by investee;
     equity method assumed

H. Cash   XX (amount received)
   Investment in XYZ Corporation   XX (amount received)
     Received cash dividend; equity method assumed

TESTING YOUR KNOWLEDGE

Matching*

Match each term with its definition by writing the appropriate letter in the blank.

_____ 1. Available-for-sale securities

_____ 2. Held-to-maturity securities

_____ 3. Cost adjusted to market method

_____ 4. Equity method

_____ 5. Parent

_____ 6. Subsidiary

_____ 7. Consolidated financial statements

_____ 8. Significant influence

_____ 9. Control

a. Ownership of more than 50 percent of the voting stock of another corporation

b. The method used to account for noninfluential and noncontrolling investments

c. Investments that a business may at some point decide to sell

d. The method used to account for influential but noncontrolling investments

e. A company that is controlled by another company

f. A company that has a controlling interest in another company

g. Combined statements of the parent and its subsidiaries

h. Investments in bonds that a business intends to keep for the full duration

i. Usually, ownership of 20 to 50 percent of another company's voting stock

---

Note to student: The matching quiz might be completed more efficiently by starting with the definition and searching for the corresponding term.

APPLYING YOUR KNOWLEDGE

Exercise

1. Jamal Corporation owns 15 percent of the voting stock of Tewa Company and 30 percent of the voting stock of Rorris Company. Both are long-term investments. During a given year, Tewa earned $110,000 and paid total dividends of $80,000, and Rorris earned $65,000 and paid total dividends of $50,000. In the journal, prepare Jamal's entries to reflect the above facts. Leave the date column empty, as no dates have been specified.

	General Journal		
Date	**Description**	**Debit**	**Credit**

APPENDIX C   THE TIME VALUE OF MONEY

REVIEWING THE APPENDIX

1. The timing of the receipt and payment of cash (measured in interest) should be a consideration in making business decisions. *Interest* is the cost of using money for a specific period of time; it may be calculated on a simple or compound basis.
   a. When *simple interest* is computed for one or more periods, the amount on which interest is computed does not increase each period (that is, interest is not computed on principal plus accrued interest).
   b. However, when *compound interest* is computed for two or more periods, the amount on which interest is computed *does* increase each period (that is, interest is computed on principal plus accrued interest).

2. *Future value* is the amount an investment will be worth at a future date if invested at compound interest.
   a. Future value may be computed on a single sum invested at compound interest. Table 1 in Appendix D of your text facilitates this computation.
   b. Future value may also be computed on an *ordinary annuity* (i.e., a series of equal payments made at the end of equal intervals of time) at compound interest. Table 2 in Appendix D of your text facilitates this computation.

3. *Present value* is the amount that must be invested now at a given rate of interest to produce a given future value or values.
   a. Present value may be computed on a single sum due in the future. Table 3 in Appendix D of your text facilitates this computation.
   b. Present value may also be computed on an ordinary annuity. Table 4 in Appendix D of your text facilitates this computation.

4. All four tables facilitate both annual compounding and compounding for less than a year. For example, when computing 12 percent annual interest that is compounded quarterly, one would refer to the 3 percent column for four periods per year.

5. Present value may be used in accounting to (a) impute interest on noninterest-bearing notes, (b) determine the value of an asset being considered for purchase, (c) calculate deferred payments for the purchase of an asset, (d) account for the investment of idle cash, (e) accumulate funds needed to pay off a loan, and (f) determine numerous other accounting quantities, such as the value of a bond, pension and lease obligations, and depreciation.

Summary of Journal Entries Introduced in Appendix C

A. Purchases   XX (present value of note)
    Discount on Notes Payable   XX (imputed interest)
        Notes Payable   XX (face amount)
            Purchased merchandise, non-interest-bearing note issued

B. Interest Expense   XX (amount accrued)
    Discount on Notes Payable   XX (amount accrued)
        Recorded interest expense for one year (see A above)

C. Interest Expense   XX (interest for period)
   Notes Payable   XX (face amount)
        Discount on Notes Payable   XX (interest for period)
        Cash   XX (face amount)
            Paid note (see A above)

D. Notes Receivable   XX (face amount)
    Discount on Notes Receivable   XX (imputed interest)
        Sales   XX (present value of note)
            Sold merchandise, non-interest-bearing note received

E. Discount on Notes Receivable   XX (amount accrued)
    Interest Income   XX (amount accrued)
        Recorded interest income for one year (see D above)

F. Discount on Notes Receivable   XX (interest for period)
   Cash   XX (face amount of note)
        Interest Income   XX (interest for period)
        Notes Receivable   XX (face amount)
        Received interest on note (see D above)

G. Tractor   XX (present value of payment)
    Accounts Payable   XX (present value of payment)
        Purchased tractor, payment deferred

H. Accounts Payable   XX (present value of payment)
   Interest Expense   XX (imputed amount)
        Cash   XX (amount paid)
        Paid on account, including imputed interest expense
        (see G above)

I. Accounts Receivable   XX (present value of payment)
    Sales   XX (present value of payment)
        Sold tractor, payment deferred

J. Cash   XX (amount received)
    Accounts Receivable   XX (present value of payment)
    Interest Income   XX (imputed amount)
        Received payment on account, including imputed interest
        earned (see I above)

K. Short-Term Investments   XX (amount invested)
        Cash   XX (amount invested)
            Invested idle cash

L. Short-Term Investments   XX (interest for period)
        Interest Income   XX (interest for period)
            Earned interest income for period

M. Loan Repayment Fund   XX (amount contributed)
        Cash   XX (amount contributed)
            Recorded annual contribution to loan repayment fund

TESTING YOUR KNOWLEDGE

*Matching**

Match each term with its definition by writing the appropriate letter in the blank.

_____ **1.** Interest

_____ **2.** Simple interest

_____ **3.** Compound interest

_____ **4.** Future value

_____ **5.** Present value

_____ **6.** Ordinary annuity

a. The amount that must be invested now to produce a given future value

b. The computation whereby interest is computed without considering accrued interest

c. A series of equal payments made at the end of each period

d. The cost of using money for a specific period of time

e. The amount an investment will be worth at a future date

f. The computation whereby interest is computed on the original amount plus accrued interest

---

Note to student: The matching quiz might be completed more efficiently by starting with the definition and searching for the corresponding term.

APPLYING YOUR KNOWLEDGE

Exercises

1. Use Appendix D of your text to answer the following questions.

   a. What amount received today is equivalent to $1,000 receivable at the end of five years, assuming a 6 percent annual interest rate compounded annually?

   $_____

   b. If payments of $1,000 are invested at 8 percent annual interest at the end of each quarter for one year, compute the amount that will accumulate by the time the last payment is made.

   $_____

   c. If $1,000 is invested on June 30, 20x1, at 6 percent annual interest compounded semiannually, how much will be in the account on June 30, 20x3?

   $_____

   d. Compute the equal annual deposits required to accumulate a fund of $100,000 at the end of 20 years, assuming a 10 percent interest rate compounded annually.

   $_____

2. The manager of City Center Lanes is considering replacing the existing automatic pinsetters with improved ones that cost $10,000 each. It is estimated that each new pinsetter will save $2,000 annually and will last for ten years. Using an interest rate of 18 percent and Appendix D of your text, what is the present value of the savings of each new pinsetter to City Center Lanes?

$_____

Should the purchase be made?

_____

3. On January 1, 20x1, Douglas Corporation purchased equipment from Courtright Sales by signing a two-year, non-interest-bearing note for $10,000. Douglas currently pays 10 percent interest on money borrowed. In the journal provided below, prepare Douglas's journal entries (a) to record the purchase and the note, (b) to adjust the accounts after one year, and (c) to record payment of the note after two years. Use Appendix D of your text for time value of money information. Omit explanations.

General Journal				
Date		Description	Debit	Credit

ANSWERS

Chapter 1

Self-Test

1. d (LO 1)		**6.** d (LO 5)	
2. a (LO 2)		**7.** a (LO 5)	
3. b (LO 3)		**8.** d (LO 6)	
4. b (LO 4)		**9.** a (LO 7)	
5. b (LO 5)		**10.** c (LO 8)	

Matching

1. h	**7.** s	**13.** u	**19.** d
2. f	**8.** c	**14.** e	**20.** g
3. o	**9.** j	**15.** l	**21.** a
4. r	**10.** v	**16.** q	**22.** p
5. k	**11.** i	**17.** m	
6. n	**12.** b	**18.** t	

Short Answer

1. (LO 6) Zeno Corporation
   Income Statement
   For the Year Ended June 30, 20xx
2. (LO 1) Bookkeeping deals with the mechanical and repetitive recordkeeping process. Accounting involves bookkeeping as well as the design of an accounting system, its use, and the analysis of its output.

3. (LO 8)
   a. *Integrity*—The accountant is honest, regardless of consequences.
   b. *Objectivity*—The accountant is impartial in performing his or her job.
   c. *Independence*—The accountant avoids all relationships or situations that could impair his or her objectivity.

d. *Due care*—The accountant carries out his or her responsibilities with competence and diligence.

4. (LO 2) Management, outsiders with a direct financial interest, and outsiders with an indirect financial interest

5. (LO 1) To earn a satisfactory profit to hold investor capital; to maintain sufficient funds to pay debts as they fall due

6. (LO 6)

Statement

a. Income statement
b. Statement of owner's equity
c. Balance sheet
d. Statement of cash flows

Purpose

a. Measures net income during a certain period
b. Shows how owner's capital changed during the period
c. Shows financial position at a point in time
d. Discloses operating, financing, and investing activities during the period

True-False

1. F (LO 5) It is the balance sheet that shows financial position.
2. F (LO 7) The IRS interprets and enforces tax laws.
3. T (LO 5)
4. T (LO 5)
5. F (LO 5) It indicates that the company has one or more debtors.
6. T (LO 5)
7. F (LO 3) The measurement stage refers to the recording of business transactions.
8. F (LO 6) Withdrawals are a deduction in the statement of owner's equity.
9. T (LO 7)
10. T (LO 4)
11. T (LO 6)
12. T (LO 6)
13. F (LO 7) That is the GASB's responsibility.

14. F (LO 4) A corporation is managed by its board of directors.
15. T (LO 7)
16. F (LO 5) Net assets equal assets *minus* liabilities.
17. F (LO 6) Balance sheets do not list revenues and expenses.
18. F (LO 3) Nonexchange transactions, such as a loss from fire or the accumulation of interest, do exist.
19. T (LO 1)
20. T (LO 6)
21. T (LO 3)
22. F (LO 2) Economic planners have an indirect financial interest in accounting information.
23. T (LO 5)
24. F (LO 1) Cash flow is a measure of liquidity.

Multiple Choice

1. a (LO 6) The answer "Wages Expense" is correct because it is an account that would appear on the income statement. The income statement is the financial statement that reports revenues and expenses.

2. c (LO 7) The SEC (Securities and Exchange Commission) is the organization that regulates financial trading. Its role is to help protect the public from incomplete information. The SEC requires that certain financial information be made available so that the public will be able to make informed investment decisions.

3. b (LO 4) The stock of a corporation is easily transferred from one investor to another. Corporations are owned through ownership of shares of stock.

4. b (LO 6) The balance sheet is a "snapshot" of the business, in a financial sense, on a given date. The account balances, as they appear on the balance sheet, are a report of the ultimate effect of financial transactions during an accounting period, not a report of the actual transactions.

5. **a** (LO 7) An audit is used to verify the information presented by the management of a firm in its financial statements. The term *fairness* refers to the ability of users of the financial statements to rely on the information as presented.

6. **d** (LO 5) Collection on an account receivable is simply an exchange of one asset (the account receivable) for another asset (cash). As a result, there is no effect on the accounting equation.

7. **d** (LO 4) The partners *are* the partnership. There is no separate legal entity in this form of organization. When a partner leaves the partnership, the original partnership is dissolved, although a new partnership may now be formed.

8. **a** (LO 6) Accounts Receivable is merely a type of asset. "Assets" is a major heading found in the balance sheet.

9. **b** (LO 5) When an owner withdraws assets, the asset account and the capital account decrease by the same amount.

10. **d** (LO 5) The purchase of an asset for cash is an exchange of one asset for another. It is an increase and a decrease, in equal amounts, on one side of the accounting equation. Therefore, it has no effect on total assets, liabilities, or owner's equity.

11. **b** (LO 6) The statement of cash flows does not list any activity called *funding activities*.

12. **c** (LO 5) The payment of a liability will reduce both sides of the accounting equation equally. The transaction produces a reduction in both assets and liabilities in equal amounts.

Exercises

1. (LO 2)
   a. Potential investors need all recent financial statements to assess the future profitability of a company and thus decide whether or not they should invest in it.
   b. The principal goal of the SEC is to protect the public. Insisting that Global make its statements public as well as examining the statements for propriety certainly will help the public make decisions regarding Global.
   c. The bank would have difficulty determining Global's ability to repay the loan if it does not have access to Global's most recent financial statements.
   d. Present stockholders must see the statements in order to decide whether to sell, maintain, or increase their investments in this company.
   e. Management needs the statements to help it pinpoint the weaknesses that caused the year's loss.

2. (LO 5) $35,000

3. (LO 6)

Mendez TV Repair Company Balance Sheet December 31, 20xx	
Assets	
Cash	$ 950
Accounts Receivable	1,500
Equipment	850
Land	1,000
Building	10,000
Truck	4,500
Total Assets	$18,800
Liabilities	
Accounts Payable	$ 1,300
Owner's Equity	
Hector Mendez, Capital	17,500
Total Liabilities and Owner's Equity	$18,800

4. (LO 5)

Transaction	Assets				Liabilities	Owner's Equity
	Cash	Accounts Receivable	Supplies and Equipment	Trucks	Accounts Payable	Bruce Hoffman Capital
a	+$20,000					+$20,000
b	−650		+650			
c				+5,200	+5,200	
d	+525					+525
e	−2,600				−2,600	
f		+150				+150
g	−250					−250
h	+150	−150				
i		+2-	−20			
j	−1,000					−1,000
Balance at end of month	$16,175	$20	$630	$5,200	$2,600	$19,425

Solution to Crossword Puzzle
(Chapter 1)

Chapter 2

Self-Test

1. a	(LO 1)		**6.** a	(LO 4)
2. b	(LO 2)		**7.** c	(LO 4)
3. d	(LO 2)		**8.** c	(LO 6)
4. b	(LO 3)		**9.** a	(LO 7)
5. c	(LO 3)		**10.** a	(LO 5)

Matching

1. k	**7.** a	**13.** e
2. f	**8.** m	**14.** n
3. q	**9.** l	**15.** p
4. o	**10.** d	**16.** h
5. b	**11.** j	**17.** c
6. g	**12.** r	**18.** i

Short Answer

1. (LO 3) Determine the transaction's effect on the accounts, apply the rules of double entry, make the entry (journalize), post the entry to the ledger, and prepare a trial balance.
2. (LO 1)
   a. July 14
   b. $150
   c. Cash and Accounts Receivable

3. (LO 4) Two examples are the purchase of any asset for cash and the collection on an account receivable.
4. (LO 4) One example is the payment of an account payable.
5. (LO 2) Revenues, expenses, investments, and withdrawals
6. (LO 3) Liabilities, capital, and revenues

True-False

1. F (LO 1) A sale should be recorded when title passes.
2. T (LO 1)
3. T (LO 2)
4. F (LO 3) The credit side of an account does not imply anything favorable or unfavorable.
5. F (LO 3) Only those accounts with zero balances have equal debits and credits.
6. F (LO 7) One quickly can determine the cash balance by referring to the ledger.
7. T (LO 2)

8. F (LO 2) Notes Payable is the proper account title; the liability is evidenced by the existence of a promissory note.
9. T (LO 2)
10. T (LO 3)
11. F (LO 3) It is possible to have all increases or all decreases in a journal entry.
12. F (LO 6) Journal entries are made before transactions are posted to the ledger.
13. F (LO 6) Liabilities and owner's equity accounts are indented only when credited.

14. T (LO 6)

15. T (LO 7)

16. T (LO 7)

17. T (LO 3, 7)

18. F (LO 2) It is a table of contents to the general ledger.

19. F (LO 5) Unearned Revenue has a normal credit balance.

20. T (LO 2)

21. F (LO 5) They are divisible by 9.

22. T (LO 5)

Multiple Choice

1. c (LO 1) Summarization of accounting data occurs at the end of the accounting cycle. Journal entries are prepared throughout the accounting period.

2. d (LO 4) When a liability is paid, each side of the accounting equation is reduced in equal proportion. The transaction results in a reduction in an asset and a corresponding reduction in a liability.

3. c (LO 6) The explanation accompanying a journal entry is a brief statement about the entire transaction. Debits and credits are elements of the recorded transaction. The explanation is entered after all debit and credit entries have been made.

4. d (LO 7) The final step in the posting process is the transfer of the ledger account number to the Post. Ref. column of the general journal. This last step is an indication that all other steps in the process are complete.

5. c (LO 5) If only part of a journal entry has been posted, the omitted information would usually be either a debit or a credit. As a result, total debits would not equal total credits in the general ledger accounts. Therefore, the trial balance would be out of balance.

6. b (LO 4) In the transaction described, the receipt of cash in payment of an account receivable, an exchange of one asset for another has occurred. Therefore, total assets would remain unchanged.

7. a (LO 3) Withdrawals account entries ultimately result in a reduction in the corresponding Capital account. Capital accounts increase with a credit entry. Therefore, accounts that ultimately result in the reduction of a Capital account would increase with a debit entry.

8. b (LO 2) Of the accounts listed, Prepaid Rent is the only account that is classified as an asset. Unearned Revenue is a liability; Jim Lutton, Capital is an owner's equity account; and Fees Earned is a revenue account.

9. a (LO 2) Of the accounts listed, only Interest Payable represents an amount owing.

10. b (LO 2) Unearned Rent would represent a liability on the accounting records of the *lessor.* The question refers to the possible entries of the *lessee,* which include entries into Prepaid Rent, Rent Payable, and Rent Expense.

11. c (LO 5) Sales is a revenue account. Revenues increase with a credit entry, and therefore Sales is referred to as having a *normal credit balance.* Revenues ultimately cause an increase in Capital, which also has a normal credit balance.

12. d (LO 5) The use of an incorrect account will not cause a trial balance to be out of balance. However, in this instance, both Accounts Receivable and Accounts Payable will be overstated.

Exercises

1. (LO 6)

		General Journal		
Date		**Description**	**Debit**	**Credit**
May	2	Cash	28,000	
		Al Mayer, Capital		28,000
		To record the owner's original investment		
	3	Prepaid Rent	900	
		Cash		900
		Paid three months' rent in advance		
	5	Printing Press	10,000	
		Photographic Equipment	3,000	
		Cash		2,000
		Accounts Payable		11,000
		Purchased a press and equipment from Vermont Press, Inc.		
	8	No entry		
	9	Cash	1,200	
		Unearned Revenue		1,200
		Received payment in advance from Ski Chalet Department Store for brochures to be printed		
	11	Printing Supplies	800	
		Notes Payable		800
		Purchased paper from ABC Pulp Supply Company		
	14	Cash	250	
		Accounts Receivable	250	
		Revenue from Services		500
		Completed job for Harrington Shoes		
	14	Salaries Expense	200	
		Cash		200
		Paid the pressman his weekly salary		
	15	Accounts Payable	1,000	
		Cash		1,000
		Payment on account owed to Vermont Press, Inc.		
	18	Cash	250	
		Accounts Receivable		250
		Harrington Shoes paid its debt in full		
	20	Al Mayer, Withdrawals	700	
		Cash		700
		The owner withdrew $700 for personal use		
	24	Utilities Expense	45	
		Accounts Payable		45
		To record electric bill		
	30	Accounts Payable	45	
		Cash		45
		To record payment of electric bill		

2. (LO 3)
   a. $1,750 debit balance
   b. $1,000 credit balance
   c. $14,600 debit balance

3. (LO 7)

General Journal					Page 7
Date		**Description**	**Post. Ref.**	**Debit**	**Credit**
Apr.	3	Cash	11	1,000	
		Revenue from Services	41		1,000
		Received payment from Lincoln Company for services			
	5	Accounts Payable	21	300	
		Cash	11		300
		Paid Middlebury Supply Company for supplies purchased on March 31 on credit			

Cash						Account No. 11	
						Balance	
Date		**Item**	**Post. Ref.**	**Debit**	**Credit**	**Debit**	**Credit**
Apr.	3		J7	1,000		1,000	
	5		J7		300	700	

Accounts Payable						Account No. 21	
						Balance*	
Date		**Item**	**Post. Ref.**	**Debit**	**Credit**	**Debit**	**Credit**
Apr.	5		J7	300		300	

Revenue from Services						Account No. 41	
						Balance	
Date		**Item**	**Post. Ref.**	**Debit**	**Credit**	**Debit**	**Credit**
Apr.	3		J7		1,000		1,000

*Previous postings have been omitted, resulting in an abnormal debit balance in Accounts Payable.

Chapter 3

1. a	(LO 1)		**6.** c	(LO 4)
2. d	(LO 5)		**7.** b	(LO 5)
3. d	(LO 2)		**8.** a	(LO 3)
4. c	(LO 2)		**9.** d	(SO 7)
5. a	(LO 3)		**10.** c	(LO 6)

Matching

1. i	**6.** q	**11.** a	**16.** j
2. d	**7.** f	**12.** h	**17.** b
3. n	**8.** k	**13.** m	**18.** g
4. r	**9.** e	**14.** p	
5. c	**10.** o	**15.** l	

Short Answer

1. (LO 4) Dividing recorded expenses between two or more accounting periods; dividing recorded revenues between two or more accounting periods; recording unrecorded expenses; and recording unrecorded revenues

2. (LO 2) The matching rule means that revenues should be recorded in the period in which they are earned, and that all expenses related to those revenues also should be recorded in that period.

3. (LO 5) Depreciation is the allocation of the cost of a long-lived asset to the periods benefiting from the asset.

4. (LO 5) Prepaid expenses are expenses paid for in advance; they initially are recorded as assets. Unearned revenues represent payment received in advance of providing goods or services; they initially are recorded as liabilities.

True-False

1. T (LO 5)
2. T (LO 1)
3. F (LO 2) The calendar year lasts specifically from January 1 to December 31.
4. T (LO 2)
5. F (LO 3) Under accrual accounting, the timing of cash exchanges is irrelevant in recording revenues and expenses.
6. F (LO 6) Adjusting entries are made before the financial statements are prepared.
7. T (LO 5)
8. F (LO 5) It is debited for the amount consumed during the period (the amount available during the period less ending inventory).

9. F (LO 5) Accumulated Depreciation (a contra account) has a credit balance, even though it appears on the left side of the balance sheet.
10. T (LO 5)
11. F (LO 5) Unearned Revenues is a liability account.
12. F (LO 4) The credit is to a liability account.
13. T (LO 6)
14. F (LO 5) If payment has not yet been received, the debit is to Accounts Receivable.
15. T (LO 5)
16. T (LO 3, 4)

Multiple Choice

1. c (LO 5) An adjusting entry normally contains at least one balance sheet account and at least one income statement account. Choice **c** does not, nor does it fit the description for any adjusting entry.

2. b (LO 5) Office Supplies are not considered long-lived assets. The use of office supplies is recorded as an expense. Adjustments to Office Supplies are the result of reconciling the ending inventory of office supplies to a cumulative total in the Office Supplies account. This cumulative total is a result of the addition of office supplies to the beginning office supplies inventory balance throughout the accounting period.

3. b (LO 5) Unearned Fees is used to record the firm's liability for amounts received but not yet earned. The use of this system of recognition is required so that revenue amounts can be represented properly and allocated in the appropriate accounting period. As the revenues are earned, the proper amounts are transferred from liabilities to revenues. Between the time those future revenues were received and the time they actually are earned, one accounting period may have ended and another accounting period begun.

4. a (LO 5) Depreciation is the allocation of the cost of an asset over the expected useful life of that asset. The matching rule requires the allocation of the cost while the asset is in use in the revenue-generating activities of a firm.

5. c (LO 6) Net income is the result of the calculation that nets revenues and expenses. The adjusted trial balance contains summary balances of each general ledger account after adjusting entries have been made.

6. d (LO 5) The adjustment debiting Interest Receivable and crediting Interest Income is required so that interest income for the period is allocated, even though the interest has not been received as yet. This income recognition is necessary for compliance with the matching rule.

7. a (LO 2) Estimates are involved in the preparation of account balances used to report net income. An example of this kind of estimate is the recording of depreciation expense. Although not exact, the reported net income of one accounting period can be compared with the net income of other accounting periods, providing a basis for conclusions about the firm.

8. d (LO 5) Until such time as Prepaid Rent is expired, and through adjustments is recorded as an expense, it remains an asset on the books of a firm.

9. c (LO 6) After preparation of the trial balance, but before preparation of the adjusted trial balance, an adjusting entry will be made to record office supplies consumed. This entry will reduce the Office Supplies account and increase the Office Supplies Expense account.

10. b (LO 3) The Cash account balance represents a dollar amount at the time the balance sheet is prepared. Cash is *never* involved in the end-of-period adjustments.

Exercises

1. (LO 5)

Bristol Transit Company
Partial Balance Sheet
December 31, 20x9

Assets		
Cash		$ 5,000
Accounts Receivable		3,000
Company Vehicles	$24,000	
Less Accumulated Depreciation,	9,000	15,000
Total Assets		$23,000

---

2. (LO 5)
a. $970
b. $1,750
c. $450

3. (LO 5)

	General Journal		
Date*	**Description**	**Debit**	**Credit**
a.	Supplies Expense	125	
	Supplies		125
	To record supplies consumed during the period		
b.	Wages Expense	2,000	
	Wages Payable		2,000
	To record accrued wages		
c.	Unearned Revenues	600	
	Revenues from Services		600
	To record earned revenues		
d.	Depreciation Expense, Buildings	4,500	
	Accumulated Depreciation, Buildings		4,500
	To record depreciation on buildings		
e.	Advertising Expense	2,000	
	Prepaid Advertising		2,000
	To record advertising used up during the year		
f.	Insurance Expense	250	
	Prepaid Insurance		250
	To record insurance expired during the year		
g.	Fees Receivable	2,200	
	Revenues from Services		2,200
	To record revenues earned for which payment has not been received		
h.	Interest Expense	52	
	Interest Payable		52
	To record accrued interest on a note payable		

*In reality, all of the adjusting entries would be dated December 31.

4. (SO 7)
   a. $6,200 ($1,200 + $8,700 − $3,700)
   b. $35,400 ($900 + $35,000 − $500)
   c. $3,000 ($1,800 + $3,600 − $2,400)

Solution to Crossword Puzzle
(Chapters 2 and 3)

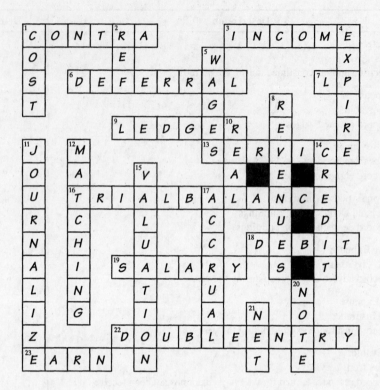

Chapter 4

Self-Test

1. b	(LO 1)	**6.** d	(LO 5)
2. c	(LO 2)	**7.** c	(LO 6)
3. d	(LO 3)	**8.** c	(LO 6)
4. c	(LO 3)	**9.** c	(LO 7)
5. b	(LO 4)	**10.** d	(LO 7)

Matching

1. e	**4.** b	**7.** c	**10.** a
2. g	**5.** h	**8.** j	
3. d	**6.** f	**9.** i	

Short Answer

1. (LO 3) Revenue accounts, expense accounts, Income Summary, Withdrawals
2. (LO 6) Trial Balance, Adjustments, Adjusted Trial Balance, Income Statement, Balance Sheet
3. (LO 4) Assets, liabilities, and owner's equity accounts will appear. Revenue and expense accounts, Income Summary, and the Withdrawals account will not appear.
4. (LO 5) Reversing entries enable the bookkeeper to continue making simple, routine journal entries rather than more complicated ones.
5. (LO 1) The steps should be numbered as follows: 3, 5, 1, 4, 2, 6.

True-False

1. T (LO 6)
2. T (LO 6)
3. T (LO 6)
4. T (LO 7)
5. F (LO 2) Income Summary account does not appear in any statement.
6. F (LO 2) Only nominal accounts are closed.
7. T (LO 3)
8. F (LO 3) The Withdrawals account is closed to the owner's Capital account.
9. F (LO 3) When there is a net loss, Income Summary will be credited.
10. T (LO 5)
11. F (LO 6) The work sheet is never published.
12. F (LO 6) The key letter is in the *Adjustments* columns to relate debits and credits of the same entry.
13. T (LO 6)
14. F (LO 4) It will not include the Withdrawals account, because that account will have a zero balance.
15. F (LO 5) Reversing entries, dated the first day of the new accounting period, serve to simplify the bookkeeping process.
16. T (LO 2)

1. c (LO 4) Of the accounts listed, Dawn Brooks, Capital is the only account that remains open after the closing procedures are complete at the end of the accounting cycle. The post-closing trial balance is a listing of such accounts, along with their account balances.

2. d (LO 7) Of the choices given, this is the only sequence that it is possible to complete in order.

3. b (LO 5) For a reversing entry to accomplish its goal (for it to "work"), it must be the opposite of the related adjusting entry.

4. a (LO 6) The amount used to balance the Income Statement columns of the work sheet and the Balance Sheet columns of the work sheet is the net income or loss. When the amount that is required to bring the Balance Sheet columns into balance on the work sheet is an entry to the credit column, there must have been a net income. The corresponding entry to bring the Income Statement columns into balance will be to the debit column.

5. a (LO 3) Of the accounts listed, Unearned Commissions is the only choice that is not involved in the closing process. Unearned Commissions is a permanent balance sheet account and will remain open from one period to the next if it contains a balance.

6. b (LO 3) When, in the closing process (after revenues and expenses have been closed), Income Summary has a debit balance (expenses have exceeded revenues), the account will be closed by a credit entry equal to the debit balance. The corresponding debit will be an entry to the owner's Capital account, reducing the balance of that account by an amount equal to the net loss for the period.

7. c (LO 2) The closing entries occur after the adjusting entries, during the end-of-period steps in the accounting cycle. The purpose of the adjusting entries is to update the revenue and expense accounts.

8. a (LO 7) All the components of a statement of owner's equity have been provided, except for net income or loss. A net income figure of $55,000 will correctly complete the statement.

9. c (LO 2) Temporary accounts are those that appear on the income statement. They also are referred to as *nominal accounts*.

Exercises

1. (LO 3)

		General Journal		
Date		**Description**	**Debit**	**Credit**
July	31	Revenue from Services	4,700	
		Income Summary		4,700
		To close the revenue account		
	31	Income Summary	700	
		Rent Expense		500
		Telephone Expense		50
		Utilities Expense		150
		To close the expense accounts		
	31	Income Summary	4,000	
		Sidney Simon, Capital		4,000
		To close the Income Summary account		
	31	Sidney Simon, Capital	2,500	
		Sidney Simon, Withdrawals		2,500
		To close the Withdrawals account		

2. (LO 7)

Sid's Fix-It Shop
Statement of Owner's Equity
For the Month Ended July 31, 20xx

Sidney Simon, Capital, July 1, 20xx	$3,000
Add Net Income for July	4,000
Subtotal	$7,000
Less Withdrawals during July	2,500
Sidney Simon, Capital, July 31, 20xx	$4,500

Frieda's Garden Service
Work Sheet
For the Year Ended December 31, 20xx

Account Name	Trial Balance		Adjustments		Adjusted Trial Balance		Income Statement		Balance Sheet	
	Debit	Credit	Debit	Credit	Debit	Credit	Debit	Credit	Debit	Credit
Cash	2,560				2,560				2,560	
Accounts Receivable	880		(e) 50		930				930	
Prepaid Rent	750			(a) 550	200				200	
Lawn Supplies	250			(c) 150	100				100	
Lawn Equipment	10,000				10,000				10,000	
Accum. Deprec., Lawn Equip.		2,000		(b) 1,500		3,500				3,500
Accounts Payable		630				630				630
Unearned Landscaping Fees		300	(f) 120			180				180
Frieda Parsons, Capital		6,000				6,000				6,000
Frieda Parsons, Withdrawals	6,050				6,050				6,050	
Grass-Cutting Fees		15,000		(e) 50		15,050		15,050		
Wages Expense	3,300		(d) 280		3,580		3,580			
Gasoline Expense	140				140		140			
	23,930	23,930								
Rent Expense			(a) 550		550		550			
Depreciation Expense			(b) 1,500		1,500		1,500			
Lawn Supplies Expense			(c) 150		150		150			
Landscaping Fees Earned				(f) 120		120		120		
Wages Payable				(d) 280		280				280
			2,650	2,650	25,760	25,760	5,920	15,170	19,840	10,590
Net Income							9,250			9,250
							15,170	15,170	19,840	19,840

4. (LO 5)

		General Journal		
Date		**Description**	**Debit**	**Credit**
Dec.	1	Cash	20,000	
		Notes Payable		20,000
		To record 90-day bank note		
	31	Interest Expense	200	
		Interest Payable		200
		To record accrued interest on note		
	31	Income Summary	200	
		Interest Expense		200
		To close Interest Expense account		
Jan.	1	Interest Payable	200	
		Interest Expense		200
		To reverse adjusting entry for interest		
Mar.	1	Notes Payable	20,000	
		Interest Expense	600	
		Cash		20,600
		To record payment of note plus interest		

Chapter 5

Self-Test

1. a	(LO 1)	**6.** a	(LO 4)
2. d	(LO 2)	**7.** a	(SO 7)
3. b	(LO 2)	**8.** b	(SO 7)
4. a	(SO 5)	**9.** c	(SO 6)
5. d	(LO 4)	**10.** c	(SO 8)

Matching

1. c	**5.** l	**9.** i	**13.** a
2. h	**6.** k	**10.** d	**14.** f
3. j	**7.** b	**11.** m	**15.** p
4. e	**8.** g	**12.** o	**16.** n

Short Answer

1. (LO 2)

Net Sales
- Cost of Goods Sold
= Gross Margin
- Operating Expenses
= Net Income

2. (SO 5)

Beginning Merchandise Inventory
+ Net Cost of Purchases
= Goods Available for Sale
- Ending Merchandise Inventory
= Cost of Goods Sold

3. (SO 5)

(Gross) Purchases
- Purchases Returns and Allowances
- Purchases Discounts
= Net Purchases
+ Freight In
= Net Cost of Purchases

4. (LO 2)

Gross Sales
- Sales Returns and Allowances
- Sales Discounts
= Net Sales

5. (SO 7) Income Summary is debited and Merchandise Inventory is credited for the beginning inventory balance. Merchandise Inventory is debited and Income Summary is credited for the ending inventory balance.

True-False

1. F (SO 5) It results in an understated net income.
2. F (LO 3) It means that payment is due 10 days after the end of the month.
3. T (SO 5)
4. F (LO 1) The dealer is more likely to use the perpetual inventory system.
5. T (LO 3)
6. F (SO 7) It would appear in the work sheet under a *perpetual* inventory system.
7. T (SO 8)
8. T (SO 5)
9. T (SO 5)
10. T (LO 4, SO 5)
11. T (SO 5)
12. F (SO 7) It is closed with a debit.
13. F (LO 2) It normally has a debit balance.
14. F (SO 5) It requires a debit to Office Supplies (office supplies are not merchandise).
15. T (LO 2)
16. T (LO 2)
17. F (SO 5) Both are done at the end of the period.
18. F (LO 3) 2/10, n/30 is a sales or purchases discount, offered for early payment. A trade discount is a deduction off the list or catalogue price.
19. F (LO 3) Title passes at the shipping point.
20. T (LO 4)
21. F (LO 4) It is treated as a selling expense.
22. F (SO 5) *Beginning* inventory is needed.

Multiple Choice

1. d (SO 8) The discount of $10 in this example (after allowing for the purchase returns) would be entered as a credit to balance the journal entry, which also would include a debit to Accounts Payable for the balance due ($500) and a credit to Cash for the balance due less the discount ($490).
2. c (SO 5) Purchases Returns and Allowances is a contra account to the Purchases account. Purchases has a normal debit balance. Its corresponding contra accounts have normal credit balances.
3. d (SO 5) Overstating ending inventory would overstate the deduction from goods available for sale. This would result in an understatement of the cost of goods sold.
4. a (SO 7) Beginning inventory appears on the debit side, and ending inventory appears on the credit side of the Income Statement columns.
5. b (LO 2) Freight out is a selling expense; it is not an element of the cost of obtaining goods.
6. c (SO 7) Beginning inventory is eliminated with a credit through the closing process. Purchases Returns and Allowances and Sales, on the other hand, are closed with debits. Income Summary is closed with a debit or a credit, depending on whether a net income or a net loss has resulted.
7. a (LO 2) Advertising Expense is considered a selling expense within the operating expenses section of the income statement. Sales Discounts appears as a contra account to Gross Sales, whereas Freight In and Purchases appear within the cost of goods sold section.
8. c (LO 4) Under the perpetual inventory system, purchases of merchandise are recorded in the Merchandise Inventory, not the Purchases, account.
9. b (LO 1) When inventory is paid for has no bearing on the length of the operating cycle.
10. d (LO 4) In addition, Credit Card Discount Expense would be debited for $50, and Sales credited for $1,000.

Exercises

1. (SO 5)

		General Journal		
Date		Description	Debit	Credit
May	1	Purchases	500	
		Accounts Payable		500
		Purchased merchandise on credit, terms 2/10, n/60		
	3	Accounts Receivable	500	
		Sales		500
		Sold merchandise on credit, terms 2/10, 1/20, n/30		
	4	Freight In	42	
		Cash		42
		Paid for freight charges		
	5	Office Supplies	100	
		Accounts Payable		100
		Purchased office supplies on credit		
	6	Accounts Payable	20	
		Office Supplies		20
		Returned office supplies from May 5 purchase		
	7	Accounts Payable	50	
		Purchases Returns and Allowances		50
		Returned merchandise from May 1 purchase		
	9	Accounts Receivable	225	
		Sales		225
		Sold merchandise on credit, terms 2/10, 1/15, n/30		
	10	Accounts Payable	450	
		Purchases Discounts		9
		Cash		441
		Paid for purchase of May 1		
	14	Sales Returns and Allowances	25	
		Accounts Receivable		25
		The customer of May 9 returned merchandise		
	22	Cash	198	
		Sales Discounts	2	
		Accounts Receivable		200
		The customer of May 9 paid		
	26	Cash	500	
		Accounts Receivable		500
		The customer of May 3 paid for merchandise		

2. (SO 7)

		General Journal		
Date		**Description**	**Debit**	**Credit**
Dec.	31	Income Summary	81,500	
		Merchandise Inventory		10,000
		Advertising Expense		5,000
		Freight In		2,000
		Freight Out Expense		4,000
		Rent Expense		3,000
		Sales Returns and Allowances		200
		Sales Discounts		300
		Wages Expense		7,000
		Purchases		50,000
		To close temporary accounts with debit balances and to close out		
		beginning inventory		
	31	Merchandise Inventory	8,000	
		Sales	100,000	
		Purchases Returns and Allowances	500	
		Purchases Discounts	500	
		Income Summary		109,000
		To close temporary accounts with credit balances and to establish the		
		ending inventory		
	31	Income Summary	27,500	
		Pam Reed, Capital		27,500
		To close the Income Summary account		
	31	Pam Reed, Capital	12,000	
		Pam Reed, Withdrawals		12,000
		To close the Withdrawals account		

3. (SO 5)

Reed Merchandising Company Partial Income Statement For the Year 20xx			
Gross Sales			$100,000
Less: Sales Discounts		$ 300	
Sales Returns and Allowances		200	500
Net Sales			$ 99,500
Less Cost of Goods Sold			
Merchandise Inventory, Jan. 1		$10,000	
Purchases	$50,000		
Less: Purchases Discounts	500		
Purchases Returns and Allowances	500		
Net Purchases	$49,000		
Freight In	2,000		
Net Cost of Purchases		51,000	
Goods Available for Sale		$61,000	
Less Merchandise Inventory, Dec. 31		8,000	
Cost of Goods Sold			53,000
Gross Margin			$ 46,500

4. (SO 7)

Kay's Mart
Work Sheet
For the Month Ended March 31, 20xx

Account Name	Trial Balance Debit	Trial Balance Credit	Adjustments Debit	Adjustments Credit	Adjusted Trial Balance Debit	Adjusted Trial Balance Credit	Income Statement Debit	Income Statement Credit	Balance Sheet Debit	Balance Sheet Credit
Cash	1,000				1,000				1,000	
Accounts Receivable	700				700				700	
Merchandise Inventory	400				400		400	620	620	
Prepaid Rent	750			(a) 250	500				500	
Equipment	4,200				4,200				4,200	
Accounts Payable		900				900				900
Kay Walters, Capital		4,200				4,200				4,200
Sales		9,800				9,800		9,800		
Sales Discounts	300				300		300			
Purchases	3,700				3,700		3,700			
Purchases Returns and Allowances		150				150		150		
Freight In	400				400		400			
Salaries Expense	3,000		(b) 500		3,500		3,500			
Advertising Expense	600				600		600			
	15,050	15,050								
Rent Expense			(a) 250		250		250			
Salaries Payable				(b) 500		500				500
Depreciation Expense, Equipment			(c) 375		375		375			
Accumulated Depreciation, Equipment				(c) 375		375				375
			1,125	1,125	15,925	15,925	9,525	10,570	7,020	5,975
Net Income							1,045			1,045
							10,570	10,570	7,020	7,020

5. (SO 6)

	General Journal		
Date	Description	Debit	Credit
	Income Summary	131,900	
	Sales Returns and Allowances		5,300
	Cost of Goods Sold		59,200
	Freight In		3,200
	Selling Expenses		39,400
	General and Administrative Expenses		24,800
	Sales	244,100	
	Income Summary		244,100
	Income Summary	112,200	
	Mary Byram, Capital		112,200
	Mary Byram, Capital	50,000	
	Mary Byram, Withdrawals		50,000

Solution to Crossword Puzzle
(Chapters 4 and 5)

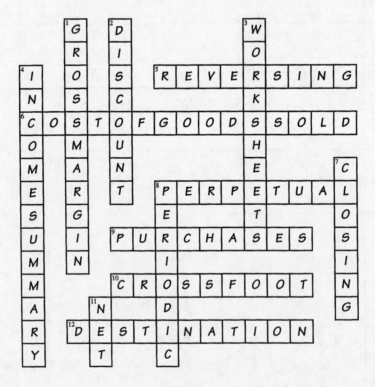

Chapter 6

1. c	(LO 5)	**6.** b	(LO 5)
2. b	(LO 2)	**7.** a	(LO 6)
3. a	(LO 3)	**8.** c	(LO 7)
4. c	(LO 4)	**9.** c	(LO 7)
5. b	(LO 5)	**10.** d	(LO 5)

Matching

1. e		**5.** h		**9.** l		**13.** a
2. k		**6.** o		**10.** f		**14.** g
3. n		**7.** j		**11.** m		**15.** d
4. c		**8.** b		**12.** i		

Short Answer

1. (LO 5)

Business Organization	Name for Equity Section
Sole Proprietorship	Owner's Equity
Partnership	Partners' Equity
Corporation	Stockholders' Equity

2. (LO 7) *Profit margin*—Shows net income in relation to net sales.

Asset turnover—Shows how efficiently assets are used to produce sales.

Return on assets—Shows net income in relation to average total assets.

Return on equity—Shows net income in relation to owner's investment.

Debt to equity ratio—Shows the proportion of a business financed by creditors and that financed by owners.

3. (LO 7) *Working capital*—Current assets minus current liabilities.

Current ratio—Current assets divided by current liabilities.

4. (LO 3) *Consistency and comparability*—Applying the same accounting procedures from one period to the next.

Materiality—The relative importance of an item or event.

Cost-benefit—The cost of providing additional accounting information should not exceed the benefits gained from it.

Conservatism—Choosing the accounting procedure that will be least likely to overstate assets and income.

Full disclosure—Showing all relevant information in the financial statements or in the footnotes.

True-False

1. F (LO 5) They are considered current assets if collection is expected within the normal operating cycle, even if that cycle is more than one year.
2. F (LO 5) The Retained Earnings account is reduced.
3. F (LO 7) Profit margin is expressed as a percentage.
4. T (LO 5)
5. T (LO 2)
6. T (LO 7)
7. F (LO 5) Short-term investments in stock should be included in the current assets section of the balance sheet.

8. F (LO 7) *Liquidity* is what is being defined.
9. F (LO 5) The operating cycle can be less than one year.
10. F (LO 5) Net worth is merely another term for owner's equity, and does not necessarily equal current net asset worth.
11. T (LO 6)
12. F (LO 6) The net income figures will be the same, although they are arrived at differently.
13. T (LO 5)
14. F (LO 7) Working capital equals current assets *minus* current liabilities.
15. T (LO 7)
16. F (LO 2) *Reliability* is what is being described.

Multiple Choice

1. c (LO 5) The conversion of inventories to cash is the basis for a firm's operations. This conversion cycle (called the normal operating cycle) is frequently less than 12 months. However, if it is *greater* than 12 months, the inventory by definition is still classified as a current asset.
2. c (LO 6) The single-step income statement does not isolate gross margin. Instead, cost of goods sold is combined with other expenses and then subtracted from total revenues to calculate net income.
3. b (LO 7) The current ratio gives management information about a firm's liquidity. Liquidity is important for anticipation of a company's ability to cover operations and current liabilities.
4. d (LO 5) The owner's Capital account would appear on the balance sheet of a sole proprietorship or partnership only.
5. a (LO 7) The ratio described is the profit margin, which describes the relationship between net income and net sales.

6. c (LO 3) Conservatism requires that losses experienced by a firm should be recognized in the period of the decline. Since inventories and short-term investments are subject to fluctuations in value, losses are recorded to reflect a negative economic impact on a firm from market conditions.
7. d (LO 1) Each choice except **d** describes an objective of FASB *Statement of Financial Accounting Concepts No. 1.* The FASB statement stresses *external* use of financial information, and management consists of internal users.
8. d (LO 7) One calculation of return on assets is profit margin times asset turnover, which in this case equals 12 percent.
9. c (LO 6) "Operating expenses" refer to expenses of running a company other than cost of goods sold and other expenses.

Exercises

1. (LO 5)

1. d	**5.** a	**9.** f	**13.** X
2. e	**6.** c	**10.** e	**14.** a
3. c	**7.** a	**11.** d	**15.** e
4. g	**8.** b	**12.** a	

2. (LO 7)

a. $40,000	**d.** 12.5%
b. 3.0	**e.** $16^2/_3\%$
c. 10%	**f.** 1.25 times

3. (LO 6)

a.

Rinaldi Company
Income Statement (Multistep)
For the Year Ended December 31, 20xx

Net Sales		$200,000
Less Cost of Goods Sold		150,000
Gross Margin		$ 50,000
Less Operating Expenses		30,000
Income from Operations		$ 20,000
Other Revenues and Expenses		
Interest Income	$2,000	
Less Interest Expense	5,000	
Excess of Other Expenses		
over Other Revenues		3,000
Net Income		$ 17,000

b.

Rinaldi Company
Income Statement (Single-Step)
For the Year Ended December 31, 20xx

Revenues		
Net Sales		$200,000
Interest Income		2,000
Total Revenues		$202,000
Costs and Expenses		
Cost of Goods Sold	$150,000	
Operating Expenses	30,000	
Interest Expense	5,000	
Total Costs and Expenses		185,000
Net Income		$ 17,000

Chapter 7

1.	d	(LO 1)		**6.**	b	(LO 7)
2.	a	(LO 1)		**7.**	d	(LO 7)
3.	d	(LO 4)		**8.**	a	(LO 7)
4.	b	(LO 5)		**9.**	c	(LO 7)
5.	c	(LO 6)		**10.**	b	(LO 7)

Matching

1.	i	**6.**	q	**11.**	j	**16.**	a
2.	p	**7.**	l	**12.**	b	**17.**	d
3.	e	**8.**	k	**13.**	h		
4.	c	**9.**	o	**14.**	f		
5.	m	**10.**	n	**15.**	g		

Short Answer

1. (LO 5)

Special-Purpose Journal	*Type of Transaction*
Purchases journal	Purchase on credit
Sales journal	Sale of merchandise on credit
Cash receipts journal	Any receipt of cash
Cash payments journal	Any disbursement of cash

2. (LO 7) As each Other Accounts item is recorded in the special-purpose journal, it is posted immediately to its general ledger account. The total for "other" items at the end of the month actually represents several items, all of which already have been posted.

3. (LO 6) A controlling account is found in the general ledger and keeps only a running total of all related subsidiary accounts. A subsidiary account keeps the balance for an individual customer or creditor and is found in the subsidiary ledger.

4. (LO 4) The Internet is a vast, global computer network; the World Wide Web is the vast storehouse of information found on the Internet.

5. (LO 6, 7) A double-posting can be made from the general journal and indicates that an amount has been posted to both the controlling account (such as Accounts Receivable or Accounts Payable) in the general ledger and the supporting account in the subsidiary ledger.

6. (LO 1)
   a. Cost-benefit principle—Benefits must match or exceed the costs.
   b. Control principle—There must be good internal control.
   c. Compatibility principle—It must be a workable system.
   d. Flexibility principle—It must be able to accommodate change.

True-False

1. T (LO 5)
2. F (LO 7) It would be recorded in the general journal (the single-column journal is only for the purchase of merchandise on credit).
3. F (LO 6) Posting to subsidiary accounts should be done daily.
4. F (LO 7) No column totals in the general journal should be posted.
5. T (LO 5)
6. F (LO 6, 7) It should have been posted to the accounts receivable subsidiary ledger.
7. F (LO 7) It should have only one posting.
8. F (LO 5, 7) Cash sales should be recorded in the cash receipts journal.
9. T (LO 6)
10. T (LO 7)
11. T (LO 7)
12. T (LO 6)
13. F (LO 4) It is called a *browser.*
14. T (LO 2)
15. F (LO 3) Microcomputer systems are critical to both large and small companies.

Multiple Choice

1. b (LO 7) The sales journal is a specialized book of original entry, designed for the efficient entry and posting of sales. Each entry represents a sale on credit. As a result, the total of the single column provides information, in aggregate, for the Sales account (a credit) and the Accounts Receivable control account (a debit).
2. c (LO 7) The appropriate posting reference for the subsidiary ledger would include a reference to the journal and page number from which the entry originated. This allows the accountant easy reference in case there is a need to search for errors.
3. c (LO 5) The cash payments journal is designed to accommodate transactions that involve a credit entry to Cash.
4. d (LO 5) The general journal is used as the book of original entry for transactions that are not appropriate for specialized journals. Each of the other choices, by design, could not accommodate a transaction involving an increase in Sales Returns and Allowances or a decrease in Accounts Receivable.
5. c (LO 7) The special-purpose journals that do accommodate transactions that include entries to Accounts Receivable are the sales journal and the cash receipts journal.
6. a (LO 6) Although daily postings to the Accounts Payable controlling account may come from the general journal, postings to that account from special-purpose journals are made at the end of the month.
7. d (LO 7) The cash payments special-purpose journal should be designed to allow for efficient entry of the most common cash credit transactions. One common cash payment that occurs in a firm is payment for purchases of merchandise. Discounts are often available and should be taken. Therefore, a typical cash disbursement entry would indicate a debit to Accounts Payable, a credit to Purchases Discounts for the amount of the discount, and a credit to Cash for the net amount of the balance owed.
8. b (LO 7) Purchases would be entered in special-purpose journals designed especially for transactions involving that account. Cash debits (entered in the cash receipts journal) would not be a part of a transaction involving purchases.
9. c (LO 1) In designing a firm's accounting system, potential changes (i.e., growth) need to be anticipated. This accommodation for potential change is known as the *flexibility principle.*
10. a (LO 4) Bulletin boards are an excellent means of exchanging information and posting questions over the Internet.

Exercises

1. (LO 5)

a. J	**d.** CP	**g.** J	**j.** CP
b. CR	**e.** S	**h.** J	**k.** CR
c. P	**f.** CP	**i.** J	

2. (LO7)

		Cash Receipts Journal							Page 1
				Debits			**Credits**		
Date		**Account Debited/Credited**	**Post. Ref.**	**Cash**	**Sales Disc.**	**Other Accts.**	**Accts. Receiv.**	**Sales**	**Other Accts.**
Feb.	3	Don Morris	✓	490	10		500		
	9	Land	135	8,000					8,000
	14	Common Stock	311	10,000					10,000
	23	Sue O'Neill	✓	150			150		
	28	Sales		25,000				25,000	
				43,640	10		650	25,000	18,000
				(111)	(412)		(114)	(411)	(✓)

3. (LO 7)

a. Cash payments journal

b. The Other Accounts total should have a check mark (not an account number) below it to signify that it is not posted at the end of the month.

c. May 1 Paid DePasquale Supply Co. for $800 of supplies previously purchased. Paid within the discount period, receiving a $16 discount.
May 7 Purchased for cash $2,000 of office equipment from Monahan Business Equipment.
May 13 Paid $350 for ad placed in the *Celestial News*.
May 19 Paid Denecker Motors for $420 of items previously purchased. Did not pay within the discount period (or no discount allowed).

d. **1.** The amounts in the Accounts Payable column were posted to the accounts payable subsidiary accounts (DePasquale Supply Co. and Denecker Motors).

2. The amounts in the Other Accounts column were posted to the general ledger accounts (Office Equipment and Advertising Expense).

3. The 315 is an error, as already explained. The other numbers refer to the account numbers within the general ledger to which the column totals were posted.

Solution to Crossword Puzzle
(Chapters 6 and 7)

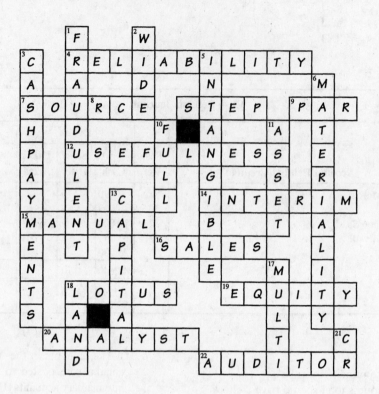

Chapter 8

Self-Test

1. c	(LO 1)		**6.** c	(LO 4)
2. b	(LO 3)		**7.** a	(SO 5)
3. b	(LO 2)		**8.** b	(SO 6)
4. d	(LO 3)		**9.** c	(SO 7)
5. b	(LO 4)		**10.** a	(SO 7)

Matching

1. f	**5.** h	**9.** o	**13.** e
2. d	**6.** b	**10.** a	**14.** c
3. n	**7.** l	**11.** g	**15.** i
4. j	**8.** k	**12.** m	

Short Answer

1. (LO 5)
   Control environment
   Risk assessment
   Information and communication
   Control activities
   Monitoring
2. (LO 3) Purchase order, invoice, and receiving report
3. (LO 1)
   Authorization for all transactions
   Recording all transactions
   Design and use of adequate documents
   Physical controls over assets and records
   Periodic independent verification of records
   Separation of duties
   Sound personnel procedures
4. (LO 4) Bank service charges; a customer's NSF check; bank charges for collecting and paying notes, stop payments, and printing checks; and an error in recording a check (only if underrecorded). (Any three would answer the question.)
5. (SO 7)
   Preparing the voucher
   Recording the voucher
   Paying the voucher
   Posting the voucher and check registers
   Summarizing unpaid vouchers
6. (LO 3) (Any six of the following would answer the question)
   Separate the authorization, recordkeeping, and custodianship of cash.
   Limit access to cash.
   Designate a person to handle cash.
   Use banking facilities and minimize cash on hand.
   Bond employees with access to cash.
   Protect cash on hand with safes, cash registers, etc.
   Conduct surprise audits of cash on hand.
   Record all cash receipts promptly.
   Deposit all cash receipts promptly.
   Make all payments by check.
   Have someone who is not involved with cash transactions reconcile the Cash account.
   Cash through the mail should be handled by two or more employees.

True-False

1. F (LO 2) It increases the probability of accuracy but does not guarantee it.
2. F (SO 5) The reverse is true.
3. T (LO 2)
4. T (SO 5)
5. T (LO 3)
6. F (LO 3) This procedure could easily lead to theft.
7. F (LO 3) The supplier is sent a purchase order.
8. T (LO 4)
9. T (LO 4)
10. F (LO 4) No entries are made for outstanding checks.
11. F (SO 6) All purchases on account are recorded in the voucher register.
12. T (SO 6)
13. F (SO 7) It is placed in the file in order of the date that payment is due.
14. F (LO 4) It begins with the September 30 balances.
15. F (LO 1) Rotating employees is good internal control because it might uncover theft.
16. T (SO 5)

Multiple Choice

1. d (SO 6) The voucher register is used to enter potential cash disbursements. Purchases on account represent the obligation to disburse cash at some future date and, therefore, would be entered into the voucher register.
2. b (LO 4) The company presumably already has recorded the deposit in transit. However, it just learned of the bank service charge, the note collected by the bank, and the bank error when it received its bank statement, and, therefore, must adjust for those items.
3. c (SO 7) The schedule of unpaid vouchers is used to verify that all vouchers paid have been recorded. Total vouchers payable (a liability) less all debits (reductions) should equal the remaining credit balance of Vouchers Payable.
4. c (SO 5) The replenishment of Petty Cash involves a credit to Cash in the amount of the difference between petty cash on hand and the total of the petty cash fund. A check is made out to Cash or Petty Cash Custodian, that check is cashed, and the cash is put into the petty cash drawer.
5. c (LO 4) Interest earned would be a component of the balance per bank, but it would not yet have been placed on the books. Because it is interest earned, it should be added.
6. d (LO 3) The purchase requisition is the initial demand for goods. The purchase requisition is prepared by the individual who ultimately needs the item. The requisition then is authorized by the appropriate person before the process of purchasing begins.
7. a (LO 1) Proper internal control procedures separate the functions of handling assets and recordkeeping in hopes of preventing employee theft.
8. a (LO 4) The error would cause the balance per bank to be understated. Therefore, the $900 should be added. The balance per books needs no adjustment for this error.

Exercises

1. (SO 5) $87.50

2. (LO 4)

1. d	3. b	5. a
2. c	4. d	6. d

3. (SO 7)

General Journal				
Date		**Description**	**Debit**	**Credit**
a.		Petty Cash	75	
		Vouchers Payable		75
		Established petty cash fund, voucher no. 200 (voucher register)		
b.		Purchases	350	
		Vouchers Payable		350
		Purchased merchandise, voucher no. 201 (voucher register)		
c.		Vouchers Payable	75	
		Cash		75
		Paid voucher no. 200 with check no. 601 (check register)		
d.		Vouchers Payable	350	
		Cash		350
		Paid voucher no. 201 with check no. 602 (check register)		
e.		Cab Fare Expense	12	
		Postage Expense	34	
		Miscellaneous Expense	7	
		Cash Short or Over	2	
		Vouchers Payable		55
		To record petty cash expenditures and to replenish fund, voucher no. 202 (voucher register)		
f.		Vouchers Payable	55	
		Cash		55
		Paid voucher no. 202 with check no. 603 (check register)		

Chapter 9

Self-Test

1. b	(LO 1)	**6.** d	(LO 4)
2. c	(LO 2)	**7.** c	(LO 4)
3. a	(LO 3)	**8.** d	(LO 5)
4. a	(LO 4)	**9.** d	(LO 5)
5. c	(LO 4)	**10.** b	(LO 3)

Matching

1. j	**6.** e	**11.** c	**16.** n
2. g	**7.** r	**12.** o	**17.** q
3. f	**8.** l	**13.** s	**18.** a
4. m	**9.** i	**14.** h	**19.** b
5. p	**10.** k	**15.** d	

Short Answer

1. (LO 4) Percentage of net sales method, accounts receivable aging method, and direct charge-off method
2. (LO 1) It means that the original payee, who discounts the note receivable, must make good on the note if the maker does not pay at maturity.
3. (LO 4) There would be a debit balance when more accounts are written off (in dollar amounts) than have been provided for in the adjusting entries for estimated uncollectible accounts.
4. (LO 3) Held-to-maturity securities, trading securities, and available-for-sale securities
5. (LO 1) Cash and cash equivalents, short-term investments, and accounts and notes receivable due within the current period.

True-False

1. T (LO 4)
2. F (LO 4) It follows the matching rule.
3. F (LO 4) The balance must be taken into account.
4. T (LO 4)
5. T (LO 4)
6. T (LO 4)
7. F (LO 5) The computation is 700 × 5/100 × 90/360.
8. T (LO 4)
9. F (LO 1) The payee must make good if the maker defaults.
10. F (LO 5) It has a duration of 62 days.
11. T (LO 1)
12. F (LO 4) Total assets remain the same.
13. T (LO 5)
14. F (LO 4) The debit is to Allowance for Uncollectible Accounts.
15. T (LO 5)

16. T (LO 4)
17. F (LO 2) Accounts Receivable are a short-term liquid asset but not a cash equivalent.
18. F (LO 1) Major credit cards involve factoring without recourse.

19. F (LO 1) It equals short-term liquid assets divided by current liabilities.
20. T (LO 2)
21. T (LO 3)
22. F (LO 3) They appear at market value.

Multiple Choice

1. c (LO 3) They are labeled Accumulated Other Comprehensive Income.
2. b (LO 5) Principal × Rate × Time for *b* equals $12. Each of the other choices results in $6.
3. c (LO 4) Using the net sales method of calculating adjustments for Allowance for Uncollectible Accounts, the amount of the Uncollectible Accounts Expense is based on the sales during the period. Therefore, it is not netted with an existing balance in the allowance account.
4. a (LO 1) Because the discounting bank has the right to extract funds from a firm's account if a note is dishonored, the firm carries that liability until such time as the note is paid to the bank. Once the note is paid, the contingent liability is eliminated.
5. b (LO 4) Under this method, Uncollectible Accounts Expense equals the amount deemed uncollectible ($850) minus the credit balance in Allowance for Uncollectible Accounts ($300), or $550.
6. c (LO 4) When an allowance account is established to record anticipated uncollectible accounts, the expense is recorded at the time the adjusting entry is made. As a result, when the actual uncollectible account is known and written off, the allowance account is reduced, and Accounts Receivable is reduced by the same amount.

7. a (LO 5) The discount rate is used as an adjustment to the maturity value of a note to calculate the proceeds on discounting that note to the bank. The details of a note would not include the discount rate because it is not known at the time the note is originated. Additionally, whether a note is going to be discounted or not is irrelevant in determining the note arrangements.
8. b (LO 4) The direct charge-off method of handling uncollectible accounts often postpones the uncollectible accounts expense of a given accounting period to subsequent accounting periods. Usually, a significant period of time elapses between a credit sale and the determination that the corresponding receivable is uncollectible.
9. c (LO 1) Inventory is not considered a short-term liquid asset. The ability of a firm to convert its inventory to cash is the basis of the firm's operations. Short-term liquid assets, by definition, are assets that can be converted quickly to cash (or are cash or near cash) to cover operating expenses and immediate cash requirements.
10. d (LO 3) The Short-Term Investments account is increased with a debit by the amount of the accrued interest. The resulting balance will reflect the investment's amortized cost.

Exercises

1. (LO 4, 5)

General Journal				
Date		**Description**	**Debit**	**Credit**
Dec.	31	Interest Receivable	75	
		Interest Income		75
		To record accrued interest on Notes Receivable		
	31	Uncollectible Accounts Expense	24,000	
		Allowance for Uncollectible Accounts		24,000
		To record estimated bad debts		
Jan.	3	Notes Receivable	10,000	
		Accounts Receivable, Kohn		10,000
		Kohn substituted a 30-day, 6 percent note for her debt		
	8	Allowance for Uncollectible Accounts	1,000	
		Accounts Receivable, O'Brien		1,000
		To write off O'Brien's account		
	25	Accounts Receivable, O'Brien	600	
		Allowance for Uncollectible Accounts		600
		To reinstate portion of O'Brien's account		
	28	Cash	200	
		Accounts Receivable, O'Brien		200
		Collection from T. O'Brien		

2. (LO 5)
  a. $16.00
  b. $910.00
  c. $43.17
  d. $4.00

3. (LO 3)

General Journal				
Date		**Description**	**Debit**	**Credit**
Nov.	17	Short-Term Investments	60,000	
		Cash		60,000
		Purchased Lopez stock for trading		
Dec.	31	Unrealized Loss on Investments	4,000	
		Allowance to Adjust Short-Term Investments to Market		4,000
		Year-end adjustment for market decline		
Jan.	12	Cash	66,000	
		Short-Term Investments		60,000
		Realized Gain on Investments		6,000
		To record sale of Lopez stock		

Solution to Crossword Puzzle
(Chapters 8 and 9)

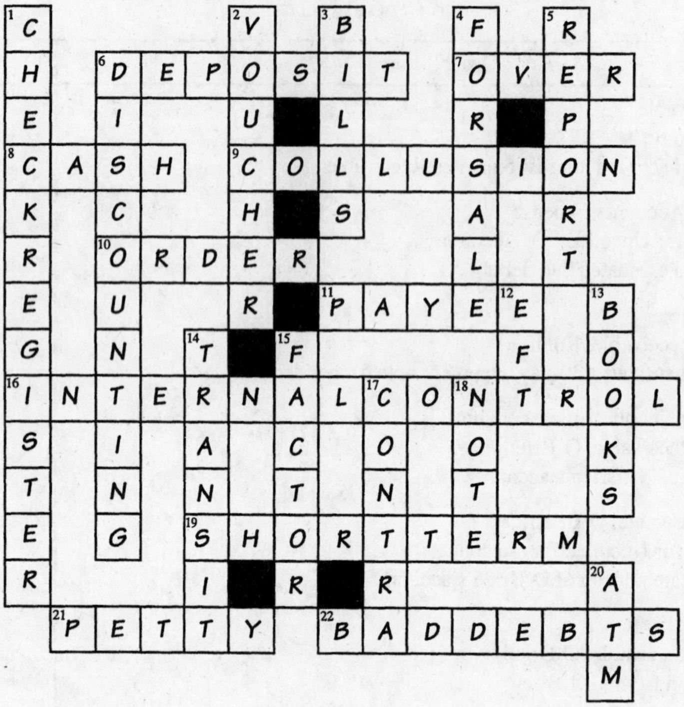
1 C 2 V 3 B 4 F 5 R
H 6 D E P O S I T 7 O V E R
E I U L R P
8 C A S H 9 C O L L U S I O N
K C H S A R
R 10 O R D E R L T
E U R 11 P A Y E 12 E 13 B
G N 14 T 15 F F O
16 I N T E R N A L 17 C O 18 N T R O L
S I A C O O K
T N N T N T S
E G 19 S H O R T T E R M
R I R R 20 A
21 P E T T Y 22 B A D D E B T S
M

Chapter 10

1. b	(LO 5)	**6.** d	(LO 1)
2. a	(LO 2)	**7.** c	(LO 3)
3. c	(LO 3)	**8.** d	(LO 6)
4. b	(LO 3)	**9.** d	(SO 7)
5. d	(LO 3)	**10.** d	(SO 7)

Matching

1. m	**5.** j	**9.** c	**13.** k
2. h	**6.** n	**10.** l	**14.** a
3. d	**7.** o	**11.** e	**15.** f
4. g	**8.** i	**12.** b	

Short Answer

1. (LO 3) Specific identification; average-cost; first-in, first-out; and last-in, first-out
2. (LO 6) Item-by-item and major category methods
3. (SO 7) Retail method and gross profit method
4. (LO 4) The periodic system does not keep detailed records of inventory; the perpetual system does. Under the periodic system, physical inventory taken at the end of each period determines the cost of goods sold.
5. (LO 1) Raw materials, work in process, and finished goods

True-False

1. T (LO 1)
2. T (LO 5)
3. T (LO 5)
4. T (LO 5)
5. F (LO 2) They belong in the buyer's ending inventory if the buyer has title to the goods.
6. T (LO 3)
7. F (LO 3) Not necessarily. The actual flow of goods is not known; the flow of costs is assumed.
8. F (LO 3) It results in the highest income.
9. F (SO 7) Items sold are recorded only at retail.
10. F (SO 7) The cost of goods sold is estimated by subtracting the gross profit percentage of sales from total sales.
11. F (LO 3) Average-cost results in a higher income before income taxes.
12. F (LO 5) The requirement is for LIFO, not FIFO.
13. F (LO 2) The consignee has possession but not title.
14. T (LO 5)

Multiple Choice

1. **b** (LO 2) The cost to store goods normally is considered too difficult to trace to specific inventory items, so it is expensed when incurred. The other costs listed are more closely related to the acquisition cost of inventory.

2. **a** (LO 5) Under rising prices, the FIFO inventory method matches current selling prices with the oldest, least expensive costs. Of the inventory methods listed, this method results in the highest income before income taxes.

3. **c** (LO 5) Forgetting to include in inventory an item in the warehouse results in an understated ending inventory, which, in turn, produces an overstated cost of goods sold. An overstated cost of goods sold produces an understated income before income taxes and, therefore, an understated stockholders' equity.

4. **c** (LO 3) With low-volume, high-priced goods, it is especially necessary to match the selling price of a particular item with its cost in order to avoid distortion in the financial statements. Only specific identification directly matches cost and selling price.

5. **b** (SO 7) In performing the retail inventory calculation, freight in is incorporated at cost, not at retail. The other choices provided are included as stated.

6. **a** (LO 1) The matching rule states that a cost must be expensed in the period in which that cost helps to generate revenue. Therefore, the cost of inventory is expensed in the period in which the inventory is sold.

7. **d** (LO 2) By definition, inventory should appear on the balance sheet of the company that has title to the goods (although not necessarily possession of them).

8. **d** (SO 7) The gross profit method is a simple way to estimate the amount of inventory lost or destroyed by fire, theft, etc. It assumes a relatively consistent gross profit ratio over time.

9. **b** (LO 1) Unlike the other three choices, office wages are not factory-related and thus would not be included in the cost of a manufactured item.

Exercises

1. (LO 3)
   a. $6,600; $8,800
   b. $7,200; $8,200
   c. $6,820; $8,580

2. (SO 7)

	Cost	Retail
Beginning Inventory	$ 70,000	$125,000
Net Purchases	48,000	75,000
Freight In	2,000	—
Cost/Retail	$120,000 ÷	$200,000 = 60%
Less Sales		156,000
Estimated Ending Inventory at Retail		$ 44,000
		× 60%
Estimated Cost of Ending Inventory		$ 26,400

3. (SO 7)

Beginning Inventory at Cost	$150,000
Purchases at Cost	120,000
Cost of Goods Available for Sale	$270,000
Less Estimated Cost of Goods Sold	
($300,000 × 80%)	240,000
Estimated Cost of Ending Inventory	$ 30,000

4. (LO 4)

May						
1	Inventory	100 units @ $10			$1,000	
4	Purchase	60 units @ $12			720	
8	Sale	50 units @ $12			(600)	
8	Balance	100 units @ $10	$1,000			
		10 units @ $12	120	$1,120		
17	Purchase	70 units @ $11			770	
31	Sale	70 units @ $11	($770)			
		10 units @ $12	(120)			
		20 units @ $10	(200)	(1,090)		
31	Inventory	80 units @ $10			$ 800	

Cost of Goods Sold = $600 + $1,090 $1,690

5. (LO 4)

May				
1	Inventory	100 units @ $10.00		$1,000.00
4	Purchase	60 units @ $12.00		720.00
4	Balance	160 units @ $10.75		$1,720.00
8	Sale	50 units @ $10.75		537.50
8	Balance	110 units @ $10.75		$1,182.50
17	Purchase	70 units @ $11.00		770.00
17	Balance	180 units @ $10.85*		$1,952.50
31	Sale	100 units @ $10.85		1,085.00
31	Inventory	80 units @ $10.84*		$ 867.50

Cost of Goods Sold = $537.50 + $1,085 $1,622.50

*Rounded.

Chapter 11

Self-Test

1. b	(LO 1)	**6.** b	(LO 6)
2. a	(LO 2)	**7.** c	(LO 7)
3. a	(LO 3)	**8.** a	(LO 8)
4. a	(LO 4)	**9.** d	(LO 8)
5. b	(LO 5)	**10.** c	(SO 9)

Matching

1. e	**7.** r	**13.** u	**18.** a
2. f	**8.** h	**14.** c	**19.** i
3. n	**9.** v	**15.** k	**20.** d
4. s	**10.** j	**16.** m	**21.** p
5. l	**11.** b	**17.** g	**22.** q
6. t	**12.** o		

Short Answer

1. (SO 9) Additions, such as a new building wing, add to the physical layout. Betterments, such as a new air-conditioning system, simply improve the existing layout.
2. (LO 5) When the cash received equals the carrying value of the asset sold
3. (LO 7) The cost of the well, the estimated residual value of the well, the estimated barrels to be extracted over the life of the well, and the actual barrels extracted and sold during the year
4. (SO 9) Ordinary repairs (a paint job, a tune-up) merely maintain the asset in good operating condition. Extraordinary repairs—for example, a complete overhaul—increase the asset's estimated residual value or useful life.
5. (LO 1) Amortization, depreciation, and depletion
6. (LO 3) Physical deterioration and obsolescence

True-False

1. T (LO 1)
2. T (LO 5)
3. T (LO 1)
4. F (LO 3) Depreciation is a process of allocation, not valuation.
5. F (LO 3) The physical deterioration of a machine is irrelevant in computing depreciation.
6. T (LO 2)
7. T (LO 3)
8. T (LO 4)
9. F (LO 4) Depreciation expense will be $1,000 in the second year also.
10. T (SO 9)
11. T (LO 6)
12. F (LO 4) It results in more net income.
13. F (LO 3) Depreciable cost equals cost minus residual value.
14. T (SO 9)
15. F (LO 8) A trademark is a name or symbol that can be used only by its owner.

16. T (LO 2)
17. F (SO 9) A betterment is a capital expenditure.
18. F (SO 9) The carrying value increases because the accumulated depreciation account is decreased (debited).
19. F (LO 5) The Accumulated Depreciation account always is debited when a depreciable asset is sold.
20. F (LO 2) *Capital expenditure* refers to the purchase of an asset; *expense* refers to the expiration of asset cost through the use or depreciation of an asset.

21. T (LO 6)
22. F (LO 5) Depreciation expense should be brought up to date before the sale is recorded.
23. T (LO 8)
24. T (LO 4)
25. T (LO 8)
26. F (LO 8) Research and development costs normally are charged as expenses in the year incurred.
27. T (LO 7)
28. T (LO 1)

Multiple Choice

1. c (LO 2) Because the relative values of the lump-sum purchase are known, a ratio can be determined and applied to the purchase price of both assets. The total appraised value of the land and building is $80,000. Of that $80,000, $20,000, or 25%, is apportioned to the land. So 25% of the purchase price for both assets, $16,500, would be allocated to land.

2. a (LO 3) The expired cost of an asset is its total accumulated depreciation to date. Depreciation is the allocation of the cost of an asset over its useful life.

3. d (LO 4) The declining-balance method would probably produce the greatest depreciation charge in the first year, although it is possible that the production method could be greater. Therefore, more information is needed to answer the question.

4. c (SO 9) The change requires an adjustment to the depreciation schedule of the asset. The remaining depreciable cost would be spread over the remaining (new) estimated useful life of the machine.

5. c (LO 8) Although the life of an intangible asset can be difficult to estimate, GAAP set a "reasonable" limit on how long a firm can amortize the costs associated with intangible assets.

6. b (LO 2) Although land is not a depreciable asset, improvements to land (buildings, street lights, pavement, etc.) are. Each improvement has an estimated useful life over which the costs will be allocated.

7. d (LO 5) In order to eliminate the asset from the company's accounting records, existing accounts pertaining to the asset must be removed from the books as part of the transaction. Because the book value of the machine was $2,000 and the original cost was $9,000, accumulated depreciation must have been $7,000 (credit balance). To eliminate that account, a debit of $7,000 should be recorded to Accumulated Depreciation.

8. b (LO 2) A new roof has an economic life of more than a year. Therefore, the expenditure for a new roof is considered a capital expenditure.

9. d (LO 2) Understatement of net income results from expensing a capital expenditure. By definition, capital expenditures should be spread over the useful life of the acquisition (more than one period). If the entire cost is put into one period, expenses for that period will be overstated.

10. b (LO 7) Depletion costs assigned to a given period are the result of calculations based on expected total output over the life of an asset. Total costs divided by total expected units of output equal the depletion cost per unit. If the expected units of output are overestimated, the unit cost will be underestimated.

11. a (LO 8) Up to a point at which the software is technologically feasible, its costs are treated as research and development and, therefore, must be expensed.

12. d (LO 8) Research and development costs are considered revenue expenditures and are recognized in the period incurred. It is difficult to estimate the useful life of research and development.

Exercises

1. (LO 4)

	Depreciation Expense for 20x2	Accumulated Depreciation as of 12/31/x2	Carrying Value as of 12/31/x2
a.	$4,800	$ 9,600	$16,400
b.	$6,240	$16,640	$ 9,360

2. (LO 4)

$$\$2,250 = \left(\frac{\$35,000 - \$5,000}{100,000 \text{ toys}} \times 7,500 \text{ toys}\right)$$

3. (LO 2)

a.	C	d.	C	f.	R	h.	C
b.	R	e.	C	g.	C	i.	R
c.	R						

4. (LO 1)

Acquisition cost ($22,000 × 1.000)	($22,000)
Present value of net annual cash flows ($4,000 × 4.623)	18,492
Present value of residual value ($3,000 × .630)	1,890
Net present value of equipment	($ 1,618)

The equipment should *not* be purchased because its net present value is negative.

5. (LO 6)

General Journal				
Date		**Description**	**Debit**	**Credit**
Jan.	2	Machinery (new)	23,000	
		Accumulated Depreciation, Machinery	17,000	
		Loss on Exchange of Machinery	500	
		Cash		15,500
		Machinery (old)		25,000
		To record exchange of machine, following GAAP		
	2	Machinery (new)	23,500	
		Accumulated Depreciation, Machinery	17,000	
		Cash		15,500
		Machinery (old)		25,000
		To record exchange of machine, following income tax rulings*		

*For income tax purposes, neither gains nor losses are recognized on the exchange of similar assets.

6. (LO 7)

General Journal				
Date		**Description**	**Debit**	**Credit**
Dec.	31	Depletion Expense, Coal Deposits	40,000	
		Accumulated Depletion, Coal Deposits		40,000
		To record depletion of coal mine for 20xx		

Solution to Crossword Puzzle
(Chapters 10 and 11)

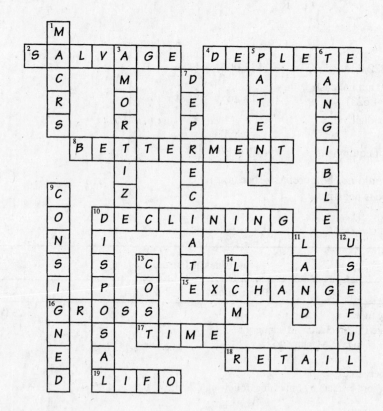

Chapter 12

Self-Test

1. b	(LO 1)	**6.** a	(LO 2)
2. d	(LO 2)	**7.** c	(LO 2)
3. d	(LO 2)	**8.** c	(LO 3)
4. b	(LO 2)	**9.** c	(SO 4)
5. b	(LO 2)	**10.** c	(SO 4)

Matching

1. b	**6.** j	**11.** f	**16.** d
2. r	**7.** h	**12.** n	**17.** p
3. g	**8.** l	**13.** a	**18.** c
4. e	**9.** k	**14.** m	
5. o	**10.** i	**15.** q	

Short Answer

1. (LO 2) Definitely determinable liabilities and estimated liabilities
2. (LO 3) Pending lawsuits, tax disputes, discounted notes receivable, the guarantee of another company's debt, and failure to follow government regulations
3. (LO 2) Income taxes payable, estimated warranty expense, and vacation pay (There are others.)
4. (LO 2) Accounts payable, bank loans and commercial paper, short-term notes payable, accrued liabilities, dividends payable, sales and excise taxes payable, the current portion of long-term debt, payroll liabilities, and deferred revenues
5. (SO 4) Social security taxes, Medicare taxes, federal income taxes, and state income taxes
6. (SO 4) Social security taxes, Medicare taxes, federal unemployment taxes, and state unemployment taxes

True-False

1. F (LO 2) Deferred revenues are a liability representing an obligation to deliver goods or services. They are shown on the balance sheet.
2. T (LO 1)
3. T (LO 1)
4. T (LO 2)
5. F (LO 2) Sales Tax Payable is a definitely determinable liability.
6. F (LO 2) A warranty is an estimated liability.
7. T (SO 4)
8. T (SO 4)
9. F (SO 4) FUTA is assessed against employers only.
10. T (LO 3)
11. F (LO 2) The account is associated with notes whose interest is included in the face amount.
12. T (LO 1)
13. T (LO 2)
14. F (LO 2) An estimate should be recorded for Product Warranty Expense in year 1, the year of the sale.
15. T (SO 4)
16. F (LO 2, SO 4) They are borne by both the employee and the employer.

Multiple Choice

1. c (LO 2) Property tax bills are not available to a firm until months after the liability actually exists. Therefore, the accountant must estimate the property taxes due for the accounting period and enter that estimate onto the books as a liabilty. On receipt of the actual tax bill, adjustments are made. This method is required by the matching rule, which allows estimates when perfect information is not available, to match the expenses of a period to that accounting period.

2. d (LO 2) Pending lawsuits, and the settlement thereof, would be recorded as contingent liabilities, but only if the outcome against the company can be estimated and is probable.

3. a (SO 4) FUTA is a payroll expense borne by the employer. There is no payroll deduction to the employee under the Federal Unemployment Tax Act.

4. d (SO 4) The withholding of income taxes on behalf of an employee creates a current liability on the employer's books. Cash is retained from the gross payroll and then submitted to depositories to be held for the employee until that employee's ultimate tax liability is known. Until the employer makes such a deposit, the amount owing on behalf of the employee is recorded as a current liability.

5. c (LO 2) Under the matching rule, estimated liabilities for vacation pay as a result of current employee status must be recorded as an expense of the current period. Therefore, by the time the employee exercises the right to a paid vacation, the expense has been recorded by the use of an allowance account, Estimated Liability for Vacation Pay. As the liability expires, it is reduced by a debit entry. The credit entry is to Cash for the disbursement of pay to the employee.

6. d (LO 2) The entry to record payment in advance of a property tax bill is a debit to the Prepaid Property Tax account and a credit to Cash. Then, as each monthly share of the prepaid amount expires, the entry is a debit to Property Tax Expense and a reduction (credit entry) to the corresponding prepaid (asset) account.

7. a (LO 2) Even though the problem states that there is no interest borne by the note, a rate must be applied. The method for doing so would be to record the note, discounted at an appropriate rate. The principal of the note less the discount is the actual "cost" of the equipment to Balboa.

8. b (LO 2) With the passage of time, Discount on Notes Payable becomes Interest Expense, in accordance with the matching rule.

Exercises

1. (LO 2)

General Journal				
Date		**Description**	**Debit**	**Credit**
Dec.	31	Product Warranty Expense	525	
		Estimated Product Warranty Liability		525
		To record estimated warranty expense for washing machines		
Apr.	9	Estimated Product Warranty Liability	48	
		Parts, Wages Payable, etc.		48
		To record the repair of a washing machine		

2. (SO 4)

		General Journal		
Date		**Description**	**Debit**	**Credit**
May	11	Office Wages Expense	260.00	
		Social Security Tax Payable		16.12
		Medicare Tax Payable		3.77
		Union Dues Payable		5.00
		State Income Tax Payable		8.00
		Federal Income Tax Payable		52.00
		Wages Payable		175.11
		To record payroll liabilities and wages expense for Pat Bauer		
	11	Payroll Tax Expense	36.01	
		Social Security Tax Payable		16.12
		Medicare Tax Payable		3.77
		Federal Unemployment Tax Payable		2.08
		State Unemployment Tax Payable		14.04
		To record payroll taxes on Bauer's earnings		

3. (LO 1)
    a. $60,000 ($100,000 − $40,000)
    b. 11 times

$$\left[(\$290,000 - \$15,000) \div \left(\frac{\$30,000 + \$20,000}{2}\right)\right]$$

    c. 33.2 days (365 ÷ 11)

Chapter 13

Self-Test

1. c	(LO 1)	**6.** c	(LO 3)
2. c	(LO 1)	**7.** c	(LO 3)
3. b	(LO 2)	**8.** a	(LO 4)
4. b	(LO 3)	**9.** c	(LO 4, 5)
5. d	(LO 3)	**10.** d	(LO 6)

Matching

1. m	**5.** c	**8.** i	**11.** d
2. k	**6.** h	**9.** a	**12.** g
3. j	**7.** f	**10.** l	**13.** e
4. b			

Short Answer

1. (LO 1) Withdrawal of a partner, bankruptcy of a partner, incapacity of a partner, death of a partner, admission of a new partner, retirement of a partner, and expiration of the partnership agreement
2. (LO 6) Selling partnership assets, paying off partnership liabilities, and distributing the remaining assets to the partners
3. (LO 1) Ease of formation and dissolution, ability to pool capital and individual talents, avoidance of the corporation's tax burden, and freedom and flexibility
4. (LO 1) Limited life, mutual agency, unlimited liability, capital limitation, and difficulty of transferring ownership interest

True-False

1. F (LO 1) A partnership agreement does not have to be in writing to be legal.
2. T (LO 1)
3. T (LO 1)
4. F (LO 3) Losses also would be shared in a 3:2 ratio.
5. F (LO 3) A net loss occurs only when expenses exceed revenues for the period.
6. T (LO 2)
7. T (LO 3)
8. F (LO 4) D's Capital account is credited for $20,000.
9. F (LO 4) The original partners' Capital accounts increase in the stated ratio.
10. F (LO 4) The original partners' accounts decrease in the stated ratio.
11. T (LO 5)
12. F (LO 6) The partners are paid according to their capital balances.
13. T (LO 6)
14. F (LO 6) The remaining partners must absorb the deficit but do not have to contribute personal assets.
15. T (LO 1)

Multiple Choice

1. b (LO 3) A partnership's income or loss cannot be determined in advance. There may be an excess of income beyond salary and interest allowances to the partners. The partnership agreement must indicate a method of distribution of that excess. In case income is insufficient to cover salary and interest allowances, provisions for dealing with the shortfall also must be included.

2. c (LO 3) The formula for the distribution of income to the partners includes the following calculation:

The net income of $5,000 is before total guaranteed payments of $10,000 to the partners. Net loss, after subtracting the salary allowances, is $5,000. That loss is distributed equally to each partner, $2,500 each. For Partner A, that $2,500 allocated loss reduces the salary allowance of $8,000 to A, resulting in a net increase in A's capital account of $5,500.

3. c (LO 4) Total equity after L's contribution is $105,000. One-third of $105,000 is $35,000, which is the amount that will be attributed to L's beginning capital. The bonus was paid to the existing partners because L paid more for the one-third interest than is entered into L's Capital account.

4. a (LO 4) Total equity after the contribution by P is $60,000. P is acquiring a Capital account with a beginning balance of $15,000 for a $10,000 investment. Therefore, Partners M and N are paying a bonus to P for investing in the partnership. That bonus is shared in the same ratio as are income and losses, 3 parts to M and 2 parts to N. M's Capital account will be reduced by $3,000 ($5,000 × 3/5), leaving a new balance of $17,000.

5. c (LO 5) The undervaluation of the assets should be shared equally among the partners. Because the assets are revalued at an amount $6,000 above their book value, each partner is credited with a $2,000 increase in capital. S will have a Capital account balance of $22,000 after the adjustment is made.

6. c (LO 3) The first calculation in solving this problem is finding the ratio of Y's capital to the total capital of the partnership. Total capital is $20,000, and Y's balance is $7,000. Therefore, Y owns 35 percent of the capital of the partnership, and 35 percent of $60,000 is $21,000.

7. d (LO 6) Liquidation of a partnership is defined in the partnership agreement. Gains and losses on liquidation are handled like gains and losses from transactions in other circumstances.

8. b (LO 1) A partnership is not a legal entity for tax purposes and need only file an informational return (the partners, however, must pay a tax based on their share of the business's earnings).

Exercises

1. (LO 3)
  a. A = $14,500 ($10,000 + $3,000 + $1,500)
  B = $13,000 ($10,000 + $2,000 + $1,000)
  C = $13,000 ($10,000 + $2,500 + $500)
  b. A = $7,000 ($10,000 + $3,000 − $6,000)
  B = $8,000 ($10,000 + $2,000 − $4,000)
  C = $10,500 ($10,000 + $2,500 − $2,000)
  c. A = ($8,000) ($10,000 + $3,000 − $21,000)
  B = ($2,000) ($10,000 + $2,000 − $14,000)
  C = $5,500 ($10,000 + $2,500 − $7,000)

2. (LO 6)
  D = $0 ($7,000 − $10,000 + $3,000 deficit absorbed by other partners)
  E = $7,200 ($15,000 − $6,000 − $1,800)
  F = $14,800 ($20,000 − $4,000 − $1,200)

3. (LO 4)

		General Journal		
Date		**Description**	**Debit**	**Credit**
a.		Cash	12,000	
		G, Capital	800	
		H, Capital	800	
		I, Capital	400	
		J, Capital		14,000
		To record purchase of one-third interest by J		
b.		Cash	15,000	
		J, Capital		15,000
		To record purchase of one-third interest by J		
c.		Cash	21,000	
		G, Capital		1,600
		H, Capital		1,600
		I, Capital		800
		J, Capital		17,000
		To record purchase of one-third interest by J		

Chapter 14

Self-Test

1. a (LO 1)		**6.** c (LO 5)	
2. c (LO 2)		**7.** a (LO 6)	
3. c (LO 3)		**8.** b (LO 6)	
4. b (LO 4)		**9.** a (LO 7)	
5. b (LO 4)		**10.** a (LO 8)	

Matching

1. f	**6.** m	**11.** d	**16.** q
2. k	**7.** g	**12.** h	**17.** i
3. p	**8.** a	**13.** c	**18.** r
4. l	**9.** o	**14.** s	**19.** j
5. e	**10.** n	**15.** t	**20.** b

Short Answer

1. (LO 1) Separate legal entity, limited liability, ease of capital generation, ease of transfer of ownership, lack of mutual agency, continuous existence, centralized authority and responsibility, and professional management

2. (LO 1) Government regulation, double taxation, limited liability, and separation of ownership and control

3. (LO 3) Contributed capital and retained earnings

4. (LO 5) When dividends are declared and when a corporation liquidates

5. (LO 3, 7) When a corporation has bought back some of its issued stock. Treasury stock is stock that has been issued but is no longer outstanding.

6. (LO 7) Treasury stock is stock that has been issued and later repurchased by the corporation. Unissued stock has never been issued.

True-False

1. T (LO 1)
2. F (LO 1, 6) It was established to protect the *creditors*.
3. T (LO 1)
4. T (LO 2)
5. T (LO 3)
6. T (LO 1)
7. F (LO 5) It may be both.
8. T (LO 5)
9. F (LO 1) Par value does not necessarily relate to market value (worth).
10. T (LO 7)

11. F (LO 5) No stockholders are ever guaranteed dividends.
12. F (LO 3) Common stock is considered the residual equity of a corporation.
13. F (LO 8) The amount of compensation is measured on the date of grant.
14. F (LO 4) Total assets and total liabilities decrease.
15. F (LO 5) Dividends in arrears are not a liability until declared. Any arrearage normally appears in a note to the financial statements.
16. F (LO 7) Treasury Stock is listed in the stockholders' equity section as a deduction.

17. T (LO 1)
18. F (LO 7) Paid-in Capital, Treasury Stock is credited for the excess of the sales price over the cost.

19. T (LO 1)
20. F (LO 1, 7) Return on equity will increase.
21. T (LO 1)

Multiple Choice

1. d (LO 7) When a company is dealing in its own stock, losses never are recognized. What would otherwise be considered a loss is recorded as a reduction in stockholders' equity. The exact nature of the transaction in this case is unknown because of the lack of detail.

2. b (LO 7) Treasury stock is still considered issued, but no longer outstanding, stock.

3. c (LO 1, 3) The number of authorized shares is the maximum number of shares a corporation can issue. Until such time as shares are issued, they are considered unissued. Outstanding shares are those shares that are issued and in the hands of stockholders (as opposed to in the treasury of the corporation). Treasury stock is considered to be issued.

4. d (LO 5) Because the preferred stock is noncumulative, there are no dividends in arrears. The current dividend declared will be distributed to preferred stockholders based on 7% of the par value of $100. Of the declaration, therefore, $7,000 will be distributed to the preferred stockholders (.07 × $100 × 1,000 shares). The remaining $33,000 will be distributed, pro rata, to the common stockholders.

5. d (LO 1) The stockholders of a corporation are protected from unlimited liability. Under most circumstances, their liability (or potential for loss) is limited to the amount of their investment.

6. d (LO 4) The declaration of a cash dividend requires a journal entry to record the liability and to reduce retained earnings by the amount of the declared dividend. On the date of payment of the dividend, a journal entry is required to record the elimination of the liability created on the date of declaration and the reduction in cash as a result of the payment. The date of record is the data-gathering date, and no journal entry is required.

7. b (LO 4) If stock is purchased after the date of record, the new owner has no rights to the dividends not yet distributed.

8. d (LO 5) The call feature on stock specifies an amount for which the corporation can buy back the stock. It is binding on the stockholder and on the issuing corporation in spite of possible differences between the call price and the market value at the time the stock is called.

Exercises

1. (LO 2, 4, 6, 8)

General Journal				
Date		**Description**	**Debit**	**Credit**
Jan.	1	Start-up and Organization Expense	8,000	
		Cash		8,000
		Paid legal and incorporation fees		
Feb.	9	Cash	575,000	
		Common Stock		500,000
		Paid-in Capital in Excess of Par Value, Common		75,000
		Issued 5,000 shares of $100 par value common stock for $115 per share		
Apr.	12	Buildings	240,000	
		Preferred Stock		200,000
		Paid-in Capital in Excess of Stated Value, Preferred		40,000
		Issued 2,000 shares of preferred stock in exchange for a building		
June	23	Cash Dividends Declared	8,000	
		Cash Dividends Payable		8,000
		Declared a cash dividend on preferred stock		
July	8	Cash Dividends Payable	8,000	
		Cash		8,000
		Paid cash dividend declared on June 23		
Dec.	20	Cash	22,000	
		Common Stock		20,000
		Paid-in Capital in Excess of Par Value, Common		2,000
		Recorded exercise of stock option by president		

2. (LO 7)

General Journal				
Date		**Description**	**Debit**	**Credit**
Jan.	12	Treasury Stock, Common	300,000	
		Cash		300,000
		Recorded purchase of treasury stock		
	20	Cash	130,000	
		Treasury Stock, Common		120,000
		Paid-in Capital, Treasury Stock		10,000
		Recorded reissue of treasury stock		
	27	Cash	116,000	
		Paid-in Capital, Treasury Stock	4,000	
		Treasury Stock, Common		120,000
		Recorded reissue of treasury stock		
	31	Common Stock	10,000	
		Paid-in Capital in Excess of Par Value, Common	40,000	
		Retained Earnings	10,000	
		Treasury Stock, Common		60,000
		Recorded retirement of treasury stock		

3. (LO 5)
   a. $18,000 (1,000 × $100 × 6% × 3 years)
   b. $33,000 ($51,000 − $18,000)

4. (LO 5)
   a. $6,000 (1,000 × $100 × 6%)
   b. $45,000 ($51,000 − $6,000)

Solution to Crossword Puzzle
(Chapters 12, 13, and 14)

```
 G        U  N  L  I  M  I  T  E  D        T
 R        C           N                    A
 N  O  P  A  R     L  I  N  E  O  F     E  X
 O        L     E     T        U     C     E
 S        L  I  Q  U  I  D  A  T  I  O  N  S
 F     A        U     A        S     N
 U     S  O  C  I  A  L     S  T  A  T  E  D
 T     S        T     C     A     I
 A  G  E  N  C  Y     E  A  R  N  I  N  G  S
       S           P  D     G
 I  S  S  U  E  D     D  I  V  I  D  E  N  D
       M        L     T  N     N        E
    S  E  C     F  I  C  A     G     T  B
       N        F     L        T        T
 R  E  T  A  I  N  E  D     B  O  N  U  S
```

Chapter 15

Self-Test

1. b	(LO 6)	6. d	(LO 8)
2. a	(LO 7)	7. b	(LO 2)
3. a	(LO 7)	8. c	(LO 3)
4. d	(LO 6)	9. a	(LO 4)
5. a	(LO 6)	10. b	(LO 5)

Matching

1. j	6. b	10. l	14. a
2. c	7. n	11. p	15. k
3. e	8. g	12. d	16. h
4. o	9. i	13. q	17. f
5. m			

Short Answer

1. (LO 6, 7) Net loss from operations, cash dividend declaration, and stock dividend declaration are the three instances discussed in this chapter. (Certain treasury stock transactions, discussed in Chapter 14, will also reduce retained earnings.)
2. (LO 7) A stock split changes the par or stated value of the stock; a stock dividend does not. Also, a stock dividend transfers retained earnings to contributed capital; a stock split does not.
3. (LO 4) It must be unusual in nature, and it must occur infrequently.
4. (LO 2, 4) Correct order: 5, 1, 4, 6, 3, 2
5. (LO 2) Within the statement of stockholders' equity, on a separate statement of comprehesive income, or on the income statement.

True-False

1. F (LO 3, 4) The net of taxes amount is less than $20,000.
2. F (LO 6) Restricted Retained Earnings is not a cash account.
3. T (LO 8)
4. F (LO 7) Each stockholder owns the same percentage as before.
5. F (LO 7) The market value of the stock is needed to calculate the dollar amount for the journal entry.
6. F (LO 7) Its main purpose is to increase marketability by causing a decrease in the market price. The decrease in par value is a by-product of a stock split.
7. F (LO 4) It does not because it is not an unusual and infrequently occurring event.
8. F (LO 4) Extraordinary items appear on the income statement.
9. T (LO 4)
10. F (LO 7) It is part of contributed capital.
11. T (LO 5)
12. T (LO 3)
13. T (LO 1)
14. F (LO 5) They are included in diluted, not basic, earnings per share calculations.
15. T (LO 7)

Multiple Choice

1. a (LO 7) A stock split simply requires replacing the number of shares outstanding before the split with the number of shares outstanding after the split. There is no adjustment to retained earnings (but the par or stated value is reduced proportionately).

2. c (LO 7) The firm distributed a stock dividend of 1,000 shares (10% of 10,000 shares). The 11,000 shares outstanding after the stock dividend then were split into 4 shares for each 1 share (11,000 × 4), resulting in total shares outstanding of 44,000.

3. d (LO 6) The restriction on retained earnings is simply an indication of the intended use of the balance. The restricted amount remains in the stockholders' equity section of the balance sheet but should be identified separately to identify the amount that is not available for dividends.

4. c (LO 7) On the date of distribution of a stock dividend, Common Stock is credited and Common Stock Distributable is debited. Retained Earnings will be reduced at the end of the accounting period when Stock Dividends Declared is closed to Retained Earnings.

5. a (LO 4) The cumulative effect of an accounting change should appear on the income statement, after extraordinary items and before net income or loss.

6. c (LO 5) For earnings per share calculations, 40,000 shares were outstanding for the entire year. An additional 20,000 shares were outstanding for 9/12 of the year. 20,000 × 9/12 = 15,000 shares. 40,000 shares + 15,000 shares is 55,000 weighted-average shares outstanding for the year.

7. b (LO 6) There was a $30,000 increase in retained earnings during the year, even after a $15,000 cash dividend. Therefore, net income for the year must have been $45,000 ($30,000 + $15,000).

8. c (LO 4, 6) Discontinued operations are shown on the income statement.

9. b (LO 8) If a corporation has just one type of stock, it would be common stock. Book value per share would be calculated by dividing total stockholders' equity (retained earnings and contributed capital) by the number of shares issued. The current year's dividends already would have reduced total stockholders' equity. Dividend information would be irrelevant to finding book value per share.

10. c (LO 6) Retained earnings accumulate over time as a result of undistributed income. Each accounting period that earnings are not entirely distributed to the stockholders through dividends, retained earnings increase. Accounting periods in which losses occur result in a reduction in retained earnings. Dividends declared and transfers to contributed capital are taken from retained earnings.

11. d (LO 1) The quality of earnings would be affected by the accounting methods and estimates chosen, and by the nature of nonoperating items.

Exercises

1. (LO 7)

General Journal				
Date		**Description**	**Debit**	**Credit**
Sept.	1	Cash	1,200,000	
		Common Stock		1,000,000
		Paid-in Capital in Excess of Par Value, Common		200,000
		To record issuance of stock		
Mar.	7	Stock Dividends Declared	65,000	
		Common Stock Distributable		50,000
		Paid-in Capital in Excess of Par Value, Common		15,000
		To record declaration of stock dividend		
	30	No entry		
Apr.	13	Common Stock Distributable	50,000	
		Common Stock		50,000
		To record distribution of stock dividend		

2. (LO 3, 4)

Operating Income Before Taxes		$100,000
Less Income Taxes Expense		40,000
Income Before Extraordinary Item		$ 60,000
Extraordinary Lightning Loss	$30,000	
Less Applicable Taxes	12,000	18,000
Net Income		$ 42,000

3. (LO 3)

General Journal				
Date		**Description**	**Debit**	**Credit**
20x1		Income Taxes Expense	24,000	
		Income Taxes Payable		16,000
		Deferred Income Taxes		8,000
		To record income taxes for 20x1		
20x2		Income Taxes Expense	12,000	
		Deferred Income Taxes	4,000	
		Income Taxes Payable		16,000
		To record income taxes for 20x2		
20x3		Income Taxes Expense	28,000	
		Deferred Income Taxes	4,000	
		Income Taxes Payable		32,000
		To record income taxes for 20x3		

4. (LO 8)

Total stockholders' equity		$680,000
Less:		
Par value of outstanding preferred stock	$200,000	
Dividends in arrears	28,000	
Equity allocated to preferred shareholders		228,000
Equity pertaining to common shareholders		$452,000

Book value per share:

Preferred stock = $228,000 ÷ 4,000 shares = $57.00 per share

Common stock = $452,000 ÷ 30,000 shares = $15.07 per share

5. (LO 5) Basic earnings per share = $\dfrac{\$50,000 - \$20,000}{10,000 \text{ shares}} = \$3.00$ per share

Chapter 16

Self-Test

1. a (LO 1)		**6.** d (LO 5)	
2. c (LO 2)		**7.** c (LO 5)	
3. b (LO 3)		**8.** b (LO 6)	
4. d (LO 4)		**9.** d (LO 7)	
5. b (LO 5)		**10.** c (LO 8)	

Matching

1. i	**6.** s	**11.** m	**16.** n
2. j	**7.** f	**12.** l	**17.** p
3. q	**8.** d	**13.** b	**18.** h
4. a	**9.** c	**14.** g	**19.** k
5. o	**10.** e	**15.** r	

Short Answer

1. (LO 2) A debenture bond is an unsecured bond, whereas a bond indenture is the contract between the bondholder and the corporation.
2. (LO 3) A premium would probably be received when the bond's interest rate is higher than the market interest rate for similar bonds at the time of the issue.
3. (LO 3) Interest = Principal × Rate × Time
4. (LO 4) The present value of periodic interest payments and the present value of the face value at maturity
5. (LO 1) Stockholders retain their level of control; interest is tax deductible; increased earnings accrue to stockholders (financial leverage).

True-False

1. F (LO 2) They are creditors.
2. T (LO 1)
3. F (LO 2) Bond interest must be paid on each interest date. It is not declared by the board of directors.
4. T (LO 3)
5. F (LO 5) It will be less than the cash paid.
6. T (LO 5)
7. F (LO 6) Bond Interest Expense is credited.
8. T (LO 5)
9. F (LO 5) It equals interest payments *plus* the bond discount.
10. T (LO 7)
11. F (LO 5) The premium amortized increases each year.
12. T (LO 5)
13. F (LO 8) The statement describes capital leases.
14. T (LO 8)
15. F (LO 7) No gain or loss is recorded.
16. T (LO 3)
17. T (LO 8)
18. T (LO 1)
19. F (LO 1) It would indicate a high risk of default.

Multiple Choice

1. d (LO 6) When bonds are issued between interest dates, the amount the investor pays for the bond includes the accrued interest as of the date of issue (the amount in choice **d** is calculated as $900,000 × .05 × 4/12). On the interest date, the full interest due for the entire period is paid out to each bondholder, including those who have held a bond for only a partial period. The issuing firm maintains the abnormal balance in the Bond Interest Expense account until the interest is paid to the bondholders.

2. a (LO 8) Interest expense on a mortgage is based on the unpaid balance. Over time, as the principal of the mortgage is reduced, the interest portion of a fixed payment becomes less. Therefore, the portion of the payment applied to the reduction of the unpaid balance increases.

3. d (LO 3) Bonds issued at a premium have a carrying value above the face value. The Unamortized Bond Premium should be shown on the balance sheet under Long-Term Liabilities after the Bonds Payable line with the two items being totaled.

4. c (LO 6) Interest expense for the period must be recorded as an adjustment at year end. In recording interest expense for bonds that were sold at a discount, the calculation includes a reduction in Unamortized Bond Discount, which has a normal debit balance.

5. b (LO 5) Using the effective interest method, the calculation of interest expense is based on the current carrying value of the bonds. As the bond discount is amortized, that carrying value increases. As a result, the interest expense per period also increases.

6. b (LO 8) The lease described in **b** does not meet the requirements for a capital lease. The arrangement does not resemble a sale. It is, therefore, an operating lease.

7. c (LO 7) Early retirement of bonds is considered an extraordinary occurrence. Therefore, when a gain or loss results from the transaction, the results are presented on the income statement as an extraordinary item. In the transaction described, the company paid $204,000 ($200,000 × 102%) for bonds outstanding with a carrying value of $195,000. The difference between the carrying value and the amount paid ($9,000) is a loss.

8. c (LO 7) The carrying value of the bonds is $612,000. If one-third of the bonds are converted, the carrying value of the bonds payable will be reduced by $204,000 ($612,000/3).

Exercises

1. (LO 3, 5)
   a. $9,000 ($600,000 – $591,000)
   b. $21,000 ($600,000 × 7% × ½)

   c. $21,450 $\left(\$21,000 + \dfrac{\$9,000}{20}\right)$

   d. $593,700 ($600,000 – $6,300)

2. (LO 3, 5)
   a. $550,000 ($500,000 × 110%)
   b. $17,500 ($500,000 × 7% × ½)
   c. $16,500 ($550,000 × 6% × ½)
   d. $1,000 ($17,500 – $16,500)
   e. $549,000 ($550,000 – $1,000)

3. (LO 5)

Interest payments ($600,000 × 8% × 10)	$480,000
Premium on bonds payable ($600,000 × 6%)	36,000
Total interest cost	$444,000 ($44,400/year)

4. (LO 8)

General Journal					
Date		**Description**		**Debit**	**Credit**
20x1 Dec.	31	Cash		50,000	
		Notes Payable			50,000
		Borrowed $50,000 at 10 percent on five-year note			
20x2 Dec.	31	Notes Payable		10,000	
		Interest Expense		5,000	
		Cash			15,000
		Made first installment payment			
20x3 Dec.	31	Notes Payable		10,000	
		Interest Expense		4,000	
		Cash			14,000
		Made second installment payment			

5. (LO 8)

General Journal					
Date		**Description**		**Debit**	**Credit**
20x1 Dec.	31	Cash		50,000	
		Notes Payable			50,000
		Borrowed $50,000 at 10 percent on five-year note			
20x2 Dec.	31	Notes Payable		8,189	
		Interest Expense		5,000	
		Cash			13,189
		Made first installment payment			
20x3 Dec.	31	Notes Payable		9,008	
		Interest Expense		4,181	
		Cash			13,189
		Made second installment payment			

Solution to Crossword Puzzle
(Chapters 15 and 16)

¹P	E	N	²S	I	O	N	P	³L	A	N		⁴S		
			H					E				⁵P	A	⁶R
⁷P	A	Y	A	B	L	E		A		⁸I		L		E
			R					S		N		I		T
⁹D	E	B	E	N	T	U	R	E		D		T		A
E										E				I
F		¹⁰Z	E	R	¹¹O		¹²B		N		¹³M		N
I				P	¹⁴M	O	R	T	G	A	G	E	D
¹⁵C	O	M	¹⁶P	L	E	X		O		U		R	
I			R		R			K		R		K	
T			E		A		¹⁷T	¹⁸R	E	D	E	E	M
			M		T		H			T			
¹⁹N		²⁰D	I	V	I	D	E	N	D	S		²¹P	
E			U		N		F				A		
²²T	E	R	M		G		²³T	R	E	A	S	U	R	Y

Chapter 17

Self-Test

1. a	(LO 1)	**6.** a	(LO 6)
2. d	(LO 2)	**7.** c	(LO 1)
3. c	(LO 3)	**8.** b	(LO 4)
4. c	(LO 5)	**9.** d	(SO 8)
5. d	(LO 6)	**10.** c	(SO 9)

Matching

1. f	**4.** g	**7.** h	**10.** b
2. j	**5.** e	**8.** c	
3. i	**6.** a	**9.** d	

Short Answer

1. (LO 3) Issuing capital stock to retire long-term debt and purchasing a long-term asset by incurring long-term debt
2. (LO 5) Because they represent noncash expenses that have been legitimately deducted in arriving at net income. Adding them back effectively cancels out the deduction.
3. (LO 6, 7; SO 9) Cash Flows from Investing Activities, Cash Flows from Financing Activities, and Schedule of Noncash Investing and Financing Transactions
4. (LO 1) Money market accounts, commercial paper (short-term notes), and U.S. Treasury bills

True-False

1. T (LO 1)
2. F (LO 3) It is considered an operating activity.
3. T (LO 6)
4. T (SO 9)
5. T (LO 5)
6. F (LO 3, 5) Depreciation, depletion, and amortization would be found in the operating activities section.
7. F (SO 8) The reverse is true.
8. T (SO 8)
9. F (LO 4) It implies that the business is generally contracting.
10. T (LO 6)
11. F (LO 5) It would be added to net income.
12. F (SO 9) Depreciation must be *deducted* from operating expenses in this case.
13. T (LO 6)
14. T (LO 3, 6)
15. F (LO 7; SO 9) Both methods produce the same net-change-in-cash figure.
16. F (LO 4) Dividends are deducted because in the long run they must be paid to retain stockholder interest.

Multiple Choice

1. a (LO 5) Cash receipts from sales, interest, and dividends are used to calculate cash inflows from operating activities. Under the indirect method, they are simply components of the net income figure presented.

2. b (LO 5) Net income in the operating activities section of the statement of cash flows includes the gain on sale of investments. That amount needs to be backed out of the operating activities section to avoid duplication of cash inflow data.

3. a (LO 5) An increase in accounts payable indicates an increase in cash available to the firm. To reflect the absence of that cash outflow, the amount by which the payables have increased is added to the Cash Flows from Operating Activities section under the indirect method of preparing a statement of cash flows.

4. e (LO 3) The purchase of a building by incurring a mortgage payable does not involve any cash inflow or outflow. The investing and financing activity is disclosed in the schedule of noncash investing and financing transactions.

5. d (LO 6) The payment of dividends is a cash outflow and would be disclosed in the financing activities section of the statement of cash flows. Investments in a corporation by its stockholders through the purchase of stock are considered a source of financing by the corporation.

6. b (LO 5) The increase in inventory represents a cash outflow and would be deducted from net income in the operating activities section of the statement of cash flows. The counter-entry is the adjustment for changing levels of accounts payable.

7. c (LO 6) Cash receipts from the issuance of stock are a cash inflow from financing activities. No adjustment to net income is required because the sale of stock is not recorded as a revenue and is not presented on the income statement.

8. d (SO 8) In the analysis of transactions for the preparation of the statement of cash flows, each operating, investing, and financing activity of the period is reconstructed. Net income results in an increase in Retained Earnings, and the analysis begins with a credit entry to that account.

9. b (SO 9) Total sales were $100,000. Of that amount, $14,000 is accounted for by an increase in accounts receivable. $100,000 less $14,000 equals $86,000 in cash receipts from cash sales and accounts receivable.

10. c (LO 4) The numerator for all three calculations is net cash flows from operating activities.

Exercises

1. (SO 9)

  a. $57,000 ($70,000 operating expenses + $1,000 increase in Prepaid Expenses + $6,000 decrease in Accrued Liabilities – $20,000 in Depreciation Expense)

  b. $360,000 ($350,000 Sales + $10,000 decrease in Accounts Receivable)

  c. $31,000 ($33,000 Income Taxes Expense – $2,000 increase in Income Taxes Payable)

  d. $221,000 ($240,000 Cost of Goods Sold – $12,000 decrease in Inventory – $7,000 increase in Accounts Payable)

  e. $51,000 (**b** – **d** – **a** – **c** above)

2. (LO 4)

  a. 2.0 times

  b. 13.3%

  c. 15%

  d. $55,000

3. (SO 8)

	Account Balances 12/31/x8	Analysis of Transactions for 20x9		Account Balance 12/31/x9
		Debit	**Credit**	
Madera Corporation Work Sheet for the Statement of Cash Flows For the Year Ended December 31, 20x9				
Debits				
Cash	35,000		(x) 6,000	29,000
Accounts Receivable	18,000	(b) 3,000		21,000
Inventory	83,000		(c) 11,000	72,000
Plant Assets	200,000	(f) 62,000	(e) 30,000	232,000
Total Debits	336,000			354,000
Credits				
Accumulated Depreciation	40,000	(e) 10,000	(g) 26,000	56,000
Accounts Payable	27,000	(d) 8,000		19,000
Bonds Payable	100,000	(h) 10,000		90,000
Common Stock	150,000		(h) 10,000	160,000
Retained Earnings	19,000	(i) 12,000	(a) 22,000	29,000
Total Credits	336,000	105,000	105,000	354,000
Cash Flows from Operating Activities				
Net Income		(a) 22,000		
Increase in Accounts Receivable			(b) 3,000	
Decrease in Inventory		(c) 11,000		
Decrease in Accounts Payable			(d) 8,000	
Gain on Sale of Plant Assets			(e) 4,000	
Depreciation Expense		(g) 26,000		
Cash Flows from Investing Activities				
Sale of Plant Assets		(e) 24,000		
Purchase of Plant Assets			(f) 62,000	
Cash Flows from Financing Activities				
Dividends Paid			(i) 12,000	
		83,000	89,000	
Net Decrease in Cash		(x) 6,000		
		89,000	89,000	

Chapter 18

1. a	(LO 1)	**6.** d	(LO 4)
2. d	(LO 2)	**7.** c	(LO 4)
3. a	(LO 3)	**8.** c	(LO 5)
4. b	(LO 5)	**9.** a	(LO 5)
5. c	(LO 4)	**10.** c	(LO 5)

Matching

1. g	**4.** e	**7.** h	**10.** d
2. b	**5.** j	**8.** i	**11.** c
3. l	**6.** f	**9.** k	**12.** a

Short Answer

1. (LO 5) Profit margin, asset turnover, return on assets, and return on equity
2. (LO 4) Horizontal analysis presents absolute and percentage changes in specific financial statement items from one year to the next. Vertical analysis, on the other hand, presents the percentage relationship of individual items on the statement to a total within the statement.
3. (LO 2) Rule-of-thumb measures, analysis of past performance of the company, and comparison with industry norms
4. (LO 1) The risk of total loss is far less with several investments than with one investment because only a rare set of economic circumstances could cause several different investments to suffer large losses all at once.
5. (LO 5) Cash flow yield, cash flows to sales, cash flows to assets, and free cash flow

True-False

1. T (LO 4)
2. F (LO 4) Common-size financial statements show relationships between items in terms of percentages, not dollars.
3. F (LO 5) The current ratio will increase.
4. T (LO 5)
5. F (LO 5) It equals the cost of goods sold divided by average inventory.
6. F (LO 5) The reverse is true because the price/earnings ratio depends on the earnings per share amount.
7. F (LO 5) Interest is not added back.
8. T (LO 5)
9. F (LO 5) The higher the debt to equity ratio, the greater the risk.
10. F (LO 5) Receivable turnover measures how many times, on average, the receivables were converted into cash during the period.
11. T (LO 5)
12. T (LO 5)
13. F (LO 5) It is a market strength ratio.
14. F (LO 4) Sales would be labeled 100 percent.
15. T (LO 3)
16. T (LO 3)
17. T (LO 5)
18. F (LO 5) A higher payables turnover will produce a *shorter* average days' payable.
19. T (LO 3)

Multiple Choice

1. b (LO 5) Interest coverage is a measure of security that a creditor can use to gauge a company's ability to cover interest payments on loans extended to the firm.

2. d (LO 5) The quick ratio measures a company's ability to cover immediate cash requirements for operating expenses and short-term payables.

3. c (LO 5) Asset turnover is calculated using net sales as the numerator and average total assets as the denominator. It is a measure of the efficient use of a company's assets.

4. a (LO 5) A high price/earnings ratio indicates optimism about a company's future. That positive outlook may be due to anticipated increases in earnings and growth of the company.

5. a (LO 4) Index numbers are calculated to reflect percentage changes over consecutive periods of time. The base year is assigned the value of 100 percent; then changes from that base are assigned a percentage so that subsequent amounts can be compared with base amounts. This method is used to identify trends, eliminating differences resulting from universal changes, such as inflation.

6. b (LO 1) Management uses financial statements to make decisions about the future of the company. Management also uses financial statements to analyze variances between actual results and budgeted results of operations. By using financial statements, management is better able to plan and control major functions of management. Each of the other choices listed is an external user of financial statements.

7. d (LO 2) Each of the factors listed in choices **a** through **c** contributes to the complications of comparing a company with the industry in which it operates.

8. c (LO 5) The turnover of receivables is the number of times receivables are collected in relation to sales in an accounting period. If the number is low, average accounts receivable balances are presumed to be high and credit policy is presumed to be weak.

9. b (LO 4) Net income is given a percentage in relation to sales, as are all other components of the income statement. Sales equal 100 percent.

10. c (LO 5) The commitments free cash flow allows for are dividends and net capital expenditures.

Exercises

1. (LO 4)

	20x2	20x1	Increase (Decrease)	
			Amount	Percentage
Sales	$250,000	$200,000	$50,000	25.0%
Cost of Goods Sold	144,000	120,000	24,000	20.0
Gross Margin	$106,000	$ 80,000	26,000	32.5
Operating Expenses	62,000	50,000	12,000	24.0
Income Before Income Taxes	$ 44,000	$ 30,000	14,000	46.7
Income Taxes	16,000	8,000	8,000	100.0
Net Income	$ 28,000	$ 22,000	6,000	27.3

2. (LO 5)

  a. 2.0 ($500,000/$250,000)

  b. $1.3 \left(\dfrac{\$500{,}000 - \$180{,}000}{\$250{,}000} \right)$

  c. 1.9 times ($350,000/$180,000)

  d. 192.1 days (365/1.9)

  e. 12.0% ($106,000/$880,000)

  f. 22.1% ($106,000/$480,000)

  g. 6.0 times ($600,000/$100,000)

  h. 60.8 days (365/6.0)

  i. 17.7% ($106,000/$600,000)

  j. 0.7 times ($75,000/$106,000)

  k. 12.5% ($75,000/$600,000)

  l. 8.5% ($75,000/$880,000)

  m. .68 times ($600,000/$880,000)

  n. $8 \text{ times} \left(\dfrac{\$40}{\$106{,}000/21{,}200 \text{ shares}} \right)$

  o. 7.0 times ($350,000/$50,000)

  p. 52.1 days (365/7.0)

Solution to Crossword Puzzle
(Chapters 17 and 18)

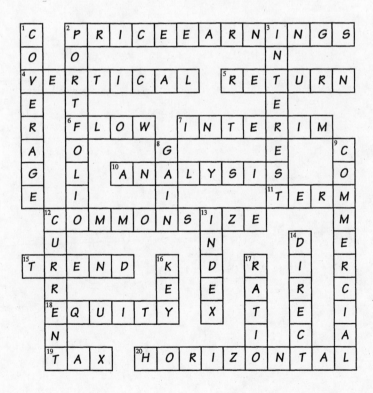

Chapter 19

Self-Test

1.	d	(LO 1)	6.	a (LO 6)
2.	c	(LO 1)	7.	a (LO 4)
3.	c	(LO 1)	8.	c (LO 6)
4.	c	(LO 2)	9.	d (LO 6)
5.	d	(LO 3)	10.	a (LO 7)

Matching

1. f	4. g	7. a	10. h
2. b	5. e	8. j	
3. c	6. i	9. d	

Short Answer

1. (LO 2) Planning, executing, reviewing, and reporting
2. (LO 3) A just-in-time operating philosophy mandates an organizational environment in which personnel are hired and raw materials and facilities are purchased and used only as needed; emphasis is on the elimination of waste.
3. (LO 7) Competence, confidentiality, integrity, and objectivity

4. (LO 5) Why is the report being prepared? For whom is the report intended? What information should be provided? When is the report due?
5. (LO 6) The difference between cost of sales and cost of goods sold is that cost of sales is equal to the cost of services sold in a service organization. Cost of goods sold is used in a merchandising organization and is equal to the beginning inventory plus net cost of purchases less ending inventory.

True-False

1. F (LO 6) They are simply called *inventory.*
2. F (LO 1) The management accountant provides management with the information needed for decision making.
3. T (LO 1)
4. F (LO 1) The reverse is true.
5. T (LO 1)
6. T (LO 1)
7. F (LO 1) Financial accounting reports must be prepared at regular, equal intervals.
8. F (LO 6) Manufacturing computations are more complex because of the three stages of inventory completion.

9. F (LO 7) It relates most closely to integrity.
10. F (LO 7) It relates most closely to competence.
11. T (LO 3)
12. T (LO 4)
13. T (LO 3)
14. T (LO 1)
15. F (LO 2) Planning is the first stage; *executing* is the second stage.
16. T (LO 3)
17. F (LO 3) The *customer,* not the manufacturer, must perceive value-adding.

Multiple Choice

1. d (LO 7) Management accountants are expected to possess the most current skills available so that they can perform their duties in a competent and professional manner. Integrity means avoiding conflict of interest situations; objectivity refers to fair and complete disclosure of information; and confidentiality forbids the unethical or illegal disclosure of proprietary information.

2. a (LO 7) To maintain their integrity, management accountants are not allowed to accept any gift or favor that would prejudice their actions. (See the answer to multiple-choice question **1** for a discussion of the other standards of ethical conduct listed.)

3. b (LO 1) The timeliness of data is an important characteristic of the information used for both financial and management accounting. The timeliness of information enhances the usefulness of the schedules, reports, and statements that are prepared from that information. The other choices presented are areas in which the two types of accounting may differ.

4. d (LO 3) Even though perfection is not attainable, JIT, TQM, and ABM all contribute to a firm's challenging goal of achieving perfection. Organizations that adhere to continuous improvement are never satisfied with what is;

they constantly seek a better method, product, service, process, or resource. Their goal is perfection in everything they do.

5. c (LO 1) The reports and schedules prepared in management accounting are generated to assist in the decision-making processes of managers. Therefore, the usefulness of the information provided by those reports and schedules is the driving force in their creation.

6. a (LO 1) Estimates are used in management accounting due to the nature of the reports and analyses. Much of the work of management accounting is based on allocations, forecasts, and projections, for which perfect information is unavailable.

7. c (LO 2) After planning and executing a decision, managers should *review* the expected performance established at the planning stage. Any significant differences are then identified for further analysis.

8. b (LO 4) Operating budgets require the use of financial information from the past to analyze differences between what was expected and what actually occurred. Operating budgets are constructed using financial data to plan for the future of a company. The other choices for this question are all based on nonfinancial data.

Exercises

1. (LO 1)

	Financial Accounting	Management Accounting
1.	e	c
2.	g	l
3.	m	b
4.	i	n
5.	a	h
6.	k	f
7.	d	j

3. (LO 3)
1. b
2. b
3. a
4. a
5. b

2. (LO 4)

Employee	Number of Pizzas Served per Hour	Employee Rating
P. Sanchez	22	Excellent
S. Wang	18	Good
R. Scotti	13	Lazy
E. Butterfield	16	Average
B. Jolita	19	Good
B. Warner	15	Average
G. Cohen	9	The Pits

Chapter 20

Self-Test

1. a   (LO 3)   6. d   (LO 7)
2. d   (LO 3)   7. d   (LO 5)
3. c   (LO 4)   8. a   (LO 5)
4. b   (LO 4)   9. b   (LO 7)
5. a   (LO 4)   10. b   (LO 8)

Matching

1. h   5. g   9. m   13. e
2. c   6. d   10. f   14. n
3. b   7. j   11. o   15. i
4. a   8. k   12. l

Short Answer

1. (LO 3) Materials Inventory, Work in Process Inventory, Finished Goods Inventory

2. (LO 3) Direct materials, direct labor, manufacturing overhead

3. (LO 3) A materials cost is considered direct when it can be conveniently and economically traced to a specific product or other cost objective.

4. (LO 1) For profit or loss determination, product pricing, inventory valuation, and planning and cost control purposes

5. (LO 5)
    Materials Inventory, beginning of period
    + Direct materials purchased
    = Cost of direct materials available for use
    – Materials Inventory, end of period
    = Cost of direct materials used

6. (LO 5)
    Cost of direct materials used
    + Direct labor costs
    + Manufacturing overhead costs
    = Total manufacturing costs

7. (LO 5)
    Total manufacturing costs
    + Work in Process Inventory, beginning of period
    = Total cost of work in process during the period
    – Work in Process Inventory, end of period
    = Cost of goods manufactured

8. (LO 7) Estimated manufacturing overhead divided by total estimated cost driver activity (e.g., direct labor hours)

9. (LO 7) Overapplied overhead is the amount by which applied manufacturing overhead exceeds actual manufacturing overhead.

10. (LO 5) Cost of goods manufactured is the total manufacturing costs attached to units of a product completed during an accounting period and moved to finished goods storage.

True-False

1. T (LO 5)
2. T (LO 4)
3. T (LO 8)
4. T (LO 3)
5. T (LO 4)

6. F (LO 1) A service firm has no direct materials cost.
7. T (LO 8)
8. F (LO 4) The purchase request is prepared first.

9. F (LO 3) They are classified as indirect labor or as manufacturing overhead.

10. F (LO 5) It must be prepared *before* the income statement can be prepared.

11. T (LO 5)

12. T (LO 4)

13. F (LO 5) The reverse is true.

14. T (LO 3)

15. T (LO 8)

16. T (LO 8)

17. F (LO 3) They would become more difficult to trace.

18. F (LO 3) It would be part of manufacturing overhead and therefore indirect.

Multiple Choice

1. c (LO 3) A direct materials cost is one that can easily be traced to the item manufactured. Other than the legs for the chair, each cost described is not distinctly traceable to the product.

2. c (LO 4) Goods must first be requested, then ordered, then received, then used.

3. a (LO 1) Salespeople are not involved in the manufacture of products. Therefore, their salaries are treated as period costs, not product costs.

4. d (LO 4) The proper document to use to buy goods is a purchase order.

5. a (LO 4) A materials request form tracks goods issued into production.

6. c (LO 8) Activities are what "drive" the costs in an ABC system.

7. b (LO 8) Costs are accumulated for a given activity pool in ABC systems and applied via the cost driver.

8. a (LO 7) One of the criticisms of traditional costing methods are that they use a single plantwide cost driver (e.g., direct labor hours) to apply manufacturing overhead to a product cost.

9. d (LO 1) Managers use product cost information in all the stages in the management cycle listed, plus the reporting stage.

Exercises

1. (LO 5)

Finished Goods, Jan. 1	$ 75,000
Add Cost of Goods Manufactured	450,000
Cost of Goods Available for Sale	$525,000
Less Finished Goods, Dec. 31	80,000
Cost of Goods Sold	$445,000

2. (LO 8)

Activity Pool	Estimated Activity Pool Amount	Cost Driver	Cost Driver Level	Activity Cost Rate
Setup	$10,000	Number of setups	200 setups	$50
Inspection	6,000	Number of inspections	300 inspections	$20
Building	8,000	Machine hours	4,000 machine hours	$2
Packaging	4,000 $28,000	Packaging hours	1,000 packaging hours	$4

	Activity Cost Rate	Product A Cost Driver Level	Cost Applied	Product B Cost Driver Level	Cost Applied
Activity Pool					
Setup	$50	70	$ 3,500	30	$ 1,500
Inspection	20	250	5,000	150	3,000
Building	2	1,500	3,000	2,000	4,000
Packaging	4	300	1,200	700	2,800
Total			$12,700		$11,300
÷ by Number of Units			1,000		2,000
= Manufacturing Overhead Cost per Unit			$12.70		$5.65

3. (LO 5)

Spencer Company Statement of Cost of Goods Manufactured For the Year Ended December 31, 20xx
Direct materials used
Materials Inventory, Jan. 1 $ 8,700
Add direct materials purchased (net)   168,300
Cost of direct materials available for use $177,000
Less Materials Inventory, Dec. 31   32,600
Cost of direct materials used $144,400
Direct labor costs   142,900
Manufacturing overhead costs
Depreciation, factory building and equipment $ 31,800
Factory insurance   2,300
Factory utilities expense   26,000
Indirect labor   42,800
Other factory costs   12,600
Total manufacturing overhead costs   115,500
Total manufacturing costs $402,800
Add Work in Process Inventory, Jan. 1   34,200
Total cost of work in process during the year $437,000
Less Work in Process Inventory, Dec. 31   28,700
Cost of goods manufactured $408,300

4. (LO 3)

a. OH	d. DM	g. DM
b. DL	e. OH	h. OH
c. OH	f. DL	i. OH

Solution to Crossword Puzzle
(Chapters 19 and 20)

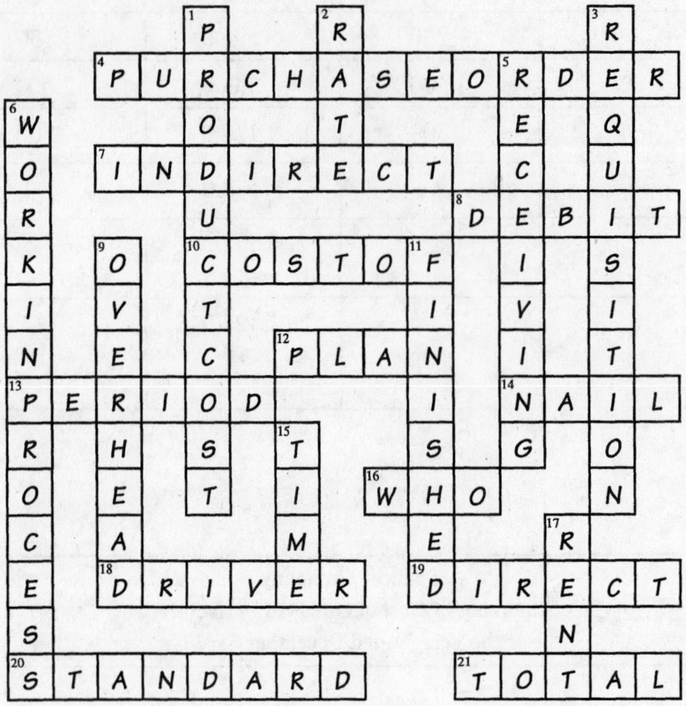
1 PRODUCTCOST
2 RATE
3 REQUISITION
4 PURCHASEORDER
5 RECEIVING
6 WORKINPROCESS
7 INDIRECT
8 DEBIT
9 OVERHEAD
10 COSTOF
11 FINISHED
12 PLAN
13 PERIOD
14 NAIL
15 TIME
16 WHO
17 RENT
18 DRIVER
19 DIRECT
20 STANDARD
21 TOTAL

Chapter 21

Self-Test

1. a	(LO 2)		**6.** c	(LO 6)
2. a	(LO 2)		**7.** b	(LO 3)
3. b	(LO 2)		**8.** d	(LO 4)
4. c	(LO 5)		**9.** d	(LO 6)
5. a	(LO 6)		**10.** b	(LO 6)

Matching

1. c	**4.** f	**6.** d	**8.** a
2. i	**5.** b	**7.** e	**9.** h
3. g			

Short Answer

1. (LO 6) Schedule of equivalent production, unit cost analysis schedule, and cost summary schedule
2. (LO 6)

   Units in beginning inventory × (100% –
      percentage of completion)
   + Units started and completed × 100%
   + Units in ending inventory × percentage of
      completion
   = Equivalent units

3. (LO 6) The cost of goods transferred out of the department and the cost of ending work in process inventory
4. (LO 1) Products such as railroad cars, bridges, wedding invitations, or any other unique or special-order products suggest the use of a job order costing system.

True-False

1. F (LO 5) Manufacturing Overhead is increased.
2. T (LO 5)
3. F (LO 5) The decrease is to Finished Goods Inventory.
4. T (LO 2)
5. F (LO 3) It uses a perpetual inventory system.
6. T (LO 4)
7. F (LO 5) A Work in Process Inventory account is maintained for each department or operation.
8. T (LO 3)
9. T (LO 6)
10. F (LO 6) Equivalent units for materials and conversion costs must be multiplied by their respective unit costs.
11. F (LO 5) Work in Process Inventory—Department 2 is debited and Work in Process Inventory—Department 1 is credited.
12. T (LO 6)
13. F (LO 6) It is made in the cost summary schedule.

Multiple Choice

1. b (LO 6) Equivalent production for conversion costs would be 14,100 units, or the sum of (1) beginning equivalent units of 2,000 (5,000 units × 40% completed this period), (2) 10,000 units started and completed during the period, and (3) ending equivalent units of 2,100 (7,000 units × 30% completed this period).

2. c (LO 6) There is no schedule of conversion costs. Conversion costs consist of direct labor and manufacturing overhead. They are the costs of converting raw materials to finished products.

3. d (LO 6) The costs necessary to complete ending inventory are costs of a future period. They would not be used in a summary of current period costs.

4. a (LO 6) Equivalent production is stated in units only. It is a schedule showing completion of beginning inventory, inventory started and completed this period, and inventory started that remain incomplete at the end of the period.

5. c (LO 2) A job order costing system is used if the goods manufactured are single large items, unique in nature. A supersonic jet is manufactured to the specifications of the buyer and is, therefore, unique in nature. Costs will be accumulated per jet.

6. b (LO 5) A process costing system accumulates manufacturing costs by department or work center, not by job or batch of products.

7. d (LO 3) All of the characteristics are those of a job order costing system.

8. a (LO 5) A process costing system accumulates costs by department, work center, or cell.

9. d (LO 7) These measurements, along with others—such as units produced per time period, special order needs of customers, and cost analysis of different technological options—will assist managers.

10. c (LO 2) A company that makes specialty suits would use a job order costing system.

Exercises

1. (LO 6)

Morris Manufacturing Company
Schedule of Equivalent Production
For the Month Ended May 31, 20xx

Units—Stage of Completion	Units to Be Accounted For	Equivalent Units	
		Materials Costs	Conversion Costs
Beginning inventory completed in this period	2,000	—	1,400
Units started and completed (19,000 – 2,000)	17,000	17,000	17,000
Ending inventory (24,000 – 17,000)	7,000		
(Direct materials costs—100% complete)		7,000	
(Conversion costs—30% complete)			2,100
	26,000	24,000	20,500

Morris Manufacturing Company
Unit Cost Analysis Schedule
For the Month Ended May 31, 20xx

	Total Costs			Equivalent Unit Costs	
	Costs from Beginning Inventory	Costs from Current Period	Total Costs to Be Accounted For	Equivalent Units	Cost per Equivalent Unit
Direct materials costs	$12,000	$114,000	$126,000	24,000	$4.75
Conversion costs	3,000	30,750	33,750	20,500	1.50
Totals	$15,000	$144,750	$159,750		6.25

Morris Manufacturing Company
Cost Summary Schedule
For the Month Ended May 31, 20xx

	Cost of Goods Transferred to New Department	Cost of Ending Work in Process Inventory
Beginning inventory		
Beginning balance	$ 15,000	
Cost to complete: 1,400 units (2,000 units × 70%)		
× $1.50 per unit	2,100	
Total beginning inventory	$ 17,100	
Units started and completed		
17,000 units × $6.25 per unit	106,250	
Ending inventory		
Direct materials costs: 7,000 units × $4.75 per unit		$ 33,250
Conversion costs: 2,100 units × $1.50 per unit		3,150
Totals	$123,350	$ 36,400
Computational check:		
Costs to next department		$123,350
Costs in ending Work in Process Inventory		36,400
Total costs to be accounted for (unit cost analysis schedule)		$159,750

2. (LO 3)

Materials Inventory

12/23	2,950	850	12/26
	2,100		

Accounts Payable

		2,950	12/23

Work In Process Inventory

12/26	800	3,900	12/29
12/27	1,200		
12/27	3,600		
	1,700		

Manufacturing Overhead

12/26	50	3,600	12/27
12/26	1,200		
12/27	300		
12/31	2,500		
	450		

Factory Payroll

		1,500	12/27

Cash

		1,200	12/26

Finished Goods Inventory

12/29	3,900	2,000	12/30
	1,900		

Cost of Goods Sold

12/30	2,000	2,500	12/31
		500	

Sales

		3,400	12/30

Accounts Receivable

12/30	3,400		

	¹F	A	²C	T	O	R	Y		³C	Y	⁴C	L	E	
⁵J			O								O			⁶P
O			N		⁷U	N	I	T	C	O	S	T		R
B			V		N					T				O
⁸O	F		E		⁹D	I	¹⁰R	E	¹¹C	T		¹²A		C
R			R		E		A		O			C		E
D			S		R		T		S			T		S
¹³E	Q	U	I	V	A	L	E	N	T	U	N	I	T	S
R			O		P			S			V			
	¹⁴C		N		¹⁵P	R	O	D	U	C	T	I	O	N
	E				L			M			T			
¹⁶P	L	A	N	N	I	N	G		M		Y			
	L				E			A			¹⁷P			
	¹⁸P	R	E	D	E	T	E	R	M	I	N	E	D	
							Y			R			

Chapter 22

Self-Test

1. c	(LO 5)	**6.** c	(LO 7)
2. a	(LO 5)	**7.** c	(LO 3)
3. d	(LO 5)	**8.** a	(LO 4)
4. c	(LO 3)	**9.** b	(LO 6)
5. d	(LO 1)	**10.** c	(LO 7)

Matching

1. i	**5.** d	**8.** c	**11.** k
2. a	**6.** f	**9.** h	**12.** m
3. g	**7.** e	**10.** j	**13.** l
4. b			

Short Answer

1. (LO 5) Just-in-time is an overall operating philosophy of management in which all resources, including materials, personnel, and facilities, are acquired and used only as needed.

2. (LO 4)
   1. Identify and classify each activity.
   2. Estimate the cost of resources for each activity.
   3. Identify a cost driver for each activity and estimate the quantity of each cost driver.
   4. Calculate an activity cost rate.
   5. Assign costs to cost objects based on the level of activity required to make the product or provide the service.

3. (LO 3) Process value analysis (PVA) is an analytical method of identifying all activities and relating them to the events that cause or drive the need for the activities and the resources consumed. PVA analysis is helpful to managers because it forces them to look critically at all phases of their operations and can assist managers in reducing nonvalue-adding activities and costs and improve cost traceability.

4. (LO 5) Just-in-time is not an inventory system, JIT is an operating philosophy. One of the goals of a JIT environment is to minimize or eliminate inventory. Unlike the traditional manufacturing approach, which requires that inventory be kept on hand to meet customer demands, JIT uses customer orders to trigger production runs. Throughput becomes much more important than the methods of costing inventories.

True-False

1. F (LO 8) ABM and JIT are similar in that they analyze processes and identify value-adding and nonvalue-adding activities.
2. T (LO 5)
3. T (LO 5)
4. T (LO 5)
5. T (LO 5)
6. F (LO 6) Product inspections are performed on a continuous basis by machine operators.
7. F (LO 6) Queue time is time spent by the product waiting to be worked on once it arrives at the next operation or department.
8. T (LO 6)
9. T (LO 6)
10. F (LO 4) The cost hierarchy of a service organization includes the unit level, batch level, service level, and operations level.
11. F (LO 4) The bill of activities, used in activity-based costing, is a list of activities and related costs that is used to compute the costs assigned to activities and the product unit costs. A bill of activities could include activity cost rates and cost driver levels used to assign costs to cost objects.
12. T (LO 7)
13. T (LO 3)
14. T (LO 3)
15. T (LO 1)

Multiple Choice

1. c (LO 4) Batch-level activities are those activities performed each time a batch of goods is produced. Installation of a vehicle's engine would be an example of a unit-level activity. Unit-level activities are those activities performed each time a unit is produced.
2. c (LO 5) Increasing emphasis on direct labor variance analysis could be an element found in any production environment. Variance analysis is a method used to isolate causes for differences between expected and actual results of operations.
3. b (LO 5) Pull-through production is a system design which depends upon demand for a product for processing to begin. The production process is a response to an order.
4. a (LO 5) JIT refers to "just-in-time" processing of materials received as needed. If inventory is delivered as needed, and not kept on hand in advance of need, the resources usually used to store, count, maintain, and move inventories could be reduced or eliminated.
5. b (LO 5) Each of the other choices does not guarantee ultimate savings to a company. Quick and inexpensive machine setups would result in a cost savings over slow and expensive machine setups.
6. d (LO 6) Decision time would have elapsed prior to the start of production. Production time begins with the requisition of raw materials and ends with the transfer of the product to finished goods.
7. c (LO 3) A value-adding activity is an operating activity that increases the market value of a good or service. An example of a value-adding activity would be using a higher-quality material that increases the value in the eyes of the customer. Recording the daily receipts would not add to the market value of the pizza; thus, it would be a nonvalue-adding activity.
8. a (LO 7) In a JIT environment where backflush costing is used, the direct materials costs and the conversion costs (direct labor and manufacturing overhead) are immediately charged to the Cost of Goods Sold account.
9. a (LO 1) In the planning stage, ABM helps managers estimate product costs, as well as identify value-adding activities, and determine the required resources for such activities.
10. b (LO 6) Processing time is the actual amount of time spent working on a product.

Exercises

1. a. (LO 4)

Direct materials cost	$28,645
Cost of purchased parts	38,205
Direct labor cost (660 × $7.00)	4,620
Manufacturing overhead (1.6 × $4,620)	7,392
Total cost of the order	**$78,862**
Product unit cost ($78,862/350 units)	**$225.32**

b.

Activity	Activity Cost Rate	Cost Driver Level	Activity Cost
Unit level:			
Parts production	$19 per machine hour	190 machine hours	$ 3,610
Assembly	$9.50 per direct labor hour	42 direct labor hours	399
Packaging/shipping	$13 per unit	350 units	4,550
Batch level:			
Work cell setup	$45 per setup	8 setups	360
Product level:			
Product design	$31 per engineering hour	38 engineering hours	1,178
Product simulation	$45 per testing hour	14 testing hours	630
Facility level:			
Building occupancy	125% of direct labor costs	$4,620 direct labor costs	5,775
Total Activity Costs			$16,502
Cost Summary			
Direct materials		$28,645	
Cost of purchased parts		38,205	
Direct labor cost		4,620	
Activity costs		16,502	
Total cost of order		**$87,972**	
Product unit cost		**$251.35**	

2. (LO 5, 6) Costs that are classified the same under both the traditional and JIT approaches: direct labor—direct cost; raw materials—direct cost.

Costs that are classified as indirect in a traditional system and direct in a JIT environment: depreciation, machinery; product design costs; small tools; operating supplies; setup labor; rework costs; supervisory salaries; and utility costs, machinery (all of these costs are traceable to a JIT work cell where, under a traditional approach, they were all included in a plantwide or departmental overhead cost pool).

The president's salary and fire insurance, plant, are indirect costs under both traditional and JIT approaches.

3. (LO 5, 6)

Work in Process Inventory	
4,890	32,750
13,300	

Finished Goods Inventory	
32,750	17,880

Cost of Goods Sold	
17,880	

Accounts Payable	
	4,890
	13,330

Accounts Receivable	
28,608	

Sales	
	28,608

Chapter 23

Self-Test

1. b	(LO 1)	**6.** a	(LO 5)
2. c	(LO 2)	**7.** c	(LO 7)
3. a	(LO 3)	**8.** b	(LO 7)
4. b	(LO 3)	**9.** b	(LO 6)
5. d	(LO 5)	**10.** c	(LO 2)

Matching

1. d	**4.** k	**7.** i	**10.** c
2. g	**5.** j	**8.** a	**11.** e
3. h	**6.** b	**9.** f	

Short Answer

1. (LO 5) Sales = Variable Costs + Fixed Costs, or Sales – Variable Costs – Fixed Costs = 0
2. (LO 3) Any cost that has both fixed and variable elements, such as telephone expense, electricity expense, and water expense
3. (LO 3) The high-low method breaks down a mixed cost into its fixed and variable components.
4. (LO 6) *Sales* refers to the gross proceeds realized on the sale of a company's product. *Contribution margin,* on the other hand, refers to the portion of sales remaining after all variable costs have been deducted. It is the amount available to cover fixed costs plus a profit.

5. (LO 6)

Sales	$XX
– Variable Costs	XX
= Contribution Margin	$XX
– Fixed Costs	XX
= Profit	$XX

6. (LO 8)
Estimating service overhead costs
Determining the breakeven point
Determining the effect of a change in operating costs
Estimating profit

True-False

1. T (LO 2)
2. T (LO 5)
3. T (LO 2)
4. F (LO 2) It is a fixed cost because it does not change with volume.
5. F (LO 2) Normal capacity is the most realistic.
6. T (LO 5)
7. F (LO 6) A contribution margin is realized on the sale of the very first unit.
8. T (LO 5)
9. T (LO 2)
10. T (LO 7)
11. T (LO 3)
12. F (LO 5) The horizontal (*x*) axis represents volume, such as units of output.
13. T (LO 6)
14. F (LO 6) Unless the selling price or variable cost per unit changes, the contribution margin per unit will remain the same.
15. T (LO 5)
16. F (LO 8) C-V-P analysis can be used by service industries after analyzing their cost behavior.

Multiple Choice

1. c (LO 3) Only a part of the taxi fare is based on an activity level. Mixed costs are those that have a fixed element and a variable element in the calculation of the total cost.

2. c (LO 5, 6) Breakeven in units is calculated by dividing total fixed costs by the contribution margin per unit. Contribution margin per unit is the selling price less variable costs per unit.

$$\frac{\$10,000}{\$10.00 - \$8.00} = 5,000 \text{ units}$$

3. b (LO 1, 2) Variable costs are directly associated with production levels. If production is zero, variable costs are also zero.

4. a (LO 6) Total contribution margin is the contribution margin per unit multiplied by the number of units sold. When profits (losses) are zero, the total contribution margin equals total fixed costs.

5. d (LO 5) The total-cost line includes all fixed and variable costs. The slope of the total-cost line is determined by the variable costs per unit. Therefore, where the total-cost line intercepts the total-revenue line, revenues equal costs.

6. a (LO 2) In preparing cost analyses and forecasting sales, normal capacity is assumed.

7. d (LO 2) When volume decreases, the number of units divided into the (same) fixed cost decreases, increasing the fixed cost per unit.

8. d (LO 6) When the selling price and variable cost per unit both increase by the same amount, the contribution margin per unit, and thus the breakeven point, remains the same.

9. d (LO 7) Solve the following equation to obtain the correct answer: $\$50X - \$35X - \$30,000 = \$45,000$, or $FC + NI \neq CM$.

10. a (LO 7) Solve the following equation to obtain the correct answer: $10,000(X - \$10) - \$40,000 = \$26,000$.

11. b (LO 6) By multiplying the contribution margin for each product by the product's percentage of the sales mix the weighted average contribution margin is computed. This in turn is used to calculate the weighted-average break-even point.

12. d (LO 8) Breakeven analysis is often used in-service industries and requires a thorough analysis of each cost component and a reliable estimate of activity.

Exercises

1. (LO 4, 5, 7)
   a. 20,000 units
   b. $260,000
   c. $32,000 loss
   d. 32,500 units

2. (LO 5)

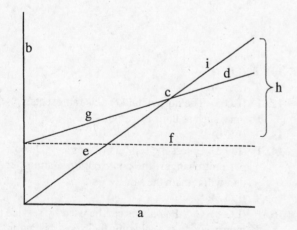

3. (LO 2, 3)
   a. Total cost = $800 + $.25/mile
   b. $4,800

4. (LO 6)
   a. $20,000 loss
   b. $10.00
   c. $50,000

Solution to Crossword Puzzle
(Chapters 22 and 23)

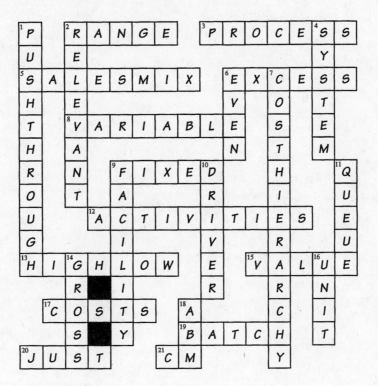

Chapter 24

Self-Test

1. d	(LO 2)	**6.** a	(LO 2)
2. d	(LO 1)	**7.** d	(LO 3)
3. a	(LO 3)	**8.** c	(LO 5)
4. c	(LO 4, 5)	**9.** a	(LO 1)
5. d	(LO 4)	**10.** b	(LO 3)

Matching

1. k	**4.** f	**7.** d	**10.** e
2. g	**5.** i	**8.** c	**11.** a
3. j	**6.** h	**9.** b	

Short Answer

1. (LO 1) Budgeting is the process of identifying, gathering, summarizing, and communicating financial and nonfinancial information about an organization's future activities. Budgeting is used in all types of organizations and is synonymous with managing an organization.

2. (LO 2) A master budget is a set of budgets that consolidates an organization's financial information into budgeted financial statements. The other supporting budgets are the sales budget, production budget, direct materials purchases budget, direct labor budget, manufacturing overhead budget, selling and administrative expense budget, cost of goods manufactured budget, capital expenditures budget, and cash budget.

3. (LO 4) The two main objectives of a cash budget are to (a) show the projected ending cash balance and (b) allow management to anticipate periods of high or low cash availability.

4. (LO 3) The three steps are to (a) calculate the total units of direct materials needed for production, (b) calculate the total units of direct materials to be purchased, and (c) calculate the total cost of direct materials to be purchased.

True-False

1. F (LO 2) A master budget is a comprehensive budget, usually for a one-year period.
2. F (LO 2) A master budget represents the entire organization's budget.
3. T (LO 3)
4. T (LO 2)
5. F (LO 4) Depreciation expense does not represent a cash outflow and therefore would not be present in the cash budget.
6. T (LO 1)
7. T (LO 3)
8. F (LO 4) Only cash collected from sales (including prior months' sales) would be included as cash receipts.

9. F (LO 3, 4) The reverse is true.
10. T (LO 3)
11. F (LO 3) External factors such as the state of local and national economies, the nature of the industry's economy, and competition are important factors in forecasting sales.
12. T (LO 3)
13. F (LO 5) The budgeted balance sheet is the final step in the development of the master budget.

Multiple Choice

1. d (LO 3) The information from detailed operating budgets is combined into the master budget. These operating budgets are prepared at the departmental level and represent the expectations of the managers responsible for each of the segments of the firm.

2. c (LO 3) The production budget is the basis for preparing the other three budgets listed.

3. b (LO 4) The cash budget presents anticipated cash inflows and outflows and the need for additional funds. Once the cash budget has been prepared, certain balance sheet account balances can be forecasted (Cash, Accounts Receivable, Notes Payable, etc.). As a result, the cash budget must be prepared prior to the preparation of the pro forma balance sheet.

4. d (LO 3) Forecasted sales would appear on the sales budget, not on the direct labor budget.

5. a (LO 4) The sales budget would provide information as to the projected *inflows* of cash.

6. d (LO 4) The cash budget consists of **a, b,** and **c** plus the beginning cash balance.

7. a (LO 3) Requirements for production in quarter 2 are 72,000 lbs (24,000 units × 3 lbs). Add 10% of the requirement for quarter 3, or 6,300 lbs (21,000 units × 3 lbs × .10). Subtract materials on hand at the beginning of quarter 2, or 7,200 lbs (24,000 units × 3 lbs × .10). The amount that should be purchased for the second quarter is 71,100 lbs.

8. d (LO 3) A manufacturing organization would prepare a direct materials budget.

9. c (LO 4) (40% × $15,000) + (60% × $10,000) + $20,000 = $32,000

10. d (LO 3) The first step in preparing the direct labor budget is to estimate the total direct labor hours by multiplying the estimated direct labor hours per unit by the anticipated units of production. The second step is to calculate the total budgeted direct labor cost by multiplying the estimated total direct labor hours by the estimated direct labor cost per hour.

Exercises

1. (LO 3)

Donlevy Company
Production Budget
For the Quarter Ended June 30, 20xx

	April	May	June
Expected sales	10,000 units	12,000 units	15,000 units
Add ending inventory	1,200	1,500	900
Units needed	11,200	13,500	15,900
Less beginning inventory	1,000	1,200	1,500
Units to produce ending inventory	10,200 units	12,300 units	14,400 units

2. (LO 4)

Monahan Enterprises
Cash Budget
For the Month Ended June 30, 20xx

Cash receipts		
Sales—May	$52,000	
Sales—June	18,000	
Proceeds from loan*	1,000	
Total receipts		$71,000
Cash disbursements		
General and administrative expenses	$22,000	
Inventory purchases—May	20,000	
Inventory purchases—June	15,000	
Purchase of office furniture	3,000	
Selling expenses	14,000	
Total disbursements		74,000
Cash increase (decrease)		$ (3,000)
Cash balance, June 1		7,000
Cash balance, June 30		$ 4,000

*Amount must be derived.

3. (LO 3)

Jeppo Titanium Company
Direct Labor Budget
For the Year Ended December 31, 20x1

	Product	Product	Year
Bending department	X	Y	
Total production units	10,000	20,000	
× Direct labor hours per unit	1	.6	
Total direct labor hours	10,000	12,000	
× Direct labor cost per hour	$10	$10	
Total direct labor cost	$100,000	$120,000	$220,000
	Product	Product	
Welding department	X	Y	
Total production units	10,000	20,000	
× Direct labor hours per unit	2	3	
Total direct labor hours	20,000	60,000	
× Direct labor cost per hour	$15	$15	
Total direct labor cost	$300,000	$900,000	$1,200,000
Total firmwide direct labor cost			
			$1,440,000

4. (LO 1) During the planning stage of the management cycle, budgeting helps managers to (a) relate an organization's long-term goals to its short-term activities, (b) distribute resources and workloads, (c) communicate responsibilities, (d) select performance measures, and (e) set goals for bonuses and rewards.

During the executing stage of the management cycle, budgeting helps managers to (a) communicate expectations, (b) challenge and motivate others, (c) coordinate activities, (d) benchmark, and (e) recognize problems.

During the reviewing stage of the management cycle, budgeting helps managers to (a) calculate variances, (b) evaluate performance, (c) determine timeliness, and (d) create solutions for continuous improvement.

During the reporting stage of the management cycle, budgeting helps managers to continuously communicate budget information and provide continuous feedback about the organization's operating, investing, and financing activities.

Chapter 25

Self-Test

1. a	(LO 1)	**6.** a	(LO 2)
2. b	(LO 5)	**7.** d	(LO 2)
3. c	(LO 7)	**8.** c	(LO 4)
4. c	(LO 4)	**9.** a	(LO 5)
5. b	(LO 4, 5)	**10.** b	(LO 6)

Matching

1. j	**5.** i	**8.** d	**11.** h
2. k	**6.** g	**9.** f	**12.** e
3. l	**7.** b	**10.** a	**13.** c
4. m			

Short Answer

1. (LO 1) During the planning stage, standard costs can be used to estimate costs for direct materials, direct labor, and variable manufacturing overhead. These estimated costs serve as goals for product costing and can also be used in product distribution and pricing. Standard costs are used in the executing stage of the management cycle to apply dollar, time, and quantity standards to work being performed. During the reviewing stage, actual costs incurred are compared with standard costs, and the variances are computed. During the reporting stage of the management cycle, standard costs are used to report on operations and managerial performance. A variance report may be tailored to a manager's responsibilities to provide useful information about how well operations are proceeding.

2. (LO 7) A favorable manufacturing overhead volume variance exists when the manufacturing overhead costs budgeted for the level of production achieved is less than the manufacturing overhead applied to production using the standard variable and fixed manufacturing overhead rates.

3. (LO 2) Direct materials price standard, direct materials quantity standard, direct labor time standard, direct labor rate standard, standard variable manufacturing overhead rate, and standard fixed manufacturing overhead rate.

4. (LO 4) A favorable direct materials quantity variable would exist when a smaller quantity of direct materials is used than was expected for a particular level of outcome.

5. (LO 5) An unfavorable direct labor rate variance would exist when a higher wage is paid than is standard for an employee doing a particular job.

True-False

1. F (LO 2) They are used in establishing direct labor time standards.
2. T (LO 2)
3. F (LO 1) It is part of the control function.
4. T (LO 4)
5. T (LO 6)
6. T (LO 5)
7. F (LO 7) The total standard manufacturing overhead rate consists of two parts: the standard variable rate and the fixed overhead rate.
8. F (LO 5) The individual variances provide more information than the total variance.

9. T (LO 8)
10. F (LO 6) A flexible budget is also referred to as a *variable* budget.
11. T (LO 7)
12. F (LO 3) Variance analysis helps managers to locate areas of operating efficiency or ineffi-ciency so that corrective action can be taken, if necessary. The mere computation of a variance is important; however, identifying the *reason* for a variance is critical if corrective actions are to be taken.
13. T (LO 6)

Multiple Choice

1. a (LO 5) The amount of wages paid is used to calculate the actual direct labor cost.
2. d (LO 4) The direct materials price variance is the difference between the standard price and the actual price multiplied by the actual quantity used. Thus, each of the responses could lead to such a variance.
3. d (LO 6) A static budget (also known as a fixed budget) forecasts sales and costs for one level of production.
4. a (LO 7) If the standard manufacturing overhead applied is less than the actual manufacturing overhead, then an organization has an unfavorable manufacturing overhead variance.
5. b (LO 6) The total budgeted cost would be:

Direct materials:	10,000 units	×	$4.00	=	$ 40,000
Direct labor:	10,000 units	×	1.00	=	10,000
Variable M.O.H.	10,000 units	×	3.00	=	30,000
Fixed M.O.H.					20,000
					$100,000

6. a (LO 6) The total budgeted cost would be:

Direct materials:	20,000 units	×	$4.00	=	$ 80,000
Direct labor:	20,000 units	×	1.00	=	20,000
Variable M.O.H.	20,000 units	×	3.00	=	60,000
Fixed M.O.H.					20,000
					$180,000

7. a (LO 4, 8) The purchasing manager is responsible for purchasing materials. Therefore, a favorable or unfavorable direct materials price variance could be used to evaluate the performance of the purchasing manager.
8. d (LO 5) If actual direct labor hours times standard labor rate is greater than standard direct labor hours times standard labor rate, an organization has an unfavorable direct labor efficiency variance.
9. a (LO 6) A flexible budget shows changes in budgeted amounts given different levels of activity. Fixed manufacturing overhead would be constant throughout the relevant range.
10. d (LO 1, 8) Standard costing can be used for all these reasons and in every stage of the management cycle.

Exercises

1. (LO 2)

Porcelain	$ .40
Red paint	.05
Blue paint	.02
Molding department wages	.12
Painting department wages	.30
Variable manufacturing overhead	
(.08 hr. x $3/hr.)	.24
Fixed manufacturing overhead	
(.08 hr. x $2/hr.)	.16
Standard cost of one dish	$1.29

2. (LO 6)

Sturchio Company
Flexible Budget
For the Year Ended December 31, 20xx

	Unit Levels of Activity			Variable Cost per Unit
Cost Item	10,000	15,000	20,000	
Direct materials	$ 12,500	$ 18,750	$ 25,000	$1.25
Direct labor	45,000	67,500	90,000	4.50
Variable manufacturing overhead	27,500	41,250	55,000	2.75
Total variable costs	$ 85,000	$ 27,500	$170,000	$8.50
Fixed manufacturing overhead	50,000	50,000	50,000	
Total costs	$135,000	$ 77,500	$220,000	

Flexible budget formula: ($8.50 × units produced) + $50,000

3. (LO 4, 5)

a. $13,140 \text{ F} = \left(\$.60 - \dfrac{\$381,060}{657,000}\right) \times 657,000$

b. $4,200 \text{ U} = (657,000 - 650,000) \times \$.60$

c. $1,105 \text{ U} = \left(\dfrac{\$100,555}{22,100} - \$4.50\right) \times 22,100$

d. $11,700 \text{ U} = [22,100 - (65,000 \times .3)] \times \$4.50$

Solution to Crossword Puzzle
(Chapters 24 and 25)

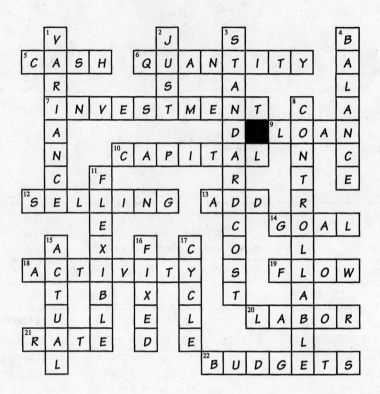

Chapter 26

Self-Test

1. c (LO 1)		**6.** a (LO 3)	
2. b (LO 4)		**7.** d (LO 4)	
3. c (LO 3)		**8.** b (LO 4)	
4. a (LO 5)		**9.** a (LO 6)	
5. b (LO 4)		**10.** c (LO 7)	

Matching

1. g	**4.** e	**7.** c	**10.** d
2. h	**5.** b	**8.** i	
3. f	**6.** a	**9.** j	

Short Answer

1. (LO 6) Economic Value Added = After-Tax Operating Income – [Cost of Capital × (Total Assets – Current Liabilities)] or Economic Value Added = After-Tax Operating Income – Cost of Capital in Dollars

2. (LO 3) Cost center, discretionary center, revenue center, profit center, investment center

3. (LO 4) In a traditional income statement all manufacturing costs are assigned to cost of goods sold. A variable costing income statement includes only direct materials, direct labor, and variable manufacturing overhead to compute variable cost of goods sold. Fixed manufacturing overhead is considered a period cost.

4. (LO 1) The purpose of a balanced scorecard is to provide a framework that links the perspectives of an organization's four basic stakeholder groups with the organization's mission and vision, performance measures, strategic plan, and resources.

True-False

1. T (LO 5)
2. F (LO 3) A discretionary center is a responsibility center whose manager is accountable only for costs in which the relationship between resources and products or services produced is not well defined.
3. F (LO 5) Return on investment is equal to profit margin multiplied by asset turnover.
4. T (LO 4)
5. F (LO 4) Performance reports should contain only costs, revenues, and resources that are controllable by individual managers.
6. T (LO 4)
7. F (LO 1) The four basic stakeholder groups are investors, employees, internal business processes, and customers.
8. F (LO 5) The asset turnover ratio is the ratio of sales to average assets invested.
9. T (LO 3)
10. F (LO 1) The reporting stage of the management cycle requires the preparation of a variety of reports to enable mangers to monitor and evaluate performance measures.

Multiple Choice

1. a (LO 4) Fixed manufacturing overhead does not change within a relevant range of volume or activity. Variable costs are added to the flexible budget by multiplying actual unit output by the standard unit cost.

2. c (LO 4) The correct answer is $180,000. The total variable cost per unit is multiplied by the number of units of output which is $8 × $20,000 or $160,000. The fixed overhead costs of $20,000 are added to the $160,000 to equal $180,000.

3. a (LO 1) The four basic stakeholder groups are the investors, employees, internal business processes, and the customers.

4. a (LO 5) The correct equation for computing return on investment is operating income divided by assets invested.

5. b (LO 5) The correct answer is profit margin which is the ratio of operating income to sales.

6. c (LO 3) A revenue center is accountable primarily for revenue and its success is based on its ability to generate revenue.

7. c (LO 4) To evaluate profit, all variable costs including costs of goods sold and variable selling and administrative expenses are subtracted from sales to arrive at the contribution margin for the center. All fixed costs are then subtracted from contribution margin to determine the operating income.

8. b (LO 3) An operating center is not one of the responsibility centers. A cost center is responsible for controllable costs. A profit center is responsible for both revenue and costs and for the resulting income. An investment center is responsible for profit generation and can make decisions about the resources the center uses.

9. c (LO 1) The reporting stage of the management cycle requires the preparation of a variety of reports to enable managers to monitor and evaluate performance measures.

10. a (LO 5) The asset turnover ratio indicates the productivity of assets or the number of sales dollars generated by each dollar invested in assets. The ratio is sales to average assets invested.

Exercises

1. (LO 4)

Corwin Company
Flexible Budget
For the Year Ended December 31, 2002

Variable Budget:	
Direct Materials (350,000 × $1.80)	$ 630,000
Direct Labor (350,000 × $.35)	122,500
Variable Manufacturing Overhead	
(350,000 × $.60)	210,000
Total Variable Budget	$ 962,500
Fixed manufacturing overhead	135,000
Total Flexible Budget	$1,097,500

2. (LO 3)

a. $5,000

[Budgeted Sales (120,000) compared to Actual Sales (125,000) = $5,000 Favorable Variance]

b. ($2,000)

[Budgeted Operating Income ($20,000) compared to Actual Operating Income ($18,000) = $2,000 Unfavorable Variance]

c. ($875)

The cost of goods sold is budgeted at $62.50 per unit, but the actual cost to produce was $63.20. Therefore, it cost $.70 more to produce each unit multiplied by the number of units sold (1,250) giving us the variance of ($875).

Chapter 27

Self-Test

1. b	(LO 3)	6. b	(LO 6)
2. b	(LO 2)	7. b	(LO 5)
3. c	(LO 3)	8. a	(LO 6)
4. a	(LO 4)	9. d	(LO 7)
5. c	(LO 6)	10. a	(LO 6)

Matching

1. g	4. e	6. f	8. h
2. b	5. a	7. c	9. d
3. i	6. f		

Short Answer

1. (LO 1) Discovering the problem or need for a change, identifying the alternative courses of action, analyzing the effects of each alternative on operations, selecting the best alternative, and judging the success of the decision
2. (LO 4) Identifying the need for a facility, evaluating different courses of action, preparing reports for management, choosing the best alternative, and rationing available capital expenditure funds among competing resource needs

3. (LO 2) Information is relevant when it differs among future alternative courses of action; information is irrelevant when it does not.
4. (LO 6, 7) Accounting rate-of-return method, payback period method, and net present value method
5. (LO 3) Purchase price of item, rent or net cash flow from vacated factory space, and salvage value of unused machinery

True-False

1. T (LO 5)
2. F (LO 2) The main concern is with the differences in costs and revenues.
3. F (LO 4) Capital budgeting does not deal with obtaining cash; it involves the purchase of plant facilities.
4. F (LO 6) The net present value method is one of the more difficult methods to apply. It is difficult to arrive at the net present value because one has to apply factors that are found in Tables 3 and 4 in Appendix D.
5. T (LO 6)
6. F (LO 7) The payback period is the *minimum* length of time to recover cost.
7. T (LO 6)

8. F (LO 6) The desired rate of return must be known.
9. T (LO 6)
10. T (LO 3)
11. T (LO 3)
12. F (LO 3) The most beneficial product is the one with the highest contribution margin in relation to capital equipment.
13. T (LO 1)
14. F (LO 1) Sources of information for making such decisions may either be internal or external to the firm.
15. T (LO 1)
16. F (LO 2) Opportunity costs are revenues forfeited when one decision is chosen over another.

Multiple Choice

1. b (LO 7) Annual net cash flow does not reflect accounting net income. For accounting rate of return, average annual net income is the numerator. (Average investment cost is the denominator.)

2. c (LO 3) Incremental analysis of two alternatives includes comparing only the costs that differ between them. This method quickly identifies only the relevant costs that should be used to make the choice.

3. c (LO 3) The decision to purchase an asset would best be analyzed using one of the various capital investment evaluation methods. A machine, once put into service, becomes an element of fixed costs through depreciation expense. The contribution approach is inappropriate for this type of decision but is useful for evaluation of product decisions: sales mix, special orders, dropping a product line, adding a product line, and so on.

4. d (LO 3) In order to solve this problem, the sales price per unit must be known. It is then necessary to determine the contribution margin in total per product.

5. b (LO 4) Depreciation represents a non-cash expense and must be added to net income to arrive at cash expenses.

6. a (LO 6) Table 3 of Appendix B can be used to determine the present value of each cash inflow. The present values of choices **a, b, c,** and **d** are $755, $741 (rounded), $727 (rounded), and $751, respectively. Accordingly, choice **a** represents the highest present value of the four choices.

7. a (LO 5) Although depreciation is a noncash expense, its deduction reduces tax liability, in effect producing a cash inflow equal to the tax benefit.

8. c (LO 3) Special decision reports are prepared by accountants to fit the needs of the decision maker or the manager.

Exercises

1. (LO 7)

a. Payback Period $= \dfrac{\$70,000}{\$8,000 + \$14,000} = 3.2$ years

(The $14,000 in the denominator is depreciation.) Because the maximum payback period is three years, the company should not invest in the machine.

b. Accounting Rate of Return $= \dfrac{\$8,000}{\$70,000 \div 2}$

$= 22.9\%$

2. (LO 6)

Year	Net Cash Inflow		Present Value Multiplier		Present Value
1	$5,000	×	.862	=	$ 4,310
2	6,000	×	.743	=	4,458
3	6,000	×	.641	=	3,846
4	6,000	×	.552	=	3,312
5	6,000	×	.476	=	2,856
Total					$18,782

The company should not purchase the machine because the present value of future net cash inflows ($18,782) is less than the cost of the machine ($20,000).

3. (LO 3) $1.75 for shipping and packaging. (All other costs are sunk and therefore irrelevant.)

4. (LO 5, 6, 7)
1. d. Depreciation = ($400,000 ÷ 5) = $80,000
2. c. Tax Benefit Resulting from Depreciation = $80,000 × .34 (tax rate) = $27,200
3. a. Accounting Rate of Return = Annual After-Tax Net Income ÷ Average Investment Cost

    Project's Average Annual After-Tax Net Income = ($160,000 − $80,000) × .66 (1 − Tax Rate) = $52,800

    Average Investment Cost = ($400,000 + 0) ÷ 2 = $200,000

    Accounting Rate of Return = $52,800 ÷ $200,000 = 26.4%
4. b. Payback Period = Cost of Machine ÷ Projected Annual Net Cash Flow

    Cost of Machine = $400,000

    Projected Annual Net Cash Flow:
    Tax Effect = ($160,000 − $80,000) × .34 = $27,200
    Projected Annual Net Cash Flow = $160,000 − $27,200 = $132,800
    Payback Period = $400,000 ÷ $132,800 = 3 years

5. a. Present value of future net cash inflows

    Tax Effect = ($160,000 − $80,000) × .34 = $27,200

    Present value factor from Table 4 in Appendix D: 5 years and 10% return = 3.791

    Present Value = ($160,000 − $27,200) × 3.791 = $503,445
6. a. Yes. The minimum desired rate of return will be earned ($503,445 is greater than $400,000).

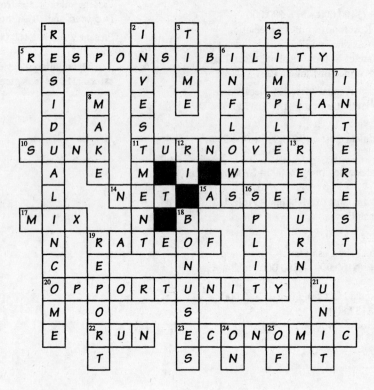

Appendix A

Matching

1. c   3. b   5. a
2. e   4. d

Exercise

1.

General Journal				
Date		Description	Debit	Credit
		Accounts Receivable, Mexican company	5,000	
		Sales		5,000
		Recorded sale of merchandise		
		($100,000 × $.05)		
		Cash	4,500	
		Exchange Gain or Loss	500	
		Accounts Receivable, Mexican company		5,000
		Recorded receipt of payment		
		($100,000 × $.045)		

Appendix B

Matching

1. c	**4.** d	**7.** g
2. h	**5.** f	**8.** i
3. b	**6.** e	**9.** a

Exercise

1.

	General Journal			
Date	**Description**	**Debit**	**Credit**
	Cash	12,000	
	Dividend Income		12,000
	Recorded cash dividend from Tewa*		
	($80,000 × 15%)		
	Investment in Rorris Company	19,500	
	Income, Rorris Company Investment		19,500
	Recognized 30 percent of income reported by Rorris Company		
	($65,000 × 30%)		
	Cash	15,000	
	Investment in Rorris Company		15,000
	Recorded cash dividend from Rorris		
	($50,000 × 30%)		

*Tewa's earnings of $110,000 are irrelevant because Jamal is using the cost adjusted to market method to account for the investment.

Appendix C

Matching

1. d		**3.** f		**5.** a	
2. b		**4.** e		**6.** c	

Exercises

1. a. $747 ($1,000 × .747)

  b. $4,122 ($1,000 × 4.122)

  c. $1,126 ($1,000 × 1.126)

  d. $1,745.81 ($100,000 ÷ 57.28)

2. Present value = $2,000 × 4.494 = $8,988

The purchase should not be made because the present value of the future cash savings is less than the initial cost of the equipment.

3.

General Journal					
Date		**Description**		**Debit**	**Credit**
(a) Jan.	1	Equipment ($10,000 × .826)		8,260	
		Discount on Notes Payable		1,740	
		Notes Payable			10,000
(b)	1	Interest Expense ($8,260 × .1)		826	
		Discount on Notes Payable			826
(c)	1	Interest Expense ($1,740 – $826)		914	
		Notes Payable		10,000	
		Discount on Notes Payable			914
		Cash			10,000